INSIGHT GUIDE
aUSTRIa

APA PUBLICATIONS
Part of the Langenscheidt Publishing Group

INSIGHT GUIDE
austria

ABOUT THIS BOOK

Editorial
Managing Editor
Maria Lord
Editorial Director
Brian Bell

Distribution
UK & Ireland
GeoCenter International Ltd
The Viables Centre, Harrow Way
Basingstoke, Hants RG22 4BJ
Fax: (44) 1256 817988

United States
Langenscheidt Publishers, Inc.
36–36 33rd Street 4th Floor
Long Island City, NY 11106
Fax: 1 (718) 784 0640

Australia
Universal Publishers
1 Waterloo Road
Macquarie Park, NSW 2113
Fax: (61) 2 9888 9074

New Zealand
Hema Maps New Zealand Ltd (HNZ)
Unit D, 24 Ra ORA Drive
East Tamaki, Auckland
Fax: (64) 9 273 6479

Worldwide
**Apa Publications GmbH & Co.
Verlag KG (Singapore branch)**
38 Joo Koon Road, Singapore 628990
Tel: (65) 6865 1600. Fax: (65) 6861 6438

Printing
Insight Print Services (Pte) Ltd
38 Joo Koon Road, Singapore 628990
Tel: (65) 6865 1600. Fax: (65) 6861 6438

©2006 Apa Publications GmbH & Co.
Verlag KG (Singapore branch)
All Rights Reserved
First Edition 1995
Fourth Edition 2006

CONTACTING THE EDITORS
We would appreciate it if readers
would alert us to errors or out-
dated information by writing to:
**Insight Guides, P.O. Box 7910,
London SE1 1WE, England.
Fax: (44) 20 7403 0290.
insight@apaguide.co.uk**

www.insightguides.com
In North America:
www.insighttravelguides.com

The first Insight Guide pioneered
the use of creative full-colour pho-
tography in travel guides in 1970.
Since then, we have expanded our
range to cater for our readers' need
not only for reliable information about
their chosen destination but also for
a real understanding of the culture
and workings of that destination.
Now, when the internet can supply
inexhaustible (but not always reliable)
facts, our books marry text and pictures to provide those much more
elusive qualities: knowledge and dis-
cernment. To achieve this, they rely
heavily on the authority of locally
based writers and photographers.

How to use this book

Insight Guide: Anybook is structured
to convey an understanding of the
state and its people as well as to
guide readers through its attractions:

♦ The **Features** section, indicated
by a yellow bar at the top of each
page, covers the natural and cultural
history of Utah as well as the
state's wide array of recreational
opportunities in a series of informative essays.

♦ The main **Places** section, indicated by a blue bar, is a complete
guide to all the sights and areas
worth visiting. Places of special
interest are coordinated by number
with the maps.

♦ The **Travel Tips** listings section,
with an orange bar, provides full
information on transportation, lodg-
ing, restaurants, sports, the arts,
adventure travel and more. An easy-
to-find contents list for Travel Tips
is printed on the back flap, which
also serves as a bookmark.

The contributors

This fully revised edition of *Insight Guide: Austria* was overseen by **Maria Lord**. She wrote the chapter on Austrian music as well as working on the Vienna chapters and adding to the Travel Tips.

For this new edition much new text was commissioned and the book was substantially reworked. **Matthew Finch** completely rewrote and reorganised the history chapters, making them more coherent and bringing them up to date. He also put together the feature on Jewish Vienna. He completely revised the chapter on Food and Drink, adding a revised feature on Austrian cafés, and wrote the fascinating new chapter on Austrian literature and film. In the places section he reordered much of the Vienna chapters and expanded the feature on Sigmund Freud. The new art and architecture chapter was written by **Dr John Lord**.

Alasdair Bouch travelled all over eastern and southern Austria to bring us the revised chapters on Styria, Burgenland and Lower Austria, while **Nicki Gander**, a resident of Salzburg, updated the Upper Austria, Salzkammergut, Salzburg (city and province), Carinthia, Tyrol and Vorarlberg chapters.

Many of the excellent photographs in the book are the work of **Britta Jaschinski**, from whom a new shoot was commissioned.

The first edition of this book was put together in the original German by Frankfurt-based Austrian author **Wilhelm Klein**. The first English translation was edited by **Tony Halliday**. Contributors to this earlier version of *Insight Guide: Austria* – and some of their work still appears in this edition – included **Rowlinson Carter** (history), **Dr Jutta Kohout** (Austrian food), **Christian Neuhold** and **Alfred Kölbel** (outdoor activities), **Evelyn Feichtenberger** and **Kurt Feichtenberger** (Lower Austria, Burgenland, Styria, Upper Austria, the Salzkammergut, Carinthia and East Tyrol), and **Dr Dieter Maier** (Salzburg, Salzburg Province, Tyrol, Vorarlberg). Previous updaters and revisers who have worked on this book include **Chris Clouter**, **Margaret de Fonblanque**, **Louis James** (who worte the original feature on Sigmund Freud) and **Paul Karr** (who wrote the features on hiking in the Tyrol, the Salzburg Festival and Melk Abbey).

Thanks go to **Paula Soper** for help with the editorial work, and to **Penny Phenix** who proofread and indexed the book.

Map Legend

▬ ▪ ▬	International Boundary
▬ ▬ ▬	Province Boundary
▬ ▪ ▬	National Park/Reserve
Ⓤ	U–Bahn
✈ ✈	Airport: International/ Regional
🚌	Bus Station
❶	Tourist Information
✉	Post Office
✝ † ⳨	Church/Ruins
†	Monastery
☪	Mosque
✡	Synagogue
🏰 🏯	Castle/Ruins
∴	Archaeological Site
∩	Cave
⚱	Statue/Monument
★	Place of Interest

The main places of interest in the Places section are coordinated by number with a full-colour map (e.g. ❶), and a symbol at the top of every right-hand page tells you where to find the map.

INSIGHT GUIDE
austria

CONTENTS

Jugendstil façade by Otto Wagner

BEHIND THE MASK

The Austrians, some of the friendliest and most down-to-earth people in Europe, inhabit a spectacular land

Before you even begin reading about Austria, it is a challenge to decide what the word means. Austria is a small European nation of the 21st century, but also a social and political grouping that has at one time or another included territories now considered Czech, Slovak, Slovene, Polish and Italian, to name but a few; and also an entity that could plausibly have celebrated its 1st birthday in 1919, its 60th in 2005, and its 950th in 1946 without contradiction. This confused state of affairs has bewildered not just past travellers and visitors to Austria, but even the country's own citizens: in 1965, a survey asking the populace "Is Austria a nation?" found less than half of the respondents answered "Yes"; as late as 1977 the percentage had only risen to 62.

Taking on the challenge of Austria means trying to penetrate this bewildering haze of identities and histories. Stereotypes abound, many perpetuated by the Austrians themselves: from glorified Habsburg splendour to the international scandals of Kurt Waldheim and Jörg Haider at the end of the 20th century, via the romanticised era of Mozart and the decadent Viennese *fin de siècle*, Austrian identity conceals itself behind shifting masks, some sweet, some shocking, every one fascinating.

In the far west, Bregenz touches the shores of Lake Constance at the junction of three nations. Heading into the Bregenzerwald, one begins to know an earthy, outgoing people. The sense intensifies in Salzburg, with its impressive position between hill and river, and its lingering echoes of Mozart, and Innsbruck, wedged between high Alps, a base for hiking, skiing and adventure. Some of the world's best spas, and countless fine vistas besides, pack themselves into the intervening folds and lakes of the Salzkammergut region. Move up through the Danube Valley's bountiful vineyards – best explored by riverside bike trail, at harvest time – and then take side trips to places such as Graz and Klagenfurt, all but unknown except to the Austrians.

And then there is Vienna. Visitors are always surprised by the Viennese – behind the imposing, astonishingly preserved architecture of the city centre, behind the apparent formality of their manners, they are gregarious and hedonistic, they enjoy their sweets, coffee, beer, banter and dining as much as anyone. Their city, although forgotten at times, now bustles with new people, new ideas and noisy construction projects reviving or restoring all but the very oldest quarters. Like Austria as a whole, it is not altogether what you had expected, and that is the joy of it. ❑

PRECEDING PAGES: the Grossglockner, Austria's highest mountain; mountains and lakes in the Tyrol; the Oberes Belvedere in Vienna.
LEFT: Otto Wagner's Am Steinhof church.
FOLLOWING PAGES: Austria in 1570, from an atlas by Abraham Ortelius.

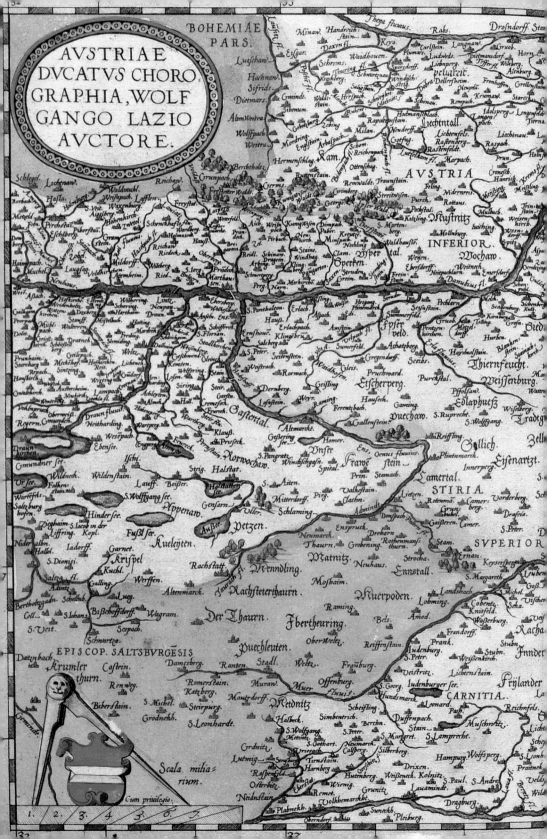

AVSTRIAE DVCATVS CHOROGRAPHIA, WOLFGANGO LAZIO AVCTORE.

Decisive Dates

circa **25,000 BC** The Danube Valley is inhabited – the Venus of Willendorf dates from this era.

800–400 BC The Hallstatt Culture inhabit the Salzkammergut, working salt mines that are still in operation today.

circa **450 BC** The Celts begin to arrive and establish the kingdom of Noreaia.

15 BC The Romans come to the Danube. They set up a garrison at Vindobona, the future Vienna.

circa **AD 280** Systematic viticulture is introduced to the Danube region.

5th–6th centuries The Völkerwanderung (migration of the peoples) takes place across Central Europe; Slavs and Bavarians immigrate into the region. In 433 the Romans are forced to abandon the area around the Danube.

798 Salzburg becomes an archbishopric.

799–800 Charlemagne repulses the advancing Avars and establishes a territory known as the Ostmark (Eastern March) in what is now Upper and Lower Austria.

907 The Magyars conquer the Ostmark.

955 At the Battle of Lechfeld, the Saxon king Otto the Great defeats the Magyars.

976 Otto II puts the Babenbergs in charge of the Ostmark.

996 The first official record of the name Ostarrichi.

1114–33 Babenberg leader Leopold III founds monasteries at Klosterneuburg and Heiligenkreuz.

1156 Heinrich II Jasomirgott moves the seat of the Babenbergs to Wien (Vienna).

1192 On his return from the Third Crusade, Richard the Lionheart is imprisoned and held hostage by Leopold V.

1246 Duke Friedrich II is killed in the Battle of Leitha against the Hungarians, marking the end of the Babenberg dynasty. Control of Austria passes to Ottakar II of Bohemia.

1278 Ottakar is killed at the Battle of Dürnkrut by the forces of Rudolf of Habsburg, the Holy Roman Emperor. Rudolf gives his sons Austria in fief, thereby founding the Habsburg dynasty, which would rule the country until 1918.

1365 Vienna University is founded by Rudolf IV.

1421 Albrecht V institutes a devastating pogrom against Jews, driving them from Vienna and demolishing the city's ghetto.

1493–1519 Cleverly exploiting several marital alliances, Maximilian I extends the Habsburg domains to include the Netherlands, Burgundy and Spain and also makes preparations for the unification of Austria, Bohemia and Hungary. During his reign the Reformation reaches the country.

1521 The Edict of Worms denounces Martin Luther.

1526 Ludwig II of Hungary dies fighting the Turks. Hungary and Bohemia fall to the Habsburgs.

1529 The Turks, under Sultan Suleiman I, reach the gates of Vienna. They almost take the city, but are forced to withdraw after the early onset of winter.

1550s Protestantism spreads, and by the late 16th century most of Austria's population has converted. The Catholic Habsburgs summon the Jesuits to Vienna to counter this.

1619–48 Fanatical Catholic Ferdinand II takes on the Protestants. The conflict spreads to the rest of Europe, resulting in the Thirty Years' War.

1620s–1730s With the Counter-Reformation comes the baroque, which sweeps the country, reaching a peak with Vienna's Karlskirche (1739).

1683 Vienna is besieged by Kara Mustapha and his 250,000-strong Turkish army. The city is liberated by Imperial forces.

1697 Prince Eugene becomes supreme commander of the army. His successes on the battlefield extend

LEFT: Maria Theresa, ruler of the Habsburg Empire 1740–80.

Habsburg control in Hungary, modern-day Croatia and large swathes of Western Europe. Austria becomes the prime mover on the European mainland.

1713 Pragmatic Sanction introduced, providing legitimacy for female succession.

1740 Maria Theresa ascends the throne.

1756 Mozart is born in Salzburg.

1765 Maria Theresa's son Joseph II becomes co-regent and rules jointly with his mother.

1805 Napoleon's troops occupy Vienna (as they would again in 1809).

1806 Franz II declares the end of the Holy Roman Empire to prevent Napoleon becoming its Emperor.

1814–15 After the fall of Napoleon, the Congress of Vienna is convened, at which Europe's princes and statesmen rearrange the political map. Under Chancellor Metternich, Austria sinks into the deathly stillness of the Biedermeier era.

1848 The March Revolution is crushed by Imperial troops; simple-minded Ferdinand I abdicates in favour of his 18-year-old nephew, Franz Joseph.

1857 Work begins on Vienna's Ringstrasse.

1870s Austrian anti-semitism begins to spread.

1890s *Fin-de-siècle* Austria (especially Vienna) sees a flowering of intellectual and artistic activity, with the appearance, among others, of Sigmund Freud, Gustav Mahler, Arthur Schnitzler, Otto Wagner and Gustav Klimt.

1914 The assassination in Sarajevo of Archduke Franz Ferdinand, the heir to the Imperial throne, ushers in World War I.

1916 Emperor Franz Joseph dies.

1918 After defeat in the war Karl I abdicates – marking the fall of the Habsburgs.

1918 The Republic of Austria is declared. In the post-war treaty Austria is forced to shrink to a 12th of its pre-war size.

1930 Robert Musil begins his epic novel of the Habsburg decline, *The Man Without Qualities*.

1934 Chancellor Engelbert Dollfuss is assassinated in an attempted putsch by Austrian Nazis.

1938 The Nazis take over – Anschluss with Germany. Hitler is welcomed in Vienna. Thousands of Jews (including Sigmund Freud) flee Austria.

1939 Outbreak of World War II.

1944–45 Bombing raids by the Allies destroy 30 percent of Vienna.

1945 Vienna is taken by the Red Army. Austria and its capital are divided into four occupation zones.

RIGHT: Bruno Kreisky, the post-war Social Democrat chancellor.

1955 The Staatsvertrag (State Treaty), between Austria and the Allied Powers, guarantees Austria's sovereignty and neutrality.

1970 Chancellor Bruno Kreisky is elected.

1979 Vienna becomes the third seat of the United Nations, after New York and Geneva.

1986 During his campaign to become president of Austria, former UN secretary-general Kurt Waldheim is accused of being involved in war-time atrocities.

1992 Thomas Klestil is elected president. Six years later he would win a second term.

1994 Austrians vote to join the European Union.

2000 Jörg Haider's far-right Freedom Party joins a coalition government, provoking rioting in Vienna

and consternation abroad. As a result, the EU imposes, and later drops, sanctions on Austria. The country's first holocaust memorial is erected in Vienna. In the worst Alpine disaster in history, 155 skiers are killed when a fire breaks out on an underground funicular train above Kaprun.

2002 The Austrian Schilling is replaced by the Euro. In parliamentary elections the Freedom Party's vote falls heavily.

2003 Right-wing chancellor Wolfgang Schüssel introduces the most restrictive asylum laws in Europe.

2005 Austria commemorates the 50th anniversary of the State Treaty and 60th of the Second Republic.

2006 Austria assumes presidency of the EU. ❑

So ich nun auff die zeytt Otto des kaysers pin ko=
men. so wil ich von den dingen sagen. die zu sei=
nen zeytten zu auffspring geschehen sind Do sich d'
kayser otto beraytett wider berengarium den künig be=
lamparden als wider ain wietrich vnd geitigen vo~
der alle gerechtikait vmb gelt gab Doch so forcht
in der selb wietrich. van er die machtikait des kay=
sers wol wisset. vnd durch ratt des herzogen bo lüt=
tringen. kam er zu dem kayser vnd begeret frid D~

CELTS, ROMANS AND CHRISTIANS

Austria has a long and complex history, from early Celtic settlements
to the mighty Habsburg Empire that dominated huge swathes of Central Europe

Comparatively little is known about the earliest inhabitants of the geographical area covered by present-day Austria; the Danube Valley was settled by around 25,000 BC, and the salt mines of the Salzkammergut, still in action today, were being worked from 800 BC. Around 450 BC, the Celts arrived. As Alexander the Great led the Macedonians east towards India, the Celts drove in the opposite direction. Austria was just one stopping-point in an unstoppable push across territories now covered by France, Spain, Italy and Britain.

Those Celts who settled in the region brought new language, new religion and urban settlements: they established a kingdom, Noreaia, whose borders corresponded with modern Austria at all but the western extremities. Celtic power did not go unrivalled, however: Germanic groups from the north were a constant threat, though not one as great as that of the Roman Empire which incorporated their territory around 15 BC. For around 50 years, the Noricans continued to govern themselves as they had done before, until Roman authorities decided that the harassment from the north justified militarisation of the region now known as Noricum.

Roman Noricum

Under the new military footing, Norican settlements were fortified; one, which was given an earth rampart and a garrison of 1,000 cavalry from Britain, was known as Vindobona. This was the future Vienna.

Rome kept up a lively trade with all corners of the empire and beyond, and as the Danube was the principal eastern artery, Noricum was bound to be in the thick of it. The supplementary network of roads and mountain passes carried a heavy traffic in Austrian gold, iron, salt and cattle south. Rome supplied olive oil and

wine, introduced bee-keeping and reformed farming practices.

In addition to these empire-approved imports, the Roman transport network also brought St Florian, an early Christian convert who, according to legend, brought the religion to the future Austria when fleeing persecution in the imper-

ial capital. In Noricum, it is said, he sat with the governor, hoping for a more tolerant reception of his beliefs. The governor had him drowned. Statues, still to be seen in many Austrian villages, of a saint pouring water over a burning house are of St Florian.

The collapse of the Roman Empire caused Rome to abandon the area around the Danube in 433 AD, leaving a power vacuum in central Europe. This occasioned an era of long-term migration: the Völkerwanderung. Noricum was taken over first by the Germanic peoples to the north, then by others from the Baltic region. Some groups remained for a generation or two and then moved on, but there were always

LEFT: the Battle of Lechfeld, 955, between the Holy Roman Emperor and the Magyars.
RIGHT: an Iron Age figure from the Halstatt culture.

others waiting to fill their space. Vandals and Huns were followed by Langobards, Avars and, later, Slavs.

Charlemagne and the Ostmark

In the 8th century AD, Charlemagne's Franks established an empire which imposed Christian order on Europe and put an end to this period of free migration and change. In 798 an archbishopric was established at the settlement of Salzburg. The area forming today's Upper and Lower Austria was named as the Ostmark, or Eastern March, and formed the new empire's easternmost boundary. In the

year 800, Pope Leo III rewarded Charlemagne with the title of King of the Romans. After his death 14 years later, the title persisted, becoming an elected one, voted for by the German nobility who had formed the core supporters of Charlemagne's regime. The support of the nobles in an election was the prerequisite to being crowned by the Pope as Holy Roman Emperor.

Over the centuries, the rules of succession were modified. The election of the king was vested in an electoral college (or diet) of seven princes, membership of which was a fiercely contested honour. A new king of the Romans was elected and kept in the wings during an

emperor's lifetime in order to speed up the eventual succession. Any Christian ruler, not merely a German one, became eligible for the throne, and this tended to make the competition hotter and less manageable.

The Babenberg dynasty

In 976, Count Leopold of Babenberg was given control of the lands that had formed Charlemagne's Eastern March; the first recorded use of the name "Ostarrichi", forerunner to today's Österreich, dates to the year 996. The Babenberg family maintained control of this region for nearly 300 years, playing power politics between the Pope, the Holy Roman Emperor, and the German princes of the electoral diet.

In 1156, Heinrich of Babenberg – usually known as "Jasomirgott" for his supposed favourite saying, "God help me!" – was awarded a duchy and at this time established the Babenberg seat of power in Vienna. His son, Leopold V, was responsible for the imprisonment of Richard the Lionheart, King of England. The ransom paid to spring Richard from Dürnstein Castle funded, among other things, Vienna's city walls.

Friedrich of Babenberg, known as "the Quarrelsome", was the last of his dynasty to hold the eastern territories. In 1246, he lost his life to Hungarian forces at the Battle of Leitha, and the territories held in the Babenberg name were awarded to King Ottakar II of Bohemia.

Enter the Habsburgs

1273 marks the entry into Austrian history of a name which remains resonant in the national culture today: Habsburg. Otto von Habsburg, a member of the European Parliament whose 90th birthday in 2002 saw official celebrations in Vienna's cathedral and presidential palace, is only the latest in a dynasty whose origins can be traced to the Swiss Habsichtsburg, "Castle of the Hawks". From the 11th century on, as knights in what is now Aargau canton, the family had gradually risen to a position of local power in the southern German region of Switzerland and Upper Alsace. By 1273 their scion Rudolf was considered a suitable candidate for the imperial election.

This is not to say that Rudolf was himself a powerful figure; indeed, it was the relative obscurity and insignificance of the Habsburg family which recommended him to the electors in the wake of King Ottakar's victory over the last Babenberg. Where Ottakar might have threatened the independence of the princes forming the diet, Rudolf seemed a "suitable nonentity", and was duly elected.

In fact, as Rudolf I, King of Germany and King of the Romans, the Habsburg "nonentity" challenged Ottakar's claim to the Austrian provinces and in 1278 defeated the Bohemian ruler at Dürnkrut, northeast of Vienna. Rudolf continued accumulating territories, purchasing the remaining Babenberg claims to the region and persuading Heinrich of Bavaria to cede land as well as taking over Carinthia.

The Diet of Augsburg in 1282 saw the electors assent to Rudolf's plan for two of his sons to jointly inherit the territories of Austria, Styria, Carinthia and Carniola. A third son, Hartmann, was intended to inherit Swabia, Alsace and Switzerland, but died travelling to England with a view to marrying Joanna, daughter of Edward III.

Habsburg-Bohemian rivalry

Rudolf intended his son Albrecht to succeed him as King of the Romans and potential Holy Roman Emperor, but Albrecht was initially rejected by the electors. Although he did attain the throne in time, he was killed only shortly afterwards by Swiss forces, and the Habsburg family lost the crown for a century. During the reign of the Bohemian Emperor Karl in the 14th century, an official document – a Golden Bull – was published removing the Habsburg right to vote in the imperial election.

Rudolf IV, then head of the House of Habsburg, was his son-in-law. He retaliated against Karl's manoeuvre by promoting his dynasty as one so illustrious and exalted that they outranked every other noble family in Christendom. These claims were based on a cache of forged documents which Rudolf claimed to have "discovered", but they were not the only element of a sustained public-relations and propaganda campaign in which the Bohemian and Habsburg rulers competed to outdo one another: the construction of St Vitus' Cathedral in Prague provoked a grand renovation of Vienna's Stephansdom in 1359, and the founding of Vienna's University in 1365 was similarly a response to Karl's creation of an equivalent establishment in Prague.

Rudolf's successor, Albrecht V, was able to reclaim the imperial throne by assisting the Bohemian Emperor Sigismund against the Hussite uprising in Sigismund's home territory. Habsburg help came at a price: their debted Bohemian monarch had to promise Albrecht the hand of his daughter and the inheritance of the Hungarian kingdom. By 1438, now crowned King of Hungary, Albrecht was in a position to be elected to the coveted title of Emperor, and this duly took place.

Immediately on attaining the throne, Albrecht took up arms against the Turks. The Ottoman Empire, which had incorporated large swathes of Asia Minor, besieged Constantinople (Istanbul) and invaded Serbia, now threatened Hungarian territory – but it was nature rather than the folly of war which caused most casualties on the battlefield, when dysentry struck both sides, and even Albrecht himself. It is reported that he declared "I shall recover if I can only once more behold the walls of Vienna."

He couldn't and he didn't see them, however, dying on his way back to the city. Immediately after he died the Hungarians snatched back their throne.

Left: Rudolf I, and, **Right:** Frederick III, from the first Habsburg window in the Ducal Chapel of Vienna's Stephansdom.

AEIOU

If Rudolf I placed the Habsburgs at the centre of the German world and of European politics, then it was Albrecht's successor, Friedrich III, who expressed the family's broad, almost cosmic, sense of calling. A geneaology as dubious as Rudolf IV's forged documents connected him to Augustus Caesar and even King Priam of Troy. His possessions were inscribed with the letters AEIOU, a device signifying *Austria est imperare orbi universo*: "It is for Austria to rule the whole world".

This rhetorical grandeur was somewhat undermined by the dire straits of the dynasty

at this time. Friedrich, who was as politically weak and insignificant as Rudolf had been when chosen in 1273, found himself in dispute with Mathias Corvinus of neighbouring Hungary, warring against his own brother, and besieged with his family in Vienna's castle, the Hofburg, by the city's residents. Legend has it that the unfortunate royals ate not only the palace pets but vultures which had gathered on the palace rooftops.

Hope for the future lay with Friedrich's son, burdened, thanks to his father's passion for the occult and astrological, with the name of Maximilian Paulus Aemilius. If Friedrich could marry his son off advantageously, it might be possible to replenish the empty Habsburg coffers and ensure the survival of the Habsburg bloodline, for all but two of Friedrich's children were dead.

Maximilian and marriage

Friedrich negotiated with Charles the Bold, Duke of Burgundy and the richest figure in Europe, for Maximilian, then aged 14, to marry Charles' daughter Mary. What the Habsburgs lacked in monetary enticements they made up for with Friedrich's sway among the electors who could make Charles King of the Romans. Achieving this exalted rank would assist Charles in his ongoing struggle against Louis XI of France, from whom Burgundy sought to secure its independence.

In fact Friedrich, lacking funds to bribe the diet, was less able to influence them than he had claimed. Charles did not become King of the Romans and, although he freed his Burgundian territories from French control, his attempts to advance his borders towards Swiss possessions were unsuccessful, and in 1477 he died in the battle for the control of Nancy. Now Mary of Burgundy, seeking a protector, chose to marry Maximilian. This alliance secured the Netherlands for the House of Habsburg, albeit precariously, and also plunged them into continual war against the French.

Maximilian managed to defeat French forces at Guinegatte in 1479, but peace of a sort was achieved only with the Treaty of Arras in 1482, in which Picardy and Burgundy were ceded to France, while the Habsburgs retained Franche-Comté and the Netherlands. This was also the year of Mary's death in a riding accident. For the next 11 years Maximilian himself acted as regent of the Netherlands before first of all handing the country over to his son Philip the Fair and later his daughter Margaret of Austria. In 1486 Maximilian became King of the Romans in his own right, and in 1490 left the Netherlands for Austria.

Renaissance man

Maximilian exemplifies the clichéd image of a Renaissance prince. He had wide intellectual interests, extensive mastery of the arts and seven languages, and a passion for jousting and hunts. He was a notable patron of art, architecture and music and had a keen eye for posterity, commissioning a series of commemorations of his own reign before his death. As he put it, "He who during his lifetime does not plan to be remembered will not be remembered."

Becoming Emperor three years later, Maximilian pursued the marriage alliance as a political policy. Maximilian's grandchildren were married into the House of Jagiellon, securing ultimate succession to the Bohemian and Hungarian thrones. Philip and Margaret were married to Juana and Juan of Spain respectively – as the children of Ferdinand and Isabella, they were heirs to the Kingdoms of Castile and Aragon. Although Juan died

In equally characteristic fashion, he did so by buying the requisite number of votes with money he did not possess.

Two other items of business on the agenda were ominous. The Pope was calling once more for a crusade against the perceived Turkish threat; and in Wittenberg the previous year, an Augustinian monk had affixed to a church door 95 theses condemning the practice of raising funds through the sale of indulgences.

Maximilian died with little intimation of what the Turks and Martin Luther would mean to the fortunes his arranged marriages had nurtured for the Habsburg dynasty.

shortly afterwards, the marriage of Philip and Juana produced not one but two emperors, Charles V and Ferdinand I. Maximilian's own marriage to Bianca Sforza, niece of the Duke of the Milan, was perhaps less successful, involving him in costly Italian wars which reaped no territorial reward.

Maximilian's last official function as Holy Roman Emperor was to attend the diet of Augsberg in 1518. In characteristic fashion, he used the occasion to ensure that his grandson Charles was crowned King of the Romans.

LEFT: a portrait of the Emperor Maximillian I.
RIGHT: a map of Vienna from 1530.

Charles V and The Reformation

Charles, Maximilian's heir, grandson and a Habsburg of the Spanish branch, was faced with challenges for the imperial throne from Francis I of France, Henry VIII of England, Lajos of Hungary and Sigismund of Poland. To see them off required bribery on a vast scale: in 1519, he secured the position of Holy Roman Emperor by purchasing votes with the wealth of the Fugger banking family.

Charles could now survey the fruits of Maximilian's dynastic scheming: through his parents he held a Spanish inheritance, including Naples, Sicily and claims in the Americas; his aunt Margaret was regent of the Netherlands and aunt Catherine, Queen of England; his sisters were queens of France, Portugal, Hungary, Bohemia, Denmark, Norway and Sweden. Charles chose to delegate the rule of the German-speaking portion of his territories to his brother, the Archduke Ferdinand.

Ferdinand is yet another Habsburg with a fair claim to be considered creator of the Austrian monarchy. In 1515 his grandfather Maximilian had arranged the marriage pact with the Jagiellonian Kings; when Louis Jagiellon died in battle with the Turks at Mohács in 1526, Ferdinand secured election to the thrones of Bohemia and Hungary, which would remain in Habsburg

THE DEFENESTRATION OF PRAGUE

The relative calm of the empire during the Reformation and Counter-Reformation was broken on 23 May 1618 when a meeting in Prague ended in "defenestration". Imperial officials acting on behalf of Ferdinand II had been despatched to curtail the activities of Protestants in the city. Tempers frayed and Bohemian delegates forced the two envoys and a secretary out of a window in the Hradčany palace, some 18 m (60 ft) above the ground. Reportedly they managed to cling to the window ledge by their fingertips, before a bang on the knuckles sent them plunging into a pile of dung. The officals made their escape and reported the insult to Vienna.

hands until the end of World War I.

This marked a significant turning point in the make-up of the Habsburg territories. Up to this point, the hereditary lands of the family had been predominantly German in character, and therefore were relatively easy to integrate under one empire. With the acquisition of Bohemia and Hungary, Habsburg rulers found themselves in possession of non-German kingdoms with long-established traditions of independence. Habsburg rule in the east was dependent on negotiation with the kingdoms' own powerful representative assemblies. Issues of multinationalism would significantly shape the future course of history in the Austrian lands.

While Charles attended to other imperial business, Ferdinand was left to grapple with Austrian affairs, including the advance once again of the Turks. In the 1520s, the forces of Suleiman the Magnificent advanced from established Ottoman territory, coming in 1529 to the walls of Vienna itself, to which they laid siege. Meanwhile the years 1525–6 saw the uprisings known as the Peasants' Wars, and Protestantism also flourished at the University of Vienna and among the Austrian nobility.

Legend has it that during the 1529 siege of Vienna by the Turks, a message was sent to the defenders: "On the third day, we will breakfast within your walls." Turkish sappers moved their trenches forward and tunnelled under the city walls to lay mines. Days passed and then weeks with the situation unchanged, until the Viennese commander was emboldened to signal his besiegers: "Your breakfast is getting cold." So was the weather and with the first snows of winter, the campaigning season closed: rather than attempt the feeding of 250,000 mouths hundreds of miles from home, the Turks struck their tents and departed.

The Counter-Reformation

While the Spanish branch of the empire pursued Counter-Reformation with brutal vigour, Austria appeared far more tolerant of Protestants. In the Bohemian lands, churches repudiating Rome predated Luther and could trace their tradition back to the Hussite risings of the early 15th century. The tradition of *pietas austriaca*, in which the realm was famed for an unswerving championship of Catholicism, began only with the accession of Ferdinand II (1578–1637), whose reign encompassed the start of the Thirty Years' War. Determined to end the privileged position of nonconformist churches in his territory, Ferdinand revoked the Letter of Majesty, a document which had granted considerable rights to non-Catholics. His officials began to harass Protestant congregations, censor their publications, and ensure that Protestant and Hussite believers did not hold office within the empire. One infamous event, the "Defenestration of Prague", provoked conflict across Europe: Protestant eyes across the continent saw symmetry between the strife in Prague and the earlier Hussite uprising and saw this as a sign that the final battle for righteousness was nigh.

Ferdinand was succeeded by Leopold I, who was no less devoted to the Catholic cause than his predecessor. Fourteen years old when he came to the throne, his piety had much impressed his Jesuit teachers. His 65–year reign would be one of the longest in the history of the Habsburg monarchy.

Besieged again

In 1683, Habsburg Vienna was once again threatened by the Ottoman Empire. The Grand Vizier Kara Mustapha sent an army of 250,000 on the long march through the Balkans. By July his forces were mere hours from the Habsburg capital: as the nobility fled to save their skins, local peasants crowded within the protection of the city walls. Leopold, of course, joined his nobles in flight. It is said that servants and courtiers left behind bolted from the Hofburg in such haste that they neglected to close the gates.

Vienna's 60,000 remaining inhabitants were defended by a mixed band of infantry and armed civilians. The city was walled on three sides and protected on the fourth by the Danube; as the Turks approached, the bridge across the river was destroyed. The imperial army itself was held in reserve further upriver, supported by forces from Poland when its ruler, Jan Sobieski, recognised the dangers for his own kingdom should Vienna fall.

On 4 September an explosion breached the city walls close to the Hofburg. Turkish soldiers attacked by the thousand, and managed to plant two standards on the wall before being

driven back. The defenders patched up the breach with rubble, furniture and any other material to hand. The Turkish commander waited for Vienna's capitulation rather than press home the advantage, but before this could happen a relief column of Polish and imperial forces charged down from the slopes of the Kahlenberg mountain and ended the siege.

Leopold was on a boat on the Danube when he was informed of the lightning victory on 12 September 1683. He ordered the postponement of any celebrations until he arrived in the city: as always, propaganda and prestige were vital. He explained, "It is true I have commanded that

I must be the first to enter the city, for I fancy that otherwise the love of my subjects for me would be diminished, and their affection for others increase."

Austria among the Great Powers

With the struggle against the Ottoman Empire ending in the Habsburgs' favour, the dynasty entered the 18th century as one of the European "Great Powers". On the western flank of the Habsburg lands, the French King Louis XIV sought to win for his heir, Philip, the Habsburg title in Spain. As England was equally opposed to a union between France and Spain, a "Grand Alliance" was formed with Austria,

---

LEFT: Martin Luther, Protestant theologian.
RIGHT: Kara Mustapha, leader of the Turks during the siege of Vienna in 1683.

and the two countries fought side by side in the 12-year War of Spanish Succession. Prince Eugene of Savoy, the most renowned military figure in Austrian history, formed a formidable partnership with England's leading general, the Duke of Marlborough. Although the French were ultimately beaten, England did not seek to win Spain for the Habsburgs and therefore broke off the alliance immediately. At the concluding Treaty of Utrecht, Philip was awarded Spain, but only on condition of forfeiting his right to the French throne; Charles VI, Leopold's Habsburg successor, was compensated with Spanish possessions – these

without the approval of the Electoral Diet. He went against precedent by permitting the crown to pass to a daughter if necessary, ensuring the inheritance of his child, Maria Theresa. Objection was raised by countries keen to see the empire disintegrate: Charles' action drew him into two costly wars before his death in 1740.

"I found myself", Maria Theresa wrote of her succession, "without money, without credit, without an army, without experience and knowledge…" The financial situation for the new empress was particularly precarious: the army had gone months without pay, the national debt was vast, and the rich nobility had

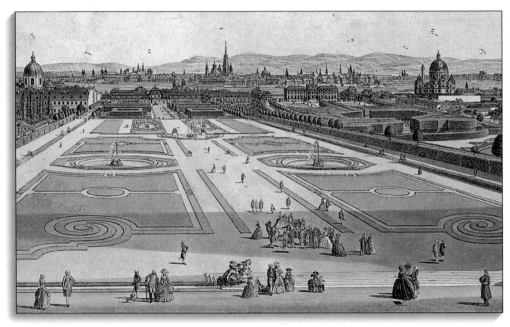

consisted of Naples, Milan, the Spanish Netherlands – and gained the territory of Sardinia, but only at the expense of Sicily.

Rivalry with France was not purely military. Schloss Schönbrunn, the famous baroque palace of the Habsburgs, was intended to outdo Versailles by its young architect, Fischer von Erlach, who was largely responsible for rebuilding Vienna following the Turkish siege.

Maria Theresa

Unable to produce a male heir, Charles VI ensured the survival of the Habsburg Empire by use of the "Pragmatic Sanction", a legal loophole enabling him to pass certain laws

been exempted from taxation by her father to ensure their loyalty. A new rival for Austria also loomed in the form of Prussia, a rising power under the rule of a man who had once been thought a suitable husband, Frederick of the House of Hohenzollern.

Seeking to expand its domain, Prussia invaded Silesia, a rich German-speaking imperial province occupying the site of present-day southern Poland. This began what came to be known as the War of Austrian Succession. France intended to dismember the Austrian possessions, giving Bohemia and Upper Austria to the Elector of Bavaria, who would then be crowned emperor; Moravia and Upper Silesia to Saxony; Lower Silesia and Glaz to Prussia; and Lombardy to Spain.

In the meantime, Maria Theresa gave birth to the child she had been carrying at the time of her succession. Recent Habsburg failure in the matter of male heirs was reversed with a spectacular emphasis: the boy Joseph was a 7 kg (15½ lb) giant at birth and apparently healthy in every respect. With invasions by both Bavaria and France imminent, she visited her Hungarian subjects, appealing for help. Hungary's representative assembly voted her six regiments, enough to repel the Bavarians and persuade the French to make peace. Maria Theresa never regained Silesia, but she did retrieve the crown of the Holy Roman Empire. As she was considered ineligible to wear it, her husband was made emperor in 1745. Joseph II, their son and heir, was elected King of the Romans in 1764, and following the death of his father in the next year, became Holy Roman Emperor in his own right.

Joseph II

Joseph, the boy on whom the hopes of the empire rested, grew up to share the throne with his mother as co-regent. The gulf between them was apparent. She always believed in absolute rule. He had travelled widely, become a student of radical French philosophy and wished to revolutionise the entire empire. On acceding to the throne on his own right in 1780, he put his liberal theories into practice. The press was given unprecedented freedom, Jews no longer had to identify themselves by wearing yellow stripes and sleeves, and education was made compulsory for all, including women. He also opened imperial parks and art collections to the public for the first time.

By the time of his death in 1790, Europe was confronted with what appeared to be the logical conclusion to unfettered liberty, the French Revolution. The only way to avoid that ghastly scenario in Austria amounted to a backlash. The unexpected death of Leopold II after only two years as emperor put the throne in the hands of his son Franz II, who quickly restored the conservative and pro-Catholic aspects of the monarchy. If the imperial ambitions of

LEFT: view of Vienna from the Belvedere in 1784.
RIGHT: a portrait of Maria Theresa by Martin van Meytens.

Napoleon were bound to bring France and the Habsburg Empire into conflict, matters can only have been exacerbated by the fact that Marie Antoinette, executed the year after Franz came to the throne, was the Emperor's aunt.

Napoleon and Metternich

Napoleon crowned himself Emperor of the French in 1804, with the clear intention of appropriating from Franz the symbolic title of Holy Roman Emperor. After a group of German princes seceded to join him in the Confederation of the Rhine, he controlled much of the empire's territory in any case. That year,

Franz proclaimed himself Franz I of Austria, a Habsburg Empire which owed nothing to the Holy Roman one. In 1805, after a series of lightning victories in Italy, Napoleon succeeded in occupying Vienna, driving the imperial family to the fortresses of Olmutz and later Teschen. In 1806, Franz dissolved the title of Holy Roman Emperor. The title which had fomented countless cunning marriages and numerous wars for 1,000 years dropped out of currency as simply as that.

Franz's immediate concern was to check Napoleon before he could do further damage to the redefined empire. Emboldened by French reverses in Spain, Austrian forces mobilised and, against all odds, inflicted a single-handed defeat at Aspern. Franz watched the victory from a nearby hill. He is supposed, after the battle, to have made only one laconic comment: "Now we can, I think, go home."

There then emerged in Austrian affairs a man whose first actions in office bore the stamp of his style. Prince Clemens von Metternich bought peace with Napoleon by persuading him to marry Marie Louise, Franz's daughter. A proxy wedding took place in Vienna in March 1810. It was quintessentially Metternich's doing that, having bought peace with the marriage, Austria then declared war on France.

Revolution and the rise of Napoleon: in the new European order, Metternich found it necessary to repress alternative and radical views and opinions through strict censorship and police intervention. Assisted by Joseph Sedlnitzky, the Chief of Police, Metternich sought to preserve the existing social and political order with draconian controls. The freedom of the press was swept away and political activity totally prohibited.

Biedermeier

With serious issues unavailable for discussion, public life settled into a pattern of withdrawn

The Congress of Vienna

Napoleon was eventually defeated by British and Prussian forces at Waterloo in 1814. Immediately afterwards the Austrian, Russian, Prussian and British allies set about carving up his conquests at the Congress of Vienna. Metternich's diplomatic skill secured Austria a generous territorial settlement from the peace conference, acquiring Salzburg and Venice and regaining much of northern Italy. The new order established at the congress proved enduring and helped to ensure relative peace in Europe for several decades.

However, the horizons of European political thought had been shifted by the French

Gemütlichkeit, staid comfort; the age became known as Biedermeier, named for a satirical figure representing the archetypal stolid middle-class burgher. Superficially, it was the emergence of a prosperous, urban middle class swept along by crazes for the waltz, floral wallpaper, beer and sausages. However, for those not secure in professional employment or with an income from property, life was almost unbearably harsh. The city's infrastructure could not support the growing working-class population and, amidst poverty, unemployment and overcrowding, diseases ran rife, including the typhoid fever that took the life of Schubert and the cholera epidemic of 1831.

Repression and revolt

In 1835, Franz II was succeeded by his son Ferdinand I, whose learning difficulties were, to put it mildly, extreme and who served only as a figurehead for Metternich's regime. Among foreign ambassadors, it was cruelly joked that the cleverest thing Ferdinand had ever said was: "I am the emperor and I want dumplings." With Ferdinand in his pocket, Metternich could use the monarch's personal power as his own, so he made sure he had plenty of it.

The Family Law promulgated in 1839 was breathtaking. It first defined the family as all the archdukes (plus wives and widows) and all

eration of the empire's desperate workers and its politically frustrated middle class in the Revolution of March 1848. Their defiance broke the false tranquillity of the Biedermeier era and people took to the streets. The army was called out, but the students of Vienna kept up the pressure.

The Paris Revolution and the numerous other European revolts of 1848 inspired the population to stage a general uprising. Soon virtually the entire empire was in revolt in five separate but interrelated actions: the Viennese, the Czechs in Prague, the Magyars in Budapest, Croats in Agram and Italians in Milan and

the archduchesses descended in the male line from Maria Theresa. They were to observe a code of conduct which amounted to undebatable obedience to the emperor's will. If any of these relatives failed to do so they would forfeit all imperial honours, titles, privileges – and income. If they married without the emperor's permission, they lost all rights for themselves and their children.

All these formal power games amongst the nobility were rendered irrelevant by the coop-

LEFT: Napoleon rides past the Schönbrunn.
RIGHT: the revolutions of 1848 in Vienna were brutally suppressed by troops.

Venice. Metternich quickly packed and escaped, reputedly hidden in a laundry basket, to England. The Monarchy, thrown off balance, fled the city; Ferdinand repealed censorship, agreed to a new constitution and in December, he abdicated in favour of his 18-year-old nephew, Franz Joseph. At the same time, however, imperial order was reasserting itself in force: the Habsburg armies under the celebrated Marshals Radetzky and Windischgrätz quashed the revolts in Vienna, Prague, Budapest and the Italian cities; Hungary, which proclaimed an independent republic in 1849, was made to capitulate by General Jellacic, aided by Russian forces at the Battle of Világos. ❑

THE REIGN OF FRANZ JOSEPH

This longest reigning Habsburg monarch saw not only a great flowering of artistic and intellectual endeavour but also the collapse of his empire

Franz Joseph's rule was a Habsburg record, lasting 68 years. It began with swift vengeance against the perpetrators of the uprising in the form of summary execution of key figures. Franz Joseph's dynasty had only survived thanks to the army's intervention in 1848–9; this weakened his position insofar as military defeats – against France in 1859 and Prussia in 1866 – weakened the empire as a whole. Austrian neutrality in the Crimean War between Russia, Britain and France weakened the Austrian Monarchy externally as well as internally, by leaving the empire in diplomatic isolation. The defeat by France, in particular, in 1859 at the battles of Solferino and Magenta, caused such a crisis within Austria that Franz Joseph was forced to introduce constitutional government in 1861.

This was the era of the rise of nationalism. The empire included nine kingdoms, and in time-honoured Habsburg fashion Franz Joseph was in every instance the king as well. Popular support for the overarching imperial identity waned: groups of people who spoke the same language and defined a common culture for themselves were beginning to envisage life as separate nations under their own autonomous government. The Austrian Empire was held together by a number of pins: bureaucracy; military force; German language and culture. But this last was double-edged. The feeling among the urban classes that they were, or had become, "German" was to drive a wedge between them and the more conservative peasants who clung to their ethnic roots. The seeds of Austro-German nationalism had been sown in Maria Theresa's reign, when the rise of Prussia under Frederick the Great offered German Austrians an alternative spiritual home. Prior to that, Germany only existed in a nebulous sense as a jumble of states that could not singly or even collectively hold a candle to the mighty

Habsburgs. As the 19th century progressed and nationalist pressures increased within the empire, Austro-German intellectuals looked increasingly to a solution involving incorporation with Prussia and, later, with Bismarck's powerful Germany. This *deutschnational* or *grossdeutsch* solution appealed across classes

and political parties, but was not to reflect the majority view until after 1918. The Austrian Empire, on the other hand, was supposedly ceding its Germanic nature to Hungary and to Slavic influence in the east, or so German nationalists feared.

Criticism of 1861's constitutional arrangement came from all sides, including liberals still faithful to the empire, nationalist groups, and particularly the Magyars of Hungary – who had only recently, albeit briefly, won their independence – and this dissatisfaction meant a further constitutional revision was necessary. It was only six years later, after Prussia's victory at the battle of Sadowa in 1866, that the final evo-

---

LEFT: Emperor Franz Joseph I, the Habsburg's longest-serving ruler.
RIGHT: a 19th-century passport.

lution of the Habsburg Monarchy, into the "Austro-Hungarian Empire" took place, with the constitution of 1867.

Ausgleich

Following the loss of Lombardy to the French in 1859, renewed demands for Hungarian independence had pushed Franz Joseph into conciliatory mode. However, the establishment of a parliament, with 85 Hungarian representatives, failed to placate their dreams of independence. In the 1867 constitutional compromise known as the *Ausgleich*, Hungary and Austria, which is to say Hungary as opposed to the rest

of the empire, would each have their own parliaments. The new set-up was to be called the Dual Monarchy of Austria-Hungary – k.u.k. or *kaiserlich und königlich* (imperial and royal). Each half of the empire bore sovereign equality. Franz Joseph, already Austria's Emperor, would be crowned King of Hungary in Budapest: yet the army, foreign affairs and finance would remain under Austrian control. In other words, there was still a pyramid and the emperor was at the top of it.

Outside Hungary, the German character of the monarchy was maintained. The Habsburg dynasty was German in origin; its administrative system and culture were both predomi-

nantly German in character. Austro-Germans were, at this time, less a nationalist force than the *Staatsvolk*, the "people of the state" who staffed Habsburg institutions, above all the civil service and the officer class of the otherwise quite multinational imperial army. The greatest shortcoming of the *Ausgleich* lay in its failure to engage with the demands of national groups other than Germans and Magyars; such groups – Poles and Ruthenians, Czechs, Croats, Slovaks, Romanians and Serbs, Slovenes and Italians – lived in both Austrian and Hungarian areas of the Dual Monarchy and in fact made up more than half of the populations, but were granted no voice and no autonomy by the new Compromise. Five groups were of particular significance for what was now the "Austrian" portion of the empire.

The Poles and Ruthenians

Poles in the Monarchy lived largely within the province of Galicia (present-day south-eastern Poland and western Ukraine), but this territory had only been acquired by the dynasty in 1772 and not all Poles actually lived within the empire. Given this fact – and Galicia's geographical remoteness relative to the imperial heartlands – the Poles could be seen as the ethnic group least connected to the "nationality issue" facing the subject peoples of the Austro-Hungarian Empire. In addition, the politics of coalition in the Viennese parliament after the Ausgleich allowed the ruling Polish Conservative Party to win major concessions in Galicia, including recognition of Polish as an official language and the "Polonisation" of the province's universities.

The Poles, rather than being a suppressed nationality, in fact dominated a minority within their own territory, the Ruthenes, an ethnic group related to the Ukrainians in Russia, but distinguished from them on religious grounds. Ruthenians responded to cultural Polonisation by building their own nationalist movement from the grassroots; Viennese authorities were content to "divide and conquer", allowing the Polish-Ruthene tension to prevent the establishment of an anti-Habsburg unity. From the 1880s on, "Young Ruthenians" agitated for union with the 30 million Ukrainians of the Tsars' Russia; in 1914, seven years after universal suffrage was introduced, they became partners of the Poles in Galicia's provincial government.

The Czechs

The Czechs, the third largest ethnic group of the monarchy, lived entirely within the empire's borders, and initially sought autonomy, rather than independence. In Bohemia, Czechs outnumbered Germans roughly three to two. A Czech middle class developed to rival the traditional one of the Germans, and this economic, political and cultural resurgence bolstered the historical claims of a nation that had been assimilated by the monarchy at the same time as the Hungarians and therefore demanded equality with them.

A key issue in the battle was over the language of administration and schooling. Czechs

The Slovenes

The Slovene people were scattered across six *Kronländer*, or crown lands, of the Austro-Hungarian Empire: Carinthia, Styria, Trieste, Istria, Gorizia and Carniola. Only in Carniola and Gorizia did they actually form a majority: in general, even the most modest demands to use their language in schools or public life were fiercely resisted, especially by German nationalists. As with the Czechs, Slovene sentiment was generally in favour of autonomy over independence, although tending towards the latter ever more by the turn of the 20th century. As South Slavs, Slovenes had ethnic links to the Serbs and Croats

sought the right to instruct children in their own language and to use it also in administrative business, something fiercely resisted by a German minority backed by fellow German speakers beyond, both in Austria and in the German Empire to the west. Czechs established their own bank, theatre and university in the second half of the 19th century and by 1910, only six percent of Prague's population was German. The conflict, raging in Viennese as well as Prague political circles, continued into World War II.

LEFT: the Imperial coat of arms of the joint monarchy of Austria-Hungary.
RIGHT: Prague around 1900.

of the Hungarian half of the monarchy – in the late 19th century they were involved in the "Trialism" movement centred on Croatia, which envisioned a tripartite empire with leadership shared between Germans, Magyars and Croats.

The Italians

Italians were the empire's smallest national group, located in the Tyrol and along the Adriatic coast. After 1861, the newly unified Italy gave Austrian-Italians a focus for nationalist sentiment. Given their numerical insignificance, the Italian presence within the monarchy never formed a "nationality question" on a par with those of the South Slavs or Czechs, but rather became a foreign-policy issue between the monarchy and the state of Italy. In 1915, the entente powers successfully used the promise of awarding South Tyrol and the Adriatic territories to Italy as an encouragement to join their battle with the Austrian monarchy.

The Ringstrasse era

The years 1867–1914 were a time of rapid change, seeing no less than 20 prime ministers in Austria – compared, for example, to just five chancellors in Germany. The imperial administration struggled to cope with the rise of nationalism and the changing tides of international ance policy against a repeat of 1848. So effective was the symbolism of Vienna's redesign that the second half of the 19th century is not known just as the *Gründerzeit*, or "Founders' Period" but also the "Ringstrasse era".

Despite this imperial flamboyance, the Liberals' time in power swiftly decayed after 1870, principally because of an economic crisis in 1873, which discredited the Liberals' laissez-faire policies. In Vienna, numerous businesses went bust and the World Exhibition being held in the capital that year caused even greater financial ruin that might otherwise have been expected. There was a marked rise in anti-

politics. For the decade immediately following the *Ausgleich*, domestic affairs were largely in the charge of the German Liberal party in Austria. Fittingly, for an administration devoted to the unitary state and centralised German administration, this period saw the building of Vienna's magnificent Ringstrasse, a circular boulevard lined with public buildings, museums and universities, which had begun with the demolition of the old city walls in 1857. Of course, for all the uplifting rhetoric, there was still a military/police aspect to this public works programme – although the city walls had gone, the ring road was in fact perfect for the deployment against civic unrest and was effectively an insur-

Semitism in response, both in Vienna and beyond, as Jews were held responsible for financial traumas which were actually caused by the massive restructuring of politics, economics and society going on across 19th-century Europe.

In 1879, Count Taaffe – a childhood friend of the emperor – headed a new government supported by German, Czech and Polish conservatives. It was nicknamed the "iron ring" around liberalism. Taaffe sought to reconcile and reintegrate imperial subjects across national and social boundaries. His first success was with the Czechs, to whom he offered language rights, increased parliamentary representation and other concessions. In addition to some modest social reforms, such as new health and safety directives, Taaffe's government brought about a franchise reform which increased the number of subjects with a right to vote, especially among the lower-middle class and even the peasantry.

The increased support for deeply conservative political parties was caused by fear of big business among the new voters; Taaffe, firmly ensconced in his position, ran the empire along bureaucratic rather than parliamentary lines, using civil servants rather than elected officials. He was nicknamed the "emperor's minister" as a result. Taaffe's balancing act between rival national groups and other political forces became known by the slightly comical name of *fortwursteln*, or "muddling through". He fell from the tightrope in 1893 when his electoral reforms were resisted by four parties in coalition – the Poles, the German Liberals, the Clericals and the Feudals – but of even greater importance, especially in the long-term, was the rise of three new mass movements: social democracy, Christian socialism and Pan-Germanism.

Social Democracy

The Social Democrats were arguably the spiritual heirs to Austro-German liberalism, although their anti-Liberal rhetoric was vitriolic. Their socialism cut across the nationalism issue, but maintained a strong centralist approach and opposed the pan-Slavist alternative, which would see the various Slavonic nations unite under Russian guidance. The Social Democratic Party was formally born in 1889, after 40 years of government repression of the labour movement in Austria. Although Marxist, the social democratic approach in Austria was reformist and the movement was criticised by Trotsky, one-time regular at Vienna's Café Central, for its lack of revolutionary fervour. Confronted by the difficulties of nationalism in a way that no Western European socialists were, the Social Democrats pursued multinational federation as the solution to Austria's social problems.

Christian Socials

The Christian Social Party were another breakaway movement from Austrian liberalism. Its founder was Karl Lueger, who became one of

Vienna's most popular mayors, serving from 1897 to 1910. He broke with the Liberal party of which he was originally a member because of the corruption he perceived within it, and sought a broadening of the franchise. Through influential speechmaking and clever political organisation, *"der schöne Karl"* ("handsome Karl") appealed to the lower middle classes and artisans frustrated by the violent upheavals in 19th-century society and their lack of a say in their own government. One of the darker rhetorical weapons Lueger brandished on behalf of the "little man" was anti-Semitism: Hitler's widely-noted admiration for Lueger's oratory

has caused later generations to see Lueger as a kind of proto-Nazi, but Lueger's prejudices were more a matter of political expediency than racist credo and Hitler himself dismissed Lueger's policies as a mere "sham anti-Semitism". Nonetheless, Lueger's actions doubtless served to popularise and legitimise anti-Semitism within the late Austro-Hungarian Empire.

Pan-Germanism

Georg von Schönerer was another former liberal who began to challenge his party's policies in the 1880s. Calls for an extended franchise and social reform were as common to Pan-Germanists as Social Democrats and Christian Socials, but von

---

LEFT: Vienna's Ringstrasse in 1900.
RIGHT: Karl Lueger, the anti-Semitic mayor of Vienna.

Schönerer brought an added call for closer links with Germany. In concert with nationalistic student associations, the Pan-Germanists sought the break-up of the monarchy so that a German-speaking Austria, stripped of Slavic and Jewish elements, might unite with Germany, then flourishing under Bismarck. He engaged in publicity-boosting campaigns such as that to nationalise a railway which had been privately financed by the Jewish Rothschild banking family. Von Schönerer's campaign failed, but it did fan the flames of a popular anti-Semitism which saw the Jews as an elite and greedy "other" people, alien to the "true" German-speakers.

The retreat into the garden?

Perhaps because of these political crises, *fin-de-siècle* Vienna flourished creatively and intellectually. Today's historians of the period describe a "retreat into the garden" on the part of the educated Viennese middle class, devoting themselves to artistic or abstract thought as the mass movements rendered them politically impotent; others point to the particular predicament of educated Viennese Jews, desperately trying to think and write their way out of rising discrimination and an increasingly apocalyptic rhetoric of prejudice.

As in Biedermeier times, social tensions were often escaped through a devoted hedonism: the waltz, a Viennese tradition derived from Austrian folk dances, became increasingly popular, as did the operetta tradition. At the end of World War I, the composer Ravel wrote of his dark piece *La Valse*, "I feel this work a kind of apotheosis of the Viennese waltz, linked in my mind with the impression of a fantastic whirl of destiny."

Ravel was not the only one to comment on the dark side of this seemingly light-hearted passion for music and theatre: Karl Kraus, who published and almost single-handedly wrote his own journal *Die Fackel (The Torch)*, aimed to skewer the hypocrisy of his Viennese contemporaries with biting aphorisms on every aspect of cultural, social and political life in the city and the empire at large. Even within the mainstream press, a newspaper section known as the *Feuilleton*, providing space for contemplative – even aimless – cultural essays, gave a forum to those wishing to satirise the urban scene around them. And the "Revolutionary Dream", one of those analysed in Sigmund Freud's ground-breaking 1900 *Interpretation of Dreams*, followed this tradition in mocking the then-prime minister Count Franz Thun.

Scandal

Viennese high society provided plenty of targets for Kraus and his fellow writers. In 1888, Franz Joseph's son and heir the Crown Prince Rudolf, married to Stephanie (the daughter of the king of Belgium), had met a young baroness, Marie Vetsera, at the Burgtheater. According to her mother's later account, the baroness and the Archduke had already noticed one another on visits to the races and the Prater – but now Marie was approached by Countess Marie Larisch-Wallersee, Rudolf's cousin and occasional procuress. On 11 December, with the Vienna Opera performing Wagner's *Rheingold*, Marie used her dislike for the composer's music as an excuse to part with her family and be smuggled by coach into the Hofburg and Rudolf's apartments. She returned to her house in Marokkanergasse in good time to welcome her mother and sister home.

Shortly afterwards, Rudolf organised a shooting trip. He invited some friends along. They would meet up at his shooting lodge, Mayerling, southwest of the captial. What he didn't tell the others was that Marie Vetsera was also invited. His brother-in-law, Prince Philip of Coburg, and Count Hoyos were Rudolf's shooting guests.

There was no sign of Mary's presence when they arrived at Mayerling, and Rudolf said nothing to indicate that she had arrived at the lodge.

Rudolf and Philip were due to return to Vienna overnight for a family dinner, while Hoyos was to stay at Mayerling – not in the lodge itself but in a nearby cottage. Rudolf and Philip would be back in time for breakfast. Rudolf then cried off. He said he did not feel strong enough for the journey and asked Philip to extend his apologies both to the emperor and Stephanie, who was expecting him to join her.

Philip having left, Rudolf and Hoyos sat down to dinner. After Hoyos went off to the stables. He had not gone far when he heard two shots. Racing back to the lodge, he could smell powder. The door was locked; he managed to smash a hole large enough to reach in and unlock the door from the inside.

"What an appalling sight," he said in a memorandum taken down by his son many years afterwards. "Rudolf, fully dressed, was lying on his bed, dead; Marie Vetsera, likewise fully dressed, on her bed. Rudolf's army revolver was by his side. The two had not gone to bed at all… It was clear at first sight that Rudolf first shot Marie Vetsera and then killed himself." The immediate response of the authorities was to con-

cottage, Marie emerged from hiding. When Rudolf and Marie withdrew to the bedroom, it was with instructions to the valet Loschek not to allow anyone in, not even the emperor.

Staying in the next room, Loschek could hear Rudolf and Marie talking late into the night but not what they were saying. His next recollection was of Rudolf walking into his room fully dressed at about 5.40 am with the request that he get horses and a carriage ready right away. Loschek got up, dressed, and made his way to

ceal all evidence of scandal: the body of the 18-year-old baroness, left for 38 hours, was loaded into a carriage at Mayerling in a way that disguised the fact of her death, and buried swiftly and without fanfare. Franz Joseph himself received news of the double death from his mistress Katherine Schratt, an actress with whom he took coffee when at liberty from official duties.

It was not until later that the scandal fully emerged and all manner of commentators permitted themselves to interpret the bizarre and gruesome event, from the professor of medicine who blamed Rudolf's actions on "premature synostosis of the cranial sutures" to Crown Princess Stephanie, who printed Rudolf's farewell letter to

LEFT: Karl Kraus, photographed in 1910.
ABOVE: Archduke Rudolf, and, **RIGHT:** Marie Vetsera.

her in her memoirs. "Dear Stephanie: You are rid of my presence and plague; be happy in your own way. Be good to the poor little girl [their daughter] who is the only thing that remains of me. Give my last regards to all friends… I am going calmly to my death which alone can save my good name. Embracing you most warmly, your loving Rudolf."

The end of Sissi

Less than a decade after the deaths at Mayerling, the empress herself – Elisabeth, popularly known as Sissi – was killed. While on holiday in Switzerland with her lady-in-waiting she was

assassinated by an Italian anarchist, who, deliberately bumping into the empress, slid a sharpened file through her rib-cage. Franz Joseph never got over the shock of his wife's death, but focused his attention on his remaining heir, his nephew the Archduke Franz Ferdinand. Of particular concern were his marital prospects, which would clearly have to conform to the long-dead Metternich's still active Family Law.

The Archduke Friedrich and Archduchess Isabella's bevy of lovely daughters had the necessary qualifications, so when Franz Ferdinand made a practice of spending weekends at their Bratislava estate the only question in the archduchess's mind, and a nagging one, was not

knowing which of the daughters he preferred. He seemed to be remarkably even-handed in dealing with them, but Isabella liked to think it was her eldest, Marie Christine.

The solution to the mystery seemed at hand when Franz Ferdinand inadvertently left his watch behind in Bratislava. Instead of a normal chain, it was attached to a string of the trinkets he collected and one of them was seen to be a locket of the kind in which lovers kept miniature portraits of their dearest. Isabella prised open the locket and stared at the portrait in total disbelief. It was Countess Sophie Chotek von Chotkova und Wognin, her lady-in-waiting.

Sophie was sacked on the spot, and the emperor would not hear of Franz Ferdinand marrying her. Her family had a respectable Bohemian background and her father was a Czech diplomat, but that was not enough, and Franz Joseph wheeled out the Family Law. Eventually, under pressure from Pope Leo XIII, Kaiser Wilhelm and Czar Nicholas, he agreed to a morganatic marriage, which meant that a wife would not assume her husband's title, rank or privileges, nor would any children. The emperor boycotted the wedding, but relented slightly in promoting Sophie to princess of Hohenberg. The title was small compensation for slights at court, such as not being allowed to share her husband's box at the theatre or sit next to him at dinner if more authentic Habsburgs were present. Despite these restrictions, Franz Ferdinand was delighted with his choice.

The decline

It is widely assumed that the Austro-Hungarian Empire was foredoomed long before the outbreak of war in 1914: the crises of nationalism and anti-Semitism, the rise of mass movements and the seeming ineptitude of the successive administrations all suggest a kind of woolly mammoth lumbering towards a belated extinction, an "over-ripe civilisation doomed beyond any possibility of reprieve." In fact, even the most radical critics calling for the empire's dissolution and dismemberment were not sure that the patient was in a critical condition. One British commentator and critic of the monarchy, Wickham Steed, remarked in 1913 that the empire's crises were "of growth rather than of decay." More measured contemporary studies suggest that the fate of Austria-Hungary was made in the decade leading up to 1914, and above all in the issue of South Slav nationalism, which transformed from an internal issue into one of foreign policy.

Archduke Franz Ferdinand's preoccupation while he waited to step into his uncle's shoes was to make up for the loss of power to Prussia in the west by consolidating the empire's hold in the east, in particular on Bosnia and Herzegovina, acquired from Turkey at the 1878 Congress of Berlin. He envisaged a multiplication of the Dual System with Hungary so that other parts of the empire could enjoy a certain degree of self-rule within the umbrella of empire.

The Archduke was not the only political figure to turn his attention to the Balkans, however: Russian interest in the region was also in resurgence. The imperial government could not decide whether to respond to South Slav nationalism and Russian provocation with oppression or concession: *fortwursteln* continued to rule the day. Imperial action was further hampered by an intelligence coup achieved by the Tsar's government in 1903. It involved the deputy head of Austria's secret service, Colonel Alfred Redl.

Redl was responsible for the reorganisation of the k.u.k. intelligence service. He modernised many of the espionage techniques used by the monarchy and introduced technological advances such as fingerprinting. However, his homosexuality had to be concealed from Austrian society of the time, and he pursued his love affairs in strict secrecy; when they were discovered by Tsarist Russia, Redl became a victim of blackmail and was forced to disclose Austrian secrets to the rival power while diverting attention from the Russians' own operations within the monarchy. This situation continued over the decade from 1903 to 1913, until another officer, Maximilian Ronge, compared the writing on a post office box application form to a secret document written by Redl. When the two hands proved to be identical, Redl was identified as a traitor: the box had been used for the drop-off of money provided by the Russian secret service. Redl committed suicide rather than face the scandal that would have ensued.

Despite this weakness in the Austrian foreign service, there was no end to the schemes devised to revitalise imperial strength in the

Balkans – up to and including a preventative war against the Serbians. Only the emperor blocked these moves, motivated by his belief in peace at all costs. The defeats of 1859 and 1866 had both occurred within the ageing monarch's reign, and war with Russia in 1914 could easily provoke further weakening of the Habsburg territories.

Baron von Aerenthal, foreign minister between 1906 and 1912, attempted to improve relations with Russia and at the same time make Serbia more dependent on the Dual Monarchy. This was to be achieved by building a railway line linking the empire directly to Turkey. Aus-

tria had the right to construct such a railway under a treaty, but overestimated Russian tolerance for such a move. Russia was angered, but there was still room for negotiation between the two powers, until the Young Turk revolution broke out in 1908. A revival of Turkey's fortunes might increase their influence over the Balkans at Austria's expense – Aehrenthal opted to annex the relevant territories before this could happen. Negotiations between Russia and the Dual Monarchy took place in Moravia in 1908. Details of the meeting remain unclear and hotly debated, but when one month later the provinces were annexed by Franz Joseph's forces, the Tsar's government was incensed. The "Bosnian

LEFT: the Empress Elizabeth, or "Sissi", painted by Franz Xavier Winterhalter.
RIGHT: the elderly Franz Joseph in 1914.

Crisis", lasting some six months, brought Europe close to the brink of war, provoked an immediate upsurge in Slav nationalism and destroyed Austro-Russian good relations once and for all. Now Italy joined with Russia in an agreement intended to preserve the status quo – unfavourable to Austria – in the Balkans.

In 1912, the Turkish Empire was shaken by events in Morocco and Libya; the Balkan states chose this time to move against Turkey and drive it out of Europe. Bulgaria, Serbia, Greece and Montenegro pushed Turkish forces back until the westernmost limits of Turkish power lay within 48 km (30 miles) of Istanbul. The Aus-

by the actions they had taken. The long term policy of peace in the Balkans and the containment of Serbian aspiration had broken down. Serbian terrorist groups operated within the monarchy while the Balkan state also attempted to build a new Balkan league with its neighbours. With such tensions in the air, Archduke Franz Ferdinand was delighted to receive an invitation to observe military manoeuvres which were to be held there in the summer of 1914.

Sarajevo

The royal party arrived at Ilidze on 25 June 1914. The trip had been publicised well in

trian historian Joseph Redlich made a sarcastic entry in his diary at the time: "The sick man is dead. Austria has every chance to be the sick man in his place." Serbian power was at an all-time high; the fear among Austria's rulers was that what Serbia held today, Russia might claim tomorrow in the name of Pan-Slavism. As Vienna's *Neue Freie Presse* expressed it, the Balkan nations in concert could be "a dagger in Russia's hand pointed straight at Austria's heart." Diplomatic action was taken to stop Serbia acquiring a port on the Adriatic coast; Russia conceded this at a conference of the "Great Powers" in May 1913, but nonetheless Serbia and Montenegro were both enlarged and empowered

advance and the resort was festooned with flags and bunting. Fully aware of Franz Ferdinand's antiques collection, the Sarejevo dealers had craftily decorated his hotel with their wares to entice him to visit their shops. Franz Ferdinand was duly enticed and decided to visit the antiques shops of Sarajevo that very day. At one point during his party's walk to the bazaar they passed close to, but probably did not notice, one youth who was not cheering.

Gavrilo Princip was 19 years old, born the fourth of nine children to the postman in the village of Oblej in the wild, mountainous region separating Bosnia from the Dalmatian coast. An ethnic Serb, he was by nationality Austro-

Hungarian and had been to school in Sarajevo. In 1912 he had gone off to live in the Serbian capital, Belgrade, and had returned to Sarajevo only four weeks prior to the archduke's visit. Only a handful of people knew that his time in Belgrade had been spent with the Black Hand, Serbian nationalists who, in the interest of a Greater Serbia, had made the assassination of Franz Ferdinand their top priority. Princip's mission in Sarajevo was to do just that, three days later on Sunday 28 June, the anniversary of Turkey's victory over Serbia at Kosovo in 1389. The choice of this date was to signify a recovery from that defeat.

Franz Ferdinand's reply showed more command of the situation: "It gives me special pleasure to accept the assurances of your unshakable loyalty and affection for His Majesty, our Most Gracious Emperor and King. I thank you cordially, Mr Mayor, for the resounding ovations with which the population received me and my wife, the more so since I see in them an expression of pleasure over the failure of the assassination attempt…"

While the Princess Sophie went upstairs to talk to a delegation of Muslim women, the archduke received local dignitaries in the vestibule. He was assured that the bomber had been arrested. Under

The first attempt on the archduke's life that Sunday was bungled by one of Princip's accomplices. Franz Ferdinand saw the bomb tossed at the imperial carriage as they made their way to the civil ceremony at the town hall and deflected it into the road, where it injured a handful of spectators. With considerable sangfroid the outraged duke carried on to the reception, where the mayor, completely thrown by the assassination attempt, could not bring himself to deviate from the prepared text of his speech.

LEFT: Archduke Franz Ferdinand and Sophie decscending the steps at Sarajevo Town Hall.
RIGHT: the arrest of the assassin, Gavrilo Princip.

the circumstances, however, aides suggested that the archduke should take an alternative route to the city museum, the finale to his tour. Inexplicably, they failed to inform the driver.

After the first bomb attack the assassins further down the route either thought the job had been done or panicked; in any case they scattered – all but Princip. Seeing another chance, he stepped forward, drew his revolver, and at a range of 1.5 metres (5 ft) fired two shots. One hit Franz Ferdinand in the neck, the second hit Sophie in the stomach. Within minutes they were dead.

Although the assassination was a shock and provoked both public and family grief, the decision to go to war was not motivated by popular calls for revenge. There was widespread apathy in the response to the death of a prince who was not particularly popular. Intimations of cataclysm were not as yet evident. An Italian foreign minister privately commented that "world peace will not be any worse off."

The assassins were quickly rounded up and under questioning revealed the part played in the assassination by senior Serbian officials and the Black Hand in particular. Army chief of staff Conrad von Hötzendorf expressed once more his long-held conviction that a preventative war was the only option; the emperor remained opposed. Aehrendorf's successor, Count

Berthold, believed that not to act emphatically would only weaken the Dual Monarchy's position amongst the Great Powers. On 23 July Vienna presented Serbia with an ultimatum: no more anti-imperial activities on its soil and the arrest of one of the implicated officials. The official in question was arrested but even more quickly "escaped", never to be found again. On 28 July, exactly one month after Franz Ferdinand's death, Austria declared war.

The stage was now set for a major European conflict, as the alliance system swung into action. War on Serbia brought in Russia, which was pledged to defend the interests of the Slavs. In mobilising against Austria, Russia triggered the Austro-Germanic mutual defence pact of 1879. Germany duly declared war on Russia and, knowing that this would activate an alliance between Russia and France, decided to get in first with an attack on France. Great Britain was still technically neutral, but when Germany invaded Belgium in order to attack the French flank, Britain could not countenance the threat to the Channel coast and threw in its lot with France and Russia. British public opinion was quickly mobilised in defence of "gallant little Serbia". Germany and Austria were joined by Turkey and then Bulgaria to create the "Quadruple Alliance". Italy remained neutral until the territory offered by the entente powers (Britain, France and Belgium) as a bribe to join them outweighed the areas Austria was prepared to cede to buy Italian favour.

Life during wartime

The Austro-Hungarian army was not the equal of the other forces arrayed on the battlefields of Europe in 1914–15. Underfunded and small in relation to the imperial population, it fielded only 48 divisions of infantry compared to Russia's 93 or France's 88. Austrian artillery, industrial capacity and transport connections were similarly inferior. Even the timetabling system of the empire's railways was outdated and impeded swift mobilisation. Before the end of 1914, Austrian forces had been driven from Serbia and routed by Russian forces in Galicia and Bukovina. 750,000 soldiers were lost in the first six months of battle alone.

Austria-Hungary became dependent on the stronger German Empire with which it was allied. With German help, Galicia was recovered and new Polish territory conquered; German and Bulgarian forces aided in the capture of Serbia and Montenegro during 1915. By 1916 virtually the entire eastern front was under the command of German officers. Less assistance was required along the River Isonzo, where Austria faced Italy in a succession of bloody battles lasting into 1917, but again a final rout of Italian forces was achieved only with Germany's intervention. Even victory weakened the overburdened resources of the Dual Monarchy, while at the same time forces within the empire turned on the administration. In 1916 Friedrich Adler, son of the prominent socialist Victor, assassinated the prime minister, Count Stürgkh, who had adjourned parliament since March 1914, preventing proper debate. Adler used the opportunity of his trial to criticise the government's conduct. Meanwhile, Czech forces deserted, negotiated directly with the allied powers, or joined underground organisations operating against the empire. South Slavs in exile promoted the anti-imperial cause and sought the creation of a new, Yugoslav state in the region. Sympathies rose for the emancipation of central and southeast Europe's subject peoples from the ancient empires. One prominent figure arguing for independence was Thomas Masaryk, future president of Czechoslovakia: "Either the Habsburgs, or a free democratic Europe; that is the question. Any compromise between the two is bound to be an unstable condition."

The end of empire

On 21 November 1916, the Emperor Franz Joseph died. His successor, Karl, was 29 years old and, like the great-uncle from whom he inherited the throne, the new emperor's overriding concern was the establishment of peace. Initial positive results to peace negotiation at the end of 1916 fell apart when Germany was unwilling to negotiate on the ceding of territory to France. Austria, now effectively a satellite of Germany, was unable to stray far from the position of its ally: in August 1918 Karl would be made to publicly denounce Austria's attempts to secure an independent peace.

Above all, the key factors in deciding the outcome of the war, and the future political geography of the imperial crownlands, were the Russian Revolution and the United States' entry into the war, both in 1917. The spectre of the Tsar's downfall haunted Austria's own shaky absolutist government and the reconvening of the long-adjourned parliament was of limited success in responding to this threat. Over the winter of 1917 a food crisis hit Austria and provoked a strike across the empire's industrialised territories. Prisoners of war returned from Russia with Bolshevik ideas and the various nationalist groups in exile began to find success in making their voices heard among the allied powers. With no need to support the Russian Empire and the USA as an ally, the entente powers were able to endorse nationalist aspirations for emancipation from the

Dual Monarchy. American President Woodrow Wilson proposed 14 points for the reorganisation of Europe in 1918, declaring that "The peoples of Austria-Hungary, whose place among the nations we wish to see safeguarded and assured, should be accorded the freest opportunity for autonomous development." If it was possible to interpret this statement in terms of reorganisation rather than dismemberment of the monarchy, events later that year made the interpretation unambiguous: by supporting Czechoslovak claims to independence in September 1918, the allied powers were calling for the acknowledgement of a new political entity within the Habs-

burg Monarchy, inevitably causing its break-up.

The last Austrian offensive of the war came in June 1918 – directed against Italy, it was as much as failure as that of Germany on the Western front. The Quadruple Alliance broke in September when Bulgaria sued for peace, but Austria, Germany and Turkey were quick to follow, seeking an armistice in October. Czechs and Yugoslavs proclaimed their independence that same month; Magyars and Poles swiftly followed. Karl's abdication formally took place on 11 November 1918. At a cost of 10 million lives and 20 million seriously wounded, the World War I was over and the Austro-Hungarian Empire had finally ceased to exist.   ❑

LEFT: women in Vienna at the 1914 mobilisation.
RIGHT: Czernin and Kühlmann negotiate the armistice with Russia at Brest-Litowsk in 1917.

Jewish Vienna

There has been a Jewish presence in Vienna for around 1,000 years. Although there had been a tradition of Babenberg and Habsburg protection of a people regarded as a vital source of finance, security was limited for the city's Jews: in 1421 a terrible pogrom, the Wiener Geserah, was provoked by non-Jews who blamed the Jewish community for times of hardship. There was persecution, a massacre and the burning down of the city's main synagogue. Today, at 2 Judenplatz there still stands a house, Zum Großen Jordan (The Great Jordan),

whose Latin inscription celebrates the "flame" of 1421 which "purged the terrible crimes of the Hebrew dogs".

The progressive Emperor Joseph II first granted his Jewish subjects substantial rights in the 1781 Edict of Tolerance, but it was in the 19th century that Vienna's Jewish community truly began to flourish. After the 1848 revolution, thousands of Jews arrived from the *shtetl*, or traditional villages, of Galicia and Bukovina to the East. The empire's Jewish population became overwhelmingly concentrated in the capital city. District II, Leopoldstadt, included all the institutions needed to supply a devout Jewish way of life, from Torah schools to kosher butchers. The area became known as the Mazzesinsel, or "Matzoth

Island", in local parlance. But for every Jew who kept tradition alive in the modern city, there were those who sought to assimilate into the mainstream of Austro-German life. The Enlightenment impulse to universal tolerance which provided the philosophical underpinning for Joseph II's edict also created *Bildung*, a humanist culture of art and education in which Jews might aspire to an undifferentiated brotherhood with non-Jews. *Bildungskultur* made a lasting impression on the generations of assimilated Jews and informed the work of many famous thinkers and writers of Jewish background. The late 19th century and *fin de siècle* saw a great flourishing of art and scholarship amongst a largely Jewish intelligentsia: the philosophy of Ludwig Wittgenstein and Karl Popper, the biting satire of Karl Kraus and Arthur Schnitzler, the music of Arnold Schoenberg and the psychology of Sigmund Freud all owe something to the Jewish situation in turn-of-the-century Vienna.

Even as Viennese Jews went from strength to strength in the new bourgeoisie, tensions were developing. From the 1880s, the Austrian liberalism which had supported *Bildungskultur* and assimilation was being replaced among German-speaking peoples of the empire with populist mass movements run along nationalist, racial and Christian lines. The modernising drive which had liberated the Jews had also unsettled vast swathes of the middle and lower classes; their discontent at events like the 1873 stock market crash turned into anti-Semitic resentment. Many nationalists denied that there could be a successful integration of Jews into "host cultures", and a pseudo-science of racism evolved, blaming Jewish people for all kinds of sexual and moral aberrations and "degeneracies". Karl Lueger, a notorious mayor of Vienna, did not subscribe to "scientific racism" – "I decide who is a Jew!" he is said to have declared – but he did play on the fears of German-speakers in the dissolving empire by presenting Viennese Jews as agents of a monolithic, international conspiracy against which all Christians needed to unite for their own survival. The anti-Semitic platform brought Lueger political success, and although his policies never matched the excesses of his electoral campaign, his rhetoric did serve to legitimise public expression of hatred against the Jews.

People of assimilated Jewish background, overwhelmingly liberal and middle class, tended to distance themselves from the poor rural *shtetl* Jews coming in from the East, although some, of whom Theodor Herzl is the most famous, instead proposed

LEFT: "We do not serve Jews" in Vienna, 1938.

an alternative solution, a Jewish nationalism.

Herzl's manifesto, *The Jewish State*, is the expression of a sense that humanism and the Enlightenment had failed and that the Jewish peoples in all their communities worldwide should strive for a common homeland. Herzl's diaries include one entry which provided a frightening prognosis for the future: "In Germany they will make emergency laws as soon as the Kaiser can no longer manage the Reichstag. In Austria people will let themselves be intimidated by the Viennese rabble and deliver up the Jews. There you see, the mob can achieve anything once it rears up. It does not know this yet, but the leaders will teach it. So they will chase us out of these countries, and in the countries where we take refuge they will kill us." In the wake of the 1914–18 War and the foundation of the First Republic, anti-Semitism did not wholly abate. The impoverished new Austria was fiercely anti-capitalist, and for many the stereotype of the Jewish entrepreneur and banker provided a focus for this ill feeling. A 1934 report from the Viennese agent of a British organisation set up to aid and protect scholars persecuted in Nazi Germany spoke, even before the Nazi annexation, of a systematic anti-Semitism in Austria, "prevalent since the 1880s...and extraordinarily strengthened in the last 12 years." Non-Jewish Austrians fervently welcomed *Anschluss* with Hitler's Germany in 1938 and wasted no time in persecuting their fellow citizens. Viennese Jews were made to scrub cobblestones with their toothbrushes, a moment recalled in Alfred Hrdlicka's *Warning Against War and Fascism* on the Albertinaplatz. Austrians were also deeply implicated in the systematic mass murder of Jews and others perpetrated by the Nazi regime: Adolf Eichmann and Franz Stangl are just two of the most notorious Austrian names associated with the *Shoah*. The principal concentration camp within Austria's borders was Mauthausen, a forced-labour site whose harsh regime included the carrying of stone blocks up 186 steps from the camp quarry. Mauthausen also administered some 60 subcamps in Northern Austria in which prisoners were worked to death. A number of Austrians of Jewish background who had fled before conflict broke out managed to preserve or resurrect in some form the intellectual and artistic strivings of the *fin de siècle*: from the writer Elias Canetti to the art historian E.H. Gombrich, these figures perpetuated or renegotiated in one form or another the values of the era of *Bildung*. For many others who became refugees, the war was spent in menial work, domestic service or even Allied internment.

After the cessation of conflict, few Austrian Jews who had survived or escaped chose to return to their former lives. Many of the displaced persons repatriated from Nazi custody chose to emigrate to Palestine; refugees tended to remain in their host country.

Gradually, Vienna's Jewish population was revived, largely by an influx from the countries of Eastern Europe. For them, Vienna has been reimagined as the cosmopolitan city of empire, home to the *Kaffeehaus* and a broad East-Central European culture that includes memories of Slovakia, Hungary and Romania. As one Jewish woman recently put it,

"These areas define me through my ancestors." If the Jewish community today numbers only a few thousand, it is nonetheless vibrant and lively. There is a Jewish festival in the city each year; Vienna's Jewish Museum is one of the most provocative, political and exciting in the world; the synagogue in the Seitenstettengasse reports rising attendance numbers; and public figures like the filmmaker Ruth Beckermann, the writer Robert Menasse and the anthropologist Matti Bunzl all communicate the concerns and experiences of the community to a wider audience. Despite all this, it can never be said that the wounds have completely healed – as one young Viennese Jew ruefully put it: "You never know when you'll have to pack again." ❑

RIGHT: Orthodox Jews in Vienna's Seegasse cemetery.

DEUTSCHÖSTERREICH

After 1918, the rump of the empire – present-day Austria – went through many changes, from Social Democracy, to Nazism to the modern nation state

After World War I ended, the map of Europe was swiftly redrawn along the lines of national self-determination. Former subject peoples within the empire were granted self-government within their own discrete territories, but Austria presented a particularly difficult case for the Allied victors: it was formed of those German-speaking territories which could not be absorbed into new nations such as Czechoslovakia, but union with Germany to the west – the obvious move if one strictly applied the rule of national self-determination – was forbidden for fear that it would strengthen the defeated enemy. As the French leader Clemenceau put it, "L'Autriche, c'est la qui reste": "Austria is what is left."

The First Republic created to replace the k.u.k. lands of the Habsburgs was granted the new name of Deutschösterreich, but retained the sense that it was a rump state, formed from the trimmings at the carve-up of the Dual Monarchy.

Life without an emperor

The disappearance of imperial tradition could be disconcerting. The top civil servant and poet Richard von Schaukal received the mixed blessing of being ennobled by Emperor Karl on 18 May 1918, only for the institution to which he had been admitted to be dissolved six months later. The satirist Karl Kraus, with rather uncharacteristic gentleness, dubbed Schaukal *der allerletzte Ritter* ("the ultimate knight"). Schaukal is reputed to have later carried a business card bearing both the dates of his ennoblement and the annulment of his title. For other Austrians, the loss of imperial rhetoric and pomp was more socially awkward than tragic: the art historian E.H. Gombrich, born 1909, remembers celebrating the birthday of the new republic instead of the emperor's birthday. He recited a poem about the revolt of a beehive against its queen. The first line was:

"The queen-bee said, 'Throw out the drones!'" An embarrassed primary school teacher discreetly suggested that "it might be better to leave out all references to the queen-bee."

After 1918, many were swift to believe that the old order had gone forever. The authorities could neither provide for, nor regulate their

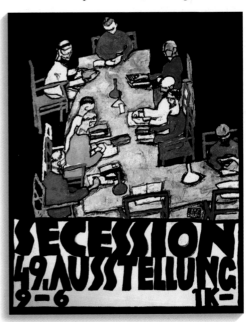

populace: food was in short supply and a thriving black market circumvented attempts at rationing. But the desperation also bred new hope for the future.

Red Vienna

Above all in Vienna, the Social Democracy movement began to implement the future visions dreamt of and planned in the years before the war. Working-class men and women and a cadre of socialist intellectuals made great political advances in the field of housing, childcare, education and social medicine. Playgrounds and hospitals grew amidst the ruins. In the national government (elected through an

---

LEFT: crowds demand a republic in Vienna, 1918.
RIGHT: Schiele's Secession poster, 1918.

admirably democratic new constitution), the socialists' old antagonists the Christian Socials always led the coalitions, although they never achieved an outright majority.

Excluded from even coalition government after 1920, the Social Democrats focused on making the capital, where their support was strong, a model community. Vienna's ground-breaking mental health clinics, TB hospitals, municipal libraries and adult education pro-grammes were all the fruit of Austrian Social Democracy. Visitors came from around the world to see social services that many today take for granted being pioneered in the city.

own experiences with frontline social work in "Red Vienna" as an after-school educator came to an end when a child under his supervision fell from a ladder and fractured his skull. He was sued by the city and, although acquitted, this marked the end of his involvement with socialist education reform.

With the capital administered as a province in its own right, the Social Democrats were able to operate relatively independently of the federal government, the still-powerful Catholic church, and the rival provinces. It was from the latter that Vienna drew the fiercest criticism. Less able than the Viennese to adjust to the change of sta-

This was the age of "Red Vienna".

Interwar Vienna produced not only one of the most comprehensive social democracies of the twentieth century, but also two men who would go on to be among the most passionate critics of socialism. Friedrich von Hayek, credited with being the architect of Ronald Reagan and Margaret Thatcher's economic policies, fought for the empire in World War I and was educated in Vienna before moving to the London School of Economics in the 1930s. Karl Popper, the philosopher and implacable critic of Marx who coined the term "the Open Society", was orig-inally a schoolteacher and social worker before likewise joining Hayek in emigration. Popper's

tus caused by loss of empire, the provinces saw the city as a *Wasserkopf*, a swollen head feeding off the national body. Ignaz Seipel, the Christian Social leader, called for the "true democracy" of a *Ständestaat*, a clerical-fascist state, to pro-tect "black", conservative Austria – pictured as God-fearing patriots true to family values – from a "red" Vienna seen as dangerously secu-lar, socialist and Jewish.

Bloody Friday and the Civil War

With the army still too much under socialist influence for Seipel to be able to use it against his political rivals, the 1920s saw his party begin to fund a paramilitary organisation, the

Heimwehr. The socialists responded in kind, founding the Schutzbund, the Republican Defence League, one year later. Street fighting began to break out between the two forces, with the Catholic press alleging that the Schutzbund had been created to lead a revolt against the federal government.

On Friday, 15 July 1927, a spontaneous demonstration broke out in objection to the acquittal of Heimwehr members in the killing of a socialist and a child. The police, unprepared, fired on the socialist demonstrators, provoking a riot in which the Palace of Justice was set alight. Eighty-five workers were killed as the police responded with more gunfire. Socialist leaders declared strikes but a combination of police and Heimwehr forces were deployed to break them. The forces of reaction had demonstrated their ability to face down the Social Democracy movement, its unions and its street fighters. The economic depression following the Wall Street Crash of 1929 only intensified the aggression of the Christian Socials, sending the Heimwehr to march in socialist areas and openly allying themselves with Austrian fascists. By the 1930s, National Socialism – a German import, albeit one led by Austrian-born Adolf Hitler – was the main force on the right wing of the nation's political spectrum, and a threat even to home-grown conservatism.

When Nazis came to power in Germany in early 1933, Austria's Chancellor Engelbert Dollfuss sensed the threatening possibility of a takeover. Foreign leaders, including Mussolini, recommended that he strengthen Austria's position by dispensing with parliamentary rule and acting against the Social Democrats. On 7 March 1933 Dollfuss declared presidential rule, suspending parliament. In the same month, the Schutzbund was ordered to disband and political meetings and demonstrations were forbidden. The socialist leadership were fearful that a civil war would benefit Nazis more than they, and wary of intervention from the neighbouring right-wing governments of Italy and Germany. They called no strike and gave no military resistance to Dollfuss' actions. Over the next year, Dollfuss brought in strict censorship and cut social security, leaving the Austrian work-

ing class weakened and demoralised. In February 1934, the latent civil war broke out in earnest, but only briefly. When Heimwehr forces tried to confiscate the weapons from an arms depot in Linz, Schutzbund members spontaneously called a strike and cut off electricity to the capital. Socialist leaders maintained their caution while a few thousand workers, both male and female, rose to take on the state. Vienna's massive Karl-Marx-Hof housing block was shelled into submission, almost 200 people were killed and resistance was quashed within just two days. The socialist organisation was liquidated, with many arrested or forced to

flee abroad. Only those political moderates who had distanced themselves from the revolt were not caught up in the purge.

Nazi Anschluss and World War II

By May 1934, Dollfuss had produced a new "corporatist" constitution whose terms provided the basis for a regime of Austro-fascism. He never fully exploited the terms of this document, however: in July, he was killed by the Nazis in an attempted putsch. Their pressure on his successor, Kurt Schuschnigg, was no less relentless as both Austrian Nazis and Hitler in Germany called for Anschluss, the union of Austrians and Germans in a "Greater

---

LEFT: workers lie murdered on a Viennese street during the demonstrations of 1927.
RIGHT: troops celebrate the Anschluss at the border.

German Reich". Mussolini, who had moved to preserve Austrian independence at the time of Dollfuss' murder, came to an understanding with Hitler in 1936.

Meanwhile, Schuschnigg tried to appease the Austrian Nazis with the offer of a couple of ministries in the government. Hitler was adamant that one of these should be the Ministry of State Security, which he proposed to hand over to Austria's leading Nazi, Arthur Seyss-Inquart. Schuschnigg was summoned to Berchtesgaden and made to understand that he had no choice in the matter.

Schuschnigg now called for a plebisicite to

cony on Vienna's Heldenplatz. Hitler might have been more interested in Linz, where he had grown up and for which he had elaborate plans, than Vienna – but the Viennese welcomed him with open arms.

Anti-Semitic pogroms, so spontaneous and impassioned that they worried the Nazi administrators, broke out in the nation's capital. Jewish men and women were dragged from their homes and businesses, forced to scrub cobblestones, beaten, splashed with acid and urinated on.

A great number of Jews and anti-Nazis managed to escape, but within the first 10 days of Nazi occupation 90,000 Austrians were

be held on 13 March 1938, in which the Austrian people were invited to confirm their commitment to a free and independent Austria. With a "yes" vote likely, the Nazis moved to intervene. Two days before the plebiscite, Germany closed its borders with Austria. On 12 March, Hitler's forces entered Austria.

A rapturous welcome was swift. Before a rescheduled referendum, Cardinal Innitzer urged good Catholics to vote for the annexation and "proclaim themselves as Germans for the German Reich" although this did not protect the Church from the Nazis' long-term plans. Two hundred thousand people welcomed Hitler when he spoke from the National Library's bal-

rounded up; most of them ended up in Dachau and Buchenwald. Resistance was unknown, and for many there seemed only one route of escape: while only 1,953 votes were cast against Anschluss by the Viennese in Hitler's referendum, the suicide rate for the city more than tripled that year to some 1,358 cases.

The country went to war in 1939 as an integral part of Germany, and while the loyalty of the Austrian officer corps to the Third Reich was considered suspect, Austrians were conscripted into the army like everyone else.

Austrian resistance was minimal over the course of the war. With the organised forces of the left already demolished by Dollfuss and widespread enthusiasm for the Nazi cause, little could be done by individuals opposed to the regime. Occasional acts of heroism were complemented by withdrawal into anonymous "internal exile" or, in the case of manual workers, deliberate incompetence, but resistance was almost entirely passive until the very last months of the war in Europe. When the Red Army was approaching the Austrian capital in 1945 a resistance group known as O5 led an attempt to abduct senior Nazis, dissolve the SS and begin an uprising. Betrayed by a junior officer, the abortive move ended in arrest and public execution, the Red Army taking more than a week to enter and finally win the city.

Vienna's Soviet liberators arranged for social democrat Karl Renner to form a provisional government. With a number of communists in key positions and the wartime alliance against Nazism already fraying, the Western Allies were swift to intercede. Austria was partitioned into zones of occupation and only then was the Renner government acknowledged, with free elections set for November 1945. The harsh attitude adopted by Soviet troops perhaps explained the poor communist showing: four seats out of 165.

The Allied victory had persuaded people that they would rather be Austrian than German; meeting the Russian troops evidently persuaded them that they would rather be in the Western camp.

Looking forward, looking back

The years since the end of World War II have been, perversely, both the most placid and the most sinister of Austrian history. Austrians have enjoyed more than six decades of wealth, peace and security – but these prosperous times were built on dark foundations, and coming to terms with this fact has been a long and painful process.

There is a blackly humorous Austrian joke, that the greatest success of the nation after 1945 was to make the world think that Beethoven was Austrian, and Hitler German. Postwar Austria – the Second Republic – swiftly distanced itself from the Nazi regime. The Moscow Doctrine formulated by the wartime Allies had

declared that Austria was the "first free country to fall a victim to Hitlerite aggression", but for many Austrians, liberation was experienced as a defeat. The battered nation was occupied and partitioned four ways by Allied forces. Symbols of the Nazi regime were swiftly destroyed or concealed: a statue of the eagle with swastika in its claws flung into the Wörthersee lake; Nazi murals overpainted and swastikas unpicked from the stripes of the Rot-Weiss-Rot flag; and Nazi insignia on official documents pasted over with plain stickers. In part these were practical moves made necessary by the scarcities of the immediate post-war period, but

they also represented a political attempt to deny Austrian complicity in Nazism, and above all the systematic mass murder of 6 million Jews and others: for example, the commemorative stamps of a 1946 exhibition purportedly acknowledging war guilt, *Niemals vergessen* (Never forget), rejected images of concentration camps and anti-Semitic persecution in favour of the Stephansdom in flames and the Austrian map pierced by a dagger with a swastika hilt.

According to one anecdote, the idea of Austria as innocent victim of Nazism was born on 18 February 1942, the occasion of the refugee Austrian Association's presentation of a mobile can-

LEFT: German troops on the Ringstrasse in 1938.
RIGHT: the Stephansdom in flames after Allied air-raids in 1945.

teen unit to the British Army. The highly-placed Sir George Frankenstein, once the First Republic's ambassador to Britain, had arranged for Sir Winston Churchill himself to accept the gift. The day was cold and the Prime Minister had fortified himself with an overcoat, Homburg hat, muffler and, allegedly, a generous measure of spirits. In such "happy" mood, he declared, "Here we see the heart of Austria trampled down under the Nazi and Prussian yoke. We can never forget here in this island that Austria was the first victim of Nazi aggression…"

The Austrian government worked tirelessly to demonstrate that it could be released from

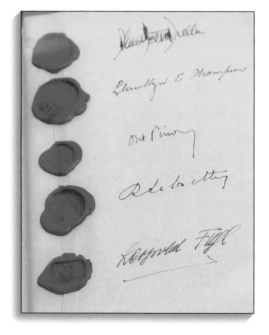

occupation. One aspect of this work was to create a new national identity. In the past there had been only support for the Habsburg Empire, or for Deutschtum – but the monarchy was gone and union with Germany prohibited. Little by little a *Willensnation* developed, distinctive "Austrianness" brought into being by an act of will. Celebrating the nation's "950th birthday" in 1946, dated back to Leopold of Babenberg's Ostarrichi, emphasised the new identity and distracted attention from the immediate past. While Austria wooed the new powers of Cold War international politics with a face of innocence, domestically it sought to charm its former Nazis. The thousands of demobilised soldiers

represented a significant proportion of the Austrian electorate and politicians greedy for votes sought their support. The political parties within Austria operated a process of mutual de-Nazification, summed up in the phrase, "If you absolve my Nazi, I'll absolve yours." Refugees or Displaced Persons, DPs, repatriated by the Allies in the wake of conflict, found themselves less welcome. Although victims of the war, they were housed once again in camps, like prisoners, and were widely perceived as an unjust burden on a still barely recovering nation. Many emigrated before the decade was up.

The new state

By 1955, the state of international politics was such that the Soviet Union was willing to withdraw from Austria on condition that its neutrality was guaranteed permanently by treaty. With the appropriate assurances given, the *Staatsvertrag* (State Treaty) was signed on 15 May, releasing Austria from occupation. For the next 30 years of the Cold War, Austria maintained a position between the rival superpowers as a neutral, but somewhat westward-looking entity. The Verein der Unabhängigen, or Society of Independents, formed of ex-Nazi servicemen, became the now-notorious Freedom Party (FPÖ) in the following year.

The mainstream parties maintained political closeness, believing that conflict between the Christian Right and socialist Left in the civil war had paved the way for Nazism. Nonetheless, they were still not averse to exploiting the legacy of 1938–45: one electoral slogan of 1957 ran, *"Wer einmal schon für Adolf war, wählt Adolf auch in diesem Jahr"* ("He who was for Adolf once before, votes Adolf this year too"). Until 1966, the parties were so close that the socialist SPÖ and conservative ÖVP (Austrian People's Party) governed in coalition. Positions of power in public life were often allocated according to *Parteibuch* (party membership), which quickly developed into a kind of cronyism.

This *Sozialpartnerschaft* (social partnership) in mainstream politics was maintained for some 40 years. Consensus was emphasised over pluralism, and private, paternalistic management of the country was preferred to open debate and dispute. The 1970s saw a spate of apparent "Nazis" being uncovered in high-profile public positions, but this largely owed to the age of the politicians in question, who had inevitably been schooled during the years of *Anschluss*. Nonetheless, it was still disturbing to hear politicians like Leopold Wagner of Carinthia unambiguously declaring their pride at having been high-level members of the Hitler Youth.

Socialist Chancellor Bruno Kreisky, despite being of assimilated Jewish background and spending the war in neutral Sweden, became embroiled in the scandals: he defended socialist colleagues with Nazi pasts and unambiguously opposed Israeli policies in Palestine, the latter move being interpreted as anti-Semitic by some Jewish groups.

Spurred by Kreisky's efforts, the 1980s saw Austria, and Vienna above all, reimagining itself as a hub of international politics, an "interface" between different peoples of the world. The number of international and non-governmental organisations based in the city proliferated, and this coincided with a great nostalgia for the Austria of the Habsburgs.

In the early 1980s conferences and art exhibitions evoked the Vienna of Freud, Schnitzler and Klimt. In popular culture, one of the first hits on MTV was Ultravox's *Vienna*, whose lyrics and video evoked a melancholic, decadent and tragic city of Central Europe. For a time, intellectuals,

The Austrian "interface"

In international politics, Kreisky's 13-year term as chancellor was less controversial. Exploiting the neutrality clause of the 1955 State Treaty, he succeeded in making Vienna a centre of international diplomacy: in 1979 it hosted the Strategic Arms Limitation Talks and the same year saw the completion of the Vienna International Centre, or "UNO-City", to the north of the Danube. This vast complex forms the third seat of the United Nations after New York and Geneva.

LEFT: the signatures of the occupying powers and the new Austrian Foreign Minister on the State Treaty, 1955.
ABOVE: Brezhnev and Carter at the SALT talks in 1979.

artists and dissidents of the former imperial subject nations exploited this nostalgia under the banner of Mitteleuropa, strengthening their identification with a culture and politics beyond those of the Soviet Union. Central Europe was envisioned as a victim of Cold War geopolitics, unjustly bisected by the Iron Curtain. Austria was, of course, very comfortable with this nostalgic revival of its role as an imperial power. However, shortly after the Soviet bloc collapsed in 1989, *mitteleuropäische* solidarity was dropped, having outlived its usefulness: the Central-East European nations preferred to pursue their own destinies independent of a remembered Habsburg multinationalism.

Waldheim

A different part of the past was, however, about to assert itself and provoke international scandal. 1986 saw the election of Kurt Waldheim as President of Austria. Some curious omissions in his campaign biography prompted a closer look at his wartime record and it quickly became clear that he had been an intelligence officer in a part of Yugoslavia notorious for Nazi atrocities. In this role Waldheim, then a young lawyer, had drawn up documents relating to the forced resettlement of countless opponents of the Ustashe, Croat fascist allies of the Nazis. Many died as a result of this policy.

While Waldheim's lapses of memory and professed ignorance of such events suggested (as one commentator acidly put it) that he must have been the "worst informed intelligence officer in history", more revealing was his failure – real or feigned – to understand the moral distinction between Nazi aggression and its victims. This lack of understanding was epitomised in his exculpatory remark, "I merely did my duty."

The resultant scandal opened the divisions and resentments that had lain beneath the *Sozialpartnerschaft*. There were many Austrians who identified with Waldheim's attitude to the past, but also many who opposed him.

The Trojan Horse

In the late 1980s, opponents of the President built the Waldheim-Pferd, a large wooden horse which was taken to demonstrations at public engagements, including a state visit to the Vatican. For critics of Waldheim, his Nazi past was concealed in political rhetoric like the Greek warriors within their gift to the people of Troy. Socialist Chancellor Fred Sinowatz phrased his criticism more sarcastically: "Waldheim wasn't in the SA", he declared, "only his horse."

The Waldheim affair revealed the price that Austria had been obliged to pay for avoiding the truth about its past. Austria could no longer be seen simply as "First Victim". The government of the USA added Waldheim to the "watch list" of people denied entry to the country. Austria began hastily to make restitution to Israel, years after West Germany had done so, and the watchword of the times was *Vergangenheitsbewältigung* – "coming to terms with the past". New Chancellor Franz Vranitzky acknowledged a "double role, namely that of victim and that of culprit" in the 1988 commemorations of Nazi Anschluss. In 1992, Waldheim was succeeded by Thomas Klestil. His inaugural speech promised the Austrian electorate a *Welt von Morgen* ("World of Tomorrow"): "Only if we live facing our history, with its bright as well as its dark hours, can we derive from it the strength to build a better, more human future."

Austria in Europe

Austria joined the European Union in 1995, after some debate as to whether this contravened the national commitment to neutrality. The new accession was the fifth most prosperous member of the Union and became the base for countless international corporations seeking access to the markets of Eastern Europe after the fall of Communism. As one commentator put it, the bittersweet truth is that "No succession of cultural congresses in Vienna, evocative meetings of intellectuals, programmes to clean the rain and air between the Carpathians and the Wienerwald will withstand the influence of Siemens or the Kommerzbank in East-Central Europe."

Austria's gradual acceptance of a new path as a minor European nation far from the cosmic Habsburg destiny "AEIOU" was complicated in the 1990s by yet another resurgence of its dark side in the form of Jörg Haider and the Freedom Party (FPÖ). This far-right organisation, revived on a basis of Nazi nostalgia and anti-immigrant populist rhetoric, established a coalition with the beleaguered ÖVP in 1999. The international community were horrified. Austria's new EU partners swiftly imposed sanctions, withdrawn when Haider resigned the following the year. The coalition broke up in 2002, with the FPÖ share of the vote declining greatly: nonetheless, far-right tendencies continue to exist within Austria, turning their attention ever more towards Muslim groups and the growing African minority.

brance and a dynamic, ongoing engagement with Austria's historical highs and lows. The country's commitment to neutrality was unwavering in the face of American pressure during the so-called "War on Terror" in the early years of the new century; this commitment, and Austria's role as host of countless international organisations, emphasises a popular dedication to peace and negotiation over conflict and strife.

Many Austrian people welcome the influx of visitors and new residents from abroad: with such a diverse history, "Austria" is a concept which can be pressed into service to encompass historical, cultural and ethnic diversity. Modern

EU ‖ AT

Despite all of this, Austrians, especially those in the younger generations, are learning to look both forward and back, acknowledging the "World of Yesterday" but also working for the "World of Tomorrow". The past need no longer represent only a burden of grievance and guilt: 1998 saw the creation of an academic *Historikerkommision* to provide an authoritative and critical account of the years 1938–1945, and the 50th anniversary of the State Treaty in 2005 occasioned a massive act of national remem-

Austria still contains a number of historical ethnic minorities, the largest and oldest being that of the Slovenes in Southern Carinthia, where the schools are bilingual. Burgenland's Croat minority is descended from families fleeing the Turkish advance into Dalmatia and Slavonia. Much of the new Austria is being built by Turkish and Central-East European *Gastarbeiter* ("guest workers"). Vienna above all has always been an immigrant destination, and would have been the poorer without it: the Viennese are *sui generis*, the product of an ethnic melting pot. The first decade of the 21st century marks a time of new opportunities and another stitch in the patchwork quilt of Austria's motley "national history". ❑

LEFT: an anti-Haider demonstration in Vienna, 2005.
RIGHT: Austria's logo for their presidency of the European Union in 2006.

FOOD AND DRINK

Hearty, filling and delicious, traditional Austrian food is
surprisingly varied and draws on many culinary sources

Fashionable refinements notwithstanding, Austrian cooking is firmly based on a collection of traditional recipes handed down over generations. Occasionally, as the empire expanded, these were supplemented by dishes from neighbouring cooking pots: damson dumplings from Bohemia, paprika goulash from Hungary, spicy braised peppers from the Balkans and rich pasta dishes from Italy. The Austrians zealously imitated all these specialities and in the end confidently claimed to have invented them.

The best example of this culinary plagiarism is the world-famous *Wienerschnitzel*, the breaded escalope of veal: when Field-Marshal Radetzky returned from Italy in the year of the 1848 Revolution, he brought back tidings not only of the quashing of the uprising, but also of a certain *costoletto alla Milanese*, a recipe which he immediately passed on to the chefs at the Imperial Court – as a closely guarded secret, of course. Ever since then, the breadcrumb coating for veal, pork, chicken or fish has been regarded as typically Austrian.

Excess

The Austrians love to eat. This devotion to gastronomic pleasures has been cultivated across the centuries. Tyrolean eagle with dumplings, roast squirrel with salad, or hedgehog in vinegar sauce with noodles were all great delicacies. During times of war and pestilence, when most of the people were starving, the nobility hardly noticed – although sieges and uprisings sometimes drove even blue-blooded stomachs to ingest whatever stray mammals could be caught and killed in the crannies of the Hofburg. When Empress Maria Theresa and her entourage visited the Monastery of Melk for just one day, the cook's duties were awesome. His shopping list included 266 kg (587 lbs) of

beef, 337 kg (743 lbs) of veal, nine calves' heads, 40 calves' feet, 2 kg (4 lbs) of marrow and four ox tongues. He also required 1,404 eggs, 138 litres (30 gallons) of dripping, nine sticks of cinnamon and five new roasting spits. At the same time, and even beyond the fall of the empire, many urban residents, known as

Bettgeher, lived in single rooms on little more than coffee, bread and meagre servings of meat, and the rural populace experienced equally hard times. No wonder that it was an Austrian, the 19th-century thinker Joseph Popper-Lynkeus, who proposed the concept of the *Nährarmee* or "nutritional army", a social-reform movement that would prepare meals for the impoverished in return for their own room and board.

At the start of the 21st century, there is sadly no *Nährarmee*, but nor is it only the nobility who enjoy the best of Austrian cuisine. It may no longer be true to say that the average Austrian is "as suspicious of nouvelle cuisine as a medieval cup-bearer faced with a goblet of

PRECEDING PAGES: the difficult task of choosing cakes in Demel.
LEFT: local firewater for sale in Ötz, Tyrol.
RIGHT: a *Wurst* or two.

hemlock", but traditional recipes continue to dominate the Austrian diet, especially when eating out. Fortunately, however, the variety of specialities on offer between Lake Constance and the Neusiedlersee is so extensive that even the most cosmopolitan guest will find plenty of novelties to sample.

The main meals

Breakfast – *Frühstuck* – consists of a pot of tea or coffee served with rolls. Even in the lowliest hostel, butter, jam and some kind of pâté will be available alongside; rising up the scale, a selection of cold meats and cheeses, cooked eggs, muesli and fruit will be available – even champagne has been spotted on the buffet table in the most prestigious of hotels.

Lunch – *Mittagessen* – is often the main meal of the day for Austrians; restaurants and *Gasthöfe* will usually offer good-value set menus, *Mittagsmenu* for the lunch hour and for the whole day a *Tagesmenu*. The evening meal – *Abendessen* or *Nachtmahl* – will offer a slightly wider range of dishes than those available earlier in the day. There is no shame among Austrians in tucking into a hearty dessert rather than a proper meal at lunchtime, and in truth, a single good slice of *Torte* or

VEGETARIANS AND VEGANS

It is scarcely easier for vegetarians, let alone vegans, to dine out in contemporary Austria than it was in Maria Theresa's day. Soups are usually made with a meat stock; and while omelettes, noodle dishes and baked cheeses are the safest bets, it is always wise to double-check with the waiter before ordering. Even a salad whose menu listing includes no meat ingredients may surprise the unsuspecting with a generous topping of bacon strips when it arrives. Even hardened carnivores need to beware: if the thought of eating veal – very common here – is unappealing, keep your eyes peeled for the word *Kalb*. Ironically, given the difficulties faced by vegetarians today, Austria's first vegetarian society was established as long ago as 1900. In the 1920s, Richard Schwartz of the society proposed a worldwide Vegetarian Demonstration on the second Sunday of September each year, although this never came to pass; a successor, Dr. Johannes Ude, combined his promotion of vegetarianism with arguments for economic reform based on humane and righteous principles in the run-up to World War II.

Help and information for today's vegan and vegetarian visitors to Austria can be obtained from the Österreichische Vegetarier-Union (Postfach 1, A-8017 Graz, tel. 0316-46 37 17, www.vegetarier.at) and the Vegane Gesellschaft Österreich (info@vegan.at, www.vegan.at).

Kuchen, heavy on the cream, should satisfy even the most ravenous. For those eating on the run, *Würstelstände* – sausage stalls – offer frankfurters, fried *Bratwurst*, *Currywurst*, spicy *Debreziner*, chips, and often kebabs and pizza slices; alternatively, Austrian supermarkets are by and large excellent for those in search of picnic supplies, with fresh fruit, various cold meats and cheeses, and an enormous range of breads widely available.

Viennese dishes

Vienna, the nation's capital, has a centuries-old culinary tradition, including the *Beisl*, traditional watering holes at which the city's residents graze and make merry. The term *Beisl* is derived from the Yiddish term for a little house. These establishments are scattered all over central Vienna, offering mighty portions of food, serious drinking, and a nostalgic atmosphere varying from the wood-pannelled and almost rustic to a Formica-and-plastic décor which is no less charming in its own bizarre, seedy way.

In addition to the *Wienerschnitzel*, the most famous speciality in this city of gourmets, is the *Tafelspitz*. This lean cut of beef is cooked in broth and served – surrounded by roast potatoes – with chive sauce, spinach and horseradish and apple purée. The *Fiakergulasch*, a local goulash variant named for the city's horse-drawn cabs, is served with a sausage and fried egg to fortify you against the cold.

Boiled beef and vegetables can be found on menus from the smallest *Beisl* to the temples of haute cuisine. A true Viennese gourmet, incidentally sometimes unflatteringly described as "a red-faced strudel-stuffer", is a great soup fan. A lunch menu without a steaming bowl of broth with semolina dumplings, liver dumplings *(Leberknödelsuppe)* or sliced pancake *(Frittatensuppe)* lurking in its depths is not a proper meal. *Gulaschsuppe*, heavy with paprika, is also common. To follow, choose roast pork with bread dumplings and sauerkraut. Or – better still – demonstrate your devotion to the Viennese way by eating *Bauernschmaus*, a heap of meat and sausages, or *Beuschel*, offal in sauce, with veal heart, lots of root vegetables, herbs and spices. Washing down this "health food" will be a cool beer, although another favourite beverage is a cool *G'spritzter*, equal quantities of white wine and sparkling mineral water. Pudding will be an apple strudel, made with a dough stretched out so thinly that you can read the newspaper through it, filled with a mixture of sliced apple, cinnamon and raisins, rolled up and baked crisply.

Alternatively, a meal may end with a choice of *Torten* (cakes). *Sacher Torte* is the best known: this rich dark chocolate cake, layered with apricot jam, is so thoroughly entwined with the image of Austria that examples are stacked high in airport duty-free shops. The

cake is named for its place of invention, the Hotel Sacher, but the paternity rights to this most popular of desserts were contested in the 1960s, when rival confectioners Demel claimed the recipe was devised by one of their chefs. A lawsuit ensued and an "official" *Sachertorte* (all one word; a legally protected name) can now only be purchased at the hotel itself on Vienna's Inner Ring: however the *Sacher Torte* you find in any *Konditorei* (bakery) is its equal. Other cakes of note include *Dobos Torte*, with a caramelised top; *Guglhupf*, a slice of ring-shaped marble cake, legendarily Freud's favourite; *Mohnkuchen*, which features poppy seeds; and *Linzertorte*, with nuts and a jam fill-

---

LEFT: a handsome piece of *Speck*.
RIGHT: *Kaiserschmarrn*, sweet pancakes cut up and served with sugar and fruit coulis.

ing. Then there are little Czech yeast dumplings, filled with damsons, painted with melted butter and served with vanilla sauce.

Regional variations

Austrian regional cuisine is no less various nor less excellent than that found in the capital. In the Vorarlberg, the most westerly province, many inns still serve meals prepared from recipes handed down across the generations. *Kässpätzle*, for instance, are home-made noodles prepared with flour, milk and egg and served with butter and cheese. A generous portion of Gouda or Emmenthaler cheese is an

of gentian spirit, fruit schnapps or rowan *eau-de-vie* (home-distilled and guaranteed to knock your hat off). It tastes best served in a remote mountain hut after an arduous hike.

For the truly ravenous there is the delicious and traditional *Bauernschöpsernes*, tender braised lamb. It is first seared with fried onion rings, then braised for half the required cooking time. Quartered potatoes are added, with parsley, a bay leaf and a glass of red wine as flavouring, and it is cooked until tender. The meal ends with special doughnuts or freshly stewed apple, and a final tot of fruit schnapps for the road.

essential ingredient in the *Marend*, the Vorarlberg mid-afternoon snack; traditionally it is served with bread and a mug of cider. Special delicacies are trout, whitefish and pike – some weighing as much as 10 kg (22 lbs) – from Lake Constance, where the Romans once fished for their supper.

The cuisine of Tyrol is both substantial and nourishing. The province, through which travellers have passed for centuries on their journey northwards or southwards across the Alps, has a long tradition of hospitality. The region's bacon and cured pork are used in Tyrolean bacon dumplings or a hearty Tyrolean snack. The latter is usually accompanied by a measure

Salzburg

The neighbouring province of Salzburg attracts visitors from all over the world, not least for its scenic beauty and works of art. But the region has far more to offer than Mozart, the festival and its celebrated churches.

Travellers should leave some time to visit the historic inns of the Old Town; here, beneath ancient vaulted ceilings or in a shady inner courtyard, you can try Salzburg braised beef, cooked in beer, or a larded veal olive – followed by bilberry soufflé or a sweet baked pudding. No-one should miss the excellent local beer, which is usually served in half-litre *Krügerl* or tankards. In times past the archbishops of Salzburg acquired brewing rights in order to improve their precarious financial situation; for many years now, beer production has been a flourishing economic sideline in this enterprising city.

Confectionery is another Salzburg speciality. Even the revered Wolfgang Amadeus is celebrated by balls of marzipan and plain chocolate – the famous and delicious *Mozartkugeln*. Like the *Sachertorte*, these omnipresent chocolates are virtually an emblem of Austrian identity and the mountains of them heaped in tourist shops and confectioners across the land – who even sell them by the 100-piece bucket – can seem positively terrifying. An alternative for the non-chocolate-lover are the Salzburger *Kokos-Rollen*, soft coconut batons, a 1950s sweet revived on the anniversary of the State Treaty in 2005.

A detour into the nearby Salzkammergut is always worthwhile, especially a visit to Zauner, the baker in Bad Ischl near the former villa of the Emperor Franz Joseph. It is a paradise for the sweet-toothed, bursting with gâteaux, *Stollen*, sweets and chocolate.

Upper Austria was once an exclusively agricultural region, as can be seen in its typical specialities. Cured pork, *Sauerkraut* and dumplings are an essential component of every menu, as is the substantial *Bauernschmaus* – which also includes sausages and bacon.

The province is considered to be the true home of the dumpling; many an inn holds an annual Dumpling Week, during which every imaginable form of the fluffy dough – savoury, piquant or sweet – will be served. The region's dumpling capital is the Innviertel, where any lunch without dumplings, however lavish it may be, is considered at best a paltry snack.

In the Mühlviertel no meal is complete unless it includes a generous measure of cider or perry. This fermented juice of apples or pears is not really intended for refined palates, for it is rather rough in texture. Many farmers still ferment their own cider; the juice is squeezed from the fruit in autumn, and allowed to settle in oak barrels. Traditionally, cider is served in a stone tankard, accompanied by a thick slice of bread topped by moist bacon.

FAR LEFT: local lake trout from the Wörthersee.
LEFT: *Spargel*, asparagus, is highly prized.
RIGHT: *Käsnudeln*, stuffed with fruit, a speciality of Carinthia.

Carinthia

In Carinthia, the southernmost province of Austria, game is served in every imaginable form, often cooked in red wine. Fish from the clear waters of the lakes, and milk and cheese specialities adorn the menus of restaurants between Villach and Klagenfurt. Best known and best loved are the *Käsnudeln*, pockets of dough filled with curd cheese and mint leaves, served with brown butter and fried diced bacon. A sweet variation is stuffed with prunes and chopped dried pears. The district around the Wörthersee is a busy tourist centre, but a few miles outside town the traveller can find peace-

ful meadows and little inns offering good plain cooking of excellent quality.

If you are lucky the landlady may even bake the bread herself, from a mixture of wheat and rye flour. One of these rustic loaves may weigh as much as 3–4 kg (6–7 lbs), with a diameter of up to 50 cm (20 inches). A thick slice topped with bacon or dripping, or just fresh farmhouse butter and honey, makes a substantial snack.

In Styria, locals and visitors alike feast on the hearty, down-to-earth dishes. Characteristic is the *Heidensterz*, fried dumplings and crackling prepared from buckwheat flour, pork dripping and water. Another classic is *Klachlsuppe*, a soup prepared from slices of leg of pork, herbs and vegetables, juniper berries and peppercorns. It is seasoned generously and served with boiled potatoes and grated horseradish. Guests who insist on something lighter, however, will find that the local market gardens can supply a huge range of fresh vegetables. The local pumpkin specialities earn eulogies from visiting gourmets.

Black gold

If the salad you ordered tastes different here from elsewhere in the world, you must ascribe the exotic flavour to the use of black pumpkin seed oil. For a long time it was scorned as "car-riage grease"; today the "Styrian black gold", darkly shimmering with an inimitable nutty flavour, is praised for its nutritious qualities and now appears on the tables of fashionable restaurants in Vienna, where it adds the finishing touch to an elegant salad buffet. *Kürbiskern-suppe* is a delicious cream of pumpkin soup, often garnished with the seeds.

Mushroom goulash and braised cabbage, poulardes and pork in every variation are other tempting – and fattening – specialities of Austria. If you decide on a fruit diet, head for the southern part of the province, along the border with Slovenia. Fruit trees form guards of hon-

COFFEE

To fully enjoy your visit to a Kaffeehaus, you will have to master at least the rudiments of Austrian "coffee speak". Essential to the whole experience is an enormous chunk of cake, the higher calorie intake the better and preferably larded with *Schlagobers* (whipped cream); one of the many types of coffee should help it to go down. Below are some of the variations on a theme:

Schwarzer or Mocca: black coffee. A *Verlängerter Schwarzer* is slightly weaker.

Brauner: black coffee with a little milk. Ask for *Kleiner* (small), *Grosser* (large) or *Verlängerter*.

Melange: large milky coffee, like a cappuccino.

Einspänner: a *Schwarzer* served in a tall glass with *Schlagobers*).

Cappuccino: confusingly, a milky coffee topped with *Schlagobers*.

Pharisäer: Strong black coffee with *Schlagobers*, served with a glass of rum alongside.

Fiaker: A *Verlängerter* containing rum and, once again, *Schlagobers*.

Kaisermelange: A *Melange* with egg yolk and brandy – an acquired taste. One tourist was asked his opinion of the concoction: "Rather…" he began weakly, "no, not rather… unbelievably vile."

our along the roads; their harvest goes to make apple juice and warming pear schnapps.

In Lower Austria, the region, like the wine, is measured in quarters: those lying above and below the Manhartsberg, those above and below the Vienna Woods, and the Wine and Woodland Quarters. The cuisine of the region is just as varied. Many dishes have been handed down from the former woodland dwellers to the present-day inhabitants.

Fresh fish

The River Danube and the region's lakes and streams are teeming with fish. A perennial favourite is trout à la meunière, in which the fish is fried in butter, seasoned with lemon and served garnished with sprigs of parsley. Game dishes – from "pheasant in a bacon jacket" to roast wild boar – are a culinary sensation. For dessert, the sweet cream strudel has achieved national fame. As a digestif, try a fine liqueur or apricot brandy from the Wachau, with its excellent country inns and ambitious cooks.

The culinary skills of the Burgenland, Austria's youngest province, are as colourful as its population. Here live Croats, Hungarians and Gypsies whose traditional dishes are gathered together under the collective title of "Pannonian cuisine". Many specialities – such as the Esterházy Roast – can trace their names back to the ancient aristocratic families of the region. Hungarian cooking is not only represented by its spicy *Gulyas* (goulash) and other stews, but also by delicious sweet and savoury pancakes, *Palatschinken*. The heady local wine can best be sampled as an accompaniment to a crispy fried *Fogosch* (freshwater fish). The Burgenland specialises in sweet wines; those from the shores of Neusiedlersee, "Vienna's sea", are particularly fine.

Drinks

Austria's spectacular variety of food is helped along by particular refreshments. In the Arlberg a perfect day is capped by a *Jagatee*, a brew of schnapps, wine and a drop of tea. Those in need of stronger fortification might turn to schnapps or *Brand*, strong, clear spirits bearing a resemblance to Italian *grappa*

and utterly unlike the sweet variants marketed abroad by large drinks concerns.

An essential part of the grape harvest are the open-air lunches of bacon, sausages and freshly pressed grape juice. It is at this time that town-dwellers flock to the Neusiedlersee, southern Styria, the Weinviertel or the hills surrounding Gumpoldskirchen to help with the hard labour in the vineyards.

Once this work is done, Austrians begin drinking of the grape straight away: not only new wine, *Heurige*, but also the rough part-fermented *Sturm* and even the grape must *(Most)* are consumed. The *Heurige* is best sampled in

an establishment of the same name, a *Heuriger* – in the vicinity of Vienna, in Grinzing, Salmannsdorf, Kahlenbergerdorf or Nussdorf.

If you see a low vintner's cottage, with the sound of laughter and the clinking of glasses echoing from the little inner courtyard, then you will have found a likely place. Some wine growers also invite travellers to a tasting in their cool cellars, among the acid smell of wooden barrels and fermented grapes, where the candlelight flickers romantically against the vaulted ceilings. Equally inviting are the attractive whitewashed houses in the vintners' districts in the Weinviertel and in southern Burgenland. ❑

LEFT: the glorious *Apfelstrudel* served with a good dollop of *Schlagobers*.
RIGHT: best eaten with a *Melange*.

THE COFFEE HOUSE

Austrians drink about twice as much coffee as beer, and *Kaffehäuser* can be found in all the major cities, including Salzburg, Linz and Graz

The coffee culture is stronger the further east one travels, and no other location can truly rival the cafés of Vienna. These are the cathedrals of caffeine, the equivalent of other countries' bars and pubs, the social centres of life in the country's capital, with their own language and etiquette. Waiters traditionally present the customer with an aloof or even irritable air, deaf to second orders or calls for the bill, but this performance is part of the pleasure and even the most practised of professional sneers has occasionally, albeit accidentally, slipped like a mask to reveal a fellow human being! Once you have been served, it is understood that you and your fellow drinkers may linger almost indefinitely, with refills to the glass of water which accompanies your coffee, often on a silver tray and sometimes accompanied by a square of chocolate.

ABOVE: The Café Central on Herrengasse, paying respects to a presiding spirit, has a mannequin of the walrus-moustached Altenberg seated at one of the tables by its entrance, although it might equally have chosen to feature Sigmund Freud, whose Wednesday Psychological Society occasionally met here, or Leon Trotsky, who famously frequented the place under the alias of Bronstein. The Central has a reputation for being somewhat touristy, although this is perhaps less than deserved.

ABOVE AND RIGHT: Café Demel on Kohlmarkt is justly one of the most famous in Vienna. It vies with the Café Sacher as the inventor of the Sachertorte (they now have an uneasy truce after a long court case). With one of the most elegant interiors of any café, it is very popular with visitors and locals alike.

INTELLECTUAL WATERING HOLES

Since Kolschitzky, the Viennese coffee legend has grown and grown. The Biedermeier period left its mark in the stereotypical décor of red velvette banquettes, marble tables, mirrors and crystal chandeliers. Countless visitors to the city today visit the Griensteidl or the Central hoping to sense the aura of those famous intellectuals and artists of the *fin-de-siècle* who came here to debate, make mock, hear the news and do business: as Stefan Zweig wrote, "The Viennese coffee house is an institution without parallel anywhere else in the world...a sort of democratic club, where the cost of admission is no more than the price of a cup of coffee." Not all Kaffeehaus business was so high-minded, of course – patrons might equally drop by to pursue their objects of desire in a discreet *Schmüseeck*, or "cuddling corner". One long-term frequenter of Kaffeehäuser, the writer Peter Altenberg, is remembered as much for the semi-pornographic postcards he sent as his pithy contributions to the *feuilleton*, or essay section, of the city press.

The dawn of the Viennese love affair with coffee has, like everything else in the city, its own pseudo-historical legend. In 1683, with Vienna on the verge of capitulation to the Turkish siege, a Pole named Kolschitzky was assigned the task of running messages to and from the beleaguered city. A Turkish speaker, he is said to have mingled easily with the Ottomans (in some variants of the myth disguised as a pasha), cheerfully accepting numerous invitations to stop for coffee. The drink was unknown in 17th-century Vienna, but Kolschitzky had developed a taste for it on his travels. As he sipped at endless cups, he studied the Turkish deployments. Kolschitzky's observations were passed on to the Duke of Lorraine and King Sobieski, and were to be of inestimable value in the plans drawn up by the Polish king for a lightning cavalry strike. Once the Turks were routed, the besieged population rushed out and fell on the food stores the Turks had left behind. One of the crowd, Kolschitzky knew exactly what he was looking for – sacks of a certain brown bean. Those who saw them asked whether they were best eaten baked, boiled or fried. The Pole kept the secrets of the bean to himself, and was rewarded for his services with a licence, the first of its kind in the Holy Roman Empire, to open his Kaffee Schrank (Coffee Cupboard). The coffee house was born.

Another famous Viennese coffee joint, the Hawelka on Dorotheergasse, which features in the video for Kraftwerk's *Trans-Europe Express*, was a haunt of artists. The husband-and-wife owners were legends in their own lifetime and occasional stars of the Viennese media. Café Frauenhuber on Himmelpfortgasse is the oldest extant café in the city, founded in 1788, and supposedly played host to performances by both Mozart and Beethoven. It is a dangerous contention to make, but Café Diglas *(above)* on Wollzeile is arguably the best in the city: the cakes are superb and once ensconced, it is almost impossible to leave its cosy velvet seats; for something a little less conventional, try the Palmenhaus in the Burggarten, set within a Jugendstil glasshouse.

etteln u. Hausieren
verboten
BEKANNT
BERÜHMT
BEGEHRT
DIE
alität

LITERATURE AND FILM

*From Freud and Fritz Lang to Jelinek and Hanneke, Austrian writers
and film makers have explored the deep recesses of the mind*

It sometimes seems that Austrian, and above all Viennese, literature has become synonymous with two things: sexual desire and the life of the mind. Depictions of sexual tension and hedonism bordering on the pornographic seem to go hand in hand with an essayistic, almost formal contemplation of life's philosophical problems. This is perhaps the legacy of the Viennese *fin-de-siècle*, in which a leisured middle class combined a high level of classical education with an incredible appetite for licentiousness. Two bodies of writing in which these concerns are yoked together are those of Sigmund Freud (1856–1939) and his contemporary Arthur Schnitzler (1862–1931).

Freud and Schnitzler

Those who have had the opportunity to read Freud in the original German know that his talents as a prose stylist were at least as significant as the quality of his thought. It has been remarked that Freudian psychoanalysis seeks to interpret its clients' life stories in the manner of literary texts: Freud himself commented that his case histories often dispensed with scientific form and rather read like novellas. Indeed, some of Freud's investigations into the sexuality and psychology of his bourgeois Viennese patients read almost interchangeably with the heady works of his contemporary and fellow doctor, Arthur Schnitzler.

Schnitzler's most famous works, *Reigen* and *Traumnovelle* (Dream Story), have both become well-known worldwide largely thanks to foreign adaptations. The play *Reigen* was filmed in the 1950s by Max Ophuls as *La Ronde*, and was revived again in the 1990s by David Hare, to some controversy, as *The Blue Room*. The latter adaptation was initially staged starring Nicole Kidman, who also appeared alongside her then-husband Tom Cruise in

Francis Ford Coppola's *Eyes Wide Shut*, a version of *Traumnovelle*. The film does not do justice to Schnitzler's short, powerful novella, which explores the sexual fantasies and jealousies of a middle-class Viennese couple and reveals a sinister and decadent underside to their seemingly prim and proper turn-of-the-

century milieu. Freud acknowledged the affinities of his work and Schnitzler's in a letter sent on the writer's 60th birthday: "Whenever I get deeply interested in your beautiful creations I always seem to find, behind their poetic sheen, the same presuppositions, interests and conclusions as those familiar to me as my own."

Grillparzer

One of the most prominent names in the literature of the imperial period is that of Franz Grillparzer (1791–1872). This Viennese civil servant, a founding member of the Austrian Academy of Sciences, began writing and translating drama at university. When his work came

PRECEDING PAGES: the Marmorsaal at Stift St Florian.
LEFT: Orson Welles as Harry Lime in *The Third Man*.
RIGHT: Nicole Kidman and Tom Cruise get close in *Eyes Wide Shut*.

to the attention of the Hofburgtheater's artistic director, Grillparzer found a mentor and after successes at the court theatre with *The Ancestress* and *Sappho*, was awarded a contract as Imperial and Royal Poet of the Court Theatre. Leaving this post early to travel, he produced a number of important works, particularly in the 1820s, but some of these brought him into disfavour with the Viennese court. An ambivalence about the politics of the time – Grillparzer objected to Metternich but was also suspicious of the 1848 revolutions – made the tension between the public and private spheres a key theme of his drama. In 1838 Grillparzer with-

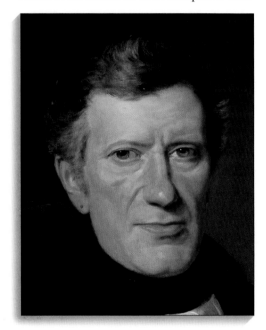

drew from theatre life and virtually all works written after that date were only performed posthumously.

Adalbert Stifter and Joseph Roth

Quiet withdrawal was also advocated by the 19th-century writer and educator Adalbert Stifter (1805–68). His values and outlook stemmed from the calm before the storm of 1848 – he equated both radical politics and personal passion with chaos and advocated a quietest approach to social and moral order. A lecturer and tutor, Stifter only found publication in his mid-thirties.

His humanitarian and poetic ideals were often at odds with those of his peers – his fiction clashed with the contemporary doctrine of poetic realism, while the educational reforms he advocated were resisted by the educational authority of Upper Austria, where he had moved in 1848. His key work is *Der Nachsommer* – translated as *Indian Summer* – in which a merchant's son gradually develops all the noble characteristics of the man of *Bildung*, the culture of German humanism. In its emphasis on simple ethics and education which affect all aspects of one's life, it exemplifies his philosophical worldview.

More than 25 years after Stifter's death, another writer, Joseph Roth, presented a very different kind of resignation in his novels. Born in Galicia in 1894, Roth worked as a journalist and novelist in Berlin, Prague and Paris as well as Vienna. In exile from the German-speaking lands from 1933 on, he was a key figure in the comumunity of émigré writers and thinkers who opposed the Nazi regime. A notoriously

---

"AUSTRIAN" PRAGUE

While Vienna has perhaps always been unambiguously "Austrian", for other locales the question is not so clear-cut. The problem of defining what "Austria" means extends to a description of its national literature. The imperial legacy means that Prague writers such as Gustav Meyrink, Leo Perutz, Rainer Maria Rilke and Franz Kafka arguably belong to "Austrian literature" and, indeed, have found themselves printed alongside writers from Vienna, Linz and beyond in various compilations.

Prague, which in the late imperial period was a rival to Vienna and Berlin in terms of German literary life, belongs today to the history of Czechoslovakia – but nonetheless its

writers, certainly into the 1920s, were shaped and affected by the Habsburg Monarchy. The image of Prague as a city of decadence and sinister, sometimes supernatural, intrigue, home to ghosts, mystics and the terrible Golem, belongs to the German-speaking, and above all Jewish, community: for Czechs of the time, Prague represented the bright hope of a future free from the imperial yoke.

The Sanatorium Hoffmann in which Kafka died of tuberculosis does lie within present-day Austria, in the village of Kierling. It is still a working institution, and one cannot visit the actual room in which he spent his last weeks, – however, there is a Kafka memorial room open to the public.

heavy drinker, Roth was haunted by never having known his father, who died before his birth, and by his identity as a Jew, feeling that the Habsburg Monarchy had given the Jewish people a protection which was lost in the post-1918 European landscape. He would ultimately die as a result of the effects of alcoholism. In virtually all his major novels, Roth's protagonists are foredoomed figures, stripped of the roles they held before World War I, living a kind of bleak afterlife in the postimperial universe.

The Radetzky March (1932) and *The Emperor's Tomb* (1938), two particularly outstanding novels, form a kind of autumnal epitaph for the empire. They give an account of the Trottas, a Slovene dynasty who rise from obscurity to nobility under the Dual Monarchy, only for their fortunes to be dashed with those of Franz Joseph in 1918. *The Radetzky March* covers three generations of the noble Trottas: the grandfather who earned the family title by saving the emperor's life in battle, his son the high-ranking civil servant, and his grandson the dissolute soldier whose drinking and gambling brings shame on the family. It is also notable for featuring Franz Joseph himself, characterised as a kindly figure, canny but passive and melancholic, isolated by the courtly routines which surround him. *The Emperor's Tomb* traces the fortunes of another branch of the family from the eve of the war through hardship in the First Republic right up to the moment of Nazi *Anschluss*.

A Viennese friend of Roth was Ödon von Horvath (1901–38) who fled the Nazis only to die in Paris in an accident. His short novel *Jugend Ohne Gott (Youth without God)* is a chilling account of a schoolteacher whose pupils are being brainwashed into fervent support for a thinly disguised Hitler figure.

Musil, Kraus and Altenberg

Another writer who sought to conjure the posthumous image of late imperial Austria was Robert Musil (1880–1942). His enormous, cerebral masterwork *Der Mann ohne Eigenschaften (The Man Without Qualities)* was written during the 1920s and 30s, but set in 1913. It is widely recognised as one of the outstanding achievements of modern Austrian literature. In the novel, the iconoclastic young intellectual Ulrich moves among the literary salons and government ministries of a Vienna unaware of the impending world war. Musil sarcastically renames the k.u.k. empire as Kakanien, the land of "caca", sparing no element of society in a work which touches on celebrity criminals, the sociology of urban life, mysticism, sexual ambiguity, anti-Semitism and big business.

Musil, who had a number of degrees and a PhD in philosophy, crammed the work with intellectually challenging material: some of the novel's chapters have even been excerpted as

essays in their own right. The publishers Rohwolt were warned that publishing this provocative, difficult work would bankrupt them, and the novel was a critical rather than popular success in Musil's lifetime.

Musil was financially supported by fellow writers who formed "Musil-Societies" to raise funding for him. Amongst these supporters was Thomas Mann, whom Musil had derided as feeding the mediocre intellectual pretensions of the middle classes. Musil's diary of 1939, when he had fled Austria for Switzerland, records the simple comment, "I am touched, particularly by Th. M. to whom I have often been unjust. I am also flattered."

LEFT: Franz Grillparzer, in a portrait by Georg Waldmüller.
RIGHT: Robert Musil.

Only the first two sections of *The Man without Qualities*, originally planned to comprise four parts, were published in Musil's lifetime. The English-language translation uses Musil's unfinished writings and drafts to produce a concluding third section. It is a rewarding read for those with the stamina, with Musil ranked today alongside Proust and Joyce in the European literary canon. Musil's earlier work *Die Verwirrungen des Zöglings Törless (The Confusions of Young Törless)*, which appeared in 1906, is an account of sex and violence among the pupils of a k.u.k. military academy on the empire's borders: although much shorter than

The Man Without Qualities, it retains the same power and intellectual quality.

More blatant in his satire and less reclusive than Musil was Karl Kraus (1874–1936), who tossed off aphorism after aphorism while almost single-handedly producing every issue of his magazine *Die Fackel*, which took no prisoners in its dissection of politics, language and culture. Kraus' play *The Last Days of Mankind*, dealing with the World War I, was a vast and almost unperformable piece composed of countless excerpts from the popular press and government statements. Kraus became such a well-known institution in his own right that Musil was provoked to write that there

were "two things you can't fight because they are too long, too fat and have no head or foot: Karl Kraus and psychoanalysis."

Writing within more conventional fields of journalism was another observer of late-imperial Viennese *Alltagsleben* (everyday life), Peter Altenberg (1859–1919). Born Richard Engländer, Altenberg's pen-name is a story in itself, the surname conjuring the place of his happy upbringing and 'Peter' being the nickname of a childhood girlfriend. Altenberg's short pieces appeared in the press *unter dem Strich*, under the line which divided news stories from the *feuilleton*, an essay section in German-language newspapers which "contained everything which did not properly belong in a newspaper". Altenberg was also an author of poems and of countless postcards, the e-mail of their day, on which he would supply friends with pictures of young girls, appending comments like, *"Idealste Beine!"* ("the most ideal legs!").

Hofmannsthal, Zweig and Canetti

A more restrained and stately writer was Hugo von Hofmannsthal (1874–1929). Even in his schooldays, his lyrical verse attracted acclaim when published in the 1890s. Around the turn of the century, Hofmannsthal suffered a loss of faith in the value of language as a tool of expression: his *Sprachkrise*, or "language crisis" led to *The Chandos Letter*, an astonishing short piece anticipating 20th-century philosophers' preoccupation with language. In it, Hofmannsthal assumes the character of an English Renaissance noble who suffers a mental collapse and is forced to retire from literary life when words rebel against him and turn into mysterious "eyes, which stared at me and into which I in turn had to stare." Hofmannsthal's later career saw him grow increasingly conservative and nostalgic for the empire: it was in this phase that he co-founded the famous Salzburger Festspiele as a bulwark against the perceived decline of modern culture.

Stefan Zweig (1882–1942) was another writer who sought to preserve the traditional values of late imperial Austria: pacifism and humanism are strong elements in his work. His novels included Freud-influenced dissections of his bourgeois peers, like *Burning Secret* (1913), as well as a vast number of biographical novels – covering subjects from Mary Stuart to Magellan via Erasmus – which provided an oblique commentary on the rising anti-Semitism of the interwar years. His book *The World of Yesterday* remains a key text for those who wish to understand *fin-de-siècle* Vienna.

His contemporary Elias Canetti (1905–94) outlived him by many decades, but his most famous work *Die Blendung* (1935; translated as *Auto-da-Fé*) also deals with the precarious place of the intellectual in the rising violence of 1930s mass politics. *Masse und Macht (Crowds and Power)* was a theoretical work on the mass movements of the 20th century which remains significant today. The novelist, poet and philosopher Hermann Broch

found literary success only after 1945, becoming a widely renowned novelist of the Second Republic before his death.

The "Land without Qualities"

The generation which has come of age since 1945 has provided an important corrective to Austrian suppression of past shames and tragedies. Aesthetic experimentalists, particularly those of the Forum Stadpark in Graz, have given way to a politically engaged generation critical of contemporary society.

Ingeborg Bachmann (1926–73) began her career as a poet aligned with the radical Gruppe

(1886–1951) similarly alternated works of narrative fiction (including 1932's *The Sleepwalkers*, an important trilogy) with more formal studies of ethics, aesthetics and the psychology of mass hysteria.

While Zweig, Canetti and Broch were all critics of the Nazi regime and fled Austria in the late 1930s, the novelist Heimito von Doderer (1896–1966) was briefly a member of the Nazi party before leaving and converting to Catholicism. Serving Hitler's Germany in the war, he became an Allied prisoner and

LEFT: Hugo von Hofmannsthal *circa* 1915.
ABOVE: an animated Stefan Zweig in 1935.

47. *The Respite* (1953) is a collection critical of the Second Republic's attempts to revive the old order; 1961's story collection *The Thirtieth Year* deals with human relationships in the aftermath of fascism. From 1965 she began a lengthy project, the Cycle of Ways of Dying, which examined women's suffering at the hands of men, but only one novel in this sequence, *Malina* (1971) was completed. The unfinished *Franza's Case* and *Requiem for Fanny Goldmann* appeared posthumously.

The 2004 Nobel Prize winner Elfriede Jelinek is a novelist, playwright, poet and translator. She was born to a Jewish father who survived World War II in relative safety thanks to his war-effort work as a chemist. *Wonderful, Wonderful Times* and *The Piano Teacher*, since made into a film, both deal critically with life in Vienna, while *Lust* takes its readers to the Austrian provinces to explore pornography and sexual exploitation from a feminist perspective. She was not the most enthusiastic of prize winners, not attending the ceremony by claiming to suffer from "social phobia".

The celebrated English poet W.H. Auden spent the last 15 years of his life in Austria, producing poetry at his farmhouse in Kirchstetten, a town to the west of Vienna. It now houses an Auden Museum (tel: 02742-200 3104; www.

Lilian Faschinger's best-known book, *Magdalena the Sinner*, features a motorcycling female renegade who kidnaps a priest so as to confess her many sins. The endless sexual scenarios of which these sins are comprised grow a little tiresome after a while; a better bet may be Faschinger's *Vienna Passion*, which sees a present-day New Yorker come to Vienna to research Anna Freud only to stumble on a neglected figure from Austrian imperial history.

The largely reclusive Thomas Bernhard (1931–89) is known for his autobiographical works, some of which treat his six years in a tuberculosis sanatorium, as well as novels and

kirchstetten.at; open by arrangement). A plaque on Vienna's Walfischgasse marks the former site of the hotel at which Auden died in 1973.

Robert Menasse has produced books of essays including *Das Land ohne Eigenschaften (Land without Qualities)* and *Die letzte Märchenprinzessin (The Last Fairy-tale Princess)*, the latter book dealing with the image of the late British Princess Diana. A former teacher at the University of São Paolo, his novels often take place in the countries of exile of Austrian Jews. Where his characters do find a "homeland", it is as likely to be in an imagined vision of the pre-war Austria as any physical location.

plays which, starting with 1963's *Frost*, present a bleak picture of human existence in general and Austrian life in particular. His play *Heldenplatz*, 1988, was an acerbic indictment of contemporary anti-Semitism which provoked a particularly high-profile response. In his will, Bernhard chose to ban all further performance of his plays and all reprints of his works within Austria – only since his estate established the Thomas Bernhard Foundation in 1998 has this been repealed.

Finally, one of the best-known Austrian authors alive today is Peter Handke. His early works were experimental texts avoiding direct social commentary in favour of a critical approach to language: "literature is created by language and not by things described by language". Later works were of more conventional form and have been compared to those of Stifter. Winner of numerous literary prizes, Handke's most widely known work is *The Goalkeeper's Fear of the Penalty*, which owes its international fame as much to the film adaptation shot in Vienna by Wim Wenders as the original text.

Austria on Film

Although Austria has never had a film industry to rival the heyday of Berlin, let alone Los Angeles, a surprising number of familiar names and faces from the world of film, and especially Golden Age Hollywood cinema, came from the territories of the Austro-Hungarian Empire. Their predominantly Jewish background forced a mass emigration of cinematic talent as the Nazis rose to power in first Germany and then Austria.

Billy Wilder, director of *Some Like it Hot* and *Sunset Boulevard*, was one of this Jewish generation. Born Samuel Wilder in the Galician (now Polish) town of Sucha in 1906, he was schooled in Vienna and worked as a reporter before transferring to Berlin. There he broke into screenwriting, fleeing Germany in 1933 when Hitler came to power. In Hollywood he shared an apartment with another one-time subject of the Dual Monarchy, Rózsahegy-born László "Lazzy" Löwenstein, better known as Peter Lorre (1904–64). Lorre had trained as an actor in Vienna, although his stage debut was in Zurich and he first came to fame as a psychopathic child killer in a German production, *M* (1931). *M* was, however, directed by an *echter Wiener*, Fritz Lang (1890–1976). Lang owed his career in film to a fortuitous injury in World War I, having fought on the imperial side. Hospitalisation in June 1916 was as much blessing as curse when it gave him the opportunity to write some film proposals; when sent home for shell-shock in 1918 he found contract work as a writer for a Berlin-based production company. A leading German director, Lang shot *Metropolis* there before emigrating to Paris when the Nazi regime refused to show his *Testament des*

Dr. *Mabuse (The Testament of Dr Mabuse)*. The stay in France was brief, and on arriving in Hollywood, Lang shot some of the great American melodramas of this period, including *The Big Heat* and *Fury*.

Wilder cast another Austrian, Vienna-born Erich von Stroheim (1885–1957), as Field Marshal Rommel himself in 1943's *Five Graves to Cairo*. Although von Stroheim is best known for his performance as Gloria Swanson's servant in *Sunset Boulevard* (1950), until the 1930s he had been a director responsible for productions including *The Wedding March*, a film about a Viennese prince who plans to

marry for wealth only to fall for beautiful-but-penniless Fay Wray, *The Merry Widow* (an adaptation of Lehár's operetta) and *Greed*, considered to be his masterpiece. Unlike the wave of Central European émigrés who fled the Nazis in the 1930s, von Stroheim had in fact emigrated to the USA before World War I. This was also the case for Josef von Sternberg, the director who made Marlene Dietrich a star. The Vienna-born von Sternberg had moved to New York City at the age of 14 and worked in a variety of film-industry roles before deciding that he could do better than the directors he saw around him. Von Stroheim had been less successful within the industry, only finding work

---

LEFT: Elfriede Jelinek delivers her Nobel Prize Lecture by video in 2004.
RIGHT: Peter Lorre in *M*.

as an assistant and bit-part actor, until America's entry into World War I presented him with a unique opportunity to exploit his ethnic background, allowing himself to be typecast as a Prussian villain in a number of productions.

A younger Viennese émigré, Otto Preminger (1905–86) would follow in von Stroheim's footsteps as a performer, repeatedly playing Nazi villains during World War II – most famously he appeared as a prison camp commander in Wilder's *Stalag 17* (1953). Before this, Preminger had been a successful stage director, directing a film *Die Grosse Liebe (The Great Love)* in 1931 before being invited to the

United States by a Broadway producer. Preminger's breakthrough movie in the US was the melodrama *Laura* (1944), a box-office success and enduring classic. Preminger went on to film *Carmen Jones*, *The Man with the Golden Arm* and *Anatomy of a Murder*, dealing with issues of race, drug use and sex crime which were shocking for mainstream US cinema of the time. Preminger's Oscar-nominated 1963 piece *The Cardinal* set its Boston-born hero at loggerheads with the real-life historical figure of Austria's pro-Nazi Cardinal Innitzer.

Another Viennese movie notable was the director of *High Noon*, *A Man for All Seasons*, *Day of the Jackal* and *Oklahoma*, Fred Zinne-

mann. Like Lang and Wilder, he first found work with the Berlin movie studios before crossing the Atlantic, in his case first to Mexico and only then the USA

In front of the cameras, it was an Austrian, Hedy Lamarr, who earned herself the title of "Most Beautiful Woman in Film" in the 1930s. Born in Vienna, 1913, Hedwig Eva Kiesler had decided to drop out of school and become an actress by the time she reached her teens. It was her fifth film, *Extase (Ecstasy*, 1932) which made her infamous when she appeared in the world's first nude scene, provoking a global sensation. Although the film was banned in the US, her notoriety attracted the attention of American studios and she signed a contract with Louis B. Mayer. Celebrity apocrypha has it that in addition to her screen work, she was responsible for the invention of a "Secret Communication System" patented in 1942 and used by the US Navy during World War II.

More recently, Austria's Michael Hanneke has found great acclaim among the ranks of contemporary European directors. Although born in the Bavarian city of Munich, he was raised in Wiener Neustadt and studied at the University of Vienna. 1997's *Funny Games* satirised both the effect of "video nasties" and bourgeois propriety in the tale of two young men who take an affluent family hostage and force them to engage in ever more degrading acts. His *The Piano Teacher* (2001) is an adaptation of Elfriede Jelinek's novel about an instructor at Vienna's music conservatory.

In the field of documentary, a contemporary Austrian filmmaker of note is Ruth Beckermann, whose *Wien Retour (Return to Vienna*, 1983) and *Jenseits des Krieges (East of War*, 1996) explore Austrian history and memories from a perspective outside the national mainstream.

Foreign takes

Austria's other great gift to cinema has been its own countryside and urban landscapes, serving as locations for a variety of famous 20th century movies.

Surely the most well-known outside Austria – within the country it was a flop and is still widely reviled – is 1965's *The Sound of Music*, in which Julie Andrews' nun Maria marries Captain von Trapp, the tough-yet-tender Austrian naval officer portrayed by Christopher

Plummer, and then must flee the Nazis or be shipped off to (gasp) Bremerhaven by the Germans. Locations from Mondsee to St Gilgen were brought in to represent Salzburg, which was insufficiently camera-friendly for the glamorous production. *The Sound of Music* managed to win an astonishing five Academy Awards at the next year's Oscars.

A close second for iconic Austro-movie status must be 1949's *The Third Man*, one of the first British films to be made chiefly on location. Renowned film producer Alexander Korda had sent the novelist Graham Greene to postwar Vienna to find "a contemporary story", which

In 1980, Art Garfunkel was the unlikely leading man for the Vienna-set final film of director Nicholas Roeg, *Bad Timing*. In it, Garfunkel plays an American psychoanalyst being interrogated by a detective (played by the equally unlikely Harvey Keitel) while his girlfriend lies in hospital after a suspicious overdose. The theme of sexual obsession and the Klimtian visual motifs both serve to conjure the heady atmosphere of *fin-de-siècle* Vienna with greater success than Francis Ford Coppola encountered in *Eyes Wide Shut*, his distant adaptation of Schnitzler's *Traumnovelle*.

Finally, 1995's *Before Sunrise* unleashed a

he promptly did, telling the tale of writer Holly Martins abroad in the partitioned city, trying to discover the identity of the "third man" seen after his friend Harry Lime's mysterious death. Filming took place with the ruined city still under military occupation: from the very start, the atmosphere of the time permeates a production very sensitive to its setting – Anton Karas' famous zither-playing made it into the film when director Carol Reed chanced upon him playing for tips in a *Kaffeehaus*.

LEFT: Hedy Lamarr in *Extase*.
ABOVE: Joseph Cotton stands on part of Vienna's old city wall during the filming of *The Third Man*.

sweeter version of Viennese charms on a generation of sentimental adolescents – Ethan Hawke and Julie Delpy play student travellers who meet on the Budapest–Vienna train and decide to spend the night wandering the city, deep in conversation, in a bid to discover whether there is potential for a deeper relationship.

While Hawke and Delpy ultimately reunited in Paris for the sequel, *Before Sunset*, and the 21st century has seen Hollywood prefer to go further east for its historic cities – Prague in particular attracting investment as a lower-budget movie location – the love affair the camera has with Austria and its unique qualities surely cannot have come to an end. ❑

MUSIC AND DANCE

From the classical greats of the western canon to

folk-derived Alpine punk, Austria has a fascinating array of musical cultures

If Austria has a claim to artistic fame it is surely in the field of music. The list of musicians and composers from the western classical canon who were born, or who have lived and worked, in Austria is quite staggering. They include: Mozart, Haydn, Beethoven, Schubert, Brahms, Bruckner, Mahler, Schoenberg, Berg and Webern. Austrian music is not, however, limited to the works we hear in the concert hall or opera house, there are also strong traditions of liturgical, folk and popular music, many of which fed into and had a significant impact on the works of the composers mentioned above.

Gluck and Mozart

The marriage of Leopold I (the "first baroque emperor") to Margherita of Spain in 1667 was celebrated by an opera held in the main courtyard of the Hofburg. This wildly extravagant spectacle entitled *Il Pomo d'Oro* with music by Pietro Antonio Cesti is the first recorded instance of an opera performance in Vienna. Subsequently the stiff Italian style of opera prevailed until Maria Theresa discovered Gluck (1714–87), whose reformist works (starting with *Alkestis*, 1767) subordinated the music to dramatic requirements. His *Orpheus* is considered one of his finest works.

He was succeeded by Wolfgang Amadeus Mozart (1756–91), regarded as one of the greatest of all western composers for his sense of melody, form and his success across all genres, from piano sonatas, to symphonies and opera. His musical talents had been recognised at a very early age, he was composing by the age of five, and he and his sister Nannerl were taken around the courts of Europe performing keyboard duets. After travels around Italy he joined the employ of the prince-archbishop of Salzburg, but this did not suit his temperament and, after literally being booted out by the chamberlain, he settled in Vienna in 1781 where he largely remained until his early death.

LEFT: Gustav Mahler in 1907.
RIGHT: Wolfgang Amadeus Mozart.

Much of his musical activity in Vienna was in aristocratic salons where his piano and chamber works were performed. However, his greatest public successes, aside from occasional concerts, were in the opera house. His most popular opera in his homeland was *Die Zauberflöte*, but he was, however, occasionally less successful at court, the emperor complaining ironically that *Die Entführung aus dem Serail* was "too beautiful for our ears… and with very many notes". When he was appointed to the court his salary was 800 Gulden a year, as compared to the 2,000 Gluck had received. "It is," said Mozart, "too much for what I do, and not enough for what I can do."

Haydn

Mozart's mentor was Joseph Haydn, a former chorister at St Stephen's, who worked for the Esterházy princes as Kapellmeister and was treated more or less like a servant. It was this position within the household that accounts for his extraordinary output. This comprises some 113 symphonies, 47 keyboard sonatas, 68 string quartets and some 23 stage works (mostly operas). His music, still one of the staples of the concert hall, is infused with a great deal of wit, but also a deep humanity. His operas, largely written for his patron, were popular in his day but have been rarely performed since his death (although the music is of undoubted genius the plots often leave something to be desired).

Towards the end of his life he managed to free himself a little from the constraints of his employer and not only started to get his music played further afield but also undertook a trip

to London which not only brought him wider European acclaim, but made him a lot of money.

Beethoven and Schubert

The third of the trio of "Viennese classics" is Ludwig van Beethoven (1770–1827). This towering figure was born in Bonn, Germany, but moved to Vienna in 1792 where he spent the rest of his life. The inheritor of the Viennese traditions of Mozart and Haydn (the so-called *Wiener Klassik*), he not only developed these but also pushed at the boundaries of form, harmony and melody, looking forward to the ideals of Romanticism. His individuality was, in part, a product of his own unhappy life and deafness, an afflic-

tion which increasingly cut him off from the world, a process which, while discernible in his works, did not lessen his concern for the human condition.

His legacy remains in, among other works, his nine symphonies, 32 piano sonatas, five piano concertos, and the opera *Fidelio*. From the revolutionary fervour of the third ("Eroica") symphony, to the programmatic nature of the sixth (witness the birdcalls of the Wienerwald), to the grand statement of the ninth and Schiller's *Ode to Joy*, Beethoven sets the ground for many of the concerns of the Romantic movement, and hence his importance for many later composers of the 19th century.

Beethoven was hero-worshipped by his near contemporary Franz Schubert (1797–1828), who might be seen as the first fully-fledged Romantic composer. In his wonderful chamber music and *Lieder*, gentle lyricism alternates with deep and sometimes melancholy passion, and whose Schubertiades (musical soirées at which he played his latest compositions to friends) are seen as typical of the burgher idyll of the Biedermeier period (1814–48). The often subtle nature of Schubert's music can sometimes fool the listener into missing its radical innovation, especially in its harmony.

Operetta and the waltz

After the post-revolutionary repression had lifted with the initiation of the Ringstrasse era, for which Franz Joseph fired the starting gun in 1857, a new feeling prevailed in Vienna. Even before the revolution, the waltz (based on rural dances called *Ländler*) had begun to sweep the country; by the mid-century it had become a craze warned against by doctors for its supposed dangers to health and by moralists for its supposed sexual provocation. In the three decades before 1848, Josef Lanner and Johann Strauss the Elder (a Habsburg loyalist and composer of the *Radetzky March*) had attracted increasingly large audiences; but it was Johann Strauss the Younger (1825–99) who became extraordinarily popular, organising his bands on a commercial basis (they played at several fashionable cafés) and even having to fend off besotted fans who wrote asking for locks of his hair (he sent them clippings from his poodle).

Although the architects may have exhibited a seriousness of purpose, the Ringstrasse era is also a by-word for frivolity, excess and irresponsibility, often summed up in the line from a Strauss operetta: "Happy is he who forgets all about what anyway cannot be changed..."

Operetta was the first and only joint cultural product of the Austro-Hungarian Empire, equally popular in Lemberg, Laibach or Ludenz. It first reached Vienna with performances of Jacques Offenbach's works in the 1850s. The genre contained a good deal of clever political satire, though this escapes today's audiences. It was also part of the world of greater sexual freedom, at least in the capital, where (as Arthur Schnitzler so well described in plays and novellas) alienation and aboulia prevailed. Well-to-

of Beethoven, and Anton Bruckner, a mild-mannered, even saintly individual, who was taken up by the standard-bearers of Wagner. The battle was carried on more by their supporters than the composers themselves (although Brahms did once describe the music of Bruckner as "symphonic boa-constrictors, the amateurish, confused and illogical abortions of a rustic schoolmaster"), who on the one hand accused Brahms of being reactionary, and on the other accused Bruckner of being long-winded and incompetent. The greatest malice came from the immensely influential critic Eduard Hanslick (memorably pilloried by Wag-

do bourgeois men assuaged their urges by consorting with poor (often immigrant) girls. These compliant *süsse Mädl* (sweet girls, as they were sentimentalised) had by no means a sweet life, often being left to cope, poverty-stricken, with an illegitimate child.

Brahms and Bruckner

Meanwhile a feud was raging in a different music world: its two protagonists were Johannes Brahms, the last representative of Romantic Viennese Classicism in the tradition

LEFT: Joseph Haydn.
RIGHT: Schubert and Beethoven.

ner as the pretentious and talentless Beckmesser in *Die Meistersinger von Nürnberg*) who was entirely on Brahms's side.

Brahms, in a sense, performs the same role for the 19th century as Bach does in the 18th; his works are the summation of a tradition. His consummate mastery of the form and harmony of the Viennese classics, allied with his melodic technique of continuous variation, produced some of the most finely and logically wrought pieces of the 19th century, but also ones that are intensely moving. Like the other great Viennese classicists, he dominated several forms: he was a symphonist, wrote *Lieder*, chamber music and produced a huge amount of piano music.

In contrast, Bruckner was brought up as a choirboy at the monastery of St Florian and was later the abbey organist. He was also deeply and naively religious (this was also pilloried by the Brahms faction as "priest-ridden bigotry") and his symphonies express a sense of the traditional Austrian piety in which he was reared. The symphonies cover huge sweeps of time and, with Bruckner's acute sense of drama and form, often build to shattering climaxes, yet he was also capable of creating the most exquisitely delicate passages, with melodies often derived from the traditional music of his native Upper Austria.

A deeply sensitive man (criticism often drove him to rewrite his works making the preparation of a critical edition of his *oeuvre* fraught with difficulty), and at one point Bruckner appealed to Franz Joseph to "stop Hanslick"; this the emperor could not do but he did give him a residence in the grounds of the Belvedere for the last few years of his life.

Mahler and Strauss

One of Bruckner's pupils at the Conservatory (although they were ill-suited) was Gustav Mahler (1860–1911), now seen as one of the greatest late-19th century symphonic composers. However, his works were not widely appreciated in Austria during his lifetime and, as a Jewish composer, his achievements were also obscured by the rise of the Nazis in Austria and Germany. Furthermore, he had also made enemies – many of them fuelled by anti-Semitism – during his tenure of the directorship of the opera (1898–1907). It was Mahler's passion and discipline that made the Vienna Hofoper the greatest house of its day and laid the foundations for its continuing pre-eminence as the Wiener Staatsoper.

His tenure coincided with the golden age of the Wiener Secession *(see page 97)*, and both musicial eclecticism (akin to the eclectic visual forms of the Secession artists) and a sense of changing times are heard in his works. A composer of songs, often with orchestra, and, above all, symphonies, Mahler, like Bruckner, worked on large canvasses, but whereas Bruckner's work is often transcendent and infused with a sense of the Almighty, Mahler inhabited a much darker and more ambiguous world. A sense of struggle is often important, against which the composer either triumphs, in the second, third, fifth or seventh symphonies, is thwarted, with the great hammer blows of fate of the sixth, or becomes quietly and beautifully resigned, as in *Das Lied von der Erde* or the ninth. At the same time he produced some of the most beautiful music of late Romanticism, and his joy in the natural world is palpable. His experiments with harmony – the continual suspension of harmonic resolutions for almost excrutiating emotional effect – look forward to the developments of Schoenberg (whom he championed), while his orchestration is endlessly inventive and often sublime.

Ironically, perhaps one of the most Viennese works of the time was Richard Strauss's opera *Der Rosenkavalier* (1913), written by a German living in Garmisch and the first performance of which was given in Dresden. However, its use of the Viennese waltz throughout not only provides a unifying motif but imparts a uniquely Viennese flavour to the whole piece. This use of the waltz was a stroke of genius on Strauss's part, and it merges beautifully with Hugo von Hofmannsthal's delightfully witty libretto. Fittingly, given Hofmannsthal's involvement in setting up the festival, it was with *Der Rosenkavalier* that the new Grosser Festspielhaus was opened at the 1960 Salzburg Festival.

The Second Viennese School

After the death of Mahler a revolutionary new direction was set by the theorist and composer Arnold Schoenberg (1874–1951). His earliest works (such as *Verklärte Nacht*) were steeped in the language of late-Romanticism, before his, at times, extreme suspension of tonality lead him to abandon tonality altogether in an "emancipation of dissonance". His first atonal works are Expressionist (Schoenberg was also a painter), though he later codified his ideas into the more classicist style of serial composition.

His serial ideas (in which all twelve notes of the chromatic scale are given equal promi-

Folk and popular musics

There is a long recorded history of local, traditional musics in Austria, the earliest sources dating back to the Middle Ages. Early Christian writings tell of "harsh, raucous and appallingly shrill" singing, a trumpet made of bark and "licentious songs"; the "harsh" singing and trumpet may have had an apotropaic purpose (for example, the ward to evil spirits). Later sources describe dances accompanied by flute, drum, fiddle and bagpipes and also a strong tradition of song. Many of these are referred to in monastic manuscripts, but the earliest sources of the songs themselves come from printed handbills and

nence) were most fully developed by his two distinguished students, Anton von Webern (1883–1945) and Alban Berg (1885–1935). Webern was ruthlessly logical, creating exquiste and sparse minatures, often lasting no more than a few seconds, whereas Berg was far more atuned to Expressionism, seen to best advantage in his two operas *Wozzeck* (1922) and *Lulu* (unfinished), or a neo-Romanticism, as heard in his violin concerto (1935).

LEFT: Johannes Brahms
ABOVE: Angelika Kirchschlager and Adrianne Pieczonka get close in Strauss's *Der Rosenkavalier* at the 2004 Salzburg festival.

songbooks from the 15th century, a number of which refer to contemporary events, such as the wars against the Ottoman Turks.

By the 19th century systematic collection of *Volkslied* (folksong) had started, both sponsored by the state and by amateur scholars. This was, in part, a response to a greater awareness of supposed national identities, and by the end of the century had become an important component of the nascent nationalisms that were sweeping the Austro-Hungarian Empire. Austrian collectors differed somewhat from those in other regions in that their focus was less concerned with text but took notice of instrumentation and the social context of the performances they observed, making these early collections still valuable to scholars today.

Although the printed collections did preserve, in some form, traditions that have since disappeared, they were also responsible for introducing a mediated version of *Volkslied* into the urban domestic sphere and the concert hall. Arranged versions of the songs were performed at home to piano accompaniment, and also in choral arrangements in large public concerts. One result of this was a concentration on certain genres, such as the Alpine *Jodler* (yodelling) which were performed in popular concerts by singers wearing traditional dress, while other tra-

ditions like narrative ballads were largely ignored. Not only did this mean these favoured styles had a greater impetus for survival, but they also lost local musical characteristics (such as tunings and rhythmic peculiarities) which were seen as "mistakes" by collectors and arrangers.

Even with this ironing out of musical differences a number of distinct regional styles can still be identified. The epic ballads that originated in Carinthia have now largely disappeared, though they were recorded well into the 20th century. Perhaps those forms most familiar to visitors will be the Alpine genres such as the *Jodler* or calls made on the alphorn. These distinctive patterns are based on the natural har-

monic series and were initially used as a form of communication across the Alpine valleys or to call in farm animals from the pastures.

A related form is the instrumental *Ländler*. These dances in 3/4 from Upper Austria and Styria, played on flute or clarinet, violin, double bass and occasionally accordian, made a great impact on composers such as Bruckner and Mahler. Good examples of this include the off-stage flugelhorn solo in the second movement of Mahler's third symphony, which is derived from the distinctive arpeggiated pattern of the *Jodler* and *Ländler*, and the rumbustious second movement of Bruckner's eighth.

While most regions of the country have a strong tradition of local wind bands which perform versions of traditional dances, Carinthia has retained a vibrant culture of song. Much of this vocal music – *Neues Kärtner Volkslied*, or new Carinthian song – is performed by choirs, and it draws on an earlier tradition of vocal polyphony.

A highly mediated form of Austrian folk music emerged in the 1970s, known disparagingly as *Lederhosenmusik*, and was broadcast widely on television both at home and abroad. This bland, kitschy conflagration of, largely, Alpine syles was performed by groups of "traditionally" clad instrumentalists (on clarinet, trumpet, tuba, accordian, guitar and drums) and sometimes a singer. It did much to promote a chocolate box- and Sound of Music-image of the country, but little to preserve or accord respect for the country's traditions.

A reaction against this came with the pan-regional genre, Alpine punk. Initially starting in Bavaria in the 1970s, and then spreading to Switzerland and Austria, it took elements of traditonal Alpine musics and gave them a twist by adding satirical lyrics, electronics (as both amplification and distortion) and driving rhythms. Other influences were brought in, especially from jazz and Latin music, to create a wholly new genre. Two of the most successful groups in Austria were Attwenger, who moved in the direction of dance music bringing in elements of hip hop, and Die Knödel (The Dumplings), who play acoustic instruments and who have an equally exciting but more traditional approach to the music.

This injected dynamism back into the traditional music scene and it has slowly started to revive. These new developments prompted some musicians to start re-examining folk music sources, and the future looks more bright for traditional music than it has for some years. A good source of these musics is the archive of the Österreichisches Volkliedwerk based in Vienna, some of which has been released on a series of CDs that cover all regions of the country. Their website (www.volks liedwerk.at) is excellent – a quite phenomenal resource – with links to each of the regions, CD reviews, listings, and publications.

Schrammel

Vienna has its own traditional music in the form of *Heurigenmusik*, after its traditional performance venue, or *Schrammelmusik* after the two brothers credited with its development. In the mid-19th century Josef and Johann Schrammel, along with Anton Strohmayer, formed a trio consisting of two violins and a guitar, to play in the *Heuriger*, or wine taverns, of Vienna's suburbs. The music consisted of songs and dances from the traditions of the many peoples who had flocked to Vienna, as the centre of the empire, from all over Central and Eastern Europe. Like many other urban genres – such as the Greek *rebétika* – it was the mix, in this case of waltzes, *Ländler*, polkas and Viennese songs *(see below)*, that gave it its particular flavour.

The Schrammel brothers subsequently added a clarinet to the ensemble and a whole new genre was born. By the end of the century the music had become phenomenally popular and entered into the life blood of the city. With its sentimental and melancholic themes it became the Viennese genre *par excellence*, or at least for that part of the city's identity that thrives on nostalgia and a mild obsession with death.

During the passage of the 20th century, and particularly after the fall of the empire, the music became highly sentimentalised and the original instrumentation contracted to a trio of violin, guitar and accordian. However, like some traditional musics, it too was rediscovered by a new generation and musicians such as Roland Neuwirth set about recreating the Viennese sound of a century ago. There is now a lively *Schrammel* scene in Vienna, with young bands such as Folksmilch and Die Neuen Wiener Concertschrammeln exploring and creating new areas of repertory.

LEFT: Arnold Schönberg in a portrait by Schiele.
RIGHT: the *Opernball*.

The music was in large part inspired by the Viennese tradition of song. This dates back to at least the 17th century and the legendary Augustin Mitte who is said to have sung the famous *O du lieber Augustin (see page 117)* in the Griechenbeisl on Fleischmarkt. However, it was during the 19th century that the songs experienced their "golden age", when they were performed in *Heurigen*. Many of these rather maudlin and sentimental compositions, such as *Wien, Wien, nur du allein* (Vienna, Vienna, only you…) and *Mei Mutter war a Wienerin* (My mother was Viennese…), are still well-known in a city that still, on occasion, harks back to a mythologised past. ❑

VIENNESE BALLS

Vienna is famous for its pre-Lenten *(Fasching)* elegant society balls, which have their antecedent in the balls held at the court from 1877 onwards. The well-known balls (many of them for particular professions) include the *Philharmonikerball* (held at the Musikverein), the *Technikercercle* and *Kaiserball* at the Hofburg, *Campagnereiterball*, the artists' balls (known as *Gschnasfeste*), the Life Ball, the Lawyers' Ball and the *Jägerball* (where the guests wear traditional costume). However, the most expensive and famous is the *Opernball* held at the Staatsoper. Stuffed full of the rich and famous, it is often the focus of demonstrations.

ART AND ARCHITECTURE

The art of Austria ranges from Stone Age masterpieces to glorious baroque

churches, and from Expressionism to elegant modern architecture

Austria's position at the centre of Europe and on the Danube, one of the principal thoroughfares of the continent, has ensured both its strategic importance and its significance to develpments in European culture. It forms, too, an important link between central and western Europe and its eastern neighbours with their own distinctive cultures.

The present state of Austria may be traced back to Charlemagne's establishment of Ostmark, 799-800, and from then until 1918, when the republic was founded, it formed a central part of the Holy Roman and Austro-Hungarian Empires. Inevitably, as part of this wider political sphere, Austrian art was knitted into the major, largely western, European movements.

The Willendorf Venus

Among Europe's earliest accomplished artefacts is the Willendorf Venus, a 10-cm (4-inch) tall limestone figure named after its Austrian place of discovery. Like other Old Stone Age dolls the emphasis on her reproductive capabilities – breasts, belly, pudenda – at the expense of legs and arms suggests its use as a fertility amulet or representation of a mother goddess. Its most extraordinary feature is the braided hair indicating an aesthetic intention in its creator some 25,000 years ago.

The limestone used suggests it may have been an import, perhaps from western Europe. The Danube and its tributaries were important in transmitting Neolithic (New Stone Age) and Bronze Age cultures into Austria and deeper into Europe, especially new ideas from Anatolia and the Aegean. Simple but beautifully shaped and decorated pottery vessels with incised or impressed decorations characterised these more settled peoples of 10,000 to 750 BC, who also created occasional stylised figurines.

By 750 BC salt mining at Hallstatt led to a settled community with an associated cemetery. At this time iron was being worked in addition to

bronze and the burial chambers have revealed many artefacts by these early Celts. The name Hallstatt has therefore been given to this earliest phase of the Iron Age. This culture (like the succeeding La Tene one of *circa* 450–100 BC) extended well beyond the Austrian borders. The Celtic interest in linear patterns and animalistic motifs may have a central Asian source and these were blended with contemporary Greek decorative ideas received through trade. The result was a lively and technically accomplished series of elaborate bronze vessels and other objects, often created as funerary offerings.

Examples from Hallstatt include a 7th-century iron sword decorated geometrically with amber and ivory, a 4th-century bronze sword scabbard uniquely depicting linear engravings of warriors with shields, perhaps indicative of Etruscan influences (Vienna, Naturhistorisches Museum), and from Dürnberg bei Hallein a 5th-century wine flagon with fantastic beasts on its handle (Salzburg, Carolino Augusteum

LEFT: Gustav Kilmt's *The Kiss*, 1907–8.
RIGHT: the Willendorf Venus.

Museum). Most remarkable is the miniature bronze wagon on which are models of horsemen, hunters and stags from the midst of which rises a goddess supporting a bowl (Graz, Schloss Eggenberg). Found in a chieftan's grave at Stettweg it shows Celtic preoccupations with animals and linear abstraction.

The Romans and Romanesque

The links with the Mediterranean indicate much early trade of salt, gold, iron and cattle to Rome from Noreaia, as Celtic Austria was known. As the Romans expanded their empire the Danube formed a natural boundary and in 15 BC they

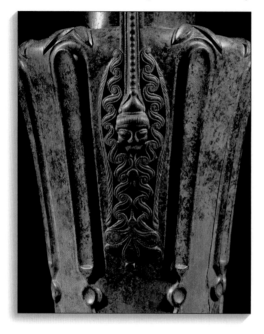

established Vindobona on the site of modern Vienna. The customary grid plan town was created as a garrison, with outlying recreational suburbs by the Michaelerplatz. Further down the Danube the Romans developed the town of Petronell-Carnutum where, alongside the fortress, baths and an amphitheatre and also a palace were built. Stone for both Carnuntum and Vindobona was quarried at St Margarethen, close to Carnuntum. The Romans introduced paved roads, ordered town plans, columned and arcuated architecture with fine ceramic, glass and further bronze artefacts to the province. Other major Roman settlements were at Villach, Aguntum close to Lavant and Brigantium

on the Bodensee (Lake Constance), where a fortified harbour was constructed.

The depredations of Germanic tribes caused the Romans to retreat from the Danube in AD 433. An unsettled period ensued. The Romans had martyred Austria's patron saint, Florian, which indicates that Christianity had been introduced at an early date. Under Charlemagne the Ostmark was founded and incorporated into the Holy Roman Empire on its foundation in *circa* AD 800. This was a brave attempt to unite Europe as it had been in Roman days, but under a Christian banner.

Not surprisingly Charlemagne's architects and artists looked for inspiration to the days of Rome's conversion to Christianity in the 4th century. Builders took the round headed arches of Rome and evolved a massive style characterised by geometric ornament and occasional figurative sculpture within strict boundaries – a style known as Romanesque. A fine late example is the abbey cloisters at Heiligenkreuz, and for sculpture the earlier apse relief at Schongrabern, which could perhaps be by French craftsmen.

During the 10th century, under the emperor Otto of Saxony, Austrian manuscript painting (and possibly murals, too) derived from work at Reichenau-Oberzell, close to the shore of the Bodensee, which had links to painting at Trier and St Gall (Switzerland). The style is vigorous and linear with broad forms and clear patterns, based on more illusionist paintings at the court of Charlemagne and his successors. These in turn refer back to Roman and Byzantine painting. The 12th century frescoes at Gurk Cathedral share a stunning linear clarity. At Klosterneuberg the altar, 1181–1216, by Nicholas of Verdun depicts 12 Biblical scenes of gilded copper and blue enamel in an architectural frame; but its animation prefigures the emergent Gothic style.

The Gothic style

Changes occurred in the 12th century in western Europe that eventually were adopted in Germany and Austria. The new Gothic style of architecture had a lighter structure that pinpointed the weight on to slender columns and buttressed walls by means of ribs deriving from pointed arched vaults and windows. The effect was one of weightlessness, verticality and light from the new large windows. often of coloured glass. Underlying the change was one in theological thought in which the world's beauties prefigured those of Heaven, and in its optimism a cult grew up of veneration of the Virgin and saints as mediators between God and mankind. With this there was a greater interest in naturalism reflected in paintings and sculptures. Stephansdom, Vienna, rebuilt from 1304 onwards, is in this style, though retaining a largely Romanesque façade. It is an example of the Germanic hall church, where the nave and aisles are of near similar height and width, thus creating a lofty interior without the usual tribune gallery above the aisles, or nave clerestory windows. The 15th century additions with their filigree overlay of detail are charac-

stone including the red Salzburg marble. External influences were also important here. The inclusion of portraits of the mason Anton Pilgram at St Stephensdom – one on a corbel, another within a false window – again reflect those of Peter Parler at Prague. In 1469 the dynamic carver, Nicholas Gerhaerds of Leiden, Netherlands, began the tomb of Frederick III at St Stephensdom, and he seems to have influenced the sculptor of the Empress Eleanora's monument at Wiener Neustadt. Ecclesiastical carving is represented by the moving *Man of Sorrows* (1478), Wiener Neustadt, by Thomas Strayff, and also by Jacob Kaschauer's addi-

teristic of the flamboyant Gothic. This love of elaboration probably owed much to Peter Parler (1332/3–99) the architect of St Vitus, Prague, and his practice is felt too at the Franciscan church, Salzburg (1408), where the elaborate vaulting may be by Hans von Burghausen (or Stethaimer).

Gothic sculpture

One of Austria's greatest Gothic arts was sculpture, aided by good supplies of timber and

tions to Stephensdom, before 1463.

Among the greatest woodcarvers Hans Klocker of Brixen, *fl.* 1478–1500, is notable for the almost organic architectural frame and portrait-like saints of the Kefermarkt Altarpiece, 1490s. A more pictorial approach is found in Michael Pacher's charming altar with *The Coronation of the Virgin* at St Wolfgang, 1471–78. The painted sculptures here have a subtlety equal in emotion to his painting of *The Coronation* (Munich); indeed his virtuosity reveals his adherence to the International Gothic with its self-conscious elegance and reference to contemporary Italian art. Some of this tender naturalism had already been seen on the

LEFT: the Dürnberg flagon, 5th century BC.
ABOVE: Anton Pilgram's pulpit in the Stephansdom.
RIGHT: his self-portrait in the same church.

Heiligenkreuz altar, *circa* 1410, depicting the *Mystic Marriage of St Catherine* (Vienna, Kunsthistorisches Museum), perhaps by a French master adopting an International Gothic lyricism, and in manuscripts executed in Vienna, especially those identified as by "Michael", *circa* 1420s.

The Renaissance and Mannerism

By 1520 the 15th-century Italian Renaissance was becoming fashionable at the Habsburg court at Augsburg, and also at Prague. Both influenced Austria, especially in court circles. The reuse of Greek and Roman architectural

forms, and figurative sculpture coupled to a sense of logic and geometry, as in perspective, was linked to a growing secularism. Italian illustrated architectural treatises by Serlio and others were influential.

The delicately detailed Armoury at Wiener Neustadt, 1524, and the cubic forms with columned arcades of the Hofburg, Vienna, from 1552, are examples of the new style. By the 1560s a more intricate, playfully self-conscious version had emerged. Known as Mannerist it often involved busy overlays of ornament – terracotta in the case of the Schloss Schallaburg (1572 onwards) – or heavily rusticated at the Linz Palace portal, 1604.

In sculpture the Hofkirche at Innsbruck shows best the transition to secular humanism, where the Tomb of Maximilian I, begun 1508, completed 1582, to designs by the painter Gilg Sesselschreiber, includes the emperor's effigy by Ludovico Scalza. Most impressive, though, are the flanking figures of his ancestors, those of King Arthur and Theodoric by Peter Vischer being especially powerful. Other Imperial sculptors and painters were involved, including Viet Stoss, Albrecht Durer, Gregor Erhart and Conrat Meit, making this venture of international significance. Later a courtly, refined mannerism appears in the work of Hubert Gerhard from Holland and Caspar Gras, whose Tomb of Maximilian III (1615–19, Domkirche, St Jakob) and Leopold Fountain (1623–30) are at Innsbruck. The latter has typical mannerist dolphin heads, grotesque masks in shells and elongated, nude allegorical figures.

Painters also explored allegorical and mythological subjects. The Rittersall at Schloss Goldegg, 1536, perhaps decorated by Hans Bocksberger I, includes these with social and hunting scenes. North Italian influences were also evident: Anton Plumenthal's frescoes in the choir of Gurk Cathedral recall Tintoretto. But north European Renaissance art was rooted in observation rather than idealisation, notable with the "Danube School" of Germanic painters.

Among these, Albrecht Altdorfer painted the St Florian Altarpiece (1518) with a dramatic sunset, ordered spatial structure and landscape interests, while Wolf Huber's vision, exemplified by his *Allegory of Salvation* was more archaic, though involving a complex spatial composition (both Vienna, Kunsthistorisches Museum). Most innovative was Lucas Cranach the Elder, who found employment at the imperial court. His interest in the nude in mythology – the first northerner to do so – and his didactically moralising paintings like the *Judith* (Vienna, Kunsthistorisches Museum), which reveals his Lutheran sympathies, added to his prolific output of prints, made him particularly admired.

Protestantism had been adopted early in Austria, especially among the aristocracy. Its rise, and the chaos of the ensuing religious wars, provoked some artists to abandon the rigid rationalism of the Renaissance for the new mannerist style, characterised by spatial ambiguities and dichotomies of scale, twisting elongated figures and compositional sophistication. At court the style became esoteric and took on erotic overtones. The Flemish painter, Bartholomaus Spranger, who was resident at Vienna before moving on to the court of Rudolf II at Prague, shows these trends. His *Venus and Adonis*, *circa* 1597 (Vienna, Kunsthistorisches Museum), is representative of the sophistication he brought to Austria, a finesse deriving from Italian precedents.

Classicism

A reaction to mannerism's artificiality set in in the 17th century. Some saw the way forward in there is something of this in Erlach's Schloss Klesheim, Salzburg, 1700–9, and Johann Lucas Von Hildebrandt's Upper and Lower Belvederes, Vienna, 1713–23. However, none of these is purely Classicist. All have strongly baroque overtones, and baroque is Austria's most characteristic style.

Austrian baroque

Catholicism, which was in the ascendancy following the disruption of the Thirty Years' War, 1619–48, embraced baroque art. Catholics wanted a mystical and theatrical style that would appeal to the emotions. Thus movement

classicism – a return to established principles based on Roman and Renaissance values. The style was not over popular in Austria, but there are elements of it in the Karlskirche, Vienna, begun 1715 by Johann Fischer Von Erlach. Its Corinthian columned portico sandwiched between triumphal columns decorated with spiral reliefs alluding to Trajan's Column reveals his antiquarian interests. Classicist architects preferred geometric, block like silhouettes and

LEFT: *Joan the Mad* from the tomb of Maximillian I in Innsbruck.
RIGHT: the Karlskirche, Vienna, between classicism and the baroque.

conveyed by curved lines and forms; a drama of light and shade resulting from sculptural surfaces and architecture that alternately advanced and receded; and colour coupled to busy, broken outlines were fundamentals of the designs. Often an overwhelming scale was important. As in the theatre architecture, painting and sculpture worked together to create breath-taking effects of a world beyond everyday experience.

The trauma of the Siege of Vienna by the Ottoman Turks, 1683, meant that a fully formed Austrian baroque dates from after that event and continued into the 18th century. By then in western Europe the baroque was being transformed into a more playful and tonally lighter manner known as the rococo. In Austria the two styles are interwoven.

Baroque began in Rome, and Italian artists frequently collaborated with northerners. Santino Solari's rebuilding of the Dom (cathedral) at Salzburg, 1614–55, looked to both Venetian precedents and also to Il Gesu in Rome. However, the Benedictine foundation of Melk, 1702–38, spectacularly sited on a bluff overlooking the Danube, is Austria's greatest baroque ecclesiastical complex *(see page 164)*.

The architects Jacob Prandtauer and Josef Munggenast set the abbey church behind a rip-

Sculpture

Sculpture was integral to baroque architecture. The decorative features were often of stucco (Feichtmayr's sculptures at Stams are particularly delicate). A favoured device was the Atlas or caryatid, as at the St Florian collegiate foundation, 1686–1724, by Leonhard Sattler, or, more famously, those introduced by Hildebrandt in the Sala Terrena, Upper Belvedere, Vienna, 1721–3. The portrait statue as hero was an important theme seen in Paul Strudel's *Duke of Alba*, 1696–1708/9 (Vienna, Hofburg Library). The concept was elaborated into allegory in Balthasar Permoser's *Apotheosis of*

pling façade of library and marble hall, above which rise twin towers before a dome, both of which employ the baroque motif of multiplied pilasters. Internally the nave walls, with their concavities between the piers, are encrusted with gilded ornaments, while Johann Michael Rottmayr's painted ceiling and dome climaxes at the high altar with saints created by Antonio Beduzzi, Lorenzo Mattielli, Giovanni Zuccalli and Peter Widerin. Among many secular structures Erlach's Hofburg Library (1722), Vienna, is notable for its rich transverse arches, oval dome and dignified exhuberance. Daniel Gran painted its frescoed ceiling in 1726, depicting Charles VI's patronage of the arts and sciences.

Prince Eugene, 1718–21 (Vienna, Österreichisches Barokmuseum) where the victor over the Turks tramples his enemy whilst Fame trumpets his achievements. This may have influenced Georg Raphael Donner's *Apotheosis of the Emperor Charles VI*, 1734 (same location), whose winged Victory haloes Charles with a snake of eternity. Donner also made fountains whose flowing waters appealed to the baroque sense of movement. The Perseus-Andromeda Fountain, 1740–1 (Vienna, Hof des Alten Rathauses) is in relief; his graceful Mehlmarktbrunnen, 1737–9 (Flour Market Fountain), commissioned by the city of Vienna, is in the round (Vienna, Österreichisches

Barokmuseum). Emotional restraint characterises his lead *Pieta* at Gurk cathedral. The anonymous wooden *Pieta* of *circa* 1620 at Annaberg im Limmertal and Michel Honel's wooden altar at Gurk cathedral, 1626–36, are emotionally restrained. Later wooden figures were more openly emotive, attenuated, with fluttering draperies well represented by those of the anonymous Vienna master's *Apostles*, *circa* 1730, at Klosterneuburg. The style's eventual virtuosity was demonstrated in Joseph Stammel's figure of Death hovering over Time's victim, one of a group of *Four Last Things*, *circa* 1760 (Admont, Abbey library). A final bizarre twist to Austrian 18th century sculpture was the grimacing character heads, 1770–83, by Franz Xavier Messerschmidt, a tutor at the Vienna Academy of Fine Arts from 1769; but these belong more to the inquiring spirit of the Enlightenment that sought to rationalise human behaviour.

Painting

Baroque painting was best seen in mural decorations. Like architecture it owed much to Italian artists. Andrea Pozzo, a foremost exponent of theatrical illusionism, and author of a book on perspective, decorated the Jesuitenkirche (Universitatskirche, 1703–5), Vienna, with an illusory dome. The foundation of the Vienna Academy in 1692, raised Austrians' confidence and they, too, tackled ambitious, allegorical works such as Johann Michael Rottmayr's dome in the Karlskirche, Vienna, 1725, and his superb *Apotheosis of Prince Eugene*, 1716 (Marmorsaal, Vienna, Lower Belvedere), where architecture and paint combine to a single effect. Paul Troger's brilliant frescoes at Altenburg, 1730–3, include an extraordinary image based on the Book of Revelation of a woman in labour lifted up to God, thus avoiding a dragon awaiting the child's birth.

Daniel Gran had a greater interest in classical imagery, better suited to secular commissions as in the Festsaal, Schloss Freidau (St Pölten), and the Hofburg Library. Generally these paintings are lighter in tone and more brilliant in colour, with a spontaneous calligraphic technique which brings them close to the rococo style. Franz

LEFT: *St James of Compostela* by Franz Anton Maulbertsch.
RIGHT: *An Archvillan* by Messerschmidt.

Anton Maulbertsch's *St Longinus* on the ceiling at Heiligenkreuz-Gutenbrunn demonstrates this in a virtuoso piece of illusionism. Contrasting with the decorators' sparkle, easel painters were more prosaic – for example the works of genre painter Johann Hartmann and the still life artist Franz Werner Von Tanm – and Dutch rather than Italian sources were uppermost. Johann Christian Brand's landscapes, however, owe more to the Venetian, Bernardo Bellotto who visited Vienna in 1759–60, while the portraitists Jan Kupecky and Jacob Von Schuppen absorbed French rococo tendencies in colour and occasional informality.

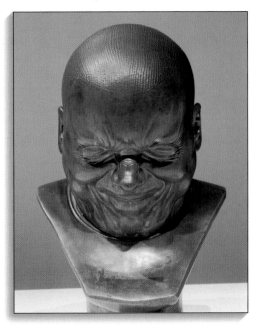

Looking back

As in Europe as a whole, two themes are evident in Austrian art after 1780: historicism – the looking back to older styles – and a quest for truth in its varying manifestations. The first movement was neoclassicism, initially provoked by the discoveries at Pompeii and the writings of the German art historian, Winckelmann. Taking antique art as a starting point, a new moral quality was found in idealised art, where the aim for truth was expressed through purity of line and form. The grand genre compositions of Peter Krafft (Vienna, Hofburg), a pupil of David, France's foremost neoclassical painter, and who settled in Vienna in 1799, emphasise these qualities. Actual antique subjects were rare, perhaps being alien to a more bourgeois taste, but portraiture flourished, especially with the academy director, Friedrich Heinrich Fuger, Barbara Krafft, and Joseph Georg Edlinger from Graz.

Artists of the contemporary romantic movement were concerned with truth to one's inner spirit. For some it was also truth to appearances. Many took to landscape. Joseph Anton Koch linked neoclassicism with romanticism in his paintings that aimed to evoke universal ideas of landscape and feeling (for example *The Bernese Oberland*, 1815, Vienna, Osterreichis-

ches Galerie; *Macbeth and the Witches*, 1835, Innsbruck, Landesmuseum Ferdinandium). Josef Rebell's interest in tranquil sunlight, and August Heinrich's concern for the minutiae of landscapes represent a more realist approach, which was the principal preoccupation of the Salzburg school of landscape. Heinrich Reinhold's *Watzmann near Berchtesgaden*, 1818, and Friedrich Loos' *The Mönchsberg near Salzburg*, 1826 (both Vienna, Osterreichisches Galerie) combine objectivity with romantic feeling. At Vienna, Ferdinand Olivier evolved a manner of unnerving precision, which glances backwards to Durer, especially in his drawn, uninhabited townscapes (see his *Quarry near*

Matzleindorf, circa 1814–16, Vienna, Albertina). The insistence of these three's vision aligns them close to the Nazarenes, a cooperative group formed in Vienna in July 1809, which aimed to revive Christian art by reference to German and Italian 15th century painting. The Nazarenes quickly moved on to Rome to live a quasi-monastic life centred on their Lucas Bund (Guild of St Luke), but the principal exponents – Johann Friedrich Overbeck, Franz Pforr, Peter Cornelius and Julius Schnorr Von Carolsfield – continued to be influential in Austria. Some echo of their romantic medievalising appears in the illustrations and murals of Moritz von Schwind (Vienna, Staatsoper).

Biedermeier

The bourgeois nature of patronage led to the Biedermeier style of 1815–48, which emphasised accessible subjects founded on a truthful study of nature, with a democratic treatment of all detail. Rejecting idealisation the Academy professor, Ferdinand Georg Waldmuller favoured landscape and portraiture (*View of the Hallstättersee*, 1838, Vienna, Historisches Museum der Stadt Wien, and *The Artist's Wife*, 1850, Vienna, Österreichisches Galerie) as did Rudolf Alt, whose landscapes and portraits are minutely detailed. Naturalist values persisted to the end of the century in still lifes by Carl Schuck and landscapes by August Von Pettenkofen, but with a painterliness anticipating Impressionism.

Sculpture, traditionally a more conservative art form, was dominated by civic monuments, well represented by Anton Fernkorn's memorials to the Archduke Charles and Prince Eugene, 1860–5, in the Heldenplatz, Vienna, or Kaspar von Zumbusch's *Monument to Maria Theresa*, 1888 (Vienna, Maria-Theresa-Platz). All subscribe to the romantic realism of the mid-19th century. Fernkorn's most dramatic sculpture is *The Lion of Aspern*, commemorating the defeat of Napoleon (1855, Aspern, cemetery). Its source lies in the *Lion of Lucerne*, 1819, by the Danish neoclassical sculptor, Thorvaldsen. There was influence, too, from the Italian, Antonio Canova, but Austrian neoclassical sculpture was less concerned with antique subjects and presentation, tending to be drily academic when doing so, as with Johan Martin Fischer's statues. However, Franz Von Zauner, who had worked on the Schönbrunn stone figures, imbued his Von Lauden Monument with vigour (Hadersdorf).

Sculptors worked closely with architects, as at the Maria-Theresa-Platz, where the buildings were by Gottfried Semper. As was common in Europe historicism was the fashion. A restrained Palladian classicism was already evident in Isidore Carnevale's Josephium, 1783–5, Vienna, which gave way to a severer neo-Greek architecture in the Burgtor, Heldenplatz, Vienna (1821–4), by Peter Von Nobile. Joseph Kornhausel's Schottenhof, Vienna, introduced ordered, stuccoed housing of restrained dignity.

The Secession

Against this the sudden appearance of the Vienna Secession brings us abruptly into modernity. Already the architect Otto Wagner had produced a group of railway stations in and around Vienna, 1894–8, that played down past styles and emphasised a linear, organic style in which the arts were to find unity, known to us as art nouveau or *Jugendstil*. The unifying ability of ornament was taken a step further in his Majolika Haus, 1898, Vienna, a block of flats with a linear, floral pattern over its façade. That year his follower, Joseph Maria Olbrich, constructed the Secession building, an exhibition hall for a group of artists

Paul Sprenger's Mint (1835–7), Heumarkt, Vienna, adopted Italian Renaissance motifs. After 1848 much of Vienna was rebuilt and the city enlarged in a mix of styles: the Gothic for Heinrich von Ferstal's Votivkirche, 1856–72; Greek revival, Theodore Hansen's Parlament, 1873–83, and Renaissance for his Academy of Fine Arts, 1872–6; and late Renaissance for the Burgtheatre, 1874–88, by Gottfried Semper, and also his Naturhistorisches and Kunsthistorisches Museums of 1872–81.

LEFT: *View from the Mönchsberg* by Rudolf von Alt.
ABOVE: the interior staircase of Gottfried Semper's Kunsthistorisches Museum.

who had broken (seceded) from the conservative Cooperative Society of Austrian Artists (based at the Kunstlerhaus).

Severely geometrical, its ornament included Medusa-like masks representing Painting, Sculpture and Architecture, with stylised trees and a dome of gilded bay leaves over glass. Josef Hoffmann designed the interiors. Hoffmann went on to design housing that incorporated the linearism of traditional Austrian timber-framed buildings (Moll and Moser houses, 1900–1), and to create unity of design between architecture and contents (Puckersdorf Sanitorium, 1904). These ideas linked all three architects to the Wiener Werkstätte, an artistic group formed by Hoffmann in 1903, modelled on C.R. Ashbee's Guild and School of Handicraft, with its belief in simplicity of design based on vernacular traditions.

Symbolism

Olbrich and Hoffmann, with the painter Gustav Klimt, were founder members of the Secession. Klimt's *Beethoven Frieze*, 1902, to accompany the exhibition of Max Klinger's statue of Beethoven, initiated a sumptuous, part gilt decoration of attenuated forms with eerie overtones. His reliance on colour and pattern emphasized design values as in *The Kiss* and

Modernism and Expressionism

Wagner's Postsparkasse (Postal Savings Bank, 1904–6), Vienna, broke with art nouveau, introducing a functional use of displayed ironwork. This modernist approach was matched by Adolf Loos in a series of Viennese buildings – the Michaeler Haus, 1909–11, the Steiner Haus, 1910, and the American Bar (Kärntner Bar) – in which ornament is stripped to geometric essentials without loss of elegance. These initiated functionalist modernism, continued by Peter Behrens for low-cost Viennese housing, 1924 (Stromstrasse and Konstanziastrasse), and for the Austrian Tobacco

many of his portraits (*Emilie Floge*, 1902, Vienna, Österreichisches Galerie).

Underlying this was Symbolism, the belief that imagery could project one's emotive preoccupations in a way that was expressive by abstract qualities of line, colour, shape and pattern. Hence the eroticism evident in much of Klimt's work and also of the younger Egon Schiele, whose output reveals much autobiography. Schiele's portraiture can be penetrating (*Edith Seated*, 1917–18, Vienna, Österreichisches Galerie), and his landscapes lyrical with a seeming peasant naivety (*Landscape at Krumau*, 1916, Linz, Neue Galerie, Wolfgang Gurlitt Museum).

Administration at Linz, 1930. Other architects, Josef Frank, Oskar Strnad and Ernst Plischke, were employed on similar social housing projects between 1918 and 1934.

The visual arts since 1900 are complex. Austria followed the major European trends, but selectively and at one remove. Although Expressionism in the German-speaking world was initially centred around Die Brücke in Dresden, there developed a distinctly Austrian school. A dominant painter in this was Oskar Kokoschka, a Secession member whose work epitomises expressionist thought. A member of the Hagenbund exhibiting group from 1910 to 1930, he was joined by Richard Gerstal (*The*

Sisters, 1904–5, Vienna, Osterreichisches Galerie) and Anton Faistauer. Schiele's influence is found in Fritz Schwarz-Waldegg (*Self Knowledge*, Vienna, Österreichisches Galerie) and Max Oppenheimer's portraits (*Egon Schiele*, circa 1907, Vienna, Historisches Museum der Stadt Wien). The darker problems of war and its chaos gave subjects to Oskar Laske (*Walpurgis Night*, lithograph circa 1919, Vienna, Historisches Museum der Stadt Wien), and the later macabre subjects of Paul Flora.

Contemporary trends

Two themes dominated painting after 1945. One was a continued interest in pattern and vibrant colour by Friedensreich Hundertwasser, which, like the mural work by Herman Boeckl (*Apocalyptic Vision*, 1952–60, Seckau Abbey) displays a puzzling naivety. The second was Aktionismus, a group of abstract expressionists including Herman Nitsch and Gunter Brus. They later became interested in "happenings" (performance art) and from that emerged the preoccupation with abstract, minimalist and conceptual art, shown in the work of Herbert Brandl and Franz West.

Much early 20th century sculpture continued older traditions. However, Klinger's *Beethoven*, and more so Carl Wollek's *Mozart Fountain*, 1905, Vienna, shows a simplification of form and fluidity of surface that suggests art nouveau. Wollek's *Memorial to Adrienne Neuman* (1912, Vienna, Historisches Museum der Stadt Wien) combines this with Renaissance and medievalising motifs. Later Anton Hanak became preoccupied with truth to materials (*Burning Man*, 1922, Langenzerdorf, Anton-Hanak-Freilicht Museum), a theme picked up by followers including Georg Ehrlich, who was interested in Lehmbruck's expressionism, as too was Fritz Wotruba. Wotruba, though, became concerned with the figure as chunkily carved, cubic forms. Sculptors of the 1950s, like Rudolf Hoflehner, developed this towards abstraction. Thereafter the boundaries between the arts blurred, especially with the installations of Bruno Gironcoli, or the media based work of Peter Weibel. An analogy also exists between the concrete solids of Manfred Walkolbinger and Rachel Whiteread's *Holocaust Memorial*, Vienna, 2000.

Austria's rebuilding after 1945 meant that there was little scope for extravagant architectural gestures until the 1970s. Nevertheless imaginative conversions were made, such as the church at Parsch, near Salzburg, 1953–6, by Wilhelm Holzbauer and partners (known as Arbeitsgruppe 4). They also designed the College of St Joseph, 1961–4 at Aigen. The postmodern mix of styles from the 1970s was led by Hans Hollein, who, in 1991, created the Haashaus, Vienna, perhaps too diversely varied in its upper stories. Helmut Richter's 1994 school, Kinkplatz, Vienna, of steel and glass displays an imaginative and humane version of high-tech construction.

Numerous housing schemes are worthy of emulation, including Anton Schweighofer's Gatterburggasse development of 1989 in which strict geometry is human in scale and adapted to modern needs. The conversion of Simmering's Gasometers by the often polemical Coop-Himmalb(l)au is interesting but less successful. Against these the Hundertwasserhaus, Lowengasse, Vienna, appears intrusive in its toytown decoration, and disappointing in its ecological aspirations. But this is exceptional. Austria's willingness to accept the new alongside the old bodes well, and the conversion of the Residenz Stables at Salzburg by Clemens Holzmeister forms a model of all that can be achieved. ❏

LEFT: Otto Wagner's Majolika Haus, Vienna.
RIGHT: a self-portrait by Egon Schiele.

PLACES

A detailed guide to the entire country, with principal sites cross-referenced by number to the maps

If one feature characterises Austria more than any other it is its towering mountains. "Land of Mountains" is the opening line of the country's national anthem, and today the people of Austria have even more reason to eulogise their landscapes. The upland pastures, which once made life so difficult for highland farmers, are now criss-crossed by ski lifts and cable-cars, evidence of the booming summer and winter tourist industry that accounts for the largest slice of the national economy.

Nestled amongst the wild Alpine scenery are hundreds of mountain lakes and idyllic watercourses that exercise an attraction of their own, especially in summer. The gentle charms of both the Salzkammergut and the lakes of Carinthia are underlined by the majestic backdrop of the mountains.

To the east, the foothills of the Alps gradually peter out in the Vienna Woods, reaching to the very suburbs of the nation's capital. Along the Danube, which crosses northeast Austria for 350 km (220 miles) of its course, stood the outposts of the Roman Empire. It was here, too, that Irish monks brought Christianity to Central Europe. Upper Austria, Lower Austria and eastern Styria have been cultivated by man since time immemorial and have been the scene of many episodes of Central European history.

Vienna, once the seat of the Babenberg dynasty and for over 600 years the centre of the vast Habsburg Empire, is today one of the loveliest cities in the world and the repository of a wealth of art treasures.

Every period of European cultural history is reflected in Austria. Romanesque, Gothic, Renaissance and baroque buildings are scattered across the land. Statues, frescoes, ceiling and wall paintings document more than 1,000 years of history.

Austrians have a reputation for being a hospitable and amenable race. The tradition stretches back a long way. For centuries Austria has been crossed by foreign peoples and tribes, by soldiers and traders. Many of them made their homes here. The inhabitants of the eastern provinces, in particular, reveal a mixture of Germanic and Slavic characteristics. In Salzburg and Tyrol, by contrast, the people are very like Bavarians. The natives of Vorarlberg, however, are of Alemannic and Rhaetian descent, and are related to the Swiss inhabitants of the Engadine and Upper Rhine.

In spite of these differences they are all proud Austrians. Since the fall of the Habsburgs and the testing period of the Third Reich they have forged a new, specifically Austrian, identity. ❏

PRECEDING PAGES: a glorious view from the Hochalpinestrasse; the Halstättersee; the Haashaus, Vienna.
LEFT: the Riesenrad on Vienna's Prater.

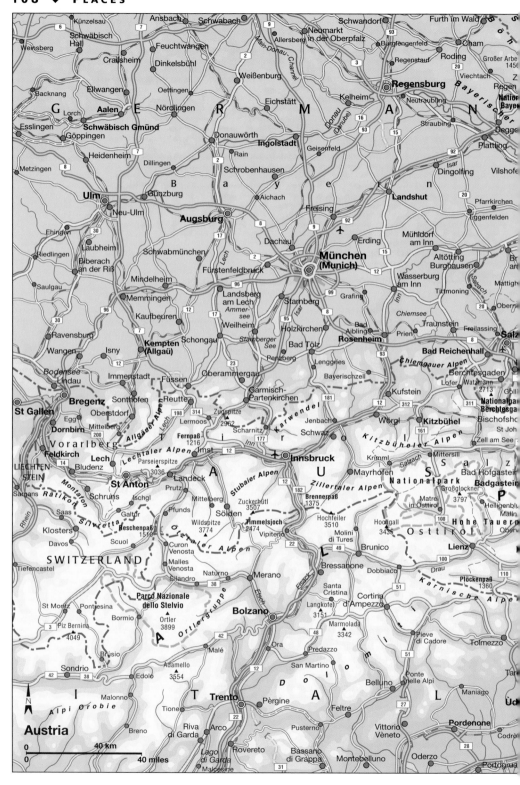

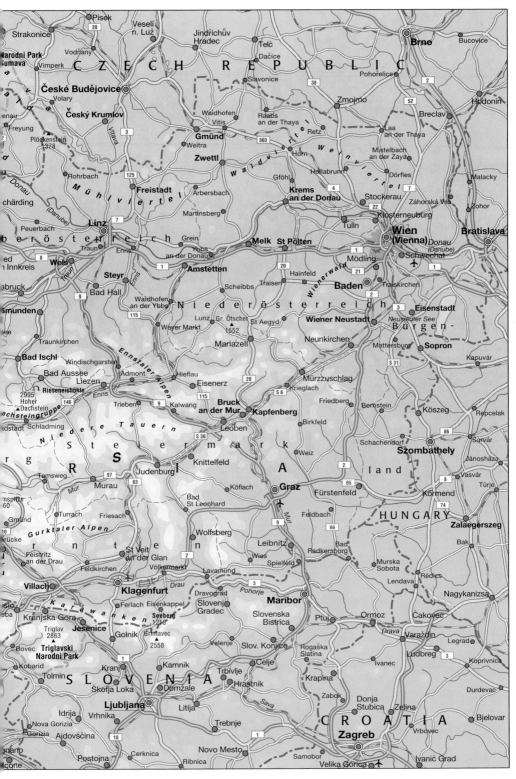

VIENNA: THE INNERE STADT

One of the world's great cities, with a staggering artistic and cultural heritage, Vienna is at once fascinating and charming, vibrant and relaxed

Map on page 112

Vienna – Wien – the city is world-famous and its name instantly evocative. Whether it is imperial grandeur that fascinates you or the romance of the baroque, excursions along the not-so-blue Danube and the Wienerwald or night-time assignations in *fiacre* and Riesenrad, Vienna will do everything in its power to seduce you. Perhaps no other world capital calls up the image of so many clichés, nor tries to bring them to life so vividly.

Of course, the city has had many human lifetimes in which to finesse these seductions. In 1815, at the Congress of Vienna which redrew the map of Europe, observers were already commenting on the host city's attempts to charm and persuade the political leaders of the day with *Gemütlichkeit*, that most Viennese brand of amiable hospitality. One historian has even remarked that as early as 1884 the famous Ringstrasse "had begun to look like a 19th-century version of Disneyland", aimed at enticing tourists to the Habsburg capital. As the head and the heart of a country with a history as chequered as Austria's, Vienna has always wrapped itself in the garments of the past: from the architecture of the Old City to the folk music of the Heurigen, from the salon waltz to the hand-kiss greeting, Vienna gilds itself with history.

LEFT: the wonderful Gothic windows and colourful roof of Stephansdom. **BELOW:** a city tram makes its way from Karlsplatz.

Beneath the façade

And yet this is only part of the story. However fascinating the mask of gold may seem, there is another city beneath. The relationship to the past is not staid, but dynamic, as the relentless works of renovation, preservation and reinterpretation bear witness. The architectural mix of baroque and Gothic, Secession and *Jugendstil* now includes the well-established "ecological postmodern" of the Fernwärme (the city's incinerator) and the striking spectacle of giant gasometers converted to housing. The accumulated statuary of the centuries is met and challenged by some of the most provocative monuments and memorials of recent years. St Rupert's Church, the earliest recorded in Vienna, lies anachronistically at one point of a now somewhat passé "Bermuda Triangle" of clubs and bars. The fiacres awaiting your command at the Stephansplatz contend with Audis and BMWs on the cobblestones, and their sharp-tongued drivers give as good as they get in the swell of 21st-century motor traffic. Sometimes it seems as if the whole urban scene awaits only a Kruder and Dorfmeister remix of the *Radetzky March* for a soundtrack – although such a tongue-in-cheek project might be more to the tastes of DJ Ötzi. In a city that never lets you forget the past, the Viennese are always moving forward, displaying their "somewhat ungraspable character – a sketch, a draft, never a completed whole…"

Viennese history

The name Wenia (later Wien) first appears in an 881 document specifying land rights.

Vienna owed its rise to its position at a commercial crossroads. The north–south axis was identified with the amber trade route, running from the Baltic to Aquilea (on the Adriatic), that existed from prehistoric times. The east–west axis is represented by the River Danube, one of Europe's great trading arteries, which runs from the Black Forest to the Black Sea. The Vienna Basin forms a gap in the Alpine and Carpathian mountain chains and it is through this gap that the Danube, Europe's second largest river, passes. The river served as the Romans' northern frontier, and their defensive forts along its banks often had garrisons and civilian settlements attached. One such was Vindobona, a Roman forerunner of Vienna dating from 15 BC, and occupying part of today's Altstadt (Old City).

Around this garrison town, the Romans resettled the indigenous Celtic inhabitants from the strategic Kahlenberg and Leopoldsberg, which make up the last eastern stretch of both the Alps and the Wienerwald (Vienna Woods). The square plan of the Roman town bounded an area now marked by the Graben to the

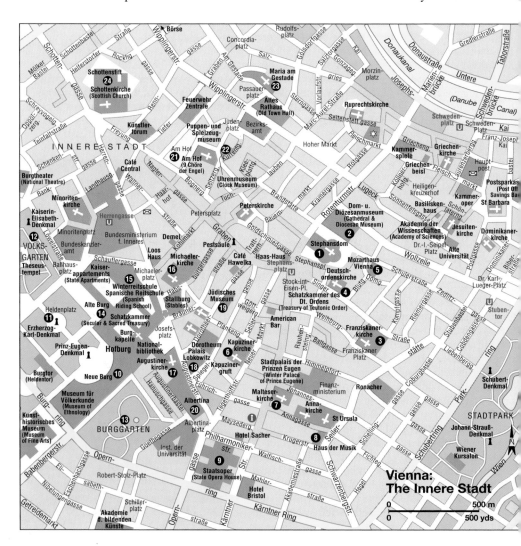

Vienna:
The Innere Stadt

0   500 m
0   500 yds

south, the Rotenturmstrasse to the southeast and the Tiefer Graben to the north-west. To the south and west of the Roman garrison lay the rest-and-recreation area, remains of which have been discovered and exposed on the Michaelerplatz in front of the Michaelertor of the Hofburg, a former imperial (and now presidential) palace within the city.

Following the retreat of the Romans in the early 5th century, Vindobona was only revived when the Babenberg Margrave (incorporating much of modern Austria) was set up by the German Emperor, Otto II, in 976 as a buffer against the insurgent Hungarians. By then it was known as Wenia, later Wien, after the old Celtic name for the small river that ran from the Wienerwald into the Danube. However, Vienna became important only when the Babenberg Margraves moved their court here in 1156, the year in which their territory was elevated to a dukedom. This was a defining moment for the city: the ducal court was set up in the area still known as Am Hof (At the Court), and Irish monks were summoned from Regensburg to found their Benedictine monastery here.

Under the Babenbergs, many of Austria's greatest abbeys and cloisters were founded along the Danube, and an agreement with the powerful bishopric of Passau led to a new parish church dedicated to St Stephen just outside Vienna's city boundary to the east. This predecessor of the great Stephansdom was consecrated in 1147 in a ceremony attended by Emperor Konrad III and his crusaders. Under Leopold VI (1198–1230), Vienna became wealthy on the backs of visiting merchants, who were obliged to sell their wares in the city, thus guaranteeing the Viennese the lion's share of the downstream Danube trade.

The Babenberg line died out when Friedrich II was killed in battle in 1246. Austria was then ruled by Ottokar II of Bohemia, and it was he who built the first fort that was to be extended gradually over the next 600 years by his successors, the Habsburgs, and which we know today as the Vienna Hofburg. After Rudolf of Habsburg defeated Ottokar in 1278, Vienna became the imperial residence of one of history's greatest dynasties.

The pious Babenbergs had already initiated the first religious building boom, which was to be repeated twice under the Habsburgs. In the late Middle Ages the city was flooded with religious orders, who built their cloisters and churches in Gothic style. A few of these, like the Minoritenkirche, have retained their Gothic aspect, but most were transformed into baroque affairs in the second great wave of religious architecture during the Counter-Reformation from 1622. If we (wrongly) think of Vienna as primarily a baroque city, it is no doubt because of the powerful impression made by the architecture at a time when Prince Eugene built the fabulous Belvedere (as well as a fine winter palace within the city walls), and other great noble families – Liechtensteins, Starhembergs, Lobkowitzes, Dietrichsteins – changed the face of the city.

This great building boom took place after the second Turkish siege of 1683 was repulsed at the last moment by armies under Jan Sobieski of Poland. After the double victory over Lutheranism (Vienna had been 80 percent Protestant in the late 16th century) and the Turks, the forces of Catholicism began

Map on page 112

2005 (Jubiläumsjahr, Jubilee Year) saw a double anniversary for Austria, being the 50th anniversary of the State Treaty which ended Allied occupation and the 60th of the Second Republic itself. Austria also commendably took this opportunity to revamp some of its most important museums.

BELOW: the Hundertwasser-haus.

to build in a spirit of triumph. Nobles built summer palaces outside the inner city walls and, later, the burghers also began to escape to the suburbs and villages that have gradually been incorporated into the city over the past 100 years. The furthest urban periphery was the Linienwall, built in the 18th century to protect against marauding Hungarian freedom fighters and demolished in 1893. Now it has been replaced by a ring road, with traffic jams by day, and prostitutes, garish lights and tacky bars by night.

By contrast, the narrow confines of the inner city present a kaleidoscopic architectural and social impression of Vienna through the ages. Perhaps somewhat incongruously, it is socialists, in power in the city continuously from 1945 to 1996, who have been the most assiduous force in preserving the city's churches, palaces and monuments – the overwhelmingly Catholic and imperialist heritage of their traditional enemies. Perhaps it is only the strange nostalgic power of a city whose motto might be "Never throw anything away, one never knows": even the Austrofascists who took over the city in 1934 did not destroy the Ringstrasse's monument to the Republic they had toppled, but rather warehoused it, allowing the post-Nazi government to restore it in 1945.

Shopping on the Graben.

BELOW: the *Heidenturme* rise above the *Riesentor*.

In the imperial epoch, much of Viennese life was clustered around an artificially confined court – after the first Turkish siege of 1529, elaborate defensive bastions in a star formation girdled the medieval town. These were not removed until the Ringstrasse boulevard was created to replace it by order of Emperor Franz Joseph in 1857.

Any modern building in this microcosmically focused environment has inevitably been controversial, whether it be the modernist house built by Adolf Loos on the Michaelerplatz in 1911, which was notoriously deemed an unfitting accompaniment to the Michaelerkirche and the Hofburg; or Hans Hollein's bold Haashaus (1990), which faces the Stephansdom, itself a building that embodies all that "Old Vienna" holds sacred. Yet people often seem to forget that Vienna has always been a jumble of old and new, outward- and inward-looking, reactionary and progressive, ascetically pious and lustily sybaritic. Today the Stephansdom, a bastion of spirituality which saw out siege, sedition, Nazism and the age of "total war", is a stone's throw from the streets of the Graben and Kärntnerstrasse, whose shop windows flaunt something to suit every fancy and price range imaginable to the 21st-century Western consumer.

Stephansplatz

The **Stephansplatz** is the focal point of the inner city, and indeed of Vienna. Conveniently for the visitor, it is well-served by the U1 and U3 underground lines, as well as being the meeting-point of the pedestrian Graben and Kärntnerstrasse. From a café table here, one might expect to see all manner of passing life: an office crowd barking into mobile phones, street performers, Hare Krishna followers, sellers of the Augustin, elderly Viennese setting the world to rights over cream cakes and *Melange*, and always the obligatory tour parties, religious and otherwise, visiting **Stephansdom** ❶ (St Stephen's Cathedral; open

Mon–Sat 6am–10pm, Sun 7am–10pm; entrance charge for towers and cata-combs; www.stephansdom.at). The glorious Gothic south tower (known affection-ately as the Steffl to the Viennese) was begun in 1365 by Michael Chnab, but only finished in 1433, and was meant to be complemented by a northerly twin, of which only a stump remains. The earliest part of the church is the west façade with two Romanesque towers known as Pagan Towers (*Heidenturme*), although their supposed resemblance to minarets is not apparent to the modern eye.

It is worth walking round the outside to admire the monumental effect of the whole, and the intricacies of the architecture of the South Tower from which Count Starhemberg directed operations against the Turks during the siege of 1683. You should also look up at the colourful tiled roof that bears the Habsburg double-eagle on one side, and the coats of arms of Vienna and Austria on the other. The entire roof of the cathedral burned out in the last days of World War II, and all the Austrian provinces contributed to its rebuilding, together with the 1951 recasting and installation in the north tower of the great bell (known as the Pummerin), which shattered in the bombing. It was partly made from abandoned Turkish cannons. Entry to the cathedral is through the **Riesentor** (Giants' Doorway), decorated with depictions of Christ, his Apostles, Samson, St Stephen, the cathedral's own master builders and a variety of humans and beasts representing the Evil of the World.

The interior is remarkable for the many baroque altars that replaced Gothic ones during the Counter-Reformation. Two particular highlights are the Alber-tine Choir, initiated by the Habsburg Albrecht II and completed under his suc-cessors in 1340, and, not far from the west door, Anton Pilgram's pulpit (*circa* 1500), whose side panels show the fathers of the Church represented as the

Map on page 112

Against the northeastern external wall of the cathedral is the pulpit from which the Dominican Giovanni Capistrano preached during the crusade against the Turks of 1454–55.

BELOW: the nave of Stephansdom.

four humours. The Pilgram self-portrait below shows him leaning out of a window, and he is also represented under the organ loft on the north wall.

One of the stranger legends of the Stephansdom is that of the Zahnwehherrgott, a relief image of a man deep in the throes of suffering. The tale goes that a group of young men made mock of the figure one drunken night, tying a bandage around his jaw to help with his "toothache". Immediately divine vengeance was wrought and the men began to suffer excruciating toothaches of their own. Only by returning to the scene of the crime and repenting could they be cured. The original image can be seen inside the North Tower, on the west wall: like many images from the cathedral, a copy can be seen on the building's exterior.

At the end of the north nave is the Wiener Neustadt Altar (1447), with its sculptured groups showing the life of Christ and of the Virgin Mary. The baroque high altar (1640), by Tobias Pock, depicts the martyrdom of St Stephen, and beyond it, at the southeastern corner, is the fine late-Gothic **Tomb of Emperor Friedrich III** (1467) by Nicolaus Gerhaert van Leyden. For a close look you have to join a guided tour, which is certainly worthwhile for this is one of Austria's best sepulchral monuments. Close by, to the north of the cathedral, is the **Dom- und Diözesanmuseum** ❷ (Cathedral and Diocesan Museum; open Tues–Sat 10am–5pm; entrance charge; tel: 01-5155 3689; www.dommuseum.at) at Stephansplatz 6. Located in the Archbishop's Palace, it includes a selection of paintings from the masters of the Austrian baroque, and exhibits from an eclectic collection including fragments surviving from the 1945 bombing, a 14th-century portrait of Rudolf IV, and an iron treasure chest, dating back to 1678, which displays an intricately crafted locking system. The Virgil Chapel, which also stood on the Stephansplatz from *circa* 1220 to 1781, can be seen through a window in the Stephansplatz U-bahn station.

Walking northeast round the church from the pulpit, you pass the entrance to the catacombs, where the embalmed entrails of many Habsburg rulers were deposited.

BELOW: the 14th-century portrait of Rudolf IV.

East of Stephansdom

From the Cathedral, Stephansplatz merges to the south with **Stock-im-Eisen** (Iron in Wood) **Platz**, named after the spruce stump on its periphery, where visiting apprentices to the iron trade would knock in a nail for luck. The tree stump, believed to be the remnant of a forest which once grew here, is bound by an iron ring which – according to legend – cannot be opened. It is now, in any case, doubly secured by a protective perspex casing.

Kärntnerstrasse is a fashionable pedestrian shopping zone leading south off of Stock im Eisen towards the opera house and the Ringstrasse, but before exploring this area, one should turn to the left: running east from this street is Weihburggasse, which is home to the **Franziskanerkirche** ❸ (open Mon–Sat 7.30–11.30am, 2.30–5.30pm; www.franziskaner.at). This church was originally built in 1383 for lay sisters before being handed over to Franciscans. While the exterior blends Gothic and Northern Renaissance styles – the gables adorning the façade are particularly striking – the interior is startling and baroque, including a *trompe l'oeil* from 1707, the work of Andrea Pozzo. Some of the altars also deserve special attention: there is a *Crucifixion* by Carlo Carlone, F.X. Wagenschön's *Martyrdom of St John Capistrano* and *The Immaculata*, from the school of Rottmayr, as well as a late-Gothic *Madonna* surviving from the 15th century.

The northern face of the Franziskanerkirche looks onto the Singerstrasse, home to another exciting church, the 14th century **Deutschordernskirche** ❹ (open daily 7am–6pm). This belonged to the Teutonic Order (*see* www.imperial-teutonicorder.org), active in Vienna from about 1200. A beautiful, winged altar within is Dutch and dates to *circa* 1500. Next door to the church is the Order's House, including a **Schatzkammer** (open Mon and Thur 10am–noon, Wed and Fri 3pm–5pm, Sat 10am–noon, 3pm–5pm; entrance charge; tel: 01-512 1065; www.deutscher-orden.at), or Treasury, whose collection includes both religious objects and more secular ones related to the crusades, including a range of exotic arms and armour. At the bottom of the staircase on the ground floor is another magnificent *trompe l'oeil* in the form of an 18th-century *sala terrena* where concerts are held (tel: 01-911 9077 or see www.mozarthaus.at for details).

The altar of the Deutschorderns-kirche

The Mozarthaus

Blutgasse, or Blood Alley, around the corner from the Deutschordenskirche, owes its gory name to a massacre reputed to have taken place here in the 14th century. Modern visitors should be able to walk the street without such traumatic incident and come safely to the entrance of the **Mozarthaus Vienna** ❺ (open daily 10am–8pm; entrance charge; tel: 01-512 1791; www.mozarthausvienna.at), formerly the Figarohaus, a museum dedicated to the Mozart family. It was on the first floor of this house that Mozart lived when he composed works including *The Marriage of Figaro*. The museum has been completely redesigned and opened to coincide with the start of the 2006 Mozart celebrations (the 250th anniversary of his birth). The new displays are spread over the top three floors and are a considerable improvement over their lacklustre previous incarnation. Below are the inevitable shop and café.

From the Mozarthaus it is a short walk back west along Schulerstrasse to the Stephansplatz; alternatively another passage leads north from the Mozart museum to Wollzeile and refreshment at Café Diglas, a plush, superlative *Kaffeehaus*.

Kärntnerstrasse to the Staatsoper

After exploring the district immediately to the east of the cathedral, it is worth taking the longer walk south towards the Opera House. Turning off the southbound **Kärntnerstrasse** along the narrow Kärntnerdurch-gang on the right hand side, one finds **Adolf Loos' American Bar** (open daily noon–4am; www.loosbar.at) whose striking exterior is matched by a marble interior which exploits mirrors to amplify its meagre floor area (5 x 2.5 m/16 x 8 ft).

Returning to Kärntnerstrasse, the next right turn brings you to the Neuer Markt and the **Kapuzin-erkirche** ❻, whose crypt – the famous **Kapuziner-gruft** (open daily 9.30am–3.30pm; entrance charge; tel: 01-512 6853; www.kaisergruft.at) – is the resting place of the Habsburg royals. Emperor Franz Stephan I and his wife Maria Theresa have perhaps the most impressive tombs – baroque sepulchres produced by Balthasar Moll – but the Franz-Joseph vault attracts more attention. There we find the last true emperor, his son the Arch-duke Rudolf who died at Mayerling, and also Empress

THE AUGUSTIN

On street corners and in U-Bahn stations, you will see the *Augustin* for sale. Homeless people are the vendors of this monthly publication, which includes listings and fiction alongside news and features. The name comes from Marx Augustin, of the 17th century, whose drunken fall into a corpse-filled plague pit is commemorated in the song "O du lieber Augustin". He is celebrated as emblematic of the twin Viennese capacities for hedonism and survival. For readers of German, it is an excellent way to get your finger on the pulse of the city: as well as the useful listings, it's a provocative forum for concerns sometimes neglected by the mainstream press. In recent years, with an increasing number of homeless Viennese coming from African backgrounds, it has challenged the dismissive and racist mainstream media stance on immigration and asylum with informative and powerful pieces. Half of the cover price goes to the vendor.

Map on page 112

An architectural detail near the Graben.

BELOW: the tombs of Franz Joseph and "Sissi".

Elizabeth or "Sissi", Franz Josef's wife, whose tomb is a focal point for Hungarian nationalism, given her sympathies for that nationality. In the last room we find the last empress, Zita, who only died in 1989 and was buried in the crypt that year with a pomp worthy of the empire's glory days. Strangely enough, the hearts and entrails of the Habsburg monarchs are located not here with their bodies, but in Stephansdom and the Herzgrüftel, or "heart crypt", of the Augustinerkirche.

Further still down Kärntnerstrasse, but this time to the left and east, lies the Himmelpfortgasse. At No. 8 is the **Stadtpalais der Prinzen Eugen**, Prince Eugene's Winter Palace, today part of the Ministry of Finance but once home to Austria's most famous general and hero of the War of Spanish Succession. Built in 1697–8 by Johann Bernhard Fischer von Erlach, it was extended by Lukas von Hildebrandt from 1708 to 1728. As a working building, only the foyer and staircase are open to the public (Mon–Fri during working hours), and permission must be asked at the entrance, but it is worth the little bother this entails: beyond the three ornamental entrances, decorated by cherubs, weapons and sculptures, lies Fischer von Erlach's astonishing interior design, featuring vast statues by Giovanni Giuliani and the stucco *Labours of Hercules*, produced by Santino Bussi. The ceilings are the work of painter Louis Dorigny.

The **Malteserkirche** ❼ (Church of the Knights of Malta; www.malteserorden.at), lies on Kärntnerstrasse. The Maltese knights had established a *dépendance* in Vienna as the Order of the Knights of St John in 1217. The Gothic building dates from 1450, but bears a classical façade added in the early years of the 19th century. The coats of arms of the Grand Masters of the Order adorn the choir, while the high altar includes statues of Saints Peter and Paul as well as Johann Georg Schmidt's *Baptism of Christ*.

The next street down on the left, Annagasse, runs past the **Annakirche** with its fine ceiling frescoes by Daniel Gran, and into Seilerstätte. On the corner is the **Haus der Musik** ❽ (open daily 10am–10pm; entrance charge; tel: 01-516 4810; www.hdm.at). This admirable "sound museum" has a twin purpose; it tells the story of the great composers who have worked in the city and its premier orchestra, the Vienna Philharmonic (whose founder lived in the building), as well as exploring more abstract concepts. It is a particularly good museum for children, with many activities and interactive exhibits on offer.

Proceeding further south, the Kärntnerstrasse's end is in sight, with the Staatsoper, or Opera House on the right. Just before is the Philharmonikerstrasse, home of the famed **Hotel Sacher**. While the accommodation and service here still lives up to its legend (and its exorbitant prices), the *Kaffeehaus* within is more for the tourist than the true Viennese coffee addict. The hotel shop on **Kärntnerstrasse** does provide the famous *Sacher Torte* in sizes to suit all appetites.

The **Staatsoper** ❾ (guided tours at 1, 2 and 3pm; entrance charge; tel: 01-514 42250; www.wiener-staatsoper.at) stands at the crossroads of Kärntnerstrasse and the Ringstrasse itself. It was built between 1861 and 1869 as part of the Ringstrasse project, designed by August von Siccardsburg and Eduard van der Nüll. Its first season opened with Mozart's *Don Giovanni*. In 1945 it was unfortunate to receive a direct hit during a bombing raid and required complete rebuilding, although this followed the original plans and was, in fact, so painstaking that it took longer than the first construction.

The safety curtain, decorated with a picture of Orpheus and Eurydice, rose again on 5 November 1955 to a re-inaugural performance of *Fidelio*. Herbert von Karajan, director of the opera company from 1956 to 1964, may have wished for a return to the days of the exclusive Hofoperntheater, or Court Opera: the Viennese are as generous with their criticism of the public arts as they are with funding for the same, and Karajan once commented that he had to contend with 1.6 million co-directors, all determined to teach him how to run an opera company.

The Hofburg

Along the Ringstrasse lies the Habsburg imperial palace, the **Hofburg**. An eagle glares down at patrons of Maria-Theresa-Platz from the Burgtor gate. Nothing more symbolises the Austria of the past than this palace, residence for Austria's rulers from Albrecht I's reign (1283–1308) to the very end of the Austro-Hungarian Monarchy. As well as being Austria's foremost heritage site, the palace complex is a working thoroughfare linking the southwestern Burgring with the city centre via two equally magnificient gateways, the **Burgtor** and **Michaelertor** (St Michael's Gate). The variety of museums, institutions and sights within the complex is such that, as with the Kunsthistorisches Museum, either multiple visits or a well-paced long day out are required to fully appreciate all that is to be seen.

The Neue Burg

Immediately to the right of the Burgtor is the **Neue Burg** ❿, built during the years 1881–1913 by Gottfried Semper and Karl von Hasenauer on the instruc-

Map on page 112

"Are all people who come to Vienna so bewitched that they have to stay here? It rather looks like it."
– Leopold Mozart, to his son Wolfgang Amadeus.

BELOW: a plaque commemorating Johann Strauss I on Kärntnerstrasse.

JOHANN STRAUSS VATER

*1804 WIEN
†1849 WIEN

tions of Franz Joseph. Today the building houses the modern reading rooms of the National Library *(see also page 124)*, the Ephesus Museum, the Hofjagd- und Rüstkammer (Court Armoury and Hunting Museum) and the Sammlung alter Musikinstrumente (Collection of Historical Musical Instruments), as well as theVölkerkundemuseum, or Museum of Ethnology.

Unlike many other European empires, Austria-Hungary's territorial possessions were relatively concentrated within Central-East Europe, the **Museum für Völkerkunde** (closed until spring 2007 for a major refurbishment; www.ethno-museum.ac.at), gathers together those Asian and American objects which the Habsburgs were able to beg, borrow or steal during their reign. The **Ephesus Museum** holds those items discovered in Turkey and Greece by Austrian archaeologists. For those fascinated by arms and armour, the **Hofjagd- und Rüstkammer** is widely recognised to be the most outstanding collection of its kind in Europe, while the **Sammlung alter Musikinstrumente** has the most extensive holdings of Renaissance instruments in the world (all museums open Wed–Mon 10am-6pm; entrance charge; tel: 01-5252 4484; www.khm.at).

For visitors interested in the ethnology of Austria-Hungary's imperial provinces, the place to visit is the **Museum für Volkskunde***, located at the junction of Lange Gasse and Laudongasse (open Tues-Sun 10am-5pm; entrance charge; tel: 01-406 8905; www.volkskunde museum.at).*

Heldenplatz and the Volksgarten

The Neue Burg looks over the **Heldenplatz ⓫** to the west. Here some 200,000 Viennese congregated to welcome Adolf Hitler in 1938, when he spoke from the balcony of the Heldenplatz, or Heroes' Square. Its monuments (1860–5) by Anton Fernkorn commemorate Archduke Karl's victory over Napoleon I at Aspern, and that omnipresent military man, Prince Eugene of Savoy. West of Heldenplatz lies the **Volksgarten ⓬**, a park laid out in 1823 on the site of the demolished Castle Bastion. It is famous for its rose garden. In addition to the Temple of Theseus by Peter Nobile (1820–3), there are memorials to figures as diverse as Empress Elizabeth, playwright Franz Grillparzer and Chancellor Julius Raab (1891–1964), who played a key rule in the drafting and signing of the Austrian State Treaty in 1955.

RIGHT: a *fiacre* lamp.

A short stroll clockwise around the Ring brings you to the **Burggarten ⓭**, laid out for the imperial family in the 19th century. It has monuments to Franz Joseph and Mozart, and a *Jugendstil* glasshouse, the **Palmenhaus**, which contains a butterfly house (*see* www.schmetterlinghaus.at) as well as a charming café (*see* www.palmenhaus.at). In the summer, rollerbladers, jugglers and groups of friends congregate on the grass.

The Alte Burg

Northeast of Prince Eugene's statue on Heldenplatz lies the **Alte Burg ⓮**, which forms the core of the Hofburg and dates back to the original fortress of 1275. Here one finds the **Burgkapelle** (Palace Chapel; open Sept–June, Mon–Thur 11am–3pm, Fri 11am–1pm; entrance charge; www.bmbwk.gv.at), home of the famed Wiener Sängerknaben (Vienna Boys' Choir). They perform every Sunday between September and June at 9.15am; tickets can be ordered in advance by fax or e-mail, and it is advisable to book well ahead, but must be paid for in cash and collected from the chapel box office (open Fri 11am–1pm, 3–5pm, Sun 8.15–9.15am; fax: 01-533 5067; e-mail HMK@aon.at).

Facing the Chapel across the courtyard of the **Schweizerhof**, whose name recalls the Swiss origins of Austria's Babenberg rulers, stands the **Weltliche und Geistliche Schatzkammer** (Secular and Sacred Treasury; open Wed–Mon 10am–6pm; entrance charge; tel: 01-525 240; www.khm.at) which includes a remarkable selection of jewels, rarities, and relics including a supposed unicorn horn and a vessel once alleged to be the Holy Grail. The first of the exhibits are die Österreichische Erbhuldigung, the insignia of the Archdukes of the Austrian territories. These are followed by the Habsburg family insignia with, most significantly, the crown of Emperor Rudolf II (1602, from 1804 also the Austrian imperial crown), and the imperial orb and sceptre (*circa* 1612). Also here are the Habsburg imperial insignia, comprising the imperial mantle, the sword of state and various ceremonial jewels. Other priceless Habsburg possessions on display include the Grand Cross of the Military Order of Maria Theresa (1765) and a diamond sabre captured from the Turks before 1683. The Habsburgs, as the last sovereigns of the Holy Roman Empire, retained its insignia and relics upon its dissolution. The Coronation robes comprise nine robes of state and the mantle of Roger II, King of the Normans, decorated with Arabic motifs. The Emperor's imperial dignity was symbolised by the crown, orb and sceptre of the Empire, as well as the swords of Frederick II and Charlemagne and the Bursa of St Stephen.

In addition to these secular possessions, a variety of sacred treasures are also held within the Schatzkammer, ranging from liturgical vestments worn in Habsburg court services to reliquaries, the most important of which house items alleged to be a splinter from Christ's crib, a tooth of St John the Baptist, and pieces of Christ's tablecloth and loincloth from the time of the Last Supper.

Map on page 112

A poster summoning the Viennese to hear Adolf Hitler give his speech in Heldenplatz.

BELOW: the Palmenhaus.

In der Burg

To the west of the Schweizerhof is **In der Burg**, a busy square thronged with tourists in addition to various horse-drawn and motor traffic cutting between the city centre and the Ring. Here is the **Leopoldischinertrakt**, official residence of the president of Austria, and the **Kaiserappartements** (open daily, Sept–June 9am–5.30pm, July–Aug 9am–5.30pm; entrance charge; tel: 01-533 7570; www.hofburg-wien.at) which housed the apartments of Franz Josef and Elizabeth. The apartments can be visited for those Habsburg devotees wishing to see how the imperial monarchs lived and worked; the rooms also house the **Silberkammer**, an extensive collection of silver and porcelain, and the **Sisi Museum** which outlines the life of the empress.

The Spanish Riding School

At the northeastern edge of the Hofburg lies the **Winterreitschule ⓯**, home of the famous **Spanische Reitschule** (Spanish Riding School; open Tues–Sat 9am–5pm, Sun 9am–1.30pm; entrance charge; www.srs.at), the last in the world to retain the classical equestrian tradition. The forthcoming programme of dressage performances and morning training sessions can be seen and booked in advance on-line. The main building, the work of Josef Emanuel Fischer von Erlach, was constructed between 1729 and 1735, its huge parade hall in particular considered a masterpiece of the baroque.

Opposite lie the stables of the Stallburg, constructed in 1558 on what is believed to have been the site of the Babenberg Duke Leopold VI's palace in 1220. Following an epidemic, the school's Lipizzaner horses can no longer be visited in their ground floor stables – however, visitors can see into the stalls via

In the Schatzkammer are the "Inalienable Treasures", wonderfully bizarre, these include: a huge agate dish once reputed to be the Holy Grail (now attributed to 4th-century Istanbul), and the unicorn's horn, taller than a man (disappointingly revealed to be the tooth of a narwhal).

BELOW: the imperial eagle over the Michaelertor.

two monitors next door in the Lipizzaner Museum (open daily 9am–6pm; entrance charge; tel: 01-5252 4583; www.lipizzaner.at), whose exhibits relate the history of the breed (named for the imperial stud at Lipizza) as well as including various riding paraphernalia.

Map on page 112

Michaelerkirche

Across the road from the Stallburg is the **Michaelerkirche** ⑯ (open 7am–10pm; www.michaelerkirche.at), former parish church of the Austrian Emperors. Dating in part from 1221, the building was extended during the 14th and 15th centuries. The tower is Gothic (1340–4), but the slender helm roof acquired its present appearance in 1590. Ferdinand von Hohenberg added the classical details to the façade, retaining nonetheless the baroque porch (1724–5) by Antonio Beduzzi, with the sculpted *Fall of the Angels* by Lorenzo Mattielli. A painted stone relief of Christ on the Mount of Olives, on the outside of the south wall, dates from 1494.

The church is well worth a visit for its fine altar paintings and remarkable number of noblemen's tombs. Past the baroque baptismal chapel is a larger than life sandstone sculpture of Christ on the Cross, dating from 1430. In the Tower Chapel are 13th-century Gothic frescoes of Saints Cosma, Thomas and Damien, and a Mass of Gregory (14th century). The altar of the magnificent Vespers Chapel contains a *Pietà* (*circa* 1430); the relief tombstone of Georg von Lichtenstein dates from 1548. Hanging above the north transept is another depiction of *The Fall of the Angels*, this time a 1751 painting by Michael Unterberger. The south choir bay was donated in 1350 by the Ducal chef Stiborious Chrezzel in grateful thanks for his acquittal on a poisoning charge. Also dating from this period are the Gothic stone statues of St Catherine and St Nicholas.

A Lippizaner and rider in the Spanische Reitschule.

BELOW: a Hussar high above Kohlmarkt.

The altarpieces of the Michaelerkirche particularly merit attention. Tobias Pock was responsible for *The Fourteen Auxiliary Saints*, dating from 1643, which adorn the altar in the Chapel of St John Nepomuk. The ubiquitous Josef Emanuel Fischer von Erlach designed the wall tomb of Prince Donat Trautson (1727). The high altar is adorned with a 16th-century portrait of the Madonna supported by angels from Iraklion (Crete); to one side are statues of the Evangelist (1781) by the junior Fischer von Erlach. At the end of the choir there recurs the theme of the Fall of the Angels in an 18th-century interpretation by Karl Georg Melville. The funeral monument to Peter von Mollart dates from 1576 and the adjacent altar is surmounted by Pock's *The Miracle of Pentecost* (*circa* 1643). In the north side choir are two epitaphs by Georg von Herbenstein (1570) and Johann von Werdenberg (1643), as well as a memorial to the court poet, Metastasio, who died in 1782.

Around the corner from the church, where Herrengasse and Kohlmarkt meet in the Michaelerplatz, stands the famous (or infamous) **Loos Haus**, whose straight lines and unadorned façade earned it the sobriquet "the building without eyebrows" and aroused the displeasure of the emperor himself when unveiled in 1910 (particularly as it faces the Hofburg). Today it is regarded as a masterpiece of Modernist architecture.

Café Griensteidl is at No. 14, Michaelerplatz. Home to imperial Vienna's literary circles until its demolition in 1897 (they moved to Café Central up the road), today's café was opened in 1990 and stands on the original site. Coffee and cakes meet the usual high Viennese standard, a range of newspapers are available, and children are welcome.

After exploring the Neue Burg, Alte Burg, Stallburg and Michaelerplatz, it is surely time for another round of *Kaffee und Kuchen*. Either try the **Café Griensteidl** *(see margin)*, or, at No. 14, Kohlmarkt, **Demel**, which offers a gilded, mirrored grandeur and prices to match. Being the former imperial bakery and confectioner's, Demel prides itself on cakes which may have a claim to being the best in the city (open daily 10am–7pm; www.demel.at).

Josefsplatz

South of the Stallburg, on Josefsplatz, is the entrance to the **National Library**. This building – the former Imperial Library – was designed by Johann Bernhard Fischer von Erlach and constructed between 1723 and 1735 under the supervision of his son, Josef Emanuel. Ascending the staircase you enter the huge baroque **Prunksaal**, which occupies both upper storeys and is the largest library room in Europe (open Tues, Wed, Fri–Sun 10am-6pm, Thur 10am–9pm; entrance charge; www.onb.ac.at). The ceiling frescoes (1730) by Daniel Gran depict the apotheosis of the library's founder, Emperor Charles VI. The painting in the oval dome portrays allegorical figures of the Sciences surrounded by patrons of the House of Habsburg; under the dome stand statues of Charles VI and 16 other Habsburg rulers (*circa* 1700, by Paul and Peter Strudel). In front of the library entrance is an equestrian statue of Emperor Joseph II.

Further on is the **Augustinerkirche** ⓱ (Church of the Augustinians; www.augustinerkirche.at/wien), founded in 1327 by Frederick the Handsome as the court parish church; it was built between 1330 and 1339 to plans by Dietrich Ladtner von Pirn. The tower was a later addition (1652). The baroque interior was removed in 1784 and the original Gothic interior reinstated.

BELOW: the Loos Haus on Michaelerplatz.

To the right of the entrance lies the marble memorial to Archduchess Marie Christine, favourite daughter of Maria Theresa, an Antonio Canova design (1798–1805) resembling a burial pyramid, with allegorical figures of Virtue and Charity depicting approaching the entrance, while a spirit leaning on the back of a lion bears the coat of arms of Marie Christine's consort, Prince Albrecht of Saxony-Teschen. The Archduchess herself can be seen on a carved medallion. Like Marie Christine's pyramid, the tomb of Emperor Leopold II, also here, is empty: both are buried within the Kapuzinergruft. The only Habsburg remains to dwell within the Augustinerkirche lie in the Habsburg **Herzgrüftel** ("heart crypt", access only by appointment), where, according to a family tradition imported from Spain, heart and entrails were removed from the body before burial and preserved separately in silver urns. The practice stretched from the reign of Ferdinand II (died 1637) to Archduke Franz Karl (died 1878).

A slice of Sachertorte.

The Theatre Museum and Dorotheergasse

Opposite the church stands the **Palais Lobkowitz** ⑱, a mansion erected in 1685 by Giovanni Pietro Tencala, acquiring a magnificent baroque doorway in 1716, courtesy of Johann Bernhard Fischer von Erlach. It was here that Beethoven's *Eroica Symphony* was first publicly performed in 1805. The palace now houses the excellent **Österreichisches Theatermuseum** (Austrian Theatrical Museum; open Tues–Sun 10am-6pm; entrance charge; tel: 01-512 8800; www.theatermuseum.at)), whose displays show the development of European theatrical architecture, while the first floor is given over to costumes, a puppet theatre and set models, as well as the beautifully decorated Eroica Saal.

BELOW: the Prunksaal of the National Library.

Also running north from the Augustinerstrasse is the narrow Dorotheergasse, which plays host to Vienna's challenging and controversial **Jüdisches Museum** ⑲ (the Jewish Museum; open Sun–Fri 10am– 6pm; entrance charge; tel: 01-535 0431; www.jmw.at). Serving as a combined research centre, library and exhibition space, the museum seeks to represent the Austro-Jewish past in all its complexity, avoiding the kind of reductive and dismissive approach characteristic of the nation at large. The ground floor, in addition to a bookshop and the excellent small Café Teitelbaum (tel: 01-512 5545), hosts US artist Nancy Spero's *Installation der Erinnerung (Memory Installation)*. Lying at the heart of the museum and visible from the balconies of other floors, Spero's work articulates the fundamental mission of the museum – remembrance. Historical images – a 1493 woodcut of Jews burnt at the stake, a 1670 bird's-eye view of Vienna's Jewish quarter, the photograph of a temple in ruins from 1941 – appear among the collection of Judaica assembled by Holocaust survivor Max Berger between 1950 and his death in 1988. Further items appear, deliberately unlabelled, on the building's top floor in a *Schaudepot*, or display depot, which represents the enormous material legacy of the city's oft-persecuted Jewish community.

The other floors are given over to temporary exhibitions covering topics such as the situation of Jewish citizens in Austria's Second Republic. The Jewish

Map on page 112

At No. 17 Dorotheergasse, you will find the Dorotheum, Vienna's "pawn shop for the rich and famous", today a leading auction house amongst whose specialist and exorbitant sales the odd affordable antique or oddity can still be found (open Mon–Sat; tel: 01-515 600; www.dorotheum. com).

Museum, with its cutting-edge intellectual approach to history and memory, has sometimes been accused of being *abgehoben*, or aloof, but its provocative qualities serve as a welcome and important antidote to the historical myths perpetuated elsewhere in the city.

Beyond the Augustinerkirche, on the street that bears its name, is the **Albertina ⑳** (open Thur–Tues 10am–6pm, Wed 10am–9pm; entrance charge; tel: 01-534 830; www.albertina.at), an 18th-century palace which today houses the Graphic Collection founded by Marie Christine's consort, Prince Albrecht. With 60,000 drawings and 1 million sheets of etchings, engravings and lithographs, it is the largest and most important collection of its kind in the world. The most valuable exhibits are works by Albrecht Dürer, Lucas Cranach, Leonardo da Vinci, Michelangelo, Raphael, Titian, Rubens and Rembrandt, although because of their value and the fragility of the graphics, only a select few are on show at any one time. Nonetheless, the Albertina's temporary exhibitions are consistently world-class, with modern showrooms and facilities to match.

On the Albertinaplatz stands the composite ***Mahnmal gegen Krieg und Faschismus*** ("Warning Against War and Fascism") erected between 1988 and 1991 by Alfred Hrdlicka. Intended to recall the horrific anti-Semitism of the days following the Anschluss, the monument provoked great criticism at the time of its unveiling *(see also page 146)*.

Stephansplatz to Schottenplatz

BELOW: Albrecht Dürer's Young Hare from the Albertina.

Opposite the Stock-im-Eisen is the stark contrast of the modern **Haashaus**, built to plans by Hans Hollein in 1990. The large, partially mirrored exterior

WIENER DIALEKT

Although High German *(Hochdeutsch)* is the official language, the Austrian variant can be so strong as to perplex native speakers of German. Wienerisch is a language within a language, full of borrowings from Yiddish and the subject peoples of the old empire, as well as the legacy of imperial Francophilia. Schönbrunnerdeutsch, originally referring to the speech of the Habsburgs' summer palace, is now a kind of Viennese blarney which you may hear from taxi drivers, waiters or at the Würstelstand. However, the further one is from the tourist districts, the more likely one is to encounter a genuine *Umgangssprache* (colloquial language) derived from everyday usage than a rose-tinted view of the k.u.k. monarchy. For the student of German, Viennese dialect can be an exciting challenge; non-German-speakers can get by with *Grüss Gott* for "Hello" and the often excellent English of your average city resident.

curves, representing a "hinge" between Stephanplatz and **Graben**, Vienna's main shopping thoroughfare, once part of the town moat surrounding the Roman camp – Duke Leopold VI had it filled in while extending the town in 1220.

Map on page 112

After extensive forays into the south, east and the Hofburg, a stroll northwest up the Graben offers a little light relief. Retail therapy is an option here, as are *Kaffee und Kuchen* in one of the innumerable outdoor cafés, or perhaps just a little Viennese people-watching. Graben is the place to see and be seen, the street that has been the centre of urban life since Maria Theresa's time. The endless bustling parade of poseurs, entertainers, tourists and ordinary Viennese going about their lives in various degrees of harassment or peace creates an impressionistic sense of the city as a whole. As Robert Musil wrote of this town, "Cities, like people, can be recognised by their walk…he would know the place by the rhythm of movement in the streets long before he caught any characteristic detail."

Between twin fountains, dedicated to Saints Leopold and Joseph and built by Johann Martin Fischer in 1804, there stands the **Pestsäule**, or Plague Column, a monument particularly striking when lit at night. Emperor Leopold I had the column erected between 1682 and 1692 in fulfilment of a vow he had made during the epidemic of 1679. Johann Fischer von Erlach took charge of the unfinished project in 1687 and sculpted six reliefs around the base: Creation, Plague, the Passover, the Last Supper, the Great Flood and Pentecost. Lodovico Burnacini designed the Cloud Obelisk, which was completed by Paul Strudel with sculptures of allegorical figures of Faith vanquishing the plague, angels bearing inscriptions, a likeness of the emperor and the Holy Trinity.

The Haashaus.

The Graben eventually gives way to the Naglergasse, and it is at the end of this street that one finds the **Heidenschuss**, a short section of street whose name derives from a house that once stood here on the corner of the Strauchgasse. It supposedly belonged to a family by the name of Haiden (Haidenschuss means "where the Haiden live"). The relevant legend tells of a baker's apprentice in 1529 whose attentiveness enabled the city to repulse the Turks, who had advanced to this point by the use of mines. The figure of a Turkish rider on the façade recalls the incident.

BELOW: young Viennese shoppers.

Am Hof

Passing through the Heidenschuss brings you via Bognergasse to **Am Hof** ㉑. This used to be the square in front of a castle built by Heinrich II Jasomirgott in 1138, which became the residence of the Dukes of Austria from 1156 to 1220, and was later given over to the Royal Mint. Today the Bank of Austria has offices on the site, but the chapel of the Mint has become Am Hof (open Tues–Sun), a Gothic church with a splendid baroque façade added by Carlo Carlone in 1662. The paintings within include the mid-17th century *Flight into Egypt* and *Jesus in the Temple* by Joachim von Sandrart and a high altar adorned by *The Virgin with the Nine Choirs of Angels*, painted by Johann Georg Däringer in 1798. On Easter Sunday 1782, Pope Pius VI, wishing to encourage Emperor Joseph II to adopt policies more favourable to the

Church, blessed the people from the balcony of Am Hof. On 6 August 1806, from the same place, the dissolution of the Holy Roman Empire and the abdication of the imperial crown by Francis II was proclaimed.

At the far end of the square stands the **Feuerwehr Zentrale**, built in 1530 as a weapons store but now headquarters to the city's fire brigade, with the obligatory baroque façade (1731–2) with relief carvings by Lorenzo Mattielli. Their museum (open Sun and Fri 9am–noon; tel: 01-531 990; www.wien.gv.at) is also on this site.

Clocks and puppets

To the left of the Church Am Hof it is possible to walk through to the **Schulhof**, a small square of magnificent baroque houses. The **Uhrenmuseum** 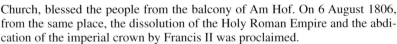 (Clock Museum; open Tues–Sun 10am–6pm; entrance charge, free Fri am and Sun; tel: 01-533 2265; www.wienmuseum.at), has an impressive 21,200-exhibit-strong collection, all beautifully displayed. It is adjacent to the **Puppen- und Spielzeug-museum** (Museum of Dolls and Toys; open Tues–Sun 10am–6pm; entrance charge; tel: 01-535 6860; www.puppenmuseumwien.com) which holds a large collection of imperial dolls, toy soldiers – including the obligatory Franz Joseph – and a thematically arranged selection of doll's houses.

The **Dokumantionsarchiv des österreichischen Widerstands** (Archive of Austrian Resistance; open Mon–Thur 9am–5pm; www.doew.at) is close by, set in the **Altes Rathaus**, Vienna's old town hall, on Wipplingerstrasse. The displays have now been updated with a broader exhibition acknowledging the rudimentary nature of resistance to the Nazis and tracing anti-Semitic tendencies to the period preceding Anschluss.

At the northern end of Wipplingerstrasse, is the **Börse**, Vienna's stock exchange. The building, remarkable for its brick-red façade, was constructed between 1871 and 1877 by the Danish architect Theophil Hansen. Underneath is a good restaurant (www.hansen.co.at).

Just off Wipplingerstrasse, between the Altes Rathaus and the Börse, is the important Gothic church of **Maria am Gestade** ❷ (http://maria-am-gestade. redemptoristen.at). Mentioned for the first time in 1158, Michael Chnab added the nave during 1394–1414. Between the nave and the choir is a pierced dome that is considered to be one of the finest surviving examples of Gothic art. Inside, there is a Gothic carving of the Angel of the Annunciation (1380) on the sixth pillar on the left, while the choir windows contain fine Gothic stained-glass panels.

The Schottenstift

Returning via Am Hof to Bognergasse and then proceeding northwest, you pass the **Harrach Palace**, today an auction house but once the residence of Count Harrach, built in the late 17th century and restored after World War II bombing with the aid of old etchings. Beyond lie the **Schottenstift** and **Schottenkirche** ❷ (Scottish Church), a church and Benedictine monastery built by Irish monks at the instigation of the Babenberg King Heinrich II Jasomirgott over the years 1155–1200. (The confusing appellation 'Scottish' derives from the 12th-century name for Ireland,

From Am Hof it is also possible to walk into the Judenplatz, via Drahtgasse, where one finds three of the most important, and contrasting, memorials to the Viennese Jewish community (see page 146), including a branch of the Jewish Museum set up to preserve the remains of a medieval synagogue.

BELOW: the beautifully decorated nave of the Schottenkirche.

Scotia minor.) The present-day baroque appearance derives, like so much in Vienna, from 17th-century rebuilding, in this case by the Allio and Carlone families; the later interior (1882–93) was supervised by Heinrich von Ferstel. A relief from 1893 on the south front of the church depicts the king approving the building plans.

Map on page 112

Within the church are a number of fine memorials, including one to Count Rüdiger von Starhemberg, defender of the city against the Turks in 1683. It dates back to 1725 and is the work of Josef Emanuel Fischer von Erlach. Von Starhemberg's tomb lies in the crypt with that of Heinrich II Jasomirgott himself. Also of note are a number of altar paintings, including Tobias Pock's 1655 *Martyrdom of St Sebastian* and *Assumption of the Blessed Virgin Mary*. On the triumphal arch we find Joachim von Sandrart's *Crucifiction* of 1654 and *Farewell of St Peter and St Paul*, from 1652.

In its centre of Hoher Markt is the baroque fountain, the Virgin's Wedding (1729–32), built by Josef Emanuel Fischer von Erlach to plans by his father.

The Schottenstift is the monastery adjoining the church. A 19th-century building, it now houses a notable **picture gallery** (open Thur–Sat 11am–5pm; entrance charge; tel: 01-5349 8600; www.schottenstift.at), of which the highlights are the Gothic paintings showing the earliest extant panoramas of Vienna. There is also a collection of 17th- and 18th-century landscapes, portraits and religious paintings.

Hoher Markt and the university

The southern end of Wipplingerstrasse runs into the **Hoher Markt**. Although its appearance does not suggest it, this is the oldest square in the city. This was the location of Vienna's Roman forum, the remains of which can be seen in the basement of No. 3 (open Tues–Sun 9am–1pm, 2–5pm; www.wienmuseum.at). Bauernmarkt runs across the southern end of the square. This narrow street is spanned by the **Ankeruhr**, a *Jungendstil* clock made between 1911–17. Every hour, for 12 hours, a figure from Austrian history appears and at noon, all the characters appear in procession.

BELOW: the art nouveau Ankeruhr.

Not far from the oldest square is the city's oldest church, the **Ruprechtskirche** (open Mon–Thur 10am–noon, Fri 10am–noon, 3–5pm; www.ruprechtskirche.at). Founded in 740, the oldest parts left standing are the Romanesque nave and the lower section of the tower; it also has some fine 13th-century stained glass.

Pass down Fleischmarkt, with Theophil Hansen's Byzantine-style **Griechenkirche** (Greek Church, 1858) and the beautifully restored central post office, to Schönlaterngasse and Sonnenfelsgasse. These are both lined with fine baroque town houses, some of which were part of the **Alte Universität** (Old University), the main building of which is on Dr Ignaz-Seipel-Platz. Facing the university building is its church, the highly ornate **Jesuitenkirche** (open daily 7am–7pm; www.jesuiten.at). The superb baroque interior has a virtuoso *trompe l'oeil* dome painted by Andrea Pozzo (1703–5).

Making your way east to the Stubenring you pass another baroque jewel, the **Dominikanerkirche** (www.kaisergruft.at), built in 1631–4. From here, taking the Dominikanerbastei, you arrive at Otto Wagner's modernist masterpiece, the **Postsparkasse** (Postal Savings Bank; *see page 98*). ❑

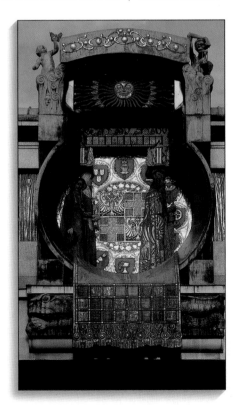

Sigmund Freud and Pyschology

Somewhat isolated from other must-sees on the Viennese museum circuit, the **Sigmund Freud Museum** (open daily, Oct–June 9am–5pm, July–Sept 9am–6pm; entrance charge; tel: 01-319 1596; www.freud-museum.at) lies some half-dozen blocks north of the Schottenstift. Schottentor underground station is the closest to the museum, which stands at Berggasse 19, Freud's former home and consulting rooms. The museum contains first editions, photographs and the various items of archaeological and ethnological art which furnished the original consulting rooms, although the famous couch itself was transported to London when he fled the Nazis, where it remains. Still, with Freud's hat, stick and flask sitting in the reproduction waiting rooms, one can daydream that the man himself has just returned from his lunchtime constitutional and is awaiting his next client. As the headquarters of the Sigmund Freud society, Berggasse 19 also houses an impressive archive, open to readers by appointment only.

Studies

Sigmund Freud (1856–1939), the eldest son of an itinerant Jewish textile merchant, was born in Moravia and brought to Vienna when he was three years old. The family settled in the Jewish quarter (the Leopoldstadt). Despite difficult financial circumstances, Freud's parents made sure he had a good education. At his Gymnasium, or high school, in the Taborstrasse, he became well-versed in Bildung, the culture of German humanism which embraced "the European family of high culture": Plato and Aristotle, Montaigne and Rousseau as well as Goethe, Schopenhauer and Schiller. This educational background served as a resource for young Sigmund, dismayed at anti-Semitic bullying of his father and other adult Jews: his childhood heroes included the historical fighting figures of Hannibal and Oliver Cromwell.

An outstanding student, Freud became a neuropathology Privatdozent (unsalaried lecturer) in 1885. He travelled to Paris to study under the famous Jean-Martin Charcot, who had pioneered the use of hypnosis in medicine. The encounter with Charcot marked the beginning of Freud's career as the explorer of the unconscious and of therapies to deal with psychological disorders. Back in Vienna, Freud worked with Josef Breuer on hysteria but was subject to the opposition of numerous rivals, and was forced by financial circumstances to work as a physician rather than pursue his research interests. It was in these years, however, that Freud was able to engage in an extended self-analysis, which provided the basis of his theories about infantile sexuality, above all the famous "Oedipus complex."

The Interpretation of Dreams

When the pioneering *Interpretation of Dreams* finally appeared in 1900, including the first full account of Freud's theories in its final chapter, it went largely unnoticed. Freud did

LEFT: the consulting room in Freud's house on Berggasse, now a museum.

not even receive an associate professorship until two years later, at the age of 45. Sardonically he commented to a friend: "The public enthusiasm is immense. Congratulations and bouquets keep pouring in, as if the role of sexuality had been suddenly recognised by His Majesty, the interpretation of dreams confirmed by the Council of Ministers, and the necessity of the psychoanalytic therapy of hysteria carried by a two-thirds majority in Parliament."

Marginalisation

The ironic references to Austrian imperial politics are as telling as any material investigated by psychoanalysis: the discipline's roots were firmly entwined with the culture of Austria's capital at the turn of the century. As a Viennese Jew in the era of rising anti-Semitism, Freud found himself increasingly marginalised and powerless. By unseating the conscious will from its throne in human psychology, he was making as dramatic a claim as Copernicus' that the Earth was not the centre of the universe, or Darwin's that the human race had come to exist in its present form thanks to evolution rather than divine ordination. Conscious, political authority was made to bow down before sexual desire and the power of dreams, albeit only rhetorically. At the same time, Freud's focus on human sexuality coincided with the *fin-de-siècle* Viennese licentiousness expressed in the writings of Arthur Schnitzler, an author, fellow doctor and contemporary of Freud. Freud remarked that Schnitzler knew by instinct what he himself discovered through empirical enquiry. But just as Schnitzler was pilloried for his candour, so Freud was often lambasted by his colleagues. In 1910 a fellow doctor denounced him at a medical congress with the claim: "Freud's theories have nothing to do with science; they are rather a matter for the police."

His legacy

Today, psychology and psychotherapy have evolved beyond these 19th-century influences, and while psychoanalysis continues to be practised, it is perhaps its legacy, the notion of the unconscious, rather than its existence in its own right, which forms Freud's bequest to the "life of the mind" in the present day. Studies of Freud today emphasise his position as an assimilated Jew in the urban culture which bred both arch-Zionist Theodor Herzl and anti-Semite Karl Lueger. The often forgotten late work *Moses and Monotheism*, exploring Jewish heritage from Biblical times, is but one example of the master psychoanalyst's concern with this issue. The book appeared in 1934 as National Socialism rose in Germany; only four years later, Freud himself was hounded from Austria, dying in London exile in 1939.

At the end of Vienna's Himmelstrasse, overlooking the Wienerwald, a plaque commemorates the site where, "on July 24th 1895, the secret of dreams revealed itself to Dr Sigm. Freud." Visitors should not allow themselves to be seduced by the seeming modesty of this memorial: although it was erected in 1977, Freud himself had enjoyed a megalomaniac fantasy about such a plaque in a letter he wrote to a friend at the time. ❑

RIGHT: Sigmund with that classic Freudian symbol, the cigar.

Map on pages 134–5

BEYOND THE RINGSTRASSE

Outside of Vienna's Innere Stadt are some of the city's greatest museums, galleries and palaces, as well as parks, wine villages and the United Nations

The Ringstrasse is one of the defining features of Vienna, the wide boulevard encircling the old city. Its design symbolises the liberal aspirations of the post-revolutionary *Gründerzeit*, with each building standing for the public values of education, democracy and culture, and the whole concept derived from Hausmann's progressive vision of Paris – even if it did conveniently allow troops to easily control crowds during demonstrations. This somewhat paternalistic project served not only to modernise Viennese public life and, of course, its traffic flow (still disconcerting for the present-day tourist who inadvertently steps out between an unstoppable tram and a speeding Audi), but perhaps it also changed the city's psychology: Freud used to walk the 5-km (3-mile) circuit in his lunch hour before returning to clinical work analysing his fellow *Wiener*. For those unwilling to emulate his habit, two trams, Nos 1 and 2, run clockwise and anti-clockwise respectively around the Ring.

BELOW: the statue of Pallas-Athene outside the Parlament.

The Kunsthistorisches and Naturhistorisches Museums

Northwest of the Burggarten is the jewel in the crown of Viennese museums, the **Kunsthistorisches Museum ❶** (Museum of Art History; open Tues, Wed, Fri–Sun 10am–6pm; Thur 10am–9pm; entrance charge; tel: 01-525 240; www.khm.at). A stellar array of famous artists worked together on the ornamentation of the interior, a stunning arrangement of marble, murals and stucco: Viktor Tilgner, Hans Makart, Michael Munkácsy, Ernst and Gustav Klimt and Franz Matsch were just some those involved. The huge collection of paintings, applied arts and archaeological artefacts can be overwhelming, and the museum is best seen over a couple of visits, rather than in one go – but, then again, you could always break for coffee in the museum café, which is run by former imperial court confectioners Demel.

The **Egyptian and Near Eastern Collections** are to the right of the main entrance. The newly renovated galleries offer a well-laid-out selection of Egyptian artefacts stretching from prehistory into the Christian era, including papyrus Books of the Dead and a reconstruction of a chamber from the pyramid of Cheops at Giza. The famous faïence model of a hippopotamus, something of a signature image for the museum gift shop, also rests here. **Greek and Roman Antiquities** include Germanic jewellery from the Time of the Great Migration and a cameo commemorating the Emperor Augustus. The **Kunstkammer** (the Gallery of Sculpture and Decorative Arts) is currently closed.

The first floor of the KHM plays host to the world-class **collection of paintings** housed here. Room X is the most popular in the museum, holding the world's largest collection of works by **Pieter Breugel the Elder** (1526–69): landscapes such as *Hunters in the Snow* (1565) sit alongside the fantastic *Tower of Babel* (1563) and the exuberant interpretations of village life in works like *Children's Games* (1559) and *The Battle Between Carnival and Lent* (also 1559), with its captivating Bosch-like grotesques.

The collection of works by **Velázquez** (1599–1660) is almost as stunning, being one of the best outside Spain itself. It includes portraits of the *Infanta Margarita Isolde* (1653–9), *Philip IV of Spain* (1632), the *Infanta Maria Theresa* (1652–3) and *The Infante Felipe Próspero* (1659). **Titian** (1487–1576) is represented by a number of pieces including *Ecce Homo* (1543) and *Woman in Furs* (1535); **Rembrandt** by a sequence of moving self-portraits (1652–7) and one of his son *Titus* (1656). **Cranach**'s *Paradise* (1530), *Judith with the Head of Holofernes* (1530), and *Three Princesses* (1535) are here, as are **Holbein** portraits including those of *Jane Seymour* (1536–7) and *Dr John Chambers* (1543).

Raphael's *Madonna of the Meadows* (1505–6) is one of the gallery's most significant works, although there are also important collections of **Van Dyck** (*Portrait of a Man*, 1620–1; *Painting of an Old Woman*, 1634) and **Dürer** (*Maria with a Child at Her Breast*, 1503, *Martyrdom of the 10,000 Christians*, 1508, the *Landauer Altar*, 1511), as well as no less than three rooms of **Rubens**. **Vermeer**'s *The Artist's Studio* (1665–6) is here, too, as are **Caravaggio**'s *Christ with the Crown of Thorns* (1603–4), *Madonna of the Rosary* and *David with the Head of Goliath* (both 1606–7).

The geological galleries in the Naturhistorisches Museum

Opposite the KHM lies the **Naturhistorisches Museum ❷** (open Thur-Mon 9am–6.30pm; Wed 9am–9pm; entrance charge; tel: 01-521 77; www.nhm-wien.ac.at), intended to complement the art-historical focus of its twin. The collections are massive and incorporate material from animal and plant exhibits to anthropological displays via a vast geological collection. Modernisation and redesign are making this notoriously outdated museum much more accessible, especially for children, but also taking some of the musty, dusty charm out of an institution which until relatively recently still labelled former imperial lands as Austrian possessions and lacked electric lighting in some of its sections.

BELOW: Raphael's *Madonna of the Meadows*.

The MuseumsQuartier.

The recently opened **MuseumsQuartier ❸**, which lies to the west of the Museums of Art and Natural History, is a vast cultural complex encompassing galleries, museums and performance spaces. A central visitor and ticket centre serves all of the institutions within (open daily 10am–7pm; www.mqw.at), which include the exhibition spaces of the **Architekturzentrum Wien** (Vienna Architectural Centre; open Thur–Tues 10am–7pm, Wed 10am–9pm; www.azw.at) and the **Kunsthalle Wien** (open Fri–Wed 10am–7pm, Thur 10am–10pm; www.kunsthallewien.at) in addition to the performance space of the Tanzquartier (www.tqw.at). Experimental media projects operate out of the site and a variety of shops, boutiques and cafés populate the "quartier 21" complex that faces Museumsplatz. These include the Lomo Shop; Lomography is a bizarre photographic movement started by two Viennese art students (*see* www.lomography.com) .

Parents and carers of young children will appreciate the Quartier's ZOOM **Kindermuseum** (Children's Museum; open Mon–Fri 8am–4pm, Sat and Sun 9.30am–3.30pm; entrance charge; tel: 01-524 7908; www.kindermuseum.at), which offers a wide variety of interactive learning and play exhibits, but booking is required. The key attractions of the MuseumsQuartier, however, are the galleries of the MUMOK and Leopold Museum.

The collection of MUMOK (Museum of Modern Art; open Tues, Wed, Fri–Sun 10am-6pm, Thur 10am–9pm; entrance charge; tel: 01-525 00; www.mumok.at) ranges from from Kandinsky (*Obstinate*, 1933) to Roy Lichtenstein (*Red Horseman*, 1974) with a special emphasis on the Viennese Actionists, 1960s avant-gardists who sought to provoke staid post-war Austria under the *Sozialpartnerschaft*.

The **Leopold Museum** (open Wed, Fri–Mon 10am–7pm, Thur 10am–9pm; entrance charge; tel: 01-525 700; www.leopoldmuseum.org) also addresses 20th-century art, along with some pieces from the 19th century. The museum is based around the collection of Rudolf and Elizabeth Leopold, and in addition to holding important works of Austrian art, there are various non-Western items, including 19th-century Japanese prints and masks from Guinea. Nonetheless the main attraction consists of the displays of Austrian work from the last century. *Jugendstil* and Secession-era work is exhibited on the ground floor, including Klimt's *Death and Life* (1911–15), and Moser's sketch for the angel window at the Am Steinhof church *(see page 148)*. The building's top floor includes some real gems of Expressionist and inter-war painting, notably by Schiele, Kokoschka and Max Oppenheimer.

North of the Ringstrasse

North along the Ringstrasse is Theophil Hansen's **Parlament** building (1873–83). Staunchly neoclassical and liberally provided with columns, friezes and statues, in front of the building is Karl Kundmann's **Pallas-Athene-Brunnen** (Pallas-Athena fountain) surrounded by river

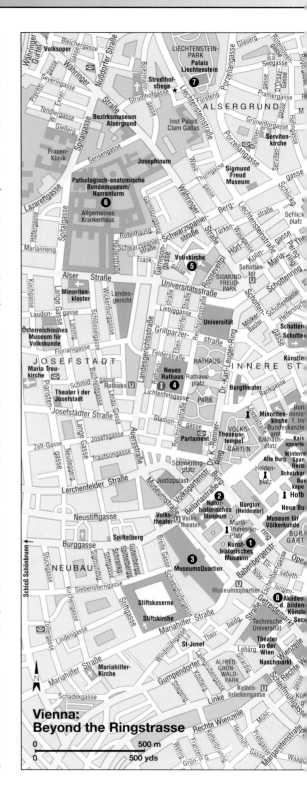

**Vienna:
Beyond the Ringstrasse**

0   500 m

0   500 yds

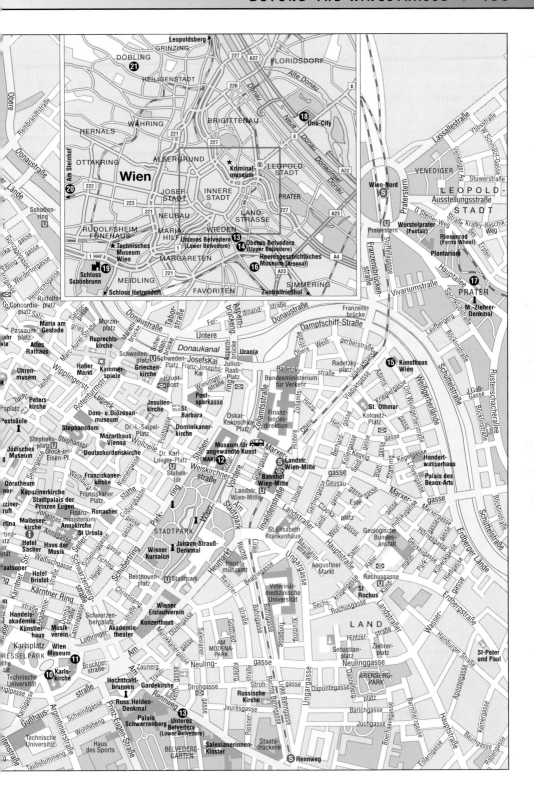

RIGHT: the grey slate façade of MUMOK.

deities depicting the Danube, Elbe, Inn and Vltava. By contrast, and almost next door, Vienna's **Neues Rathaus** ❹ (New Town Hall) is a neo-Gothic confection. Built in 1872–83 to a design by Friedrich von Schmidt, it too has a series of sculptures on its façade, these ones depicting seminal figures from Austrian history. Rathausplatz in front of the imposing building is the location of an ice rink in winter, and a Christmas market during December, while during the summer a large screen is erected to show films of operas and concerts.

Continuing the Gothic theme is the **Votivkirche** ❺ (open Tues–Sat 9am–1pm, 4–6.30pm, Sun 9am–1.30pm; www.votivkirche.at), which lies to the north of the Rathaus on Rooseveltplatz. Built in 1856–79, it commemorates a failed attempt on the life of Franz Joseph in 1853. A superb example of neo-Gothic architecture, the dark interior is very atmospheric. The church's small museum contains the ornately carved 15th-century **Antwerp Altar** (open Tues–Fri 4–6pm, Sat 10am–1pm; entrance charge).

The **Pathologisch-anatomische Bundesmuseum** ❻ (the Museum of Pathological Anatomy; open Wed 3–6pm, Thur 8–11am, 1st Sat in the month 10am–1pm; entrance charge; tel: 01-406 8672; www.narrenturm.info) is located on the Spitalgasse. This lies on the site of the former city hospital, within the Narrenturm, or Fools' Tower, in which the mentally ill were interned in the late 18th and early 19th centuries. Nowadays the museum seems determined to rival the Kriminalmuseum *(see page 145)* in displaying the most horrific and provocative exhibits.

To the north of the Ringstrasse (take tram D to Porzellangasse) is the **Liechtenstein Museum** ❼ (open Fri–Mon 10am–5pm; entrance charge; tel: 01-319 576 7252; www.liechtensteinmuseum.at). Lying on Fürstengasse, this was the garden palace of the princes of Liechtenstein. Now beautifully restored, the build-

ing itself is a museum of the baroque, with frescoes by Rottmayr above the staircases and well-preserved stuccowork. The private collection is exceptionally fine, including Italian and northern European Gothic, Renaissance and baroque works, but above all an excellent array of paintings by Rubens.

Map on pages 134–5

Karlsplatz

Moving south from the MuseumsQuartier, beyond the Opernring, is **Die Gemäldegalerie Akademie der bildende Künste** ❽ (Picture Gallery of the Academy of Fine Arts; open Tues–Sun 10am–6pm; entrance charge; tel 01-5881 6225; www.akademiegalerie.at). This small but wonderful collection includes Hieronymous Bosch's powerful, terrifying triptych of *The Last Judgement*, as well as a number of Flemish and Dutch works, including sketches by Rubens. The students' pinboard on the ground floor is a good place to look for avant-garde cultural events, and in the Schillerplatz, the pleasant, placid square on which the building stands, the benches are often covered with stickers promoting the art students' latest radical movement.

To the rear of the Academy of Fine Arts is one of Vienna's most iconic pieces of architecture, the **Secession Building** ❾ (open Fri–Tues 10am–6pm, Thur 10am–8pm; admission charge; tel: 01-5875 36721; www.secession.at). The building, designed and built by Joseph Olbrich in 1897–8, was conceived as a "temple to art" and as the home of the Secessionist painters who had broken away from the conservative Künstlerhaus *(see page 97)*. It now functions as an exhibition space for contemporary art, while downstairs is Klimt's *Beethoven Frieze*, painted for the 14th Secession exhibition in 1902. A further space for contemporary art is the glass **Kunsthalle Project Space** (open Sun and Mon 1–7pm, Tues–Sat 4pm–midnight; www.kunsthallewien.at), just across from the Secession in Resselpark on Karlsplatz.

At the far end of Karlsplatz is one of Vienna's finest churches, the **Karlskirche** ❿ (open Mon–Sat 9am–12.30pm, 1–6pm, Sun 1–6pm; entrance charge; www.karlskirche.at). The building of this highly classicised baroque church was begun by Johann Bernard Fischer von Erlach in 1716 and completed by his son, Josef Emmanuel in 1737. It was built to commemorate a plague that hit the city in 1713. Flanked by two heroic columns (modelled on those of Trajan and Marcus Aurelius in Rome), and with a strictly classical façade, the greatest glory of the church is perhaps the dome frescoes, painted by Rottmayr in 1725–30.

The renovated **Wien Museum Karlsplatz** ⓫ (previously the Museum of the City of Vienna; open Tues–Sun 9am–6pm; entrance charge; tel: 01-5058 7470; www.wienmuseum.at) is sometimes overlooked but it includes significant memorabilia including Wiener Werkstätte pieces, reconstructions of interiors from famous city apartments and notable Viennese works of art.

To the north is the **Musikverein** (tours Fri–Mon, Wed, usually at 1.30pm; entrance charge; tel: 01-505 8190; www.musikverein.at). This is the home of the Wiener Philharmoniker, who perform in the gilded Grosse Saal, famous for its acoustic; chamber concerts take place in the smaller Brahms-Saal.

Opposite the Musikverein are Otto Wagner's two art nouveau Karlsplatz U-bahn pavilions built from 1899 to 1901. Neither are now used as an entry to the underground; one is a café, the other a temporary exhibition space.

BELOW: a quiet moment in the Leopold Museum.

MAK (Museum für Angewandte Kunst)

The MAK  (Applied Arts Museum; open Wed–Sun 10am–6pm, Tues 10am–midnight; entrance charge, free on Sat; tel: 01-711 360; www.mak.at) is opposite the Stadtpark. One of the most exciting museums in the city, its unfaced brick exterior, built by Heinrich von Ferstel between 1868 and 1871, has been completely renovated, with a modern extension. Within, familiar artefacts – chairs, ceramics and carpets – are showcased in a variety of rooms which were each given over to the vision of a different contemporary artist at the time of the 1993 refurbishment. The wide range of approaches to design and curating gives an added edge to the already eclectic variety of arts and crafts on display here. Particularly noteworthy are the featured products of the Wiener Werkstätte and the collection of baroque and rococo glass.

The Unteres Belvedere

To the south-east of the city centre lies the **Belvederegarten** (open Apr–July daily 10am–6pm weather permitting), incorporating the botanical gardens of the city university. The Unteres und Oberes Belvedere (Lower and Upper Belvedere; open Tues–Sun 10am–6pm; Oberes Belvedere until 8pm Thur; entrance charge; tel: 01-795 570; www.belvedere.at), to the north and south of this park respectively, form one of the most striking places to visit in Vienna. Originally the baroque summer palace of renowned military commander Prince Eugene of Savoy, the buildings now house three highly recommended museums: the Baroque Museum, the Austrian Gallery, and the Museum of the Art of the Middle Ages.

In Prince Eugene's time, the **Unteres Belvedere** ⓫ housed the living quarters. Built 1714–16, highlights include a two-storey marble hall, decorated with stucco reliefs and statues and bearing on its ceiling a fresco, the work of Martino Altomonte, depicting Prince Eugene's victory at Peterwardein in 1714, with Apollo and the nine muses watching over the Austrian general. In the prince's sleeping quarters next door, another Altomonte fresco depicts Luna and Endymion, Daphne and – again – Apollo, who was the favoured figure for allegorical reference to Prince Eugene.

Today the Lower Belvedere is home to the **Barock Museum**, a collection of Austrian painting and sculpture from the baroque, including artists such as Franz Anton Maulbertsch, Daniel Gran and Peter Strudel. The strange, grimacing busts of sculptor Franz Xavier Messerschmidt rest in the appropriately named Hall of the Grotesques. Balthasar Permoser's statue, *The Apotheosis of Prince Eugene*, stands in the highly ornate Goldkabinett, a cabinet of mirrors decorated in 23-carat rococo gilt.

Adjoining the Lower Belvedere is the former Orangery, now the **Museum Mittelalterliche Kunst** (Museum of Art in the Middle Ages). Covering art of the Romanesque and late Gothic periods, particularly outstanding among its collection are Conrad Laib's 1449 *Crucifixion* and *The Mystical Marriage of St Catherine of Alexandria* (1380–90) by the Master of Heiligenkreuz. There are also a series of works by Michael Pacher.

The Wiener Werkstätte ('Vienna Workshops', 1903-32) were a firm founded in the collaboration of an architect, Joseph Hoffmann, a designer, Kolo Moser, and a textile merchant, Fritz Wärndorfer. From fashion to furniture, jewellery to interiors, for almost thirty years the Wiener Werkstätte produced innovative designs.

BELOW: "To each age its art, to art its freedom" proclaimed on the Secession building.

South of the Unteres Belvedere lies the magnificent park itself. Laid out between 1700 and 1725 by Dominique Girard, it conforms to classical French style and is decorated by fountains, pools, little waterfalls and avenues bordered by trimmed hedges.

Map on pages 134–5

The Oberes Belvedere

At the end of the terrace lies the **Oberes Belvedere ⓮**, regarded widely as the greatest masterpiece of its architect, Johann Lukas von Hildebrandt. Completed over the years 1721–3, its interior was designed by Claude le Fort du Plessy, while the stucco work is that of Santino Bussi. The ceiling fresco *Apollo and Aurora* in the Garden Room to the right of the entrance hall is by Carlo Carlone. The central hall on the upper floor, its walls clad in red marble, hosted the signing of the Austrian State Treaty on 15 May 1955. Carlone frescos also adorn this room *(The Allegory of Fame)* and the dome in the palace chapel *(God the Father with the Holy Ghost)*.

The Oberes Belvedere today houses the **Österreichische Galerie** (Austrian Gallery), a stunning collection of 19th- and 20th-century painting. Of the neoclassical works, the portraits by Angelica Kaufmann are particularly fine; Romanticism is well represented by the landscapes of Casper David Friedrich, but the most famous works here are those of Gustav Klimt, notably *The Kiss*, *Avenue in the Park at Schloss Kammer* and *Farmhouse in Upper Austria*. Klimt's contemporaries Oskar Kokoschka *(Still Life with Dead Mutton)* and Egon Schiele *(The Family)* are also here. There are also some superb French Impressionist canvases, including Renoir's *After the Bath* and *Bather with Loose Blond Hair*, and Monet's *Anglers on the Seine at Poissy* and *Pathway in the Garden at Giverny*.

Klimt's Stoclet Frieze *from the collections of the* MAK.

BELOW: the glorious Oberes Belvedere.

Hundertwasser and military history

To the east of the Belvedere, on the junction of Löwengasse and Kegelgasse, is the **Hundertwasserhaus** (signposted from Rochusgasse U-bahn station; www.hundertwasserhaus.at). These council flats were designed and built by Friedensreich Hundertwasser in 1983–5. His trademark colourful surface decoration can also be seen at the **Kunsthaus Wien** ⓯ (www.kunsthauswien.com) a gallery dedicated to his life and works. The building was once the factory of Thonet, known for their ground-breaking bentwood furniture.

The **Heeresgeschichtliches Museum** ⓰ (Museum of Military History; open Sat–Thur 9am–5pm; entrance charge; tel: 01-795 610; www.hgm.or.at) also lies in the 3rd district, within the Arsenal, one of the barracks built in the city as a counter-revolutionary move in the wake of 1848. Military paraphernalia here ranges from 17th-century trophies of the Turkish defeat to 20th-century armoured vehicles; of particular morbid note is the tunic of Franz Ferdinand, stained with blood from his assassination.

The Zentralfriedhof

To the south of the city lies the vast **Zentralfriedhof**. Laid out in 1874, this cemetery is the largest in Austria, covering some 243 hectares (600 acres). Harry Lime may not really be buried here, but almost every other resident of note is. The sector devoted to illustrious figures lies at the main entrance, Gate No. 2. Politicians buried here range from "der schöne Karl" ("handsome Karl"), the anti-Semitic mayor whose mausoleum has its own church (built 1910), to Socialist chancellor Bruno Kreisky (1911–90). Writers include Karl Kraus (1874–1936), Arthur Schnitzler (1862–1931), Johann Nestroy (1801–62) and Anton Wildgans (1881–1932); actors range from Hans Moser (1880– 1964) to Curt Jürgens (1915–1982); amongst the many composers are Christoph Willibald Gluck (1714–87), Ludwig van Beethoven (1770–1827), Franz Schubert (1797–1828), Josef Lanner (1801–43), Johann Strausses Elder and Younger (1804–49 and 1825–99 respectively), Johannes Brahms (1833–97), Hugo Wolf (1860–1903) and Arnold Schoenberg (1874–1951), the latter buried under a striking monument created by sculptor Fritz Wotruba. Even Mozart (1756–91) has a monument, although he was actually buried in a pauper's grave at the **St Marxer Friedhof** (Leberstrasse 6–8): a statue of an angel in mourning there marks the supposed resting place.

The Prater

The **Prater** ⓱, an enormous area of parkland, lies east of the city centre across the Donaukanal, and extends southwards from the **Praterstern**. The name, for foreign visitors, is often largely synonymous with the Wurstelprater (open 15 Mar–31 Oct daily 10am–midnight; www.prater.at), the famous amusement park which forms just one element of Vienna's largest outdoor leisure site. The **Grüner Prater** is an extensive nature park with spacious meadows, streams, and clumps of trees. Here, in contrast to the gaudy funfair, one understands how the Austrian *Prater* was derived from the Spanish *prado*, or meadow, in the time of the Habsburgs. Until the intervention of Joseph II in 1766, the area had been reserved for members of the court and aristocracy. With these privileges abolished, the park became welcoming and positively invited the public to take a leisurely walk: the Hauptallee, or main avenue, nearly 5km (3 miles) long and dating back to the reign of Ferdinand I, is bordered by chestnut trees which are particularly beautiful in May, when they are in flower. There are also various wine and beer taverns and cafés for those in need of refreshment.

The **Kriminalmuseum** (open Thur–Sun 10am–5pm; entrance charge; tel: 01-214 2678; www.kriminalmuseum.at) on Grosse Sperlgasse, perhaps understandably for a city as safe as this, demonstrates a dark fascination with the evil-doers of the imperial and post-imperial past. The displays, detailing the most bizarre and scandalous cases from Austrian criminal history, are often in German, and photographs from crime scenes and executions are gruesome, bordering on the disturbing – not for children or the squeamish.

Vienna International Centre and the Donau

East of the city centre is the **Donaukanal**: this channel is only one of three bearing the name of the Donau (Danube). A variety of flood defence measures since the mid-19th century have created three parallel channels: the canal, the Alte Donau, and the Neue Donau. The sliver of land between the New and Old Danubes, the **Donauinsel**, 40km (25 miles) in length, has been transformed into a sister park to the Prater. Cyclists and roller-bladers come here for exercise, and you will also find picnickers, bathers and nudists colonising the island.

Peering over at this scene of pastoral delight are the grey towers of **UNO-City** ⑬, the Vienna International Centre. It hosts the International Atomic Energy Agency, United Nations Industrial Development Organisation, the

Map on pages 134–5

*The landmark **Riesenrad** (big wheel, built in 1897; www.wienerriesenrad. com), famous for its appearance in* The Third Man, *is the last remaining example of a series erected by Walther Basset. Vienna's wheel slowly takes you 64m (210ft) off the ground, offering a magnificent view of the city; rides last approximately 20 minutes.*

BELOW: UNO-City.

*Ascending the Schönbrunn Hill, you will finally reach the **Gloriette**. The colonnade (1775) was intended as a memorial to the soldiers who had fallen for the imperial court. It offers a stunning panorama of the city of Vienna. To the east of the Gloriette proper lies the Little Gloriette, with wall paintings by Paccassi.*

BELOW: a buccolic afternoon on the Donauinsel.

Nuclear Test Ban Treaty Commission, and UN offices for everything from Drugs and Crime to Outer Space Affairs. The building of UNO-City by Johann Staber between 1973 and 1979 was part of Bruno Kreisky's programme to internationalise and revitalise the city, and almost brought Vienna to bankruptcy. Thankfully the city's finances survived and the UN has since provided a much-needed regular source of income – at times, the sheer numbers of conference and diplomatic visitors can almost overwhelm hotels and restaurants, a problem worth bearing in mind for the tourist and traveller. Guided tours are available (Mon–Sat from 9.30am; entrance charge; tel: 01-2606 03328; www.unis.unvienna.org): security has always been tight, as might be expected of the third seat of the United Nations, and visitors should always bring a passport; fear of terrorist action may bring further restrictions on entry to the centre in the future.

Schloss Schönbrunn

Schloss Schönbrunn  (open daily, April–June, Sept and Oct 8.30am–5pm; July–Aug 8.30am–6pm; Nov–Mar 8.30am–4.30pm; entrance charge; tel: 01-8111 3239; www.schoenbrunn.at), favourite residence of the Imperial family, lies about 6km (4 miles) from the city centre. Take the U4 underground line to Schönbrunn or Hietzing. The Kattermühle (mill) that originally stood on the site was mentioned in records for the first time in 1311. A castle, the Katterburg, was added in 1471, and in 1568 the property passed to Maximilian II, who had it converted into a hunting lodge and later added a zoo. In 1619 Emperor Matthew was credited with the discovery of a "beautiful spring" – *schöner Brunnen* – whilst hunting. This supplied the palace's water needs until the end of the 18th century. The hunting lodge was destroyed by the Turks in 1683 and a grandiose new palace, intended to outshine Versailles, was designed by Johann Bernhard Fischer von Erlach. It was to have been built on the Gloriette Hill, but costly military campaigns thwarted the project. A less elaborate building in which Joseph I (1705–11) stayed was completed by 1700.

Joseph's successor Charles VI neglected the building, and it was not until the reign of Empress Maria Theresa (1740–80) that the Schönbrunn was completed. In 1744 she commissioned Nicolaus Paccassi to rebuild and extend the palace, which was completed in 1750. It took a further 15 years for the interior to be finished in accordance with Paccassi's design. The initial layout for the park was designed by Jean Trehet in 1705–6, but the present appearance dates from Ferdinand von Hohenberg's designs of 1753–75. The Neptune fountain was added in 1780.

Every one of Schönbrunn's 1441 rooms and halls were needed to maintain the court. Some 390 of these were residential apartments and audience chambers; there were 139 kitchens. Almost 1,000 people lived in the vast complex, which together with its park covers 176 hectares (435 acres). When Napoleon I occupied Vienna in 1805–6 he used the palace as his headquarters, and when the map of Europe was redrawn at the end of the Napoleonic wars, the Schönbrunn played host to the Congress of Vienna in 1815. Emperor Franz Joseph I was born here and died here in 1916. Here, too, Karl I renounced his right to rule in 1918, mark-ng the end of the monarchy. Even then the palace's association with international ower politics had not fully come to an end: in 1961 it hosted a summit between he then-leaders of the USA and USSR, Kennedy and Khruschev.

Map on pages 134–5

The palace

The palace itself is 175 m (574 ft) long and 55 metres (180 ft) wide, the entire edifice painted in a distinctive shade of yellow to which it lent its name, *Schön-runnergelb*. On the courtyard and garden side it boasts two similar, richly decorated baroque façades. Two staircases bordered by rococo balustrades lead up to the balcony terraces, situated above a carriage thoroughfare with five magnificent wrought-iron gateways. The hall, decorated with two statue groups portraying Hercules (*circa* 1700, by Adrian de Vries), leads on the right to the sleeping quarters, with a large number of fine works of art.

Ascending the Blue Staircase, with an 18th-century ceiling painting depicting the apotheosis of Joseph I, you will reach the rooms open to the public. Of particular interest are: the Death Chamber of Franz Josef, the Hall of Mirrors (in which Mozart, six years old, performed for Maria Theresa), the Chinese Round Cabinet (conference room for the Empress and her Chancellor of State), the Great Gallery and the Small Gallery, adorned with ceiling paintings by Gregorio Gugliemi, *The Seven Years War* and *The Clement Rule of Maria Theresa* (1759–61). Other rooms worth visiting are the Napoleon Room, recalling the era of Napoleonic occupation, the Gobelin Room which hosts a number of tapestries, and Maria Theresa's private salon, the Room of Millions – overwhelming in its ornamentation. The Bergl-Zimmer are elaborately decorated rooms with *trompe l'oeil* landscape paintings, the work of Johann Bergl (1780), but are subject to restricted access. The Palace

Baroque statuary on the Schönbrunn's Gloriette.

BELOW: the Schönbrunn.

BELOW: in the Schönbrunn gardens.

Chapel (also entry by appointment only) includes a high altar adorned with *The Marriage of the Virgin Mary* painted by Paul Troger and Raphael Donner's relief of *The Suffering Madonna*. The altar itself is by Franz Kohl.

In front of the palace is the 24,000 sq. m (260,000 sq. ft) courtyard. The main gateway is flanked by two obelisks, and was given French imperial eagles after Napoleon's victory of 1809. On the right is the Schönbrunn Court Theatre, a rococo edifice fitted out by Ferdinand von Hohenberg in 1766–7. The two large fountains in the courtyard depict allegorical versions of the empire's rivers, the Danube, Inn and Ems, and its subject nations, Transylvania, Galicia and Lodomeria. The nearby **Wagenburg** contains a large collection of imperial coaches, state carriages, sedan chairs and sledges from 1690 to 1917.

The **Neptune Fountain** by Franz Anton Zauner (1780) lies at the far side of the flower beds from the palace, flanked by rows of statues. To its left is von Hohenberg's mock Roman Ruin, dating from 1778. It was completed a year after the obelisk, a pastiche like the Roman Ruin, whose hieroglyphics depict scenes from the history of the Habsburg family. Not far from the obelisk lies the *schöner Brunnen* itself, surrounded by a pavilion built in 1779.

At the foot of the Schönbrunn Hill lies the **Tiergarten** (zoo). Extensively modernised only the original central pavilion (1752) remains, now as a café. Although, as in most zoos, the animals are unhappy, its aquarium, with a "walk through" flooded Amazon rain-forest and a spectacular coral reef, is worth a visit.

The outskirts

The **Technisches Museum Wien** (open Mon–Fri 9am–6pm, Sat and Sun 10am–6pm; entrance charge; tel: 01-8999 86000; www.tmw.at), Vienna Technical Museum, is just to the north of the Schönbrunn, at Mariahilfer Strasse 212. This newly renovated, child-friendly museum pays tribute to the empire's quite astonishing number of engineers and inventors.

Visitors who have made it to Schönbrunn should also take the opportunity to visit Schloss Hetzendorf and Am Steinhof, worthwhile stops only a short distance from the palace. Lying to the south of Schönbrunn, **Schloss Hetzendorf** is a former hunting lodge, built in 1694 but redesigned in 1743 and now host to the Vienna School of Fashion. The collection of 19th- and 20th-century clothing, numbering some 18,000 items, including hats, handbags, and jewellery is open in part to the public, as is the 12,000 volume library (open Mon–Fri 7.30am–3.30pm; entrance charge; tel: 01-804 2795; www.modeschulewien.at)

The church **Am Steinhof** ❷⓿ (tours Sat 3pm only; entrance charge; tel: 01-91060 11204; www.wienkav.at), located in the psychiatric hospital grounds also close by, is one of the crowning achievements of Viennese art nouveau and also a humane and pioneering piece of institutional design which put the needs of its patients and clients at its heart. Built 1904–7 in accordance with the visions of Otto Wagner (he even designed special robes for its priests), the building's unique character is highlighted by its unmistakable copper cupola, white marble cladding and *Jugendstil* statuary *(see page 106)*.

Döbling

Map on pages 134–5

Lying on Vienna's outskirts, the widely-spread region of **Döbling** ㉑ is one of the most attractive areas of the city. It falls into the outer metropolitan districts, but also marks the beginning of the forests and vineyards that make up the **Wienerwald** (Vienna Woods). Most of the villages that now form the XIX district of the city can trace their origins back to the 11th and 12th centuries. From the reign of Maria Theresa, these former wine-growing villages were popular summer retreats for Viennese society.

The most famous district in Döbling is **Grinzing**. Known as the archetypical *Heurige* village, it overflows with tourists as a result. For the best *Heurigen*, avoid those with coaches parked outside and head for the sign of the *Buschen*, a green Scots pine, over the entrance. Nestling between gardens and vineyards are houses dating back to the 16th and 17th centuries.

Sievering is another wine-growing village of the district. Its parish church was built in the 14th century, although the interior largely dates from the 18th. Those on a Beethoven pilgrimage may wish to visit **Heiligenstadt**, the oldest of Döbling's wine-growing villages, a place where Beethoven often stayed and where he wrote the *Heiligenstadt Testament*, a bitter complaint about his incipient deafness. A memorial to the composer dating from 1862 exists along the Beethovengang in this village; the **Heiligenstädter-Testament-Haus** (open Tues–Sun 10am–1pm, 2pm–6pm; entrance charge; www.wienmuseum.at) includes various exhibits such as Beethoven's death mask.

Another figure from the history of music remembered in Döbling is Emanuel Schikaneder, librettist of Mozart's *Magic Flute*. He lived in **Nussdorf** from 1802 to 1807. The **Palais Schickaneder** is just one of the charming 18th century buildings in this ancient village, including a baroque parish church on the Greinergasse. Nussdorf also has a promenade along the banks of the Danube: this is the starting point of the Donaukanal, and the extensive lock system is an Otto Wagner design.

The **Höhenstrasse** is a road meandering along the northwestern borders of the city through the Vienna Woods. From the car park a footpath leads through the woods to the summit of the **Hermannskogel**, the highest of the mountains on the northern boundary of Vienna (542 m/1,778 ft). It was on the **Kahlenberg** (483 m/1,585 ft), previously known as the Sauberg for its sizeable population of wild boar, that Vienna's relief forces gathered during the siege of 1683. In the sacristy of the Church of St Joseph there are memorials to Jan Sobieski, who led the Polish army which saved Leopold I's capital.

The nearby **Leopoldsberg** (423 m/1,388 ft), approached by a woodland path some 2 km (1¼ miles) long, is named after a Babenberg duke, Leopold III, "the Saintly", who built a castle here around 1100 and made it his seat of government. The castle was a casualty of the 1529 Turkish siege, but is commemorated by St Leopold's Church on the same site. Like the Kahlenberg, the Leopoldsberg offers an amazing view which covers the Innere Stadt, the plains of the Marchfeld, which extend to the Carpathians, and across the Danube to the Leitha mountains. ❑

The best way to explore the Grinzing district is by 38a bus, which begins at Heiligenstadt U-Bahn station and ascends all the way to the highest points of the mountain range.

BELOW: Kolo Moser's windows for Am Steinhof.

MONUMENTS OF VIENNA

Although Habsburg statuary dominates among Vienna's monuments, and you are never far from some general on horseback or allegorical monarchic figure, there are also Mahnmale and Denkmale, monuments of warning and reflection, acknowledging a darker period in Austrian history

The most controversial of all Vienna's monuments to the Nazi era was intended as a positive anti-fascist statement. In the 1980s, Mayor Helmut Zilk commissioned the Albertinaplatz's *Mahnmal gegen Krieg und Faschismus (below) – Warning against War and Fascism –* from the sculptor Alfred Hrdlicka. It comprises a Gate of Violence, a representation of Orpheus entering Hades and a stone commemorating the birth of the Second Republic, but at its heart is a small bronze of a Jewish man crouched to scrub the street clean. While Zilk had to defend the monument from conservative critics, it also came under attack from Jewish residents, who found the statue demeaning. Hrdlicka's response in a radio interview was, to say the least, ill-considered: "if the Jews complain that I use an act of humiliation as a symbol, it's their problem." When passers-by on the Albertinaplatz thoughtlessly began to use the statue as a bench, barbed wire was added to the figure's back.

At the time of Anschluss in 1938, Mexico was the only country to protest to the international community at the League of Nations. Out of gratitude, the Second Republic honoured Mexico with its own square, the Mexikanerplatz *(top)*, close to the Danube.

The Nazi policy of systematic mass murder affected not just Jews, but also the Roma and other peoples, including the patients of mental hospitals, whose tragedy is commemorated in the memorial at the Kirche am Steinof *(centre)*.

The memorial to victims of the Gestapo on Morzinplatz *(bottom)* was temporarily adapted to acknowledge gay and lesbian victims of Aids during a recent *Regenbogenparade*, or Rainbow Parade.

ABOVE: Hitler's 1938 speech at the Heldenplatz exemplified the Nazi preference for exploiting Habsburg imperial architecture rather than rebuilding the city, but National Socialism did leave one architectural legacy in the form of the Flaktürme, six enormous, bleak anti-aircraft towers in the Augarten, Arenberg Park, Stiftskaserne and Esterhazypark. The tower at Esterhazypark is open to the public, containing an aquarium and bearing a climbing wall offering dramatic views of the city for those skilled enough and willing to brave the ascent (Aquarium open daily 9am–6pm; Thurs 9am–9pm; entrance fee; tel: (01) 587 14 17; www.haus-des-meeres.at; climbing wall open Sept–June Mon–Fri 10am–10pm; July-Aug Mon–Fri 10am–6pm, Tues and Thurs 10am–10pm; Oct–May Sat–Sun 2pm–8pm; tel: 01-405 26 57; www.kletterzentrum.at).

OCCUPYING FORCE

The troubled relationship of Austria with its 1945 liberators, the Soviet Army is represented by the mixed feelings the Viennese hold towards the celebratory Russendenkmal behind the fountain on Schwarzenbergplatz *(above)*. One black joke in Cold War Vienna claimed that the city could survive a Third World War, but never a Second Liberation. Out of town, near the church on the Leopoldsberg, is a memorial to Austrian prisoners of war held by the Soviets after World War II.

RIGHT: Judenplatz plays home to three significant memorials: Zum Grossen Jordan, a house whose 15th-century relief celebrates the pogrom of 1421; a statue of Gottfried Lessing, whose play *Nathan the Wise* promoted tolerance, which was destroyed by the Nazis but re-erected in 1982; and British artist Rachel Whiteread's haunting inverted library monument, which recalls Nazi book-burnings by displaying a concrete cast of a library and its contents, giving material form to absence. Close by is Museum Judenplatz (*see page 128 and* www.jmw.at).

Map
on page
152

LOWER AUSTRIA

*The country's largest province is a subtle landscape of rolling
hills and vineyards, scattered with monasteries and
castles and bisected by the River Danube*

The region of Lower Austria (Niederösterreich) completely surrounds
Vienna. Cut across by the River Danube, it is renowned for moated castles
and thermal springs, bustards and Waldviertel carp, cider taverns and wine
cellars, abbeys and Richard the Lionheart's prison. You will find something of
everything here – forests and vineyards, plains and mountains.

The Vienna Woods

Leaving Vienna in a northwesterly direction, the road leads past the city's twin local
mountains: the Kahlenberg and the Leopoldsberg to **Klosterneuburg ❶**. Visible
from afar is the formidable Augustinian Monastery (open daily; charge for obligatory tours; tel: 02243-411 212; www.stift-klosterneuberg.at), its church topped by a
dome in the form of the Imperial Crown. The Romanesque monastery was founded
in 1114 by Margrave Leopold III of Babenberg, also known as Leopold the Pious.
The present interior is of 17th-century origin. Highlights are the magnificent 12th-
century enamel-and-gilt Verdun altar and the treasures of the **Stiftsmuseum** (open
Tues–Sun, May–mid-Nov; entrance charge). The town is also home to the splendid new **Essl Collection** of modern Austrian and international art (open Tues–Sun,
entrance charge; tel: 02243-3705 0150; www.sammlung-essl.at).

The picturesque road between Klosterneuburg and
Hütteldorf is known as the Vienna High Road; it leads
back along the upper slopes of the two mountains, past
cafés and panoramic terraces with magnificent views
of Vienna, the Danube and the Marchfeld beyond.

The way leads over the Sophienalpe, with more rustic cafés and picnic meadows (all only a short drive
from Vienna), through fairy-tale woods to Mauerbach,
which has the remains of a Carthusian monastery
founded in 1314. The combination of the baroque
church, added some three centuries later, and the
monks' cells built on to the outside presents an interesting architectural ensemble.

Purkersdorf ❷, just south of Mauerbach, was the
site of the first staging post on the old Imperial Road to
Linz. The post house, built in 1796 in an early neoclassical style, is decorated between the windows with
reliefs depicting in symbolic manner the secrecy of the
postal service. The **Sandstein-Wienerwald Nature
Park** (tel: 02231-63601; www.naturparke.at) on the edge of
town, includes walking paths and wildlife enclosures.
Just west of Purkersdorf is a reservoir, the Wiener-
waldsee, surrounded by a district that is elegantly discreet as regards both landscape and inhabitants.
Tullnerbach, Pressbaum and Rekawinkel are typical of
the recreation areas in the vicinity of the capital.

Further west is **Neulengbach ❸**, the "Pearl of the
Vienna Woods". It lies on the western fringe, nestled

PRECEDING PAGES: a
garden statue at
the Scholss
Greillenstein.
LEFT:
Klosterneuberg
abbey.
BELOW: breakfast in
Mödling.

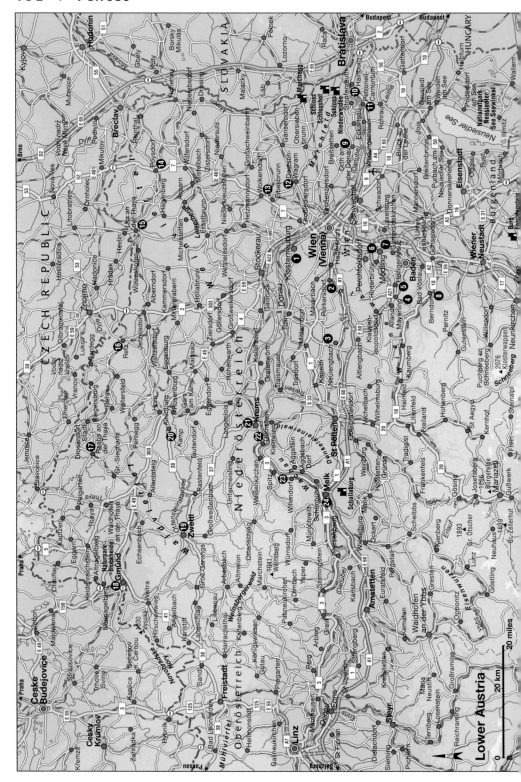

Map on page 152

between the Buchberg and the Kohlreith, two mountains that are popular excursion destinations. The town centre was built in about 1200 around the (private) castle of the lords of Lengbach. Its present-day countenance is characterised by well-maintained Renaissance buildings. Egon Schiele was placed under investigation here, and a small exhibition decorates his cell in the Bezirksgericht. It is well worth walking from Altlengbach, which lies to the south and is dominated by a 16th-century late-Gothic church, to the Schöpfl. Its 895-metre (2,935-ft) summit makes it the highest promontory in the area, affording a spectacular panoramic view across the entire Vienna Woods.

Circling back east from here along the Schwechat River via Klausenleopoldsdorf – where the main defile of the Schwechat with its twin wooden attendants' huts provides an attractive scene – one eventually reaches Alland and Mayerling. **Alland** was once the home of the Babenbergs and the birthplace of Friedrich of Austria. Today, its main attraction is its stalactite cave, the **Tropfsteinhöhle** (open Apr–Oct, opening times vary; entrance charge; tel: 02258-6666). **Mayerling ❹**, became a household name when it rocketed to fame as the setting for the tragic suicide of Crown Prince Rudolf *(see pages 36–38)*, which occurred in the hunting lodge here. On the spot where the prince shot first his mistress, Baroness Mary Vetsera, and then himself, there now stands a Carmelite convent of atonement (open daily; entrance charge), founded by Emperor Franz Joseph.

Plaque on the Beethovenhaus, Mödling.

A stroll through history and nature

From this point it is possible to drive directly along the wild and much-sung Helena Valley (Helenental) to the neighbouring town of Baden bei Wien; before doing so, however, it would be a pity not to make the acquaintance of some of the other villages in the Vienna Woods which lie on an alternative route.

At **Heiligenkreuz ❺**, the majestic **Cistercian abbey** is an architectural gem (open daily; charge for obligatory tour; tel: 02258-87030; www.stift-heiligenkreuz.at). The basilica, begun in 1133, has Austria's oldest example of ribbed vaulting; the Gothic hall chancel was a model for many South German hall churches. Encrusted with mineral deposits, a tiered well complements the simple beauty of the Romanesque cloisters. The ornate chapter house entombs dukes and margraves – including the last of the Babenbergs – while skeletons dance in the adjoining Chapel of the Dead.

Nearby **Mödling ❻** has been a settlement for almost 8,000 years. It has lured countless artists, writers and composers from Vienna here; from Johann Strauss, to Arnold Schönberg and Oskar Kokoschka. Ludwig van Beethoven lived at Hauptstrasse 79 from 1818 to 1820.

A stroll through the pedestrianised Old Town is recommended, to the Romanesque charnel house and church of St Othmar, the magnificent Plague Column and the stunning Town Hall on the Schrannenplatz. The views from the Black Tower merit the visit alone. In nearby Hinterbrühl is Europe's largest underground lake, the mysterious, labyrinthine **Seegrotte** (open daily; entrance charge includes boat ride; tel: 02236-26364; www.tourist-net.co.at/seegr1.htm). A tip for avid

BELOW: a baroque column at Heiligenkreuz abbey.

The neo-Gothic Burg Liechtenstein is north of Mödling in Brunn am Gebirge.

BELOW: the rolling hills of the southern Vienna Woods.

mountaineers: on the way there, the almost vertical rock faces serve as popular practice crags for enthusiasts and climbing schools.

Further east is **Schloss Laxenburg** (grounds open daily; entrance charge; tel: 02236-71226; www.schloss-laxenburg.at). The 18th-century (private) palace is resplendent in yellow. The surrounding park has been designed to look as natural as possible. A large artificial lake stretching from the central area towards the east invites visitors to take a boat trip or to visit the **Franzensburg** (open daily; charge for obligatory tour) on an islet. Reached by ferry or via the "Roman" bridge, this medieval-style folly, built by Franz II in 1798, houses a museum and a café. At the end of a long, straight avenue of poplars, beside a canal, lies a recreation centre with a restaurant, swimming pool, and mini-golf course.

Just south of Mödling is **Gumpoldskirchen ❼**, the most popular wine-growing village to the south of Vienna. A stroll through the hilly vineyards conveys something of the district's convivial atmosphere and serves as an ideal preparation for the pleasures of the world-famous Gumpoldskirchner vintages, or a visit to the **Fire-Brigade Museum** (open May–mid-Oct, Sun and bank holidays; tel: 02252-62222).

With its thermal baths, theatre and casino, the spa town of **Baden** has a nostalgic air of faded empire. A slightly decadent, 19th-century charm continues to pervade the architecture and the spa park; an impression underlined by events such as the Operetta Summer. The **Römertherme** (open daily; tel: 02252-45030; www.roemertherme.at) and sandy open-air **Strandbad** (open daily May–Sept; tel: 02252-48670) should satisfy any aquatic desires, while the lovingly curated **Puppenmuseum** (doll museum; open Tues–Sun; tel: 02252-41020) and **Rollettmuseum**, full of oddities from near and far (open Wed–Mon; tel: 02252-48255) provide suitable diversions.

After a wallow in the pleasing ambience of the outdoor thermal spa complex (open May–Sept daily; tel: 02252-762 660; www.thermalbad-voeslau.at) at Bad Vöslau, 5 km (3 miles) south, continue west to **Berndorf** ❽. The undisputed cultural focal point, not only of the town, but of the entire valley, is the magnificent **Municipal Theatre**, built in the spirit of Vienna's Ringstrasse architecture with an interior which resembles a rococo stage at the court of a minor prince.

The neo-baroque **Church of St Margaret**, whose gleaming green cupola tops the roofs of the town, also deserves attention. The church building is flanked by two apparently unremarkable school buildings constructed in 1808, but their interiors are anything but everyday: the classrooms have been decorated in 12 important architectural styles, ranging from Moorish to Gothic, Egyptian and Doric (opening times vary; charge for guided tours; tel: 02672-82253).

An abundance of castles

Heading east of Vienna, any journey through the March-Donauland is an excursion back in time, as the visitor wends through unspoilt countryside, liberally peppered with castles. Many little villages in the northern part of the Marchfeld have retained their amiable rural character. **Orth an der Donau** ❾ is the site of a moated castle straight out of a fairy tale. The forbidding complex was founded in the 12th century, but acquired its present-day appearance in 1532. The New Castle on the western flank was added in 1784. Acquired by the Habsburg family in 1824, it subsequently became one of the favourite residences of Crown Prince Rudolf. Today it houses the **Danube Park Centre** (open Easter–Oct daily; entrance charge; tel: 02212-3555; www.donauauen.at), with a gallery, café and a new underwater hall. The charming local church nearby also deserves a peek.

Next on our eastward journey is the hunting lodge at **Eckartsau** (open Apr–Oct Sat–Sun; entrance charge with obligatory tour; group bookings in advance; tel: 02214-2240; www.bundesforste.at), the last Austrian home of the last emperor in 1918. Set amongst rambling parkland, it was destroyed in 1945 but has since become an example of superb restoration work. The original 12th-century castle was completely rebuilt in the 18th century, the creation of which testifies to the consummate skills of such great masters as Bernhard Fischer von Erlach, Lorenzo Mattielli and Daniel Gran.

Further east is **Stopfenreuth**, where the Danube meadows have attracted much public attention as a result of local initiatives and WWF campaigns. An observant and careful walker will find a unique biotope that is home to kingfishers, beavers and cormorants as well as herons and freshwater turtles. It is one of the last primeval forests to be found in Europe. The river can be explored by boat or canoe.

Bear north for **Schloss Hof** (open mid-Apr–Oct daily; tel: 02285-20000; www.schlosshof.at), the real centre of royal and aristocratic life in the Marchfeld. Prince Eugene acquired a 17th-century fortress here, and in 1729 Johann Lukas von Hildebrandt completed the extensive alterations. With the addition of two wings and the resulting courtyard, the beautiful fountain and the sweeping staircases, the building was intended to be the most lavish and magnificent sum-

Map on page 152

At the southwest boundary of Niederösterreich, Semmering sits comfortably amongst the wild Süd-Alpin landscape. The world's first high Alpine railway (now a World Heritage Site) was built here, via a fine ensemble of bridges and viaducts, and the rich swarmed here for summer breaks at the turn of the last century.

BELOW: Schloss Hof.

mer residence far and wide, capable of being defended in an emergency. A few kilometres further north lies the eye-catching (private) hunting lodge of Marchegg, where, every summer, it is possible to witness a large colony of white storks.

Returning south and crossing the Danube, one reaches the well-fortified citadel of **Hainburg** ❿. The most striking of the three town gates, the 13th-century western Wienertor, leads to a fine town centre of architectural and historical interest. Following a laborious restoration programme, the castle today provides an elegant setting for special exhibitions and is surrounded by a glorious baroque garden.

After the castle passed into the possession of Maria Theresa in 1755, she immediately embarked upon a programme of alterations and extensions, which rapidly made Schlosshof a favourite residence of the Imperial court.

Apart from sections dating from the 11th century, the forbidding fortress on the Schlossberg still has a massive round-arch gateway, a keep with ribbed vaulting constructed in 1120, and an entrance hall built in 1514. The complex has been uninhabited since the 17th century, but has nevertheless been constantly modernised and restored. Visitors yearning for wider horizons should continue their journey along the panoramic road (E 58) on the Braunsberg. The view is breathtaking, especially at sunset, and will bring you very nearly to Bratislava at the Slovakian border.

Roman ruins

Heading west on the south bank of the Danube, you will shortly come to **Petronell-Carnuntum** ⓫ (open mid-Mar–mid-Nov daily; entrance charge; tel: 02163-33770; www.carnutum.co.at), the site of the most extensive Roman excavations in Central Europe. During its heyday, the town of Carnuntum had a population of 70,000; including a military camp, it covered an area of 10 sq. km (4 sq.

BELOW: the river near Hainburg.

miles). The open-air museum includes the floor plans of an entire section of the town, indicating the position of houses, baths and workshops, while a well-stocked exhibition hall shows local finds. The highlights include the main baths, the palace ruins, an amphitheatre and the Heidentor, once more than 20 metres (65 ft) high and now reduced to 12 metres (40 ft), but still arresting.

Joseph Haydn was born in **Rohrau**, to the south, on 31 March 1732; today his enchanting birthplace houses the **Haydn-Geburtshaus** (open Tues–Sun; entrance charge; tel: 02164-2268). **Schloss Rohrau** (open Easter–Oct Tues–Sun; entrance charge; tel: 02164-2253; http://har-rach.nwy.at), dates from the 16th century but has been rebuilt several times. It now contains the largest private gallery in Austria; its delightful collection represents a complete cross-section through the Dutch, Flemish, Italian, Spanish and French schools of painting.

Wine country

The village of **Deutsch-Wagram** ⓬, 20 km (12 miles) northeast of Vienna, lies on the edge of the Marchfelden route to the Weinviertel (Wine Country). This little community is first mentioned in records as long ago as 1250, and the church belfry is actually 1,000 years old. The village owes its fame, however, to Napoleon Bonaparte, who established his base camp here in 1809 in the Battle of Deutsch-Wagram. The memorial stone on the relevant spot, as well as numerous mementoes in the local museum (open Mar–Nov Sun and bank holidays; entrance charge), provide information concerning this period. Here, too, is the ever-popular **Marchfelderhof** (tel: 02247-2243, reservations recommended) restaurant, which provides traditional culinary delights in an outrageously opulent environment.

Roughly 10 km (6 miles) north of Deutsch-Wagram is **Wolkersdorf** ⑬, often mentioned as the true gateway to the Wine Country. Here, too, the Battle of Deutsch-Wagram left traces: first of all, the Emperor Franz I set up his base camp in the priest's backyard; shortly afterwards, following the victory of his army, Napoleon took up residence in the Schloss. Built in 1050 as a moated castle, it was subsequently converted into a hunting lodge in 1720 by Karl VI, and has become the landmark of this little town.

There is an entire **museum village** (open Apr–Oct daily; entrance charge; tel: 02534-333; www.museumsdorf.at) in **Niedersulz**, 23 km (14 miles) northeast. The open-air collection includes over 40 complete original buildings in representative vernacular style –chapels, various workshops, wine-pressing sheds, a water mill and the obligatory tavern complete with bowling alley – all presenting a picture of a Weinviertel village before industrialisation.

The quiet market town of **Wilfersdorf**, lying in the midst of a fertile agricultural and wine-growing region to the north, presents a completely different character. As early as the 14th century it was the seat of the local assizes. The most eye-catching element is undoubtedly the pale yellow **Liechtenstein Castle** (open Apr–Nov Tues-Sun; entrance charge), housing exhibitions on local history and the omnipotent Liechtensteins, an all-embracing Heimatmuseum, a cellar Heuriger and Vinotek.

Train enthusiasts will be in seventh heaven at Das Heizhaus (Apr–Oct Tues–Sun entrance charge; www.heizhaus.com) in Strasshof, a depository for all things rail-oriented.

BELOW: Petronell-Carnuntum.

The fertile Wienviertel north of Vienna is Austria's chief wine-producing area.

BELOW: dawn in the hills.

Head 10 km (6 miles) north of here to find **Poysdorf** , with its picturesque Kellergassen (historic alleys lined with taverns) and fine vintages – a highlight for wine buffs. Twenty-nine winegrowers from the municipality have joined together to form a syndicate in the **Weinmarkt** (open daily; tel: 02552-20371; http://tourismus.poysdorf.at). This permits an expert selection from approximately 250 different wines, predominantly Grüner Veltliner, Welschriesling, Rhine Riesling, Chardonnay and white Burgundy, but also several red wines of excellent quality.

Continue southwest to **Mistelbach** to find a large sports centre offering a wide range of facilities, an open-air swimming pool and a mini-golf course. A Gothic hall church, a 12th-century charnel house, a former Barnabite cloister with frescoes by Maulbertsch (guided tours by appointment) and a small, private baroque castle (with occasional exhibitons) provide cultural interest.

Asparn an der Zaya lies just west in the foothills of the Leiser Mountains. The heart of the old wine-growing market town is undoubtedly the fortress complex, complete with moat, church, battlement walk and monastery. Housed in a section of the commanding castle is a **museum of prehistory** (open Apr–Nov Tues–Sun; entrance charge; tel: 02577-8039; www.urgeschichte.com), and in the grounds, an archaeological park, while the **wine museum** (open Apr–Oct Sat–Sun) is situated in the adjoining Kloster.

North of Asparn, at the Czech border, is a settlement with a 5,000-year history. **Laa an der Thaya** was fortified as a bulwark against Bohemia by the Babenbergs around 1200. Sections of the town walls and Laa's general appearance both date from this time. So, too, does the dilapidated castle – now the home of a **beer museum** (open May–Oct Sat and Sun pm; entrance charge). The town's chief promise lies in its modern **Therme** (open daily; entrance charge, tel: 02522-84700260; www.thermelaa.at) and brand new hotel complex.

Some 42 km (25 miles) west, is the town of **Retz** . The ground under Retz has a life of its own: an extensive subterranean network (the largest historic wine cellar in Austria) covers a larger area than the streets above ground. The tunnels often extend three levels deep into the underlying sand. Guided tours of the vaults (open Mar–Dec daily; Jan–Feb Sat and Sun; entrance charge; tel: 02942-2700; www.retz.at) only encompass 5 percent of the system, but still include 900 metres (2,955 ft) of tunnel. The town also possesses museums, a large number of stunning baroque and Renaissance buildings – the Rathauskapelle interior is particularly special –and a landmark 1772 windmill that is still in working order.

The region south of Retz where the city of **Eggenburg** now stands was settled in prehistoric times, but the first fortified town was erected here around 1160. The wonderful Hauptplatz boasts a number of notable buildings, including a fantastic example of the Sgraffito technique. Other diversions include the chilling charnel house, the fascinating **Krahuletz Museum** (open April–Dec daily; entrance charge; tel: 02984-3400; www.krahuletzmuseum.at) of geology and folklore, and the **Austrian Motorbike Museum** (open early Jan–mid-Dec; tel: 02984-2151; www.motorradmuseum.at). There are over 320 motorcycles exhibited here.

East of Eggenburg stands the beautiful 13th-

century Romanesque church of **Schöngrabern** (guided tours available; tel: 02952-2132), known as the "Stone Bible" due to the rich sculptural reliefs adorning the outer wall of the apse. The three sections represent the Fall of Adam and Eve, the story of Cain and Abel, and Man's struggle against evil. The interior of the church features 14th-century frescoes.

The Waldviertel

The **Waldviertel** (Woodland Country) possesses a singular, austere charm of its own. One becomes particularly aware of its northerly latitude at night, when jackets are automatically buttoned a little higher against the persistent cool breeze. One will seldom experience here the frenetic outdoor activity that characterises the balmy summer nights of Southern Austria. In any case, the visitor comes here in search of peace and quiet.

Northwest of Retz, on the Czech border, is the hamlet of Hardegg. Perched on a high mountain ridge overlooking it, is a forbidding 12th-century **castle** (open Apr–mid-Nov daily; entrance charge; tel: 02949-8205). Here, the bridge over the river Thaya will make the heart of every fisherman beat faster, for the waters below are teeming with trout. It is also a good starting place for a hike through the meandering valleys that distinguish the cross-border **Nationalpark Thayatal** as a haven for rare flora and fauna.

Eight kilometres (5 miles) to the west lies the magnificent lakeside baroque castle of **Riegersburg** (open Apr–mid-Nov daily; entrance charge; tel: 02916-400; www.schloss.riegersburg.at) with its art gallery and unique dog cemetery, a must-see en route to Geras. A peaceful holiday village, **Geras** runs popular arts and crafts courses from the Stiftshotel Alter Schüttkasten, while the **Stift** (open Easter–Oct, Tues–Sun; tel: 02912-345 289; www.stiftgeras.at) itself warrants a visit for its engaging exhibitons. **Drosendorf**, in a northerly direction from Geras, merits a mention for its peaceful medieval Hauptplatz, where the local MOKA café sells homemade poppyseed cake, a Waldviertel speciality.

The next town of any size, **Raabs an der Thaya** 🄗 has been nicknamed "The Pearl of the Thaya Valley". If you look down on this congenial little town from the picturesque 11th-century **castle** (open June–Sept Fri–Sun; entrance charge; tel: 02856-3794), you'll agree that the name is justified. On a steep cliff high above the confluence of the German and Moravian Thaya rivers, the castle hosts cultural festivals and art exhibitions.

West of Raabs, the situation of the market town of **Thaya im Waldviertel** was determined by the sunny climate and healthy, bracing air. Two Renaissance fountains adorn the market place, surrounded by beautifully renovated merchants' houses and a Romanesque parish church. In a wood just beyond the town boundary you will find the excavations of the medieval village of Hard.

Further west, a massive moated **castle** (open Apr–Oct Tues–Sun; entrance charge; tel: 02862-52268; www.kinsky-heidenreichstein.at) lends a fairy-tale aura to the romantic town of **Heidenreichstein**, first mentioned in records in 1205. The fortress is still approached via

Maissau lies a short distance south of Eggenburg, and claims the largest deposit of banded amethyst in the world, as evidenced by Amethyst Welt (open daily; entrance charge; tel: 02958-848400; www.amethyst welt.at), a child-friendly, interactive themed museum.

BELOW: the monastery of Altenburg.

medieval drawbridges. The local moor is now a **Naturpark** with a museum (open May–Sept Sat–Sun; entrance charge; tel: 02862-52619) and walking routes.

With two border crossing points into the Czech Republic and its standing as an administrative and educational centre, **Gmünd**  is the main town in the north-west district of the province. It is also the terminus of the **Waldviertel Narrow Gauge Steam Railway**, which runs south from here to Grossgerungs. Situated on its main square are two wonderful 16th-century castellated Sgraffito houses and a number of local museums. The principal attractions, however, are the mystical granite formations found in the nearby **Naturpark Blockheide** (open daily; free).

Head south to **Weitra**, Austria's oldest brewing town and home to the country's smallest brewery, the Brauhotel. The handsome **castle** (open May–Oct Wed–Mon; entrance charge; tel: 02856-3311; www.schlossweitra.at) boasts a theatre, a splendid outlook tower and no less than three museums, covering regional interest, brewing and the fascinating history behind the Iron Curtain. Also worth the diversion are the town's **Textile Museum** (Alte Textilfabrikmuseum; open May–Oct Tues–Sun; www.members.aon.at/textilmuseum) and the Russ glassblowing studio on Böhmstrasse.

Turning southeast, we begin our journey back towards the Danube. Some 24 km (15 miles) away is the romantic town of **Zwettl** , where the brewing theme continues – this is the seat of the largest privately owned brewery in Austria, and the beer ought to be sampled. Visit the engaging **Stadtmuseum** (open July–Aug Tues–Sun; May–Oct Fri–Sun; entrance charge; tel: 02822-503 129) in the old Sgraffito Rathaus – listen out for the chiming bell tower – and the Hundertwasser fountains in the Hauptplatz. On the outskirts lies a magnificent **Cistercian abbey** (open May–Oct daily; entrance charge; tel: 0800-242480; www.stift-zwettl.at) built in 1138; a little further in the opposite direction is the baroque **Schloss Rosenau** (open Apr–Oct daily, book in advance Nov–Mar; entrance charge; tel: 02822-5822 115; www.freimaurermuseum.at), where an initiation into the mysteries of Freemasonry awaits the curious visitor.

Just east at the very heart of the Waldviertel lies **Ottenstein Reservoir**, with its countless fjord-like inlets and the secluded **Schloss Ottenstein** (open Easter–Oct Wed–Sun; book for group tours; tel: 02826-254). Rastenfeld is an ideal starting point for this water sports centre, which attracts anglers, swimmers, sailors and surfers; for landlubbers there are 35 km (20 miles) of signposted hiking trails, bicycle rental, an 18-hole golf course, tennis courts and bowling greens.

Baroque treasures

About 25 km (15 miles) northeast of Rastenfeld, is a baroque masterpiece, **Stift Altenburg** ㉑ (open Easter–Oct daily; entrance charge; tel: 02982-345114; www.stift-altenburg.at). Primarily the work of Josef Munggenast, the monastery displays the splendours typical of the more famous abbeys – a wonderful library and plenty of frescoes by Paul Troger, who lived here for many years. Not far from the abbey is the 16th-century Renaissance **Schloss Greillenstein** (open Apr–Oct daily; entrance charge; tel: 02989-

Many of the towns and villages around Gmünd, including Alt- and Neu-Nagelberg and Hirschenwies, are home to the famous Waldviertel glasscutters, and are the best places to buy good-quality glassware.

BELOW: Krems old town.

Map on page 152

808021; www.greillenstein.at), which is noted for its exotic baroque statuary, bath-house and wonderfully preserved interior.

Southeast of Altenburg, **Schloss Rosenburg** (open May–Sept daily; April and Oct Tues–Sun; charge for obligatory tour; tel: 02982-2911; www.rosenburg.at), rises high above the River Kamp. First mentioned in 1175, the magnificent structure possesses a unique jousting yard and houses a large number of works of art and weapons in the splendid rooms. Twice daily, it is possible to catch a free-flight performance of eagles, falcons and other birds of prey.

Travelling south of Rosenburg brings you to **Gars am Kamp**, a pretty market village lying at the foot of a ruined castle that once belonged to the Babenbergs. Highlights of the village include the Romanesque-Gothic church of St Gertrude, a number of fine patrician houses and an exhibition documenting the local excavations, which have revealed that the Gars district has been a site of human settlement for at least 5,000 years. Further south towards Krems is the prepossessing town of **Langenlois**, notable for the recent **Loisium** development (open Feb–Dec daily; entrance charge; tel: 02734-322400; www.loisium.at), a journey through the winemaking process.

The Wachau

South of Langenlois, you enter the **Wachau**, the most charming river region in Austria – a land of apricot blossoms, ruined castles, rolling vineyards and, of course, the Danube. Every visitor should taste the region's fine wines and in particular, its apricot brandy. On its eastern extremity is **Krems ㉑**, the "Model Town for the Preservation of Historical Monuments". A few hours are required to appreciate the proliferation of historic churches and townhouses in the delight-

If you have generously partaken of the prize-winning spirits in the tiny Garser Schnapskeller (Wed–Sat) in Gars am Kamp, it is possible to recuperate in one of a trio of health spas founded by late fitness guru Willy Dungl in the vicinity.

BELOW: colourful housing and steep streets, Krems.

ful Altstadt and neighbouring Stein, while the **Karikaturmuseum** (open daily; entrance charge; tel: 02732-908020; www.karikaturmuseum.at) and the **Kunsthalle Krems** (open daily; entrance charge; tel: 02732-908010; www.kunsthalle.at) should be first port of call for art lovers.

Across the river lies one of the highlights of the area, the fine **Stift Göttweig** (open late Mar–mid-Nov daily; entrance charge; tel: 02732-8558 1231; www.stift-goettweig.at), a mighty 11th-century monastery that was later reworked in baroque style after a fire in 1718. The plans of the emperor's architect Johann Lukas von Hildebrandt were only ever partly realised, but his masterly Imperial Staircase (Kaiserstiege) – with a ceiling fresco by Paul Troger – and the frescoed banqueting hall (Altmannsaal) can be seen on the guided tour.

Back at the river, head west to **Dürnstein ㉒**, probably the most popular – and beautiful – town in the Wachau. Dürnstein was made famous by the legend of King Richard the Lionheart and Blondel, his minstrel. At the end of the 12th century, the king of England, captured by Leopold V on his return from the Third Crusade, languished as a prisoner in the dungeons of the town's impregnable castle. Only one faithful follower, his minstrel Blondel, refused to believe that his beloved master was no longer alive. He took his lute and set off to find him. Eventually, striking up the first bars of Richard's favourite song beneath Dürnstein Castle, he was answered by the familiar voice of his master. Soon afterwards, Richard was released upon payment of a huge ransom by the English. (The money was used to finance the construction of Vienna's first city wall.)

Aside from the ruined castle on the hill overlooking Dürnstein, the primary tourist destination is the elaborate baroque **monastery church** (open Apr–Oct; entrance charge; tel: 02711-375; www.stiftduernstein.at) that hosts concerts and exhibitions. Its stunning blue-and-white steeple is best viewed from the river (Blue Danube ferries run regularly between Krems and Melk; tel: 01-58880). The entire village is pervaded by an unusual charm to which it is easy to succumb.

The former monastery of Und now houses a winegrowers' college and a Vinotek restaurant containing the choicest vintages from Austria's wine-growing valleys; visitors are able to taste and purchase them to their heart's content.

BELOW: Dürnstein castle.

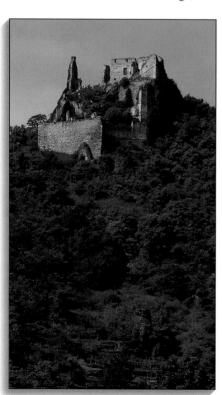

The road to Melk

Beyond Dürnstein is **Weissenkirchen**, a picturesque village with narrow alleys, historic houses and ancient gleaning yards. The community is dominated by an imposing fortified church dating from 1190; next door is a museum dedicated to the Wachau and wine-growing culture (open Apr–Oct Tues–Sun; entrance charge; tel: 02715-2600; www.weissenkirchen.at).

Further south is **Spitz**, a famous wine-growing town that sprawls around the Tausendeimerberg. The mountain's name refers to the claim that, during a good year, the yield from its vineyards will total 1,000 buckets of wine. Romantic souls are bound to fall deeply in love with the ruined Fortress of Hinterhaus. Schloss Erlahof now contains a diverting **Shipping Museum** (Schifffahrtsmuseum; open daily; entrance charge; tel: 02713-2246). The late-Gothic parish church has a triple nave and a baroque high altar with an altarpiece by renowned painter Kremser Schmidt.

Upstream from Spitz is **Willendorf ㉓**, famous for the discovery of the "Venus of Willendorf", a neolithic limestone statue. The soil here is the repository of many a fascinating historical detail; it has revealed, for instance, that a camp of mammoth hunters was situated here during the Ice Age.

Across the river from Willendorf are the awesome ruins of **Aggstein Castle** (open Mar–Oct daily; entrance charge; tel: 02753-82281; www.sch-agg.at), almost 700 years old and perched about 300 metres (985 ft) above the Danube. Here the Kuenringers, a lawless tribe of robber barons, barricaded the river with chains in order to plunder passing ships.

Staying on the same side of the river, **Aggsbachdorf** contains a former Carthusian monastery dating from the 14th to 16th centuries, as well as the tombs of the founding Maissau family, embellished with coats of arms. About 5 km (3 miles) further upstream lies the private Schloss Schönbühel. Dating from the 12th century, the castle occupies a dominant site on a 40-metre (130-ft) high cliff above the river. On one of its exterior walls is an interesting relief depicting the Last Supper.

Without a doubt, the most impressive sight in the Wachau is the magnificent **Stift Melk ㉔** (open Easter–Oct daily; Nov–Easter guided tours only; entrance charge; tel: 02752-555 232; www.stiftmelk.at), set on a steep hill above the Danube. Best viewed initially from the river, the monastery's yellow-and-white walls stretch for an extravagant 362 metres (1,187 ft) on its southern façade. *(See pages 166–67 for a full description of the monastery).*

The Mostviertel

Just a few kilometres south, **Schloss Schallaburg** (open May–Oct daily; entrance charge; tel: 02754-6317; www.schallaburg.at) has miraculously preserved a 16th-century Renaissance interior courtyard, recalling the glories of Florence or Venice. Parts of the Romanesque 12th-century fortress still remain. Every year, the castle puts on an archaeological or historical exhibition, and a pleasant garden lies without the castle walls.

Returning east towards Vienna brings one to **St Pölten**, the sprawling capital of Niederösterreich. Unjustly scorned by some, the city holds many surprises for the discerning visitor. The modern governmental quarter may possess little charm, but it does house the engaging **Landesmuseum** (open Tues–Sun; entrance charge; tel: 02742-908090; www.landesmuseum.net), encompassing natural history and art, and the **Klangturm** (opening times vary; free; tel: 02742-908050; www.klangturm.at), a glass tower featuring interactive soundscapes on each level.

In the Altstadt, the **Diözesanmuseum** (open May–Oct Tues–Sun; entrance charge; tel: 02742-324331; www.dz-museum.at), in an attractive cloister next to the cathedral, displays religious artworks and the wonderfully maintained Stiftsbibliotek. Other places of interest include the Jugendstil Olbrichhaus, the **Stadtmuseum** (open Tues–Sat; tel: 02742-3332640; www.stadtmuseum-stpoelten.at) and the rococo Franziscan Church.

Further south again is the impressive baroque **abbey** (Mon–Sat; entrance charge; tel: 02762–52420; www.stift-lilienfeld.at) at Lilienfeld, founded in 1202. Before you leave the Mostviertel, however, don't forget to taste some of the pear cider (or *Birnenmost*) that gave the region its name. ❑

Map on page 152

Today the main attraction of Aggstein Castle is undoubtedly the fine panoramic view: upstream towards Melk, south to the foothills of the Dunkelsteiner Wald and north to the highland plateau of the Waldviertel.

BELOW: the monastery tower, Dürnstein.

MELK ABBEY

The Abbey of Melk (known in German as Stift Melk), standing high above the Danube, is among Austria's most prized baroque treasures

The abbey, easily seen from the train en-route to Vienna, was rebuilt in its present form after the Turks burnt it down in 1683. The abbot at the time, Berthold Dietmayr, was an enthusiastic supporter of baroque master Jakob Prandtauer, but other monks were reluctant to commit large funds to the rebuilding. Dietmayr prevailed and Prandtauer produced a masterpiece. Antonio Galli-Bibiena created the magnificent high altar in marble and pure gold. The central scene is of Peter taking leave of Paul. Especially impressive are the ceiling frescoes by J.M. Rottmayr in the abbey church, a breathtaking depiction of the life, death and ascension of Italian monk St Benedict (*circa* 480–547).

BELOW: the Prälatenhof courtyard unifies the monastery buildings. Its ornate fountain dates from the early 19th century.

A MODERN MONASTERY

Originally a castle stood on the site of Melk Abbey – the Babenberg family's first residence after they gained power in 976. The Order of Benedictines was given the land by Leopold II in 1089, and monks have lived and worked here ever since.

While only half of its three-dozen or so monks live in the grounds, the abbey continues to operate much as it always has. Monks still carry out forestry and agricultural tasks; and nearly 800 children attend the religious primary and secondary schools here, which are collectively known as the Stifts Gymnasium. There is a strict emphasis on biblical scholarship, and the monks are renowned throughout Europe for their instruction. There is also the ongoing task of maintaining the huge structure, which has long been a concern.

The monks also run a busy museum, host concerts, commission modern artists to add new frescoes and curate occasional art exhibitions which are held inside the abbey walls.

ABOVE: The Gutenberg Bible was once sold by the Melk order to finance the renovation of the abbey's aging façades. Depicted above is the west façade, which faces the river. The 61-metre (200-ft) octagonal dome sits atop the abbey church at the centre of the complex, a fine example of baroque design.

THE FRESCOES AND ABBEY LIBRARY

The ceiling frescoes in the church depict the combat of good and evil, and Benedict's assumption into heaven, as seen by two monks in a vision. There is little marble in the Marmorsaal (Marble Hall), whose columns are faux, but it is also worth a visit for the splendid Paul Troger frescoes. The frescoes are a mere appetizer to the abbey library. One of the finest in the world, it is said to have inspired Umberto Eco to write his medieval thriller *The Name of the Rose*. Some 100,000 ancient hand-copied books and illuminated manuscripts – carefully rebound in leather and leafed in gold – line the wooden shelves of the enormous room. The abbey also possesses important religious items, such as a piece (the monks claim) of the Calvary Cross.

BURGENLAND

Map on page 168

This border region, with its long history of contested ownership, is a land of vineyards, castles and nesting storks, it also contains one of Europe's largest lakes

The name Burgenland does not, as one might think, derive from the numerous castles (Burgen) within its boundaries. Rather, it stems from a complex and decisive period of history played out on the world stage. The large area of land called German West Hungary consisted of four administrative districts: Pressburg, Wieselburg, Ödenburg and Eisenburg, each with a county town bearing the same name. The inhabitants were predominantly German-speaking. After World War I, the victorious and defeated powers sat down together to negotiate the new national boundaries. Peace conferences were held – among other places, at the Trianon in Paris – which is where Austria's territorial claims with respect to Hungary were debated. In the Venice Protocol, the eastern boundary of Austria was finally agreed – with the proviso that the inhabitants of Ödenburg themselves should decide to which country they wished to belong.

Austria's agreement to the 1921 plebiscite was, in fact, tantamount to surrender at the outset, for the area in question was inhabited predominantly by Hungarians. There was no alternative, however, for this was the price Austria had to pay in order to gain the rest of the territory.

After the plebiscite, most of German West Hungary was ceded to Austria. It was named the "Burgenland" after the suffix "Burg" which formed part of the former names of the constituent districts. Of the former county towns, three now lie in Hungary and one – Pressburg (now Bratislava) – in Slovakia.

The community of Ödenburg – now called Sopron – forms a "peninsula" which appears to jut into Austria and which, had it not been for the plebiscite, would probably have become the "natural" capital of the Burgenland. And so, since 1925, the province's capital – succeeding Mattersburg – has been Eisenstadt. Five years later, the regional government of the Burgenland was also transferred there.

The Esterházys

Eisenstadt ❶ is the smallest provincial capital of Austria, claiming a population of around 13,500 people. The settlement was first recorded as Castrum Ferreum in 1118, and was given trading rights in 1388. As a result, the 13th-century Gothic castle was enlarged, and strong city walls constructed. The Habsburgs pledged the castle to Count Nikolaus Esterházy as a bond in 1622 and it fell under the powerful Hungarian family's ownership in 1649. The city has been dominated by their name ever since.

Eisenstadt is best served by exploring on foot. All notable sights are easily accessible. Instead of merely admiring the baroque façades and late-Gothic arches of the fine old houses, it is worthwhile stealing into the lovely inner courtyards of some of them.

LEFT: Burgenland vines.
BELOW: the entry to Schloss Esterházy.

The magnificent baroque **Esterházy Palace** (open Apr–Oct daily; Nov–Mar Mon–Fri; entrance charge; tel: 02682-719 3000; www.schloss-esterhazy.at) should be any visitor's first stop. The future Prince Paul I, the son of Nikolaus, commissioned the reconstruction of the existing medieval fortress, and it began in 1663 under the direction of Carlo Carlone, the Italian master builder. Over 120 years later, his French successor, Charles Moreau, added pyramid-shaped roofs to the corner towers, previously topped by onion-shaped domes. He also designed a colonnaded portico and completely rearranged the garden, even filling in the moat that had surrounded the castle. His Leopoldine Temple and the sumptuous Orangerie grace the pleasant park. When the work was complete the complex comprised a total of more than 200 spacious rooms and six ballrooms, of which the Haydn Room, with its late 17th-century frescoes by Carpoforo Tencalla, is undoubtedly the jewel.

Below your feet in the Schlosskeller, you can learn about local winemaking traditions at the **Weinmuseum Burgenland** (open daily; entrance charge; tel: 02682-63348).

Haydn is Eisenstadt's most revered adopted son. Near the castle, in pretty Haydngasse, is the **Haydnhaus** (open Apr–Oct daily; entrance charge; tel: 02682-719 3900; www.haydnhaus.at), where the composer lived from 1766 to 1778. It displays rare artefacts including a Hammerflügel grand piano from 1780 and first editions of his works. His Mausoleum can be seen in the **Bergkirche** (open Apr–Oct daily; entrance charge; tel: 02682-62638; www.haydnkirche.at), also the site of an elaborate Kalvarienberg.

The city plays host to three more excellent museums: the **Diözesanmuseum** (open May–Sept Wed–Sat; entrance charge; tel: 02682-777 234; www.kath. kirche.eisenstadt.at) in the Franciscan monastery, displaying sacred art, the highly informative **Austrian Jewish Museum** (open May–Oct Tues–Sun; entrance charge; tel: 02682-65145; www.ojm.at) and the varied **Landesmu-**

seum Burgenland (open Tues–Sat; entrance charge; tel: 02682-600 1234; www.burgenland.at/landesmuseum) offer something for everyone.

Neusiedler See

With 300 days of sunshine a year, Burgenland's temperate weather positively encourages outdoor activity. Largely flat, its 1,900 km (1,181 miles) of cycle routes and 700 km (435 miles) of bridle paths leave no excuse for the unfit. What is more, just a few kilometres east of Eisenstadt and barely 70 km (45 miles) from Vienna, is Europe's largest (320 sq. km/125 sq. miles) and westernmost steppe lake – an ideal destination for watersports. The shores of **Neusiedler See** also harbour one of the last major breeding grounds for almost 300 rare species of bird and more than 40 species of mammals. The lake has no outflow and loses most of its water through evaporation. Only a handful of celebrated places in the world can stand comparison with this region as a bird haven. There are 15 nature conservation areas to choose from – a real paradise. One can even tour the lake via a circular cycling path that takes you into Hungary before completing the circuit.

Here, the last foothills of the Alps subside into the Pannonian plain, creating a steppe-like climate, which ranges from very hot summers to bitterly cold winters. Low rainfall and a steady breeze are other characteristics of this particular microclimate. In some of the lakeshore communities, the average temperatures in July and August lie only one degree below those of the French Riviera. This Mediterranean characteristic, combined with the varying saline levels of the ponds and lake (made up of soda, Glauber's salt, Epsom salts and common salt), provide ideal conditions for unique flora and fauna.

Map on page 168

The Haydn Museum, Eisenstadt.

BELOW: the Esterházy palace.

A tour of the lake

The main road around the lake heads northeast from Eisenstadt and soon reaches the winemaking village of **Donnerskirchen ❷**. Those lucky enough to visit the area between mid-April and the beginning of May will be able to witness a splendid natural spectacle – the cherry blossom. Laden with white blossom, the thousands of cherry trees on the slopes of the Leitha Mountains surrounding Donnerskirchen are truly spectacular. The sight puts local inhabitants in a festive mood, too. The entire village takes to the streets for a high-spirited celebration of the arrival of spring. Donnerskirchen is also famous for its highly successful village restoration project, which accounts for its well-cared-for appearance.

Since the parish church here is dedicated to St Martin, it seems appropriate to mention a few facts about the patron saint of Burgenland. The local version of the legend has it that St Martin, pursued by a number of persecutors, sought refuge here, but his hiding place was betrayed by the loud gabbling of some geese. The day for a traditional St Martin's goose dinner (not only in Burgenland, but also in Lower Austria and Vienna) and when the new wine, Heuriger, is broached is now 11 November.

There are a few more points of interest in Donnerskirchen: the **Weinforum Leisserhof** (open Wed–Sun; tel: 02683-8636; www.leisserhof.at) is devoted to the viticulture of Burgenland. In the Wine Vault there's an exhibition assembled by dozens of vineyards offering more than 100 wines, and the Wine Exchange stores tens of thousands of bottles of rare vintages. Whoever can keep their eye on the ball in spite of a glass or two can try their hand on the magnificent local 18-hole golf course or clear their head with a short walk up the Martinsberg to the three Celtic burial mounds.

Beware of stormy weather on Neusiedler See. It is a mistake to underestimate the lake, as even experienced sailors often struggle with incredibly high waves, despite the shallow depth.

BELOW: summer lake activities.

Most of the lakeshore villages share a typical infrastructure, including a bathing area, boat rental, sailing and windsurfing facilities, a campsite and bicycle rental. There is a simple explanation for the predominance of sailing and windsurfing; the lake is very shallow – mostly only 1–2 metres (3–7 ft) deep – and on most days you can be sure of finding a force six wind whipping across its surface.

Northeast of Donnerskirchen is **Purbach**, whose community suffered badly during the Turkish Wars. In 1683 it was virtually razed to the ground, explaining the origin of its Hungarian name, Feketevaras, meaning "Black Town". Still standing today are parts of the original city wall and gates – rare relics dating from the Turkish era. According to local legend, the stone figure peeping out of the chimney of the Türkenkeller represents a single remaining Turk. The intoxicatingly beautiful Kellergasse, dating from 1850, gives one the perfect excuse to experience the fruits of the local labour.

In **Breitenbrunn ❸**, near the northern end of the lake, a friendly atmosphere greets the visitor. The 30-metre (98-ft) high watchtower known as the **Türkenturm** is another reminder of the wars against the Turks. It is the town's principal landmark and figures prominently on every postcard. From the balcony of the freestanding edifice there is a fine panoramic view of the lake. Baroque farmhouses and dark, picturesque alleys complete the picture of this pretty village set in the water meadows.

A marina on the Neusiedler See.

At nearby **Jois**, a Roman double grave containing the skeletons of a mother and daughter was discovered in 1982. Another skeleton discovered a few years later, the so-called Lame Woman of Jois, showed evidence of two badly healed breaks in the lower leg. One of the most gruesome finds, however, is the family grave of a Bronze-Age prince. It was flanked on all sides by 12 further graves containing male skeletons. All the skulls had been smashed, indicating unequivocally the barbaric customs of the Scythians, who were wont to dispatch a number of courtiers into the next world to accompany a dead ruler.

BELOW: lakeside rushes.

The eastern shore

Just east of Jois, we come to the shopping town of **Neusiedl am See ❹**. Overseeing the daily bustle is the Ruine Tabor (daily; free), a modest ruined tower that offers a decent prospect over the lake and town. If the walk to the Strandbad is too much to bear, a swimming pool will meet you halfway. A note for sailing aficionados: Neusiedl was afforded the privilege of hosting the ISAF World Sailing Games 2006. Southeast of Neusiedl, at the foot of a geological formation known as the Parndorfer Platte, is the wine village of **Weiden**, which has retained its true rural character. Every day in summer, women sell produce from their doorsteps along the main road: fresh fruit and vegetables from their own gardens, and hand-made items of straw woven during the long evenings of the previous winter.

Before continuing your journey along the lakeshore, a short detour southeast will take you to a modern Vinotek at **Gols** – the **Weinkulturhaus** (open daily; tel: 02173-20039; www.weinkulturhaus.at) – where it is possible to sample the various local wines, and the enthralling open-air **Village Museum** (open Apr–Oct

Tues–Sun; entrance charge; tel: 02173-80642; www.dorfmuseum.at) at **Mönchhof**.

Ten kilometres (6 miles) from Weiden, the charming village of **Halbturn** ❺, just before the Hungarian border, is recommended. The castle here (open summer–autumn; times vary; entrance charge; tel: 02172-8577; www.schlosshalbturn.com) is one of the most famous baroque buildings in Burgenland, and served the Habsburg family as a hunting lodge and summer residence for over 300 years. Situated on the edge of the village, the castle was built at the beginning of the 18th century by Lukas von Hildebrandt for Count Harrach. Emperor Karl VI joined hunting parties here, and it served his wife Elisabeth as a dower residence. Empress Maria Theresa finally had it rebuilt, and it is thanks to her that it contains priceless frescoes by Maulbertsch. She gave it to her favourite daughter, the Archduchess Maria Christina, as a wedding present, and it has remained in the private possession of the Habsburg-Lothringen branch of the family, from whom the present owner is descended.

Extensively damaged during World War II and in a disastrous fire in 1949, the structure underwent a major restoration campaign beginning in 1971. Today the building serves as an attractive venue for exhibitions and concerts. A short distance south of Mönchhof is **Frauenkirchen**, a popular pilgrimage destination notable for its impressive baroque Basilika, Kalvarienberg and Franciscan monastery.

Back beside the lake, head south along the eastern shore to the tourist centre of **Podersdorf** ❻, the "Pearl of Neusiedler See". The largest campsite in Austria, a yachting marina and the town's location directly on the 3 km (2 miles) of reed-free shoreline account for its popularity. An integral part of its charm is one of the last working windmills in the Burgenland, whose sails continue to turn in spite of an advanced age of over 200 years.

The great bustard, Europe's heaviest bird, is a local inhabitant but is difficult to spot. One of the best places to see it is in the marshland southeast of Tadten, a village east of Illmitz.

BELOW: nesting stork in Rust.

South of Podersdorf, in the elbow of the lake, is the village of **Illmitz** ❼. It is at the centre of a bird watcher's paradise known as the Seewinkel. Exploratory trips into the wildlife reserves lying along the shore of the lake, guided by knowledgeable ornithologists from the excellent **National Park Centre** (open Apr–Oct daily; Nov–Mar Mon–Fri; tel: 02175-34420) at the edge of town, can be made by horse-drawn carriage, bicycle or even on foot. A well-signposted nature trail provides interesting information about the scientific work of the Biological Field Station. Lange Lacke, the conservation area near Apetlon, is closed to the public but you can walk or cycle along a footpath skirting its perimeter.

Generally considered the prettiest house in Illmitz is the Florianihaus, with its original thatched roof and narrow baroque courtyard. Almost as old is the Pusztascheune, a Magyar-style barn and now a well-known *heuriger* often resounding to impassioned folk music. To avoid retracing your steps, it is possible to take a ferry (Gangl; tel: 02175-2158; www.schifffahrt-gangl.at) from Illmitz to Mörbisch on the western side of the lake.

Storks and wine

Back on the western side of the lake is **Rust** ❽, which is world famous as the summer retreat for families of storks. In conjunction with the WWF, a Stork Post Office (postal code A-7073) has been set up here. It is open all year round, and the special postmark depicting a stork is much sought-after among philatelists and animal lovers. You can also buy special "stork" envelopes and postcards in the town's shops. With the proceeds, the local inhabitants and the WWF aim to acquire new food sources for the long-legged visitors, and to create additional breeding places on the roofs of the houses in the Old Town, their traditional nesting sites. These measures will, it is hoped, secure stocks of the much-loved bird at their present levels.

Rust is at least as famous for its wine as for its storks. Pleasantly full-bodied, it is well rounded and easily digestible. No other Austrian community has such a large number of special-quality wines; every cork bearing the brand-marked "R" guarantees the Rust origins of the wine. Here, the Austrian Wine Academy offers seminars and commentated wine tastings (for group bookings in advance; (02685) 6853; www.weinakademie.at). Artistically and historically speaking the most significant building in the town is the glorious **Fischerkirche** (Fishermen's Church; open Mar–Oct; tel: 0676-970 3316). Romanesque in origin, it later acquired a Gothic extension, and medieval frescoes were discovered during renovation in the 1950s. With a bit of luck you may even be able to enjoy a romantic classical concert there. Climb the Pfarrkirche tower for a stork's perspective of the townhouses' baroque and Renaissance façades.

Four kilometres (2 miles) west are the Roman quarries at **St Margarethen** (open Apr–Oct; entrance charge; tel: 02680-7060; www.st-margarethen.at). Stone has been quarried from here for 2,000 years and was used to build Carnuntum (*see page 156*) and Vindobona (Roman Vienna). In the summer, artists from all over the world converge here for an international sculpture school (tel: 02680-2188; www.roemersteinbruch.at). The quarry also hosts spectacular summer operas

A quiet corner of Rust.

BELOW: *Heuriger* entrance, Rust.

and passion plays *(see page 296)*, not to mention the largest colony for jackdaws in Europe. Beware, it is widely regarded as the hottest place in Central Europe: in 1936, a temperature of 48°C (118.4°F) in the shade was recorded here.

Operetta on the lake

South of Rust is **Mörbisch** ❾. The town has been famous since 1957 as the site of the Mörbisch Lakeside Festival *(see page 296)*, which takes place on a pontoon built out over the lake. The themes chosen are those from light music; every year a different operetta is performed during July and August. In order that nothing should spoil the evening's entertainment, here is a tip: it is advisable to smear yourself liberally with insect repellant, for the pesky mosquito also enjoys warm evenings on the water.

A wayside shrine.

The Hungarian border, only 2 km (1¼ miles) south of Mörbisch, makes its proximity felt in the appearance of old houses, ablaze with a riot of flowers and displaying the characteristic dried sheaves of maize. Window boxes bright with geraniums and large tubs overflowing with blossoming oleander conjure up a Mediterranean atmosphere, redolent of warm sunshine in long alleys and courtyards bordered by gleaming whitewashed houses.

Heading west now, away from the lake, the next place of interest is **Burg Forchtenstein** ❿ (open Apr–Oct daily; charge for obligatory tour; tel: 0226-81 212; www.burg-forchtenstein.at), situated 20 km (12 miles) southwest of Eisenstadt. Few other fortresses make such a strong, multi-faceted impression. Nothing remains of the oldest section, dating from the 14th century, apart from the keep with a roof that recalls the keel of a ship. After the rest of the complex was completely destroyed, Count Nikolaus Esterházy began the construction of the New Castle in 1635.

BELOW: a Turk's head in St Margarethen.

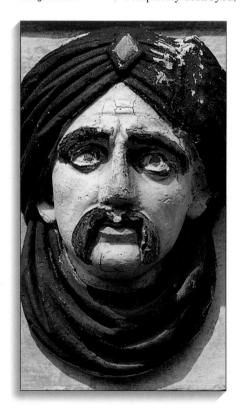

On his instructions were built the entrance tract in the inner courtyard, the vaulted passage linking it to the higher section of the ramparts, the true castle entrance, the arsenal and the chapel. In the middle of the 17th century, his successor Count Paul continued the extensions and gave the castle its present form. Many doorframes and doors with exquisite hand-wrought locks, some of the original window glazing, tiled floors and fireplaces date from this period, as does the 142-metre (465-ft) deep "Turk's Well", which has a fine echo.

Another 25 km (15 miles) south lies the roadside village of **Stoob**. A mecca for potters, Stoob is home to the only specialist ceramics academy in Austria and a traditional potters' guild. The original round-bellied clay pots with thin necks known as *pluzer* are manufactured here. The small market town of **Raiding**, northeast of Stoob, was the birthplace of composer Franz Liszt in 1811.

Southern reaches

The town of **Lockenhaus** ⓫, lying in the Günstal some 20 km (12 miles) south of Stoob, is first mentioned as a settlement at the end of the 9th century. The imposing Romanesque castle (open daily; entrance charge; tel: 02616-2394) – today the scene of chamber music festivals and other cultural events – once belonged to the Order of Templars, officially dis-

Map on page 168

banded in 1311. Around the beginning of the 17th century, the castle was owned by the Nádasdy family, one of whose members, Erzsébet Báthory, the so-called Blood Countess, was responsible for the murder of 600 women. The Italian master builder Orsolini constructed a baroque parish church in Lockenhaus in 1669. Today it is a place of pilgrimage. Peculiarly, whiskey lovers may also like to make the pilgrimage here – the local cellar bar and a tiny bar attached to the hairdressers' are well stocked with imported brands.

Continuing south through the Naturpark Geschriebenstein will take you to the market town of **Rechnitz**, where the moving Kreuzstadl – a Jewish memorial – stands at the town's boundaries. Attractive side streets lead to the Badesee, a swimming lake and beyond that, untaxing woodland walks.

Bernstein ⑫, 15 km (9 miles) west, is the world's only known source of the gleaming green semi-precious stone known as serpentine. Interested parties can learn more about Bernstein itself, the history of the village and its mining development from the laboriously executed details with which Otto Potsch, the painter and sculptor, adorned the **Felsenmuseum** (Rock Museum; open Mar–Dec daily; entrance charge; tel: 03354-6620; www.felsenmuseum.at). The Chinese astronomical sphere on display is also his work.

The castle, which dates from the 13th century, was of great strategic importance in the border skirmishes between Austria and Hungary – in contrast to the fascinating **Burg Schlaining**, (open Easter–Oct Tues–Sun; entrance charge; tel: 03355-2306; www.aspr.ac.at) 12 km (7 miles) south. Originally in the possession of the Babenbergs, it was predominantly involved in local plots and treachery. It is now busy with intriguing permanent and temporary exhibitions on the themes of justice in the Middle Ages, Austrian history and local handicrafts.

Bad Tatzmannsdorf, just west of Schlaining, offers a comprehensive range of treatments for patients suffering from rheumatism or coronary, circulatory, spinal, metabolic or vascular disorders. As long ago as the 17th century, the medicinal baths (open daily; entrance charge; tel: 03353-89900; www.burgenlandtherme.at) in this spa town – previously a Magyar and before that a Croatian settlement – were popular with the aristocracy. The peaceful town contains a **Freilichtmuseum** (open daily, free) with relocated, well-preserved old farmhouses. There are a number of jogging and walking arenas and a choice of golf courses.

The large shopping town of **Oberwart**, the next town to the south, is notable for a significant Hungarian population, as evidenced by the presence of a Calvinist church, rare in Austria. Finally, **Güssing** ⑬ – a further 35 km (21 miles) south – is famous for its mineral water and is dominated by a magnificent hillside **castle** (open Easter–Oct Tues–Sun; entrance charge; tel: 03322-43400; www.burgguessing.info). Dating from the 12th century, it contains a museum, an ancestral portrait gallery containing some pictures attributed to Brueghel, an armoury and the oldest organ in Burgenland. West of Güssing, the village of **Gerersdorf** has an open-air museum with farm buildings dating from the 18th and 19th centuries (open daily; entrance charge; tel: 03328-32255; www.freilicht-museum-geresdorf.at). ❑

Oggau, on the western side of the lake.

BELOW: grapes ready for pressing.

STYRIA

*Known as the "Green Province", the southern region
of Styria combines splendid mountain scenery,
thermal spas and gently rolling hills*

Maps:
City 178
Area 180

The "green heart of Austria" is an appropriate slogan for Styria (Steiermark). The second-largest Austrian province combines the Alpine landscape of perpetual ice and deeply cut ravines, with extensive expanses of forest that give way to rolling ranges of hills skirting the lower Hungarian plains.

For some, Styria may at first seem exotic: dark, nutty pumpkin seed oil, rosé Schilcher wine, and a dialect that may be unintelligible to unpractised ears. But here, in fact, Austria shows itself at its best: pithy and natural, with a genuinely hospitable attitude to visitors and affordable prices. The mountainous north, with its countless opportunities for active and adventure holidays, can claim the largest interconnected Alpine pasture area in Europe. In the green hills of the romantic south, the unhurried visitor can wander along routes dedicated to castles, apples, flowers and of course, wine. It's never too far to the local bounteous *buschenschank* (vineyard restaurant) or *heuriger* (wine tavern), serving homegrown delicacies like *brettljause* (assorted meat and cheese specialities) and wine. These favourable conditions are underlined by the fact that the Austrians themselves regard the "Green Province" as their favourite holiday region within their own borders.

LEFT: giant pumpkins.
BELOW: statue of St Peter in the Mausoleum of Ferdinand II.

The Styrian capital

With a population of 240,000, the province's capital, **Graz ❶**, is the second-largest city in Austria. Situated on the Mur River, it is an economic and cultural centre (it was Cultural Capital of Europe 2003), settled as long ago as AD 800, but was first mentioned in records in 1128. The town was awarded special privileges under the Habsburg King Rudolf I, who seized it from his archrival Ottokar, and from 1379 it became the chief residence of the Leopoldine line. A bastion against the Turkish threat, Graz was fortified between the 15th and 17th centuries and withstood a succession of sieges. The Italian influence on the architecture is unmistakable.

A stroll around the Old Town, designated by UNESCO as a World Cultural Heritage Site, is a joy. Its appearance is characterised by numerous gabled houses dating from the 17th and 18th centuries, some of which still display fine stucco decorations. A favourite meeting place is the **Erzherzog-Johann-Brunnen Ⓐ** (Archduke Johann Fountain) on Hauptplatz. The four female figures on the bronze fountain are allegorical depictions of the Enns, Mur, Drau and Sann – the four principal rivers of Styria before the partition. The neo-Renaissance **Rathaus Ⓑ** (Town Hall; built in 1888) here is a classic example of historicist architecture.

The **Landhaushof Ⓒ**, behind the Rathaus, built by Domenico dell'Allio between 1557 and 1565, is con-

sidered one of the finest intact Renaissance buildings in the south German-speaking area. A stunning courtyard, with three tiers of arcades and a bronze well canopy, hosts summer concerts. Also not to be missed are the Rittersaal (Knights' Hall) and Landstube (Parliament Chamber), with their magnificent stucco ceilings depicting the four elements, signs of the zodiac and scenes from local history.

Armour for a medieval army

On the south side of the Landhaus stands the 1642-built **Landeszeughaus** **Ⓓ** (Arsenal; open daily; entrance charge; tel: 0316-8017 9660), which boasts the world's largest collection of ancient weaponry. In the 17th century it could easily have equipped a 28,000-man army of mercenaries. Sixteenth-century suits of armour (for man and beast), two-handed swords, chain mail, rifles, decorated pistols and musical instruments are all on view here.

The social focal point of the Old Town is the Herrengasse, a fashionable shopping street with a number of noteworthy townhouses. The Herrengasse eventually leads to the square Am Eisernen Tor, with the central Mariensäule (Virgin's Column). North of here are a number of architectural jewels. The 15th-century **Burg** **Ⓔ** (Castle) on Hofgasse now contains government offices, however there is access to a late-Gothic double spiral staircase dating from 1499 in the northwest wing. Opposite the Burg is the late 15th-century **Domkirche** **Ⓕ** (Cathedral) whose interior combines Gothic and baroque features. Beside the cathedral is the magnificent **Mausoleum of Ferdinand II** **Ⓖ** (opening times vary; entrance charge), a Mannerist-baroque construction begun in 1614. The interior contains some eye-catching stucco and frescoes by Johann Bernhard Fischer von Erlach and a red marble sarcophagus of Ferdinand's parents, Charles II and Maria.

Agriculture is a hugely important part of the Styrian economy.

Glorious views over the red city roofs and beyond are afforded from the **Schlossberg** **Ⓗ**. This dolomite rock is 472 metres (1,548 ft) high and can be ascended by funicular railway, glass lift or on foot (in 20–25 minutes). It is crowned by the 28-metre (90-ft) **Uhrturm** **Ⓘ** (Clocktower), a city landmark erected in the 13th century that is visible for a great distance around.

Graz is also a student town (it has two universities and a music conservatory) and has an active cultural life. Every autumn it hosts the avant-garde arts festival, Steirischer Herbst, and in summer, the Styriarte, devoted to classical music.

Contemporary art lovers are well catered for, with the consistently reliable **Neue Galerie** (contact for exhibitions info; entrance charge; tel: 0316-829 155; www.neuegalerie.at), in an old townhouse on Sackstrasse, and on the west bank of the Mur, the estimable **Kunsthaus Graz** (open Tues–Sun; entrance charge; tel: 0316-8017 9200; www.kunsthausgraz.at). This shimmering, blue, biomorphic bubble – known

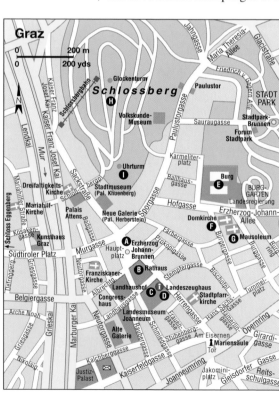

Graz

locally as the friendly alien, is complemented by the nearby Murinsel, a shell-like haven in the middle of the river, and a peaceful spot to relax over a drink.

As expected, Graz can offer a wide range of gastronomic pleasures. Those in need of refreshment after an extended exploration of the city on foot will find it in one of many fine restaurants. If you don't want the evening to end there, the Bermuda Triangle (just ask for the Mehlplatz) is a fine place to get lost, while many venues in town host live music.

The environs of the Styrian capital are also worth exploring. Approximately 2 km (1 mile) west of Graz stands **Schloss Eggenberg** 1625–35 (grounds open daily; entrance charge), commissioned to reflect cosmic harmony. Thus the four towers represent the seasons, twelve gates the months and 365 windows, the days of the year. The Planet Room and rich Staterooms are decorated with magnificent stucco and ceiling paintings. Also in the 19th-century landscaped grounds are a museum of prehistory and antiquity, the Alte Galerie, and the Roman Provincial and coin collections belonging to the provincial museum, the **Joanneum** (museums open Tues–Sun; entrance charge; tel: 0316-08017 4830; www.museum-joanneum.at).

Some 40 km (25 miles) west of Graz and 3 km (2 miles) northeast of Köflach, lies the **Piber Stud Farm** ❷ (open Apr–Dec daily; charge for obligatory tours; tel: 03144-3233; www.piber.com). This is where the Lipizzaner stallions of the Spanish Riding School in Vienna *(see page 123)* are bred and trained. The oldest classic horse breed in Europe dates back to 1580, when Archduke Karl II founded a stud in Lipizza, near Trieste.

The nearby town of **Bärnbach** is notable for its local glassblowing craftsmen and possesses a church that was given an unique makeover in 1987 by Viennese

Maps:
City 178
Area 180

Every year about five Lippizaner stallions are sent from Piber to the riding school in Vienna

BELOW: a sunny cherub in Graz.

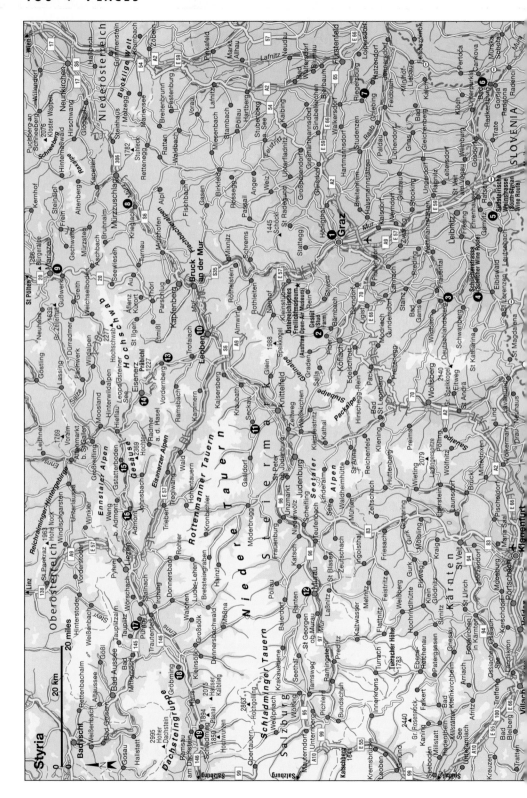

Map on page 180

architect Friedensreich Hundertwasser. **Pfarrkirche St Barbara** now has irregular windows, a golden onion dome, a bowed roof and other typical Hundertwasser touches.

Northeast of Graz near Weiz is **Puch**, the apple capital of Styria. Since 80 percent of Austrian apples come from more than a quarter of a million trees in Styrian orchards, they have a lot to celebrate about at the Apple Blossom Festival in April. However, you don't need to wait until spring to sample the local *apfelsturm* (cider) at one of the stops along the 25-km (15½-mile) apple route.

Where the Schilcher grows

South of Graz lies Styria's principal wine-making district. At present, more than 4,000 hectares of land are devoted to viticulture in the province. This means that it only contributes around 5 percent of the national total wine production, but the 3,200 wine-growing concerns produce predominantly high-quality vintages. The wines produced here are, in the main, piquant Rhine Riesling and Welschriesling varieties. However, the Schilcher, the Styrian speciality produced in the western part of this region, is not so much a wine as a staple of life.

Southern Styrian grapes.

The Schilcher claims to be the oldest Styrian wine; it was probably first cultivated from a wild vine stock by the Celts. Pope Pius VI reported on the occasion of his journey to Vienna in 1782, that he had been served at the foot of the Koralpe mountain a "light-red, sharp-tasting wine, agreeable and refreshing." In the 16th and 17th centuries, the Wildbach grape was widely grown in Styria. Archduke Johann, the popular younger brother of Franz I and an enthusiastic supporter of Styrian wine growing, had the Wildbach grape bred in his own vine nurseries. At the end of the 19th century, however, the vine louse destroyed most of the Schilcher stocks; the continuation of the strain could only be assured by grafting the Wildbach grape on to an American stock. In the middle of the 1960s this ancient Styrian grape species was rediscovered and cultivation along modern lines was begun.

BELOW: Pfarrkirche St Barbara.

The Schilcher, whose name derives from the word *schillert* (shining) – as its colour shimmers from light pink to dark red – is one of the more rare Austrian wine varieties. Its production is the only one to be protected by law and restricted to a specific area. It is characterised by a fruity yet lively sharpness, a mild yet distinctive bouquet and a balanced, slightly acidic taste.

The central village in the Schilcher District is **Deutschlandsberg ❸**, 35 km (22 miles) southwest of Graz. Dominated by the fortified Landsberg Castle, it is an excellent place for resting in one of the numerous rustic taverns. Those who prefer to live more healthily should pay a visit to the neighbouring spas or the mudbaths at Schwanberg. Castles and country houses are dotted across the area. The Renaissance Schloss Hollenegg is just to the south, as is Schloss Limberg; to the north, there are castles at Frauental and Stainz, the latter being the magnificent ancestral home of the Counts of Merano. Another castle in the area that should not be overlooked is at Wildbach, near Frauental. Franz Schubert stayed here in 1827. Schilcher is pressed here too, from the Blue Wildbacher grape.

The Schilcher lends its name to the panoramic **Schilcherstrasse** ❹ (Schilcher Wine Route). It leads across attractive ranges of hills and past pretty wooden vintners' houses, winding from Ligist (in the north) via Greisdorf to Stainz, Bad Gams, Deutschlandsberg and thence to Eibiswald, almost on the Slovenian border, where it joins the South Styrian Wine Route (*see below*).

Colourful doorway in St Veit am Vogau near Ehrenhausen.

More wine country

To the southeast of the Schilcher region is the South Styrian Wine Country, which stretches from Leutschach, near the Slovenian border, east and north through Ratsch, Gamlitz and many other famous wine-making villages to Kitzeck (Europe's highest lying wine-making village) near Leibnitz. Gamlitz, with a total of 350 hectares (865 acres) under cultivation, is regarded as the largest wine-making village in the province.

This region is served by the **South Styrian Wine Route** ❺, which takes you through a land of hills that radiates peace, calm and a salubrious air. The vineyards cascade down the hillsides to the valley floors; farmhouses are scattered as if by some caprice across the scene; and the graceful poplars recall the cypresses so familiar in the Tuscan landscape. In fact, "The Styrian Tuscany" is the nickname given to this corner of the Green Province. Visitors enjoying the 40-km (25-mile) drive or rail journey south from Graz to Ehrenhausen, the gateway to the South Styrian Wine Country, may find themselves making this comparison.

Maize, another important component of the local economy, is also much in evidence; only the olive trees are missing. In their place grow sweet chestnuts, known here as *Maroni* and roasted over the countless stoves that proliferate beside woodland and roadway when they are harvested in autumn. The chestnuts are especially good accompanied by Sturm, lightly fermented (thus slightly alcoholic), cloudy grape juice, which can be sampled at the long tables placed near the chestnut stoves or in the kitchens of the farmhouses. Musicians perform on accordion and dulcimer by some chestnut stands well into October.

BELOW: Riegersburg castle.

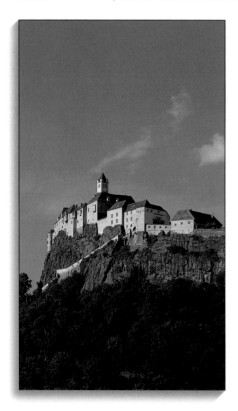

The *klapotetz*, a kind of windmill, is a regular sight in the area. Six or eight slanting wings, fixed to a powerful shaft, carry small hammers positioned to hit an anvil – either furiously if a strong wind is blowing or intermittently if only a breeze is stirring. The actual purpose of the contraption is to scare away the starlings, which may have designs on the grapes. Each of the bird-scarers has an individual sound. The vintners start up their *klapotetz* each year on St Jacob's Day (25 July) and shut them down on St Martin's Day (11 November).

The land of spas

The southeastern corner of Styria is one of the healthiest regions in Austria. Here, spa resorts invite the visitor to relax, regenerate or draw from the medicinal effects of the thermal waters. **Bad Radkersburg** ❻ lies right in the southeast corner of this region, some 75 km (46 miles) southeast of Graz. The River Mur, flowing along the southern side of the town, marks the border with Slovenia.

The Styrian spa with the longest tradition retains its elegant mid-19th century Biedermeier character.

Map on page 180

Bad Gleichenberg, 25 km (15½ miles) north of Bad Radkersburg, was highly esteemed during Imperial times for its efficacy in the treatment of circulatory and pulmonary disorders. In recent years cure programmes for children suffering from respiratory disorders have been available here. The village is surrounded by a 20-hectare (50-acre) nature park and offers an excellent 9-hole golf course.

North of Bad Gleichenberg, **Riegersburg** ❼ is home to a monumental **castle** (open Apr–Oct daily; entrance charge; tel: 03153-8670; www.riegersburg.com). Standing majestically on a basalt cliff, it was built in 1170 on the site of a Roman fort. It received its present appearance in the 17th century. The castle, which became the country's main bulwark against Turkish invasion, is today one of the best-preserved medieval castles in Europe. Since 1987 it has housed a number of temporary exhibitions.

The extraordinary development of a thermal resort in the village of **Blumau**, 30km (18 miles) northeast of Riegersburg, partially owes its success to visionary artist Hundertwasser. His playful, otherworldly designs at **Rogner-Bad Blumau** (open daily; entrance charge; tel: 03383-51000; www.blumau.com) make any visit a cheerful occasion.

Bad Waltersdorf, a little further north, specialises exclusively in relaxation and fitness. In addition to the wide range of curative facilities on offer, there are walks through peaceful woods, past vineyards, fishponds and fairy-tale castles. A family-oriented alternative can be found just south of Fürstenfeld, at **Therme Loipersdorf** (open daily; entrance charge; tel: 03382-82040; www.therme.at), the biggest spa in Europe, with a wave bath, waterslide and a comprehensive menu of therapies and massages; there's something for everyone.

Bad Radkersburg is an attractive town, characterised by well-preserved merchants' and noblemen's houses from the Gothic, Renaissance, baroque and art nouveau periods – it was recently given a European Gold Medal for Historic Preservation. Today the town is devoted to health and fitness.

BELOW: a southern Styrian wine estate.

Highly decorated façade, Mariazell.

In Rosegger's forest home

North of Graz, on the right bank of the Mur near Stübing, is the **Austrian Open-Air Museum** (open Apr–Oct Tues–Sun; entrance charge; tel: 03124-53700; www.freilichtmuseum.at). It is home to a collection of old farmhouses, barns and mills from all over Austria. It presents 90 exhibits over 61 hectares (150 acres), from cattle troughs to a complete farmyard.

North again you will eventually reach **Bruck an der Mur**, at the confluence of the Mur and Mürz rivers. An exquisite late-Gothic residence, the Korn-messerhaus, stands on Bruck's large central square, by an intricate 17th-century wrought iron well. Overseeing the scene on the Schlossberg, is an attractive Uhrturm and the ruins of Landskron, one of the oldest fortresses in the country.

A 30-km (18-mile) detour east to **Krieglach** ❽ is strongly recommended. Here, at Roseggerstrasse 44, the celebrated Styrian writer Peter Rosegger lived and died. It now houses a newly renovated museum, and an adjoining **Heimatmuseum** (open Tues–Sun; tel: 03855-2375, www.waldheimat.at) displays local curiosities. A memorial recalls the famous local son, whose grave you'll find in the village cemetery. Krieglach is also the starting point for walking tours through "Rosegger's native country".

A side road south to **Alpl** will transport the visitor into a forest landscape that could have come straight out of a Grimm's fairy tale. The Waldschule, the community school where Rosegger taught, includes a **Wandermuseum** (Austrian Walkers' Museum; open Apr–Oct Tues–Sun; entrance charge; tel: 03855-8238), while the short walk to Rosegger's rustic **Geburtshaus** (birthplace museum; open Apr–Dec Tues–Sun; entrance charge; tel: 03855-8230) through the famous woodlands, make the village an attractive stopping point.

THE VIRGIN OF MARIAZELL

Mariazell is a place with an importance out of all proportion to its small size. This scenic mountain village takes in a deluge of visitors every year, particularly in August and September – all because of a single wooden statue believed throughout Austria, Hungary and the Balkans to possess both healing and protective powers. Mariazell's basilica, Romanesque in origin, was rebuilt in the 14th century as a Gothic-style hall church before being transformed into a larger baroque edifice between 1644 and 1683. The goal of all pilgrims, however, is the late-Romanesque, wooden statue of the Virgin Mary, a plain rendering which in 1157 was claimed by a local monk to have delivered his party from danger. Soon a small chapel was constructed in the woods, and a cult began to develop. In 1377, the Virgin of Mariazell was given direct credit for preventing a Turkish victory over the Hungarians.

Today she is housed within the basilica in the Gnadenkapelle (Chapel of Miracles) behind a Viennese silver grille. Two important religious holidays, Assumption Day and Mary's birthday (8 September) bring even more than the usual throngs to see her, as do Saturday evenings in summer, when the village streets are lit by torches and filled with processions.

Map on page 180

Northern pilgrimage

If, however, you continue your exploration of Styria in a northerly direction from Bruck an der Mur, you will soon enter the Hochschwab region. **Thörl** claims a surprising variety of interesting buildings for its size, and the ruins of the 15th-century Burg Schachenstein ought to have artists reaching for their sketchbooks. Beyond Thörl, and only 18 km (11 miles) north of Bruck, lies the resort village of Aflenz, often referred to as "the Davos of Styria". The region also provides the headwaters for the freshwater supply network of Vienna.

The village of **Mariazell** ❾ is 40 km (25 miles) north of Aflenz and almost on the provincial boundary between Styria and Lower Austria. This northern-most part of the province is the country's major focal point for religious pilgrims, thanks to a simple wooden statue of the Virgin Mary *(see page 184)*. She is kept in the town's breathtaking basilica (open daily; treasury May–Oct Tues–Sun; entrance charge; tel: 03882-25950), which was built to display her. Fischer von Erlach created the magnificent baroque high altar (1704) of various coloured marble, dominated by a larger-than-life silver Crucifixion group. The grave of the famous Hungarian, Cardinal Mindszenty, is in the church.

Mariazell also offers a variety of attractions that make it suitable for a longer stay. These include a Kneipp cure complex, hang-gliding, a natural toboggan run, fishing on Lake Hubertus, canoeing on the Salza River and various excursions – up to the Bürgeralpe via a cable-car (closed Apr and Nov, www.mariazell-buergeralpe.at) or with the Museum Tram to **Lake Erlauf** (July–Sept Sat–Sun; tel: 03882-3014; www.museumstramway.at). The **Heimathaus** offers an eclectic collection of local treasures (open May, June, Oct: Wed and Fri; July–Sept daily; entrance charge for obligatory tours; tel: 03882-43126; www.mariazeller-schaetze.at). While in Mariazell, don't pass up the opportunity to try the Mariazeller Honig-Lebkuchen, spicy honey and gingerbread biscuits.

Southwest of Bruck is **Leoben** ❿, the second-largest town in Styria (37,000 inhabitants) and the centre of the province's iron industry. Here we find not only the seat of an iron and coal university with a worldwide reputation, but also much to appeal to the culturally-interested traveller – not to mention the celebrated **Gösser brewery** (museum open Apr–Nov Sat–Sun; entrance charge; tel: 03842-2090 5802; www.goesser.at). Visitors walking under the "Mushroom Tower" – as the local populace lovingly calls the 17th-century Mautturm (Customs Tower), in reference to its toadstool-shaped roof – en route to the attractive, spacious Hauptplatz, pass the **Municipal Theatre** (founded in 1791) on the right-hand side. It is one of the oldest public theatres in Austria, but no longer has a resident troupe of players. Apart from productions from the stages of Vienna and Graz, it also hosts touring groups from Germany and Switzerland.

Culture vultures will find much to devour in the nearby **MuseumsCenter** complex (open Tues–Sun; entrance charge; tel: 03842-4062 408; www.leoben.at), housed in what was formerly the castle of the local prince, and **Kunsthalle** (opening times vary; entrance charge). The museum is devoted to local socio-political history and craftsmanship over the centuries.

Those wishing to recuperate in Aflenz can either take a Kneipp cure or simply enjoy the healthy, bracing air by taking a long walk – the Hochschwab is a designated conservation area.

BELOW: a wayside shrine near Mariazell.

The Murtal

Castle fanatics should not fail to visit Teufenbach, along the Upper Mur Valley. The village has a population of barely 600, but houses a whole series of castles: Alt-Teufenbach (12th century), Neu-Teufenbach (16th century), the ruins of Stein Castle (12th century) and Pux Castle (12th–14th century).

If you are heading west from Leoben, you should include an excursion through the Upper Mur Valley. The countryside here is mountainous and dotted with idyllic little villages where old traditions are still cultivated. The setting is ideal for a restful holiday. Protected by the Schladminger and Rottenmanner mountains, many of the village resorts here are renowned for their healthy climate. Walking enthusiasts will find excellent conditions at any time of year.

First stop is the famous Benedictine Abbey in **Seckau** ⓫. It was founded in 1140 and, following a fire, rebuilt in the original style in 1259. The abbey is one of the finest Romanesque buildings in Central Europe. A cloister courtyard with Tuscan-style pillars, the Romanesque basilica, the Imperial Hall, the Homage Hall and the so-called Black Hall are all worth seeing. Some distance to the southwest lie the villages of Zeltweg, Judenburg, St Peter and Unzmarkt-Frauenburg;all good starting points for walking tours through the Seetaler Alps or the Niedere Tauern.

Murau ⓬, a few miles west, is a centre for Nordic sports, woodcarving and the local speciality, Murauer beer. The village contains a number of ancient trees dating from medieval times. In the neighbouring village of St Georgen stands the **Holzmuseum** (Styrian Wood Museum; open daily; entrance charge; tel: 03534-2202), which documents the links between the province's inhabitants and their lush green forests.

Those wishing to continue their journey towards Carinthia and Klagenfurt should turn left on to Road 95 near Predlitz. It leads steadily uphill through the romantic Turracher Graben between the Gurktaler Alps. The summit is the Turracher Höhe, at 1,783 metres (5,840 ft), which forms the natural boundary between Styria and Carinthia. A trio of lakes, the Turracher See, the Grünsee and

BELOW: the wine country of southern Styria

the Schwarzsee, invite the visitor to explore the district on foot. In winter, the area is a favoured ski centre; in summer, the mountain pastures and forests attract almost as many visitors.

Map on page 180

An industrial past

Back at Leoben, the road northwest leads to **Trofaiach**, an archetypal summer resort. It was once the main resting place at the heart of the Styrian Iron Road that ran northwest from Leoben to Steyr in Upper Austria. Today, thanks to its castles – Mell, Stibichhofen (museum open Sat and Sun; tel: 03847-30250) and Oberdorf – it is an attractive goal for excursions.

Beyond Trofaiach is **Vordernberg** ⓫, once a centre for iron production. Archduke Johann was largely responsible for the development of the Vordernberg coal and steel industry, the history of which can still be traced in many places. Vordernberg is one of the foremost towns in the history of European iron manufacture. Apart from numerous old mineworkers' houses and the Meran House (Archduke Johann's house), there are the **Erzbergbahn Museum** (opening times vary; entrance charge; tel: 03849-832) a rack railway museum, the **Hochofenmuseum** (open daily; tel: 03849-283; www.radwerk-vordernberg.at) an iron-smelting plant and an old blacksmith's shop to see.

The Eisenerz Alps from the Präbichl Pass.

The Präbichl Pass, which reaches 1,227 metres (4,035 ft), links Vordernberg and Eisenerz via 12 km (7 miles) of twisting road. The Erzberg railway, which traverses the pass through a series of tunnels, was not completed until 1892. As recently as 1978, steam engines still puffed up the steep rack railway over the pass. Nowadays the Präbichl is held in high regard as a first-class ski resort.

The town of **Eisenerz** ⓬, another important mining centre, lies in a wild valley basin, at the mouth of the Krumpen and the Trofeng valleys. Rising more than 700 metres (2,300 ft) above the valley floor is the 1,470-metre (4,820-ft) Erzberg, or "ore-mountain", its slopes scarred by opencast mining into ochre-coloured ridges and terraces. Tours of the mountain and mining works are offered (open daily; May–Oct; entrance charge; tel: 03848-3200; www.abenteuer-erzberg.at), including a 90-minute journey underground and a ride around the terraces in a huge lorry.

BELOW: the Erzberg, scarred by opencast mining.

The town's present-day appearance owes much to its economic heyday in the 15th and 16th centuries. There are a number of sights worth visiting: the Schichtturm bell-tower (1581); the Bergmannsplatz with its fine miners' union houses; the remains of the Rupprechta furnace; the Kammerhof (once the seat of the mining overseer), which now contains the **Municipal Museum** (open May–Oct daily; Nov–Apr Tues–Fri; entrance charge; tel: 03848-3615); the Kaiser-Franz-Stollen, where the ore was prepared for smelting; remains of the ore consignments at the railway station; and the huge slag heaps in Münichthal. In addition Eisenerz has a well-developed infrastructure for tourists: campsite, climbing school, fitness circuit and walking trails.

Northwest of Eisenerz is the **Leopoldsteiner See**, 1,500 metres (4,920 ft) long by 500 metres (1,640 ft) wide. A mountain lake impressively surrounded by craggy rock walls, it recalls the fjords of Scandinavia.

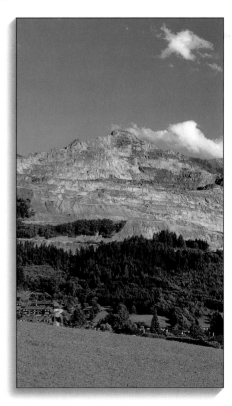

According to local legend, a malevolent water sprite once brought bad luck to the lake's fishermen. Eventually they gathered up their courage and caught the wicked fellow, but the sprite, somewhat subdued, made his captors a proposal: "A golden river, a silver heart or an iron hat" in exchange for his release. His captors wisely chose the iron hat, whereupon the sprite pointed at the nearby Erzberg mountain. It is said that this incident marked the beginning of the history of ore mining in Upper Styria.

In the Gesäuse Ravine, between mountains that rise up to 2,400 metres (7,870 ft) high, the River Enns laboriously carves its way through precipitous rock faces. The rushing torrents and majestic mountains make this countryside one of the most bizarre and fascinating in Austria.

The Gesäuse Ravine

About 15 km (9 miles) northwest of Eisenerz is **Hieflau**, the principal traffic intersection in the Gesäuse region. At this point Road 115 (the Iron Road) meets Road 146 (the Gesäuse Road), and the Amstetten-Selzthal railway line meets the Erzberg line to Leoben. Hieflau marks the eastern end of the Gesäuse Ravine.

A few miles along Road 146, **Gstatterboden** ⓕ deserves its epithet of "Capital of the Gesäuse". It lies exactly in the middle of the Enns corridor, between Hochtor Range in the south and the Buchstein Group and the Tamischbachturm in the north. Gstatterboden is a good starting point for a variety of Alpine pursuits. Walkers, mountaineers, climbers, ski enthusiasts, wild-water canoeists and fishermen are all well catered for here. The new **Nationalparkpavillon** (open June–Oct daily; entrance charge; tel: 03613-2100 041; www.nationalpark.co.at) contains a helpful information centre for the surrounding area and a modern, interactive exhibition for all ages that explores the region in depth.

Johnsbach, south of the main road, is regarded as the second most important climbing centre in the Gesäuse. It is linked to the Enns valley by a 6-km (4-mile) long gorge, and lies in an idyllic high-altitude valley between the Hochtor range in the northeast and the gentler Eisenerz Alps and the Admonter Reichenstein to the south and west. A moving Mountain Church (14th century) with a world-famous climbers' cemetery, and, a little further down the road, short walks to the Wolfbauer Waterfall and the Odelstein Stalactite Caves make Johnsbach a welcome diversion.

One of the highlights of any tour of Upper Styria is a visit to **Stift Admont** ⓖ, Austria's oldest male monastic institution. The Benedictine monastery (open Apr–Oct daily; entrance charge; tel: 03613-231 2601; www.stiftadmont.at) was founded by Archbishop Gebhard of Salzburg in 1074 and was for centuries the artistic and cultural centre of the Enns valley.

The abbey library is one of the finest examples of baroque architecture in the world, with superb ceiling frescoes by Bartolomeo Altomonte and sculptures by Joseph Stammel. It contains around 150,000 volumes, 1,400 manuscripts and 900 early printed works, making it the largest and most valuable monastery library in the world. The foundation buildings also include the oldest neo-Gothic church in Austria, contemporary and fine art museums, a multimedia monastery presentation and, perhaps not for the phobic, a natural history museum with an insect collection consisting of no fewer than 252,000 exhibits.

To the west is **Liezen**, the capital of the Styrian section of the Enns valley. With over 7,000 inhabitants, it

BELOW: autumn colours in the Styrian forest.

is primarily a transport hub and, thanks to the nearby Wurzeralm, a small ski resort. Southwest of Liezen is the town of **Bad Wörschach** with its famous sulphur springs – also notable for hosting the World Championship 24 Hour Run. The Wörschach Gorge is one of the most striking in the land, and there is a fine panorama from the ruins of Wolkenstein Castle (1186), which overlooks the town.

Beyond Wörschach is the delightful village of **Pürgg** ⑰, site of some of the oldest surviving frescoes in Austria, completed around 1160. They decorate the Romanesque Chapel of St John, set on a hill on the edge of town. The subjects portrayed are the Annunciation, the Nativity and the Feeding of the Five Thousand. The classic wood-framed houses and painted facades of the village only add to Pürgg's allure.

The next port of call is the romantic 13th-century **Trautenfels Castle** (open Easter–Oct daily; entrance charge; tel: 03682-22233; www.museumtrautenfels.at). It was built to defend the Enns valley and acquired its present-day appearance in 1664. In fact, its observation tower affords a spectacular view of the middle Enns Valley. With frescoes by Carpoforo Tencalla and a splendid countryside museum, Trautenfels is a must-see. Taking a northwesterly route from here will lead you to the Styrian part of the Salzkammergut, including Bad Aussee and Altaussee *(see page 205)*. Carry on in a southwesterly direction and you will reach **Gröbming** ⑱. This picturesque, sleepy village and ski resort is a popular holiday destination because of its sunny climate. The beautiful late-Gothic parish church (15th century) contains the largest altarpiece in Styria. Things get busy in late July, when the Ennstal Classic car rally comes to town. Families with small children are particularly welcome in Gröbming. Childcare and babysitting services have been set up to relieve parents of some of the strain of holidaymaking.

Around the Dachstein

If you travel still further southwest, you soon arrive in the town of **Schladming** ⑲ (population 4,000), and the area surrounding the Dachstein Massif. It boasts the largest Lutheran church in Styria – built in 1862 but containing a much older altarpiece from around 1570 – and in 1982 held the Alpine Skiing World Championships. It is also a candidate for the Skiing World Championships in 2011, and every January sees the return of the men's slalom Night Race. The winter-sports infrastructure is correspondingly well developed. Linking the surrounding four mountains' ski centres are 120 km (75 miles) of avalanche-free pistes, a cable-car network and chair and draglifts. Around 30 national cross-country ski teams train on the Dachstein Glacier and other outdoor pursuits are catered for too: golf, paragliding, mountain-biking, climbing and rafting. Meanwhile, the strong of stomach can enjoy the bird's eye view from the Dachstein Sky Walk (open daily; (03687) 81241; www.dachsteingletscher.at). The spectacular viewing platform is at an altitude of 2,700 metres (8,858 ft) above sea level. Ramsau, a neighbouring village reached by a meandering road north, has meanwhile developed into a fine resort – it hosted the Nordic Ski World Championships in 1999. In the warmer months the entire region is ideal for mountain and walking tours. ❏

Map on page 180

Ramsau-Rössing is a textile-manufacturing town, and is the site of the oldest loden-dyeing factory in Austria (open Mon–Fri; free) – it exports its wares to fashion houses worldwide. Loden is the hardwearing, heavy green woolcloth beloved by Germans and Austrians for their short pile overcoats.

BELOW: a miniature from the Stift Admont library.

UPPER AUSTRIA

*Between the baroque monasteries of St Florian and Kremsmünster
and the historic towns of Steyr and Freistadt, Upper Austria hides
large swathes of remote countryside*

Map
on page
194

Frrom the Dachstein peaks in the south to the Bohemian woods in the north, from the Inn River to the Enns River – these are the boundaries of Upper Austria (Oberösterreich). The province is also sub-divided into regions: the Mühlviertel, the Innviertel, the Hausruck Forest and the Traunviertel. The most scenic region, the Salzkammergut, is covered in the next chapter.

Upper Austria can offer its visitors a wide range of holiday facilities: adventurous souls, for example, will get their money's worth hang-gliding (Windisch-Garsten), potholing (Dachstein Caves), wild-water canoeing (on the Steyr) or scaling one of the region's many peaks. The more than 70 lakes in the Salzkammergut cater for every type of water sport. If you prefer a more tranquil atmosphere, the Mühlviertel will prove a paradise for extended cycle tours and walking holidays, while those whose interests lie more on the cultural side will find much to explore in the countless monasteries and convents, and in the pretty villages with their quaint houses.

PRECEDING PAGES:
in the Dachstein
mountains.
LEFT: the café at the
Neue Galerie, Linz.
BELOW: *Portrait of
Maria Munk* by
Klimt in the Neue
Galerie.

Linz

A popular rhyme, claiming that "It all begins in Linz", arouses the new arrival's curiosity about the provincial capital of Upper Austria. **Linz ❶** proves to be a city that at once invites the visitor to stroll through its streets, to watch the world go by, to eat, drink and shop. The third-largest city in the country has been the capital of the "Land around the Enns" since 1490.

The city's roots stretch back to before the time of the Romans, whose records mention "Lentia" for the first time in AD 410. The name is of Celtic origin, and it is even claimed that the site was settled in neolithic times. In approximately 700 Linz became the eastern base of the Bavarian kingdom.

At the start of the 13th century it came into the possession of the Babenbergs and received its town charter soon afterwards; at the end of the 15th century Linz even became the royal seat for a short while. In 1672 a wool factory (which later employed as many as 50,000 home workers) was founded. In 1832 Austria's first (horse-drawn) railway commenced operations between Linz and Budweis, and 1842 saw the foundation of the shipyard, which made the first iron ships in Europe. Thanks to the nitrogen works and the Voest steelworks, Linz has become one of the principal industrial cities in Austria.

Within the city, the attractive Old Town has preserved its predominantly baroque appearance, inviting the visitor to take a leisurely stroll followed by a *kleiner brauner* (a coffee) in one of the many welcoming cafés – perhaps with a piece of *Linzertorte*, the traditional local cake.

*Just outside Linz, to the west, is the small town of **Wilhering**. The abbey church here is one of the finest surviving examples of Austrian rococo architecture with splendid decoration (see www.stiftwilhering.at).*

The town's landmark, the white marble **Plague Column**, was dedicated in 1723. It dominates the Hauptplatz, whose dimensions – 220 by 60 metres (720 by 195 ft) – make it the largest enclosed square in Austria. Between the stately patrician houses with their baroque and Biedermeier façades stands the imposing Renaissance Old Town Hall. South of Hauptplatz are the sophisticated shops of the pedestrianised Landstrasse.

The fact that Linz was long the seat of the local bishop and hence a town of considerable importance explains the presence of the numerous churches. Worthy of special mention is the Jesuit church just off Hauptplatz, known as the **Old Cathedral**, where the composer Anton Bruckner was once organist. Bruckner, "God's musician", as he was dubbed, is a great favourite among the Austrians. The citizens of Linz honoured him by naming the **Brucknerhaus** after him. Opened in 1974, this concert hall beside the Danube has since become one of the most famous in Europe. Just north of the river is the **Ars Electronica Museum** (open Wed–Sun; entrance charge; tel: 0732-72 720), devoted to the

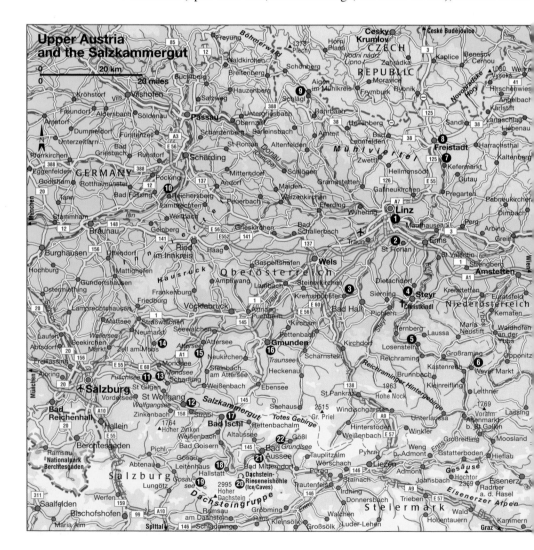

Map
on page
194

internet, virtual reality and other cyber-trickery. It's definitely worth a look if you're tiring of more traditional culture. An art and technology festival with same name, Ars Electronica, takes place in Linz every September.

Elsewhere in town, you can admire paintings by Klimt, Kokoschka and Schiele at the **Neue Galerie** (Blütenstrasse 15; open daily, Thur until 10pm; entrance charge); ride the Pöstlingbergbahn, the steepest tramway in Europe; and see a fine cactus collection in the **Botanical Gardens** (open daily; entrance charge) southwest of the city centre.

Stift St Florian

An easy day-trip southeast of Linz takes you 15 km (9 miles) to the beautiful baroque abbey **Stift St Florian ❷** (open Easter–Oct daily; charge for obligatory tour; tel: 07224-890 20), built in 1686, where composer Anton Bruckner first rose to prominence and is now buried. Regular tours take in the heavily stuccoed and frescoed abbey church, the remarkable library (with a ceiling fresco by Altomonte) and other highlights such as the grand Marmorsaal and the world's largest collection of paintings by Albrecht Altdorfer (1480–1538). The abbey's patron saint was a Roman official drowned in the nearby Enns River as punishment for his conversion to Christianity; he is believed to protect from both drowning and fires, and is usually depicted as a boy throwing water onto a fire.

Another building of outstanding beauty is **Kremsmünster Abbey ❸** (open daily; Observatory Tower closed Nov–Apr; entrance charge), founded in 777, which overlooks the Krems Valley about 35 km (22 miles) southwest of Linz. It was remodelled in the baroque style in the late 17th century. The frescoes are well worth a visit, as are the library and the Kaisersaal. The 8th-century Tassilo Chalice – the most valuable exhibit – is made of gilded copper and housed in the treasury. Also worth visiting is the Sternwarte (Observatory Tower), which has a varied museum collection; and the Fischkalter – five fish ponds dating from the late 17th century, complete with statues and arcades.

A detour west of Kremsmünster brings you to **Lambach**, whose Benedictine abbey contains some unique treasures (open Easter–Oct: one tour daily at 2pm). The highlights are the Romanesque Adalbero Chalice, an unusual rococo theatre and, best of all, a series of extremely well-preserved Romanesque frescoes dating from the 11th century.

Steyr

About 20 km (12 miles) south of St Florian is the old iron town of **Steyr ❹**, situated where the Steyr River flows into the Enns. Here the medieval Old Town offers an impressively harmonious countenance. The Bummerlhaus (1497), on the Stadtplatz, and the Parish Church (15th–17th centuries) are real jewels of Gothic architecture. Between 1886 and 1894 Anton Bruckner put his finishing touches to his last great compositions in the Priest's House next door to the church. Only a few yards away from the Stadtplatz, across the Grünmarkt, is the Innerberger Getreidestadel (1612). This former granary now contains the **Municipal Museum** (open Apr–Oct Tues–Sun;

A collection of Gothic stained glass is on display at Stift St Florian.

BELOW: the Marmorsaal at Stift St Florian.

Nov–Mar Wed–Sun; free) and the Steyrer Kripperl, a famous mechanical puppet theatre (performances held only in December and January).

The Wehrgraben district, north of the River Steyr, has retained all its fine 16th- to 18th-century architecture, making it an enchanting setting for a stroll. It also contains the **Arbeitswelt Museum** (World of Work Museum; open Mar–Dec Tues–Sun; entrance charge) which displays industrial history in a lively manner.

A worthwhile short excursion into the surrounding countryside is to the pilgrimage church of **Christkindl**, situated only 3 km (2 miles) from Steyr and constructed during the 18th century by the baroque master builders Giovanni Carlone and Jakob Prandtauer. The special post office set up every year at Christmas in the town sends letters bearing the coveted special stamp to all the corners of the earth.

An ornate shop sign on Stadtplatz in Steyr.

The Iron Road

The so-called Iron Road in Styria continues into Upper Austria and winds through the province's southeast corner to reach Steyr. After the decline in the European steel industry, this part of the province was largely forgotten, but in recent years new life has been injected into this once-important trading route. South of Steyr the Iron Road (No. 115) runs along the Enns through densely wooded Alpine foothills. **Losenstein ❺**, the highlight of the Enns valley, lies beneath the peak of the Schieferstein. Perched on a cliff above the village stand the ruins of a castle. Worth seeing are the Gothic parish church (*circa* 1400), the Castle Tavern and the Klausgraben ravine. Nearby is **Laussa**, one of the prettiest and neatest villages in Austria.

BELOW: Steyr's Michaelerkirche.

The next town, Reichraming, was once an industrial centre with hammer mills and a brass factory; today it is primarily the gateway to the popular but unspoiled countryside of the Reichraminger Mountains. Brunnbach, in the hills to the south, is a good starting point for mountain walks through the hinterland.

Map on page 194

The Golden Market

Further up the valley, the former "golden market" of **Weyer Markt** ❻ was reputedly founded in the 13th century, receiving its charter as a market town as early as 1460. Nowadays the resort area is a perfect base for walking tours, riding holidays, fishing, and in winter both Alpine and cross-country skiing. Visitors who are interested in the town's past should view the impeccably restored market place, the late-Gothic Church of St John and Egerer Castle.

Also of interest is nearby **Kastenreith**. Formerly known as Kasten and today the site of the **Enns Museum**, it was an important trade centre when the rafting and boat traffic on the Enns was in its heyday. The Iron Road continues via Kleinreifling to Altenmarkt, by which time it has crossed the provincial border into Styria.

About 25 km (16 miles) northeast of Weyer Markt, over the border into Lower Austria, is the famous pilgrimage church of **Sonntagberg**. Built on a hill long associated with miracles, the present church was completed in 1733.

Schubert returned to Steyr twice more after 1819, in 1823 and 1825. Today his stay here is commemorated by a stone plaque on the side of the so-called "Schuberthaus", where he sometimes resided while composing.

The Mühlviertel

The name of this remarkable region derives from its two principal rivers, the Greater and Lesser Mühl. It stretches out to the north of Linz, between the Danube and the Czech border, and consists of a granite plateau whose densely

LEFT: the first page of Schubert's *Die Forelle* (The Trout), composed in Steyr.

SCHUBERT IN STEYR

The composer Franz Schubert came to the wealthy industrial city of Steyr in 1819 at the invitation of a fellow musician, opera singer Johann Vogl. He was instantly smitten with the place and stayed the better part of a year. While here, he gained a commission to write what would become one of his best-known works, the *Trout Quintet*, and set a number of poems to music.

It was a time of creative growth for Schubert. He met painters, musicians and writers, was trailed briefly by intelligence authorities (he ran with an impetuous university crowd) and generally had a good time, while staying with an assortment of doctors and other patrons. One dispatch home stated, "The country around here is extremely beautiful. In Steyr I've always had good conversations.... [and] in the house where I live there are eight girls, nearly all of them pretty. You can see that there's much to be done." His spirits seemed to rise above the malaise of what had been a rather diffuse life back in Vienna.

wooded slopes remain largely untouched, even by tourism. The rural scene is interspersed with the occasional castle or ruined fortress and little market towns which look as though they have been nestling in the hills since time immemorial.

Kefermarkt , about 40 km (24 miles) northeast of Linz, is famous for the huge Gothic altarpiece in the church of **St Wolfgang** (open daily; free; tel: 07947-6203). Carved from limewood by an unknown master, it measures 14 by 6 metres (44 by 20 ft). There are life-size of St Wolfgang in bishop's robes flanked by St Christopher and Peter. The village is dominated by Schloss Weinberg to the north, which is now an art and music school.

Freistadt ❽, 11 km (7 miles) north of Kefermarkt, is regarded as the capital of the lower Mühlviertel and one of the most interesting sights in Austria. Founded by free merchants in 1200, today the town retains its medieval fortifications: the double defensive wall, moats, circular towers and the late-Gothic town gates – the Linzertor and the Böhmertor. The former merchants' houses surrounding the main square still have their original Gothic interiors behind magnificent Renaissance and baroque façades. Also of note is the parish church, the so-called **St Catherine's Cathedral**, with two masterpieces of late-Gothic architecture: the chancel and the baptism chapel (1483–1501). To the northeast is the Schloss – the former residence of the local rulers – whose medieval keep (14th century) is well preserved . It contains the **Mühlviertel Museum** (open daily, Sat–Sun pm only; entrance charge), which houses an extensive collection of stained-glass pictures. The 15th-century Church of Our Lady stands outside the Böhmertor. The town is also home to an outstanding local brewery – try some of the thick, dark Freistädter Bier.

Freistadt's brewery has been in operation since 1777 and, unusually, is owned communally by all the households within the medieval town walls. A share in the brewery comes with ownership of a house (and in no other way), making a takeover effectively impossible.

The mountains

Sandl, some 15 km (9 miles) northeast of Freistadt, is a destination which is still a closely-kept secret amongst winter sportsmen. The 1,110-metre (3,645-ft) Viehberg offers some very acceptable Alpine ski pistes, whilst the network of cross-country ski runs has made the town a centre for Nordic skiing.

There are also a number of worthwhile destinations west of Freistadt. **Bad Leonfelden** is a peat and Kneipp spa about 20 km (12 miles) away. The nearby Sternstein (with winter-sports facilities) is, at 1,125 metres (3,690 ft), the highest peak in the entire Mühlviertel. By continuing through Rohrbach, which is encircled by the dense pine and spruce forests of the Bohemian Woods, our tour brings us to **Aigen-Schlägl** ❾. Here a highlight is the Premostratensian monastery in Schlägl, rebuilt in the baroque style in the 17th century.

South of Rohrbach lies another of the Mühlviertel's special attractions: the **Altenfelden-Mühltal Nature Park**. Its 80 hectares (200 acres) house over 700 animals, including ibexes, wild horses, antelopes and deer.

A cable car casts its shadow over the forest.

BELOW: all kitted up for a day's hiking.

The Innviertel

The northwest part of Upper Austria is separated from Germany by the River Inn. **Schärding**, a little town perched high above the river, is famous today as the home of the largest Kneipp cure clinic in Austria. Its appearance is characterised by its medieval silhouette, which is dominated by a ruined castle (15th century) and the town ramparts and gates. Close by is Austria's only Trappist monastery (former Cistercian Abbey). This is at Engelhartszell, on the Danube, to the east of Schärding.

In **Reichersberg** ⑩, 18 km (11 miles) south, stands an imposing Augustinian abbey. Founded in 1084, the buildings were badly damaged by fire in 1624 and rebuilt over the course of the rest of the century. During summer months a variety of craft courses and cultural events are held in Reichersberg.

Turning away from the river, Road 143 brings us to **Ried im Innkreis**, the economic focal point of this region, the Innviertel. A number of scenic roads from Ried thread through the Hausruck Forest to **Frankenburg**. This town was the setting for a macabre spectacle in 1625; citizens and peasants alike were forced to throw dice to decide which of them would die and which would live. As a reminder of this gruesome event dating from the Peasant Wars, the Frankenburg Game of Dice is staged every year.

Ampflwang, a little further to the east, has earned a reputation during the past few years as an equestrian centre. The entire village has dedicated itself to the sport all year round, and novices and professionals alike will find a wide range of activities to suit them.

To the south of here is Upper Austria's most beautiful region, the Salzkammergut, which is covered in full in the next chapter. ❑

Map
on page
194

Austria's only Trappist monastery is at Engelhartszell, on the Danube east of Schärding.

BELOW: thick forest in the mountains.

Map on page 194

SALZKAMMERGUT

Lofty peaks and placid lakes provide the Salzkammergut with a succession of near-perfect scenes, but the region also has historic sites and superb facilities for outdoor adventure

Vienna

BELOW: St Gilgen on the edge of the Wolfgangsee.

The Salzkammergut is famous for its lakes, which provide unequalled possibilities for summertime recreation. There are 76 of them altogether, strung out like a necklace of pearls, each possessing its own inimitable charm. There are lakes for bathing in, like the Mondsee and the Wolfgangsee; yachting centres (the Attersee or the Traunsee), apparently bottomless gleaming "emeralds" (the Grundlsee and the Hallstätter See), and romantic retreats like the Gosausee and the Altausseer See. The area is also known for its numerous salt mines (Salzkammergut means "salt chamber estate"), at one time an important source of revenue.

It is difficult to encompass the Salzkammergut within a single geographical term, but it extends from the Fuschlsee and Wolfgangsee in Salzburg Province to the Toplitzsee in Styria. If Salzburg is your point of departure, the quickest route to the lakes is the motorway leading via Thalgau to Mondsee. If you have sufficient time at your disposal, however, a short detour to the south is recommended. The **Fuschlsee** ⑪ lies only minutes away from the busy main road, its dark, cold waters nestling between forested slopes. The pristine hills surrounding the lake were used as a backdrop for the famous opening scene in *The Sound of Music (see page 78).*

Not far from the road stands the **Fuschl Hunting Lodge**, with a museum containing a number of rare trophies (open daily). The nearby **Schlosshotel Fuschl** stands on a promontory above the northwest end of the lake. It was built in 1450 as a hunting lodge for the archbishops of Salzburg, and in the 20th century it became the property of the Nazi politician Ribbentrop. It is now a luxury hotel offering guests every imaginable facility: beach, fishing jetties, indoor swimming pool, tennis court and one of the most scenic golf courses in Austria. Walking through the castle's magnificent grounds, the visitor follows in the footsteps of the many monarchs, film stars and politicians (Nixon and Khrushchev, for instance), who have slept or conferred here.

Wolfgangsee and Mondsee

Skirting the south side of the Fuschlsee we soon reach **St Gilgen** on the Wolfgangsee. Of particular interest here is the birthplace of Mozart's mother, Anna Maria Pertl (1720–78). Today the building houses the local courthouse, but includes a Mozart memorial room (open June–Sept Tues–Sun; entrance charge). One should not miss a boat trip on the lake itself, which covers an area of 13 sq. km (5 sq. miles).

The excursion to the village of **St Wolfgang** ⑫, on the northern shore, is highly recommended. The landing stage is near the Weisses Rössl, the "White Horse Inn", made famous in an operetta by Ralph Benatzky. Strolling along delightful alleys, the visitor arrives at the village's main attraction, the **Pilgrimage Church** (open daily; free; tel: 06138-2321), which contains one of the most remarkable examples of Gothic art in Austria. The magnificent winged altar, created by Michael Pacher between 1471 and 1481, has 16 panels, depicting scenes from the lives of Christ, the Virgin Mary and St Wolfgang. The central sculpted scene shows the Coronation of the Virgin, flanked by saints Wolfgang and Benedict.

The village is also the starting point for a unique highlight. A steam-driven train (commissioned in 1893) chugs along unhurriedly to the summit of the 1,785-metre (5,855-ft) Schafberg. From here there is a breathtaking panorama of the Lake District, a stunning view of 12 lakes: Wolfgangsee, Fuschlsee, Attersee, Mondsee, Zeller See, Wallersee, Obertrumer See, Niedertrumer See, Grabensee, Abtsdorfer See, Chiemsee and Waginger See.

Those who choose St Gilgen as their base for further exploration of the Salzkammergut can take Road 154 north to the **Mondsee** ⑬. The lake lies in the shadow of the dominant silhouettes of the Drachenwand and the Schafberg; 11 km (7 miles) long and over 2 km (1¼ miles) wide, its waters are among the warmest in the region. Lakeside bathing beaches and sailing schools lend the lake a carefree holiday atmosphere.

The Fuschlsee in autumn.

The village of **Mondsee**, founded in 748 by Odilo II, a Bavarian count, when a Benedictine monastery was established here, offers a number of historical sights. The local museum, for example, has a display of finds dating from the Mondsee's prehistoric culture (open May–Oct Tues–Sun; entrance charge), while the market place is surrounded by well-preserved houses dating from the 16th–18th centuries. The **Parish Church** was redesigned in the baroque style at the end of the 17th century and contains some particularly fine altars carved by Meinrad Guggenbichler. Retained Gothic elements include a beautiful sacristy doorway. The wedding scene in the film *The Sound of Music* was filmed here *(see page 78)*.

(see page 78).

The villages surrounding the Mondsee offer yet another attraction: gourmets will discover more illustrious restaurants here than in almost any other region of Austria – creative nouvelle cuisine of the highest quality, with strong local influences, can be found almost everywhere.

The lakes beyond Mondsee

Continuing from Mondsee you are spoilt for choice between the vast eastern waters of the Attersee and the Traunsee and the untamed romanticism of the south – the Hallstätter See, Grundlsee, et al – quite apart from the enchanting lakes of the Alpine foothills to the north. To get a better perspective, make a detour north into the neighbouring flatlands and the Salzkammergut catchment area.

Road 154 leads off in a northerly direction from Mondsee, reaching **Zell am Moos** ⑭ some 6 km (4 miles) later. The village lies on the eastern shores of the Zeller See (or Irrsee), a nature conservation area. The lake's waters reach temperatures of 27°C (80°F)

BELOW:
St Wolfgang on the Wolfgangseee.

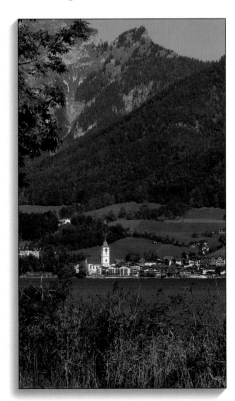

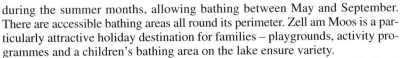

BELOW: couple by
the Halstätter See.

during the summer months, allowing bathing between May and September. There are accessible bathing areas all round its perimeter. Zell am Moos is a particularly attractive holiday destination for families – playgrounds, activity programmes and a children's bathing area on the lake ensure variety.

Returning to our original starting point, the Mondsee, you can then take Road 151 to Unterach, on the **Attersee** ⑮. The lake's dimensions – 20 by 3 km (12 by 2 miles) – make it the largest in the Salzkammergut. It is an El Dorado for sailors and is encircled by a succession of picturesque villages ideal for holidaymaking: Unterach, Nussdorf and Attersee on the western shore, Seewalchen and Kammer to the north and Weyregg, Steinbach and Weissenbach to the east. Most have camp sites, sailing and windsurfing schools and boat rental. The Attersee is the only lake in the Salzkammergut which never freezes in winter. Its waters are also considered to be very clean, and the underwater topography makes it ideal for divers (courses available).

Those wishing to explore the **Traunsee**, yet another jewel of the Salzkammergut, should follow the road round the southern tip of the Attersee before continuing via Neukirchen to **Gmunden** ⑯ (population 12,000). Lying in a picture-postcard setting on the northern shore of the Traunsee and offering a wide variety of water-sports facilities as well as traditional cures (salt-water baths), Gmunden is a typical summer resort. Architecturally, it also has much to offer: there is the Renaissance-era Town Hall with its porcelain-tiled glockenspiel, as well as a number of fine townhouses and numerous castles (Cumberland, Württemberg and Freisitz-Roith). Southwest of the town is the so-called Landschloss Orth, which is linked by a 130-metre (425-ft) long wooden bridge to the Seeschloss (Lake Castle), built in the 14th century on an artificial island.

One should also make a point of visiting the town's famous porcelain factory, with its characteristic greenglazed china (Keramikstrasse 24; tours Mon–Sat am; entrance charge). Gmunden, once the salt capital and residence of the local prince, documents its close links with the "white gold" in a museum in the **Kammerhof**, which was for centuries the seat of the Salt Authority (open May–Oct Mon–Sat, Sun am only; entrance charge; tel: 07612-794 244). It contains displays tracing the development of the salt industry and that of the local pottery. In addition there is a collection of original manuscripts by the town's famous sons Johannes Brahms and 19th-century playwright Friedrich Hebbel.

The famous salt town of **Ebensee** lies at the southern end of the Traunsee. As early as 1607, its townfolk were refining brine from the salt mined in the area. Ebensee is a good starting point from which to make excursions into the nearby Totes Gebirge and Höllengebirge mountains. Particularly recommended is a visit to the romantic **Langbathsee** lakes, 8 km (5 miles) to the west.

Following the course of the River Traun southwest from Ebensee, the visitor will duly arrive in the spa town of **Bad Ischl** ⑰. This is where the emperor used to come for a cure, and it is still well worth a visit today. Its inimitable late 19th-century aura greets the traveller everywhere, not only in the **Kaiservilla**

Map
on page
194

(Imperial Villa; open May–Oct daily; Nov–Apr Wed pm; entrance charge) and the **Lehárvilla** (open May–Sept Wed–Mon; entrance charge), the summer home of operetta composer Franz Lehár. The oldest saline baths in Austria now have ultra-modern therapeutic equipment; even a short cure is relaxing. It is pleasant to follow such a session with a stroll along the esplanade beside the Traun and then to sample coffee and cakes at **Café Zauner**, the legendary pâtisserie at Pfarrgasse 7.

Thus fortified, the 11-km (7-mile) journey south to **Bad Goisern** will prove child's play. A resort with sulphur and brine baths, the town is also the shopping centre of the Salzkammergut. Manufactured here and nowhere else are the "Original Goiserer" mountain boots – one of the best of their kind in the world.

Baroque jewel

If there is a single village which fully deserves to be the subject of a postcard, then it must be **Hallstatt ⑱**, to the south. Predominantly baroque in style, the pastel-coloured houses cling precariously to the steep mountain slopes on the edge of the Hallstätter See. The historic part of the town looks as if, by some superhuman effort, it has reclaimed a narrow strip of land from both the mountains and the lake. From the village church there are numerous hikes into the surrounding hills.

No cars are allowed through central Hallstatt, which has helped to preserve its character. If you do drive here, you'll be required to park your car in one of two car parks; one is in a tunnel down the approach road, while the second is a little further along.

The past 4,500 years have left their mark here. Salt was the basis of wealth in the town even for the Celtic and Illyrian tribes. An entire epoch, marking the first

In Traunkirchen, a former fishing village on the Traunsee's western shore, the parish church has an unusual baroque pulpit from 1753. It is in the form of a fishing boat and is carved with the New Testament scene of the miraculous haul of fish.

BELOW: looking out over the lake from Hallstatt.

phase of the European Iron Age, between 800 and 400 BC, has been christened the "Hallstatt Period". Sophisticated artefacts were produced by this ancient culture, and Hallstatt achieved world fame when many were unearthed from a 2,500-year-old burial site. Some can be seen at the **Hallstatt Museum** (open Apr–Oct daily; Nov–Mar Tues–Sun; entrance charge) in the village.

Visitors with an interest in the macabre should take a look inside the Beinhaus (charnel house) beside the parish church. Since space is at a premium here, the bones have to be removed from the tiny cemetery after 10 years. They are stacked up, but not before the skull has been artistically labelled and painted.

The Hallstätter See is very popular with people who are into fresh-water diving, shipwrecks and the recovery of sunken treasure. Gerhard Zauner, proprietor of the diving school and Divers' Inn in Hallstatt, spends almost more time underwater than above it. Even experts can learn from his classes. He offers more than 20 courses, from a basic introduction to diving, to such esoteric topics as "Fish Language" and "Cutting and Welding Under Water".

The hundreds of skulls in Hallstatt's Beinhaus are labelled with the names of their former owners.

RIGHT: the Dachsteinbahn cable car.

Dachstein delights

Opinions are divided, but the **Gosausee** ⑲ – 17 km (11 miles) southwest of the Hallstätter See – can certainly lay claim to be the loveliest lake in the Salzkammergut. Whether you are visiting it for the first or fifth time, you will not fail to be captured by an indescribable emotion as you gaze upon the view of the lake set against the slopes and glaciers of the Dachstein Massif. It is best to stay here until the late afternoon, taking the last funicular to Zwieselalpe. The benches in front of the shelter are perfectly placed for watching the Alpine pyrotechnics at sunset.

THE GISELA

A particular attraction in Gmunden is a trip on the oldest coal-fired paddle steamer in the world. The 52-metre (170-ft) long *Gisela* was built in Vienna and then taken apart and transported to the Traunsee, where she was reassembled for her maiden voyage in 1872. After being saved and declared a historic monument it has been ploughing through the waters of the Traunsee ever since. The steamer even transported Emperor Franz Joseph to his cool summer retreat in the heart of the Salzkammergut every year. (Gisela, not coincidentally, was the name of his first daughter.) In fact, the Habsburgs used it as a transport link between Vienna and Salzburg – at the time there were no roads between Gmunden (at the head of the lake) and Bad Ischl (en route to Salzburg) – and an especially luxurious "*Kaiserkabine*" was designed for their exclusive use.

Obertraun, at the southeastern tip of the Hallstätter See directly across from Hallstatt, is regarded by winter-sports enthusiasts as a place where snow is assured. A funicular leads up the 2,110-metre (6,920-ft) Krippenstein facing the lake's southern shore, providing another impressive view of the Dachstein.

From Schönbergalm, the intermediate station, one can visit the famous **Dachstein Ice Caves** ⓴ (open May–Oct daily; entrance charge). Here, imposing vaults and corridors lead into the interior of the mountain. The highlight of this chilly excursion is undoubtedly the **Mammuthöhle** (Mammoth's Cave), which consists of several storeys with a total combined height of 300 metres (985 ft). Equally impressive is the **Koppenbrüllerhöhle**, with its fantastically-shaped stalactite sculptures.

Into Styria

From Obertraun, the road climbs steeply and crosses into the Styrian Salzkammergut. Here the regional capital is **Bad Aussee** ㉑, which lies between the Dachstein foothills and the Totes Gebirge. It is a lively town with a number of architectural jewels: the 15th-century Parish Church of St Paul, the Spital Church (14th century), with a very fine altarpiece (1449), and the Gothic **Kammerhof**, once the office of the salt works in the region, and now housing the local museum (open June–Sept daily; Apr–June and Oct Tues, Fri–Sun; entrance charge). A sleepy enchantment hangs over the place; some houses give the impression that time has stood still. The modern spa complex is a stark contrast.

From Bad Aussee it is well worth seeking out a panoramic view of the nearby **Altausseer See**. The best one can be reached by heading northwards from the lake itself towards the Loser. This brilliantly-engineered toll road requires 15 hairpin bends to reach an altitude of 1,600 metres (5,250 ft). From this height one has a magnificent eagle's-eye view of the entire lake and its fairy-tale surroundings. If you are lucky, you may even see a hang-glider or parasailing enthusiast launching himself towards the glittering depths below.

Northeast of Bad Aussee is the **Grundlsee** ㉒, whose emerald waters shimmer like a jewel. The largest lake in the Styrian Salzkammergut, it is 6 km (4 miles) long and popular with sailors and windsurfers; anglers, too, like to try their luck from its shores. A three-hour boat trip from Bad Aussee gives great views of the lake.

In summer, a horse-drawn post coach (tel: 03622-8666 or 72 160) plies the route between Gössl (at the far end of Grundlsee) and the next lake, **Toplitzsee**. Gerhard Zauner *(see page 204)* has salvaged large quantities of treasure buried here during World War II. His activities have also contributed to the lake's fame. The visitor surveying its dark waters, secluded shores, steep rocky cliffs and roaring waterfalls will understand why he chose this lake to search rather than any other.

A 10-minute walk through the forest beyond Toplitzsee, including a steep track with 71 steps, leads to the tiny, idyllic Kammersee. Eerie reflections, utter peace and a sense of seclusion engender a delusion of having escaped from the world. ❑

Map on page 194

Pumpkins for sale on the way to Styria.

BELOW: a Dachstein rock face.

SALZBURG

*With a splendid architectural legacy of the prince-bishops,
its many associations with Mozart and the annual music festival,
Salzburg is one of the best-loved towns in Austria*

Map
on page
208

Many towns in Austria are blessed with fine churches, squares and ornamental fountains. In none but Salzburg, however, do they enjoy such a vibrant, cosmopolitan atmosphere and such magnificent surrounding scenery. Salzburg is one of the most visited cities in Austria, especially during the Salzburg Festival, its annual tribute to local hero Wolgang Amadeus Mozart (1756–91), when music lovers flock here from all corners of the globe.

The Mönchsberg and the Kapuzinerberg – the two mountains within the city boundaries – tower over the narrow alleys of the Old Town, with their tall, narrow merchants' houses, hidden arcaded courtyards, baroque-domed churches and the palaces and spacious squares of the prince-bishops' quarter. Clinging to the side of Mönchsberg, and dominating the Old Town, is the fortress of Hohensalzburg, a symbol of the power base that shaped so much of the city's history.

Princes and archbishops

The Celts were the first to recognise the region's attractions; and it was here that the Romans built Juvavum ("the seat of the god of heaven"), their administrative centre. Over the course of a few hundred years, the monastery founded by St Rupert shortly before AD 700 grew into the mightiest spiritual principality in South Germany. In the 13th century its archbishops were given the title of Princes of the Holy Roman Empire. Thanks to their considerable income from the salt and silver mines of the area they were able to express their power in fine buildings. Three bishops in particular, all possessing an awareness of aesthetics as well as of their own might, stamped the town with the characteristics it still bears today.

Wolf Dietrich von Raitenau (archbishop from 1587) was a typical Renaissance prince, who dreamed of creating a "Rome of the North". He charged the Italian architect Scamozzi with the task of constructing a cathedral larger than St Peter's in Rome. At the same time he commissioned Mirabell Palace for his mistress Salome von Alt, by whom he had 12 children. His successor, Marcus Sitticus von Hohenems (archbishop from 1612), reduced the cathedral to a more modest scale, but commissioned a summer residence, Schloss Hellbrunn, set in an extensive park and surrounded by an elaborate system of fountains. Paris Lodron (archbishop from 1619) was finally able to dedicate the cathedral in 1628; it was during his term of office that the new Residenz (Bishop's Palace) was also completed.

In Renaissance and baroque times, the starting point for the building activity of the prince-bishops was the **Residenzplatz**, an excellent place to begin a tour of the town. In the square stands the 15-metre (50-ft)

LEFT: looking out over the city from the fortress. **BELOW:** the Residenzplatz fountain.

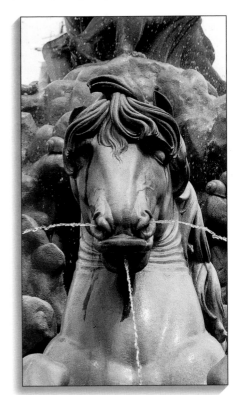

baroque Residenzbrunnen (Residenz Fountain; 1661). Grouped around this focal point – partly following the dictates of history and partly the whims of the prince-bishops – stand the most important episcopal buildings. On the south side is the **Dom ❶** (Cathedral), begun according to Renaissance precepts in 1614 and completed in the baroque style in 1655. If you walk across from the Residenzplatz to the Domplatz, you will gain a view of the West Front, built of light-coloured Salzburg marble and framed by twin towers topped with cupolas, which are themselves surmounted by lanterns.

As a result of the annual performances of Hofmannsthal's *Jedermann (Every man)* here, the three arcaded porticos with their four statues have achieved worldwide fame. The latter depict the apostles St Peter and St Paul flanked by two local saints, St Rupert and St Virgil. Watchfully surveying the scene are statues of the four evangelists, plus Moses and Elijah, while a statue of Christ dominates the ensemble. The contemporary bronze doors are dedicated to the themes of Faith, Hope and Charity. The baptismal font in the left aisle, dating from

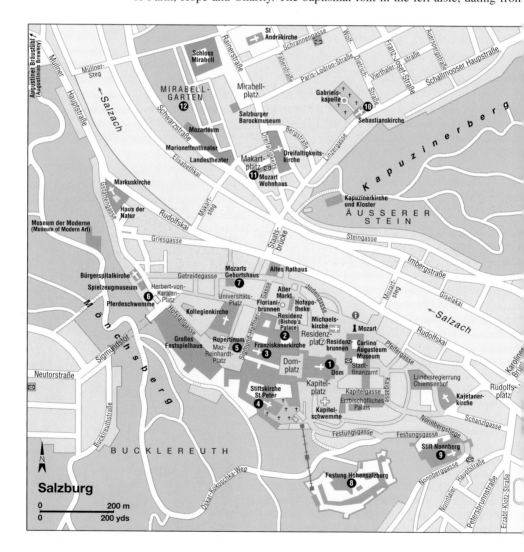

1321, is a relic from the previous Romanesque church. So, too, is the crypt, in which traces of the original walls have been exposed. The mosaic-tiled floor shows the ground plans of the three cathedrals built in succession upon this site. The priceless treasures assembled by the bishops across the centuries can be seen in the **Cathedral Museum** (open mid-May–Oct daily; entrance charge).

Map on page 208

The Alter Markt.

Palaces and churches

Forming the western boundary of the Residenzplatz is the **Residenz ❷** (Bishop's Palace; open daily; entrance charge; tel: 0662-8042 2690). Archbishop Wolf Dietrich von Raitenau (1559–1671) had it constructed from 1595 to replace the previous 12th-century building. The state apartments of the Residenz are predominantly decorated in late-baroque and classical style. A total of 15 rooms are lavishly appointed with murals, stucco, paintings, tapestries and statues. The young Mozart frequently performed in what is now the Conference Hall. The **Residenzgalerie** on the floor above (open July–Aug daily; Sept–Mar Tues– Sun; entrance charge; tel: 0662-840 4510) contains paintings from the 16th–19th centuries. Opposite the Residenz, on the east side of the square, is the Glockenspiel, erected in 1705 and containing 35 bells cast in Antwerp. It sounds several times daily.

To the west of the Domplatz stands the **Franziskanerkirche ❸** (Franciscan Church), dedicated in 1221 and demonstrating an interesting transition between the Romanesque and Gothic styles. The nave is still completely Romanesque, and creates a rather austere impression due to the massive columns and capitals decorated with stylised foliage and animal figures. The late-Gothic chancel dates from the 15th century and features stellar vaulting supported by cylindrical pillars with palm-tree capitals. Of the late-Gothic winged altarpiece created by Michael Pacher in 1496, only the Madonna remains; it is integrated into the baroque high altar.

BELOW: the Dom, seen from the Modern Art Museum.

Tucked into the north side of the Mönchsberg, and accessed from Franziskanergasse, are **Stiftskirche St Peter ❹** and its cemetery. The church itself is a Romanesque triple-aisled basilica dating from 1147, but in the 18th century it was completely redesigned and as a result acquired the baroque ostentation – elaborate frescoes and ornate stucco – that makes it so striking. The nave vaulting contains frescoes depicting scenes from the life of St Peter; the walls above the great arches are decorated with a Passion and a Crucifixion scene. Beneath the clerestory are scenes from the life of St Benedict on the left and St Rupert on the right.

The cemetery is flanked on three sides by arcades housing family tombs; hewn from the rock face above are the catacombs (tours daily), in which early Christians celebrated Mass during the 3rd century. In the church's courtyard is the entrance to an atmospheric, subterranean restaurant and watering hole. Said to be Austria's oldest, it has been a tavern for 1,200 years.

Mozart's birthplace

Just west of the Franziskanerkirche is the **Rupertinum ❺** (open Tues–Sun, Wed until 9pm; entrance charge; tel: 0662-8042), an art gallery with a perma-

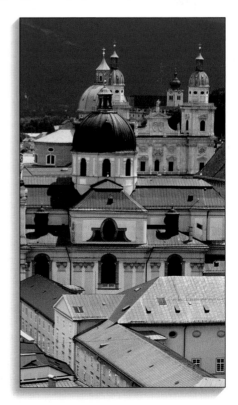

nent collection of 20th-century work and space set aside for temporary exhibitions. Highlights include pieces by Gustav Klimt and Oskar Kokoschka.

West again and you reach Hofstallgasse, which leads past the Festspielhaus (a concert venue used during the Salzburg Festival) to the **Pferdeschwemme** ➏. What appears to be a fountain was actually a pool for washing horses, built in 1700. It is decorated with equine frescoes. To the northwest is the Gstättengasse lift up the Mönchsberg and the **Museum der Moderne** (Museum of Modern Art; open Tues–Sun; entrance charge; tel: 0662-842 220-401). From the top of the ridge, the views are splendid, and there are wooded walking trails leading along the ridge to Festung Hohensalzburg *(see page 211)*.

Not far away is the **Getreidegasse**, one of the principal thoroughfares of Old Salzburg. The houses lining the street were built between the 15th and 18th centuries; they are characterised by lovely arcaded courtyards, wrought-iron signs and carved stucco window frames. Passageways occur at regular intervals; the people of Salzburg call them *durchhäuser* (through houses). The house at Getreidegasse 9 is the **Mozarts Geburtshaus** ➐ (open daily; entrance charge; tel: 0662-844 313), where the composer Wolfgang Amadeus was born on the third floor on 27 January 1756. It was while living here that Mozart wrote almost all of his juvenile works. Today the house contains many mementoes of the composer's childhood including his original instruments: concert violin, viola, fortepiano and clavichord.

The Getreidegasse leads on in an easterly direction towards the **Rathaus** (Town Hall) and the **Alter Markt** (Old Market), with its St Florian Fountain. At Alter Markt 6, the rococo interior of the Hofapotheke, founded in 1591, retains the fittings of the original chemist's shop.

Looking down in the Rupertinum.

BELOW: the impressive Hohensalzburg fortress.

Shortly after this, the Getreidegasse joins the Judengasse, once the centre of Salzburg's thriving Jewish quarter; it, too, is characterised by numerous, elaborate, wrought-iron shop signs.

Map
on page
208

Wealth and power

For many the **Festung Hohensalzburg** ❽ (open daily, entrance charge, tel: 0662-8424 3011) is the highlight of a trip to Salzburg. It stands south of the old town, 15 minutes up the hill on foot, or a short ride up the Festungsbahn funicular. A symbol of the worldly power of the prince-bishops, the fortress was begun by Archbishop Gebhard on the site of a Roman *castrum* in 1077 and was continuously extended until the 17th century. It was Leonhard von Keutschach, Archbishop of Salzburg from 1495 to 1519, who had the most significant influence on its present structure and furnishing. Conducted tours around the state apartments, dungeons and torture chamber take place throughout the day. One particularly interesting item is a monumental porcelain tile stove, dating from 1501, kept in the so-called Golden Room. It portrays Biblical scenes and the princes of the time.

To the east of the fortress lies **Stift Nonnberg** ❾, a Benedictine convent founded at the beginning of the 8th century by St Rupert, which makes it one of the oldest convents still in existence. Its late-Gothic church dates from the end of the 15th century. Look out in particular for a Gothic winged altarpiece, created by Veit Stoss in 1498, and remarkable 12th-century frescoes to the rear of the nave.

If you visit the church at Stift Nonnberg in the late afternoon, you may be lucky enough to hear the nuns singing Evensong – an experience that greatly enhances the beautiful Gothic interior.

The right bank

If you cross the river on the Staatsbrücke and continue straight on, you'll find yourself on **Linzergasse**. The street is lined with shops and always bustling

BELOW: the Mirabell gardens.

BELOW: in Schloss
Hellbrunn.

with activity. The **Sebastianskirche** 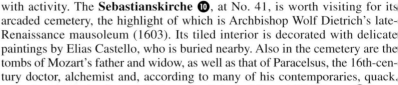, at No. 41, is worth visiting for its arcaded cemetery, the highlight of which is Archbishop Wolf Dietrich's late-Renaissance mausoleum (1603). Its tiled interior is decorated with delicate paintings by Elias Castello, who is buried nearby. Also in the cemetery are the tombs of Mozart's father and widow, as well as that of Paracelsus, the 16th-century doctor, alchemist and, according to many of his contemporaries, quack.

Back towards the river, at Makartplatz 8, is the **Mozart Wohnhaus** ⑪ (open daily; entrance charge), where the composer lived for seven years from 1773. It now houses original manuscripts, period furniture and, most interesting, various multimedia displays covering his life and times.

The nearby **Mirabell Garten** ⑫ form the most attractive park in Salzburg. Designed by Fischer von Erlach at the beginning of the 18th century, they enchant visitors with their statues, fountains and well-tended flower beds. One of the loveliest views is towards Hohensalzburg fortress from the terrace of the former palace, which now houses government offices. The original palace, built here in 1606, was the Altenau, commissioned by Wolf Dietrich to accommodate his celebrated Jewish mistress, Salome von Alt. Between 1721 and 1727 it was rebuilt by J. Lukas von Hildebrandt, but this structure was destroyed by a catastrophic fire in 1818. The present palace is a reconstruction of that building by Peter von Noble.

On the outskirts

The pilgrimage church of **Maria Plain** stands on a hilltop about 5 km (3 miles) north of the city. Built in 1674, it has a façade framed by two towers. The interior is exceptionally attractive, representing the transition from baroque to Rococo.

Schloss Hellbrunn (open Apr–Oct daily; entrance charge; tel: 0662-820 3720), 5 km (3 miles) south of Salzburg proper, symbolises pleasures of a primarily worldly nature – even though the complex, surrounded by a spacious park, was the summer residence of Archbishop Marcus Sitticus. It was designed by Santino Solari, the architect who was also responsible for Salzburg's cathedral (an unfinished sketch of this is kept in the castle's dining-room). The most interesting aspect of the interior appointments are the ballroom's *trompe-l'oeil* paintings by Arsenio Mascagni. The main attraction of Hellbrunn, however, is undoubtedly the collection of fountains in the park. Elaborate waterspouts and grottoes with countless figures, scenic representations and a mechanical theatre in which no fewer than 113 marionettes are set in motion by water power, were designed for the prince-bishop's private amusement.

Southwest of the city, the **Untersberg** makes a good day-trip. Begin by renting a bicycle at the railway station, then take it with you on a bus to Moosstrasse on the western side of Mönchsberg. Here, climb onto the saddle and head straight down Moosstrasse. You soon leave the city behind and roll down a perfectly straight road past farmhouses, schools and cows. After a time, the road brings you to the base of the Untersberg. Here you can hike or, more easily, take the cable-car to a mountain-top restaurant with excellent views. ❑

The Salzburg Festival

Two annual festivals in Salzburg highlight the genius of Wolfgang Amadeus Mozart. Born in the city in 1756, Mozart was pushed into music at an exceptionally early age by his court-musician father, who recognised his son's abilities at once. The boy began composing and performing while practically a toddler, and first toured Europe at the age of six. He later moved to Vienna, where he wrote such classics as *The Magic Flute* and *The Marriage of Figaro*.

Despite wide acclaim, he never knew enduring wealth and security – his gambling and philandering suggest he had little time for such bourgeois virtues. The archbishop of Salzburg would not countenance his applications for prestigious positions, and he was later hounded by unappreciative music critics. At 35 he died of fever and was buried a pauper in an unmarked grave.

In 1848, supported by donations from the Mozart family, a group of enthusiasts formed the International Mozarteum Foundation to "perform and propagate Mozart's music and music in general, to broaden the public's knowledge of Mozart and his creative work and to preserve the memory of Mozart, his work and his family". Today the foundation runs two Mozart museums in Salzburg. Its extensive collections include the composer's original letters and sheet music and numerous performances of his work.

But the foundation is best known for its two long-running concert series. For almost half a century, it has kicked off each year with Mozart Week (Mozartwoche) in late January. This 10-day presentation of the composer's works marks his birthday – 27 January. The idea is to present the entire oeuvre through successive years. Performances usually include traditional concerts by the Vienna Philharmonic Orchestra and concertos performed by star pianists.

In July and August every year, the foundation's Mozart concert series forms an integral part of the annual Salzburg Festival (Salzburger Festspiele). The festival dates from 1920 and the decision of local theatre director Max Reinhardt to keep his performers employed during the traditionally slow summer holiday season. Supported by the composer Richard Strauss and the poet Hugo von Hofmannsthal, he initiated an annual programme of opera, drama and music, performed in spectacular settings around the city. Venues include Domplatz (in front of the cathedral), the Mozarteum, the Landestheater, the Kollegienkirche, the Grosses Festspielhaus and the Kleines Festspielhaus. Particularly oustanding are the Marionettentheater's ornate puppets, which sing opera in perfect pitch beneath the Mirabell's fine ceilings. Huge crowds arrive in the city to see it all.

For Mozart Week information and tickets, contact the Mozarteum Foundation's Ticket Office at Theatergasse 2 (tel: 0662-873 154; fax: 0662-874 454). For Salzburg Festival schedules and tickets (available from November), visit the festival website at www.salzburgfestival.at ❏

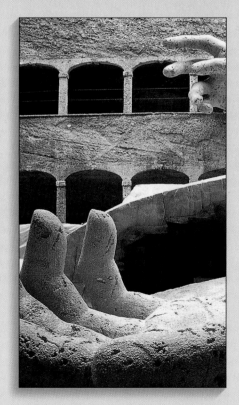

RIGHT: a new set goes up at the Festival Halls.

Map on page 216

SALZBURG PROVINCE

Away from its capital, Salzburg Province is where the Austrian Alps begin for real, with rushing streams, soaring peaks and beautiful lakes

Most visitors to the province will begin with the capital **Salzburg ❶** *(see pages 207–12)*, the baroque city that spawned both Mozart and *The Sound of Music*. But the rest of the province deserves some exploration, starting with the so-called German Corner, a pocket of Bavaria that juts provocatively into Austrian territory just south of Salzburg.

To reach it from the capital, take Road 160, which soon crosses into Germany and the beautiful foothills of the Bavarian Alps, heading towards the town of **Berchtesgaden ❷**. There was once an important Augustinian priory here, which served as one of the bastions of the Bavarian House of Wittelsbach against the predations of the archbishops of Salzburg. The Wittelsbachs themselves appointed three powerful prince-provosts to the priory between the 16th and 18th centuries. The entire region was finally ceded to the Kingdom of Bavaria in 1809, which explains why this territory now belongs to Germany and not Austria. The town today contains the former priory, with its 13th-century cloisters and Gothic dormitory. The monastery's salt mine is still in operation and can also be viewed.

BELOW: at the salt mines

The main attractions nearby are the **Königssee**, with its remote Church of St Bartholomä; the panoramic drive via the Rossfeld-Ringstrasse to the **Obersalzberg**, the site of Hitler's infamous Eagle's Nest; and the ascent to the **Kehlsteinhaus**, Hitler's former "tea house", at 1,834 metres (6,015 ft). All these destinations afford spectacular views of the surrounding countryside.

Salt and water

Hallein ❸, which lies east of Berchtesgaden and back in Austria, was one of the most prized possessions of the archbishops of Salzburg. From the 13th century onwards they refined salt from the brine extracted from the Dürrnberg, a practice that had been carried out at various points in history. Even the Celts had exploited this source of "white gold"; traces of their civilization can be seen in the **Museum of Celtic History** (Pflegerplatz 5; open Apr–Oct daily; entrance charge; tel: 06245-80 783).

The **salt mine** is still in operation today, and is open to visitors (open Apr–Oct: daily; entrance charge; tel: 06245-852 8515). Part of the tour includes riding on a toboggan down the salt miners' wooden slide, a trip in a punt across a salt lake and a thundering journey on the underground train that goes deep into the caverns. It is strongly recommended; both children and adults thoroughly enjoy it.

Opposite the parish church in the picturesque Old Town is the house where the organist and choirmaster, Franz Xaver Gruber (1778–1863) lived. It was he who in 1818 composed the world-famous carol *Silent Night, Holy Night* for the Christmas Mass in Oberndorf, north of Salzburg.

South of Hallein, the Salzach Valley is increasingly dominated by flowing water. The karst water from the 2,523-metre (8,276-ft) Hoher Göll plunges in an awe-inspiring curtain of water, foam and mist known as the **Gollinger Waterfalls**, cascading over a 76-m (250-ft) precipice.

Further south, the Salzachöfen and Lammeröfen are two narrow gorges carved through the limestone rock over many millions of years by the rivers Salzach and Lammer. In the case of the Lammer, the walls of the gorge, known locally as *öfen* (ovens), are narrow, only 1 metre (3 ft) apart in some places. The Salzachöfen is a vast jumble of rocks, crevices, caves and erosions. It is accessible from the Lueg Pass.

Schwarzenberg, a prince-archbishop of Salzburg, commissioned the construction of the footpath to the top of the Gollinger falls.

Tennengebirge to the High Tauern

Beyond Golling, the Salzach is forced into narrow, forbidding ravines by the mountain ranges of the Hagengebirge in the west and the Tennengebirge in the east. Near the village of Werfen the naturally impregnable countryside gives way to defences of a man-made nature: here, dominating the scene from a rocky eminence, stands **Burg Hohenwerfen** ❹ (open Nov–Oct daily; entrance charge). As in the case of Festung Hohensalzburg *(see page 211)*, the stronghold was begun by the archbishops of Salzburg in the 11th century. It was enlarged to its present form towards the end of the 16th century by the addition of an extensive system of outer defences in the Italian manner. For the present-day vis-

BELOW: Burg Hohenwerfen in autumn.

itor the fortress provides an excellent impression of medieval defences.

Opposite Hohenwerfen, hidden away between the cliffs of the Tennengebirge, lie the **Eisriesenwelt Caves** (open May–Oct daily; entrance charge). They form one of the most extensive cave complexes in the world; to date, about 50 km (30 miles) of galleries, subterranean halls and labyrinths have been systematically explored. Since the entrance to the caves lies at an altitude of 1,641 metres (5,385 ft), the approach by bus and cable-car is an experience in itself. The cave is illuminated only by the carbide lamps of the visitors and the magnesium lamps of the guides; the effect of this is magical. Some of the individual ice structures are as much as 20 metres (65 ft) thick.

Further south, the parish church of **Bischofshofen** is one of the finest examples of Gothic architecture in the Austrian Alps. The transept dates from the 11th century and the chancel from the 14th century, whilst the nave was built in the hall style with groined vaulting in the 15th century. On the left wall are 16th- and 17th-century frescoes depicting the Passion of Christ. The north

From the Eisriesenwelt cave entrance there is an exceptionally fine view westwards to the glaciers of the 2,941-metre (9,647-ft) Hochkönig.

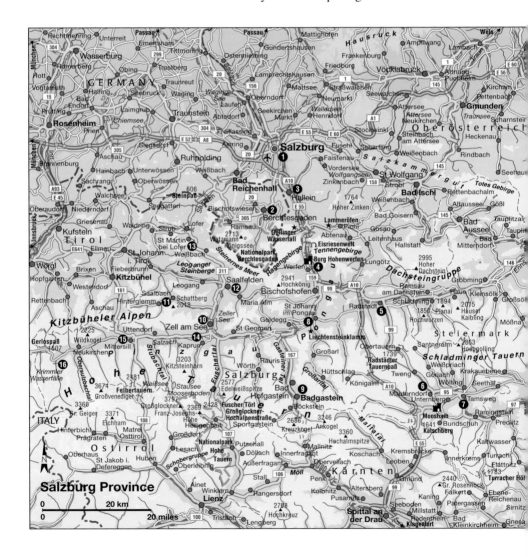

transept contains the marble tomb of Sylvester, Bishop of Chiemsee, completed in 1462. It is the only example of a Gothic standing tomb in the Salzburg region.

About 25 km (15 miles) to the east is **Radstadt ❺**, a medieval town situated at the foot of the pass through the Radstätter Tauern, which lost much of its importance following the construction of the A-10 motorway. As a result, its protected position behind moats and turrets enhances its charm for the visitor. Once upon a time, however, the ancient walls had a more crucial role to fulfil: they were built between 1270 and 1286 on the orders of the prince-bishops of Salzburg as a border defence against the neighbouring province of Styria. Furthermore, Radstadt served as a point of control over access to the northern approach to the Radstädter Tauern Pass.

Since the construction of the motorway, the 1,738-metre (5,700-ft) pass, which marks the boundary between the Low and the High Tauern ranges, has become a quiet country road once more. On both sides of the village there are cable-cars for the journey to the summit and the ridge.

On the southern side of the pass is the town of **Mauterndorf ❻**. King Henry II gave Archbishop Hartwik not only possession of the area, but also the right to levy customs duties. Thus the first occupied toll-booth in the Eastern Alps was founded. As a result, Schloss Mauterndorf was built at the beginning of the 14th century. It was extended in about 1500 by Archbishop Leonhard von Keutschach. The residential apartments, the chapel and the frescoes on the wall of the triumphal arch are of particular interest (open May–Oct daily; entrance charge).

Schloss Moosham, just south of Mauterndorf, was also once a stronghold of the prince-bishops of Salzburg. It served as a bastion of local defence in the Lungau, this remote but strategically important region. As the seat of the ordinary court in the 17th and 18th centuries, the fortress achieved notoriety through numerous trials of witches, sorcerers, beggars and other "miscreants". The judicial procedure was usually extremely brief, thanks to the intervention of the executioner (on the instructions of the bishop). Today the castle functions as a local history museum (open daily; entrance charge).

To the east is the principal town in the Lungau, **Tamsweg ❼**, first mentioned as Tamswick in 1160. The town's most famous monument is the ancient pilgrimage **Church of St Leonhard**, situated on one of the foothills of the Schwarzenberg. Its turretted surrounding wall lends it the appearance of a fortified church. It houses a number of notable treasures, including stained-glass windows manufactured between 1430 and 1450. Most famous of all is the church's "gold window", composed almost entirely of blue and gold pieces. Hardly less precious is a choir stall dating from around 1415 and decorated with intricate carvings and inlaid woodwork.

The Pongau

It is only upon reaching **St Johann im Pongau ❽**, 6 km (4 miles) south of Bischofshofen, that the Salzach, which in its upper reaches flows in a precise west-easterly direction, finally decides to change its course towards the north. Characteristic of the entire upper stretch are the tributaries, some of which flow

Map on page 216

Encouraged by the excellent walking possibilities in summer and the reliable snow conditions in winter, a holiday village has grown up at the top of the Radstädter Tauern Pass.

BELOW: stained glass in the Church of St Leonhard, Tamsweg.

through deeply cut north–south valleys. They all descend from the main Alpine crest and were previously the cause of frequent flooding. The area surrounding the elbow of the Salzach was once the domain of the counts of the Pongau, who also gave it their name.

In the immediate vicinity of St Johann, the Grossarl Valley branches off before opening into the remarkable **Liechtensteinklamm**. This gorge is reached by a path which in many places has been blasted through solid rock; after passing through the first section of the gorge, it opens out into a basin enclosed by 300-metre (985-ft) high walls of rock. Then the gorge narrows down again, becoming sometimes no more than 2 metres (6 ft) wide; finally, in order to reach the 60-metre (212-ft) high waterfall at the end of the gorge, one must pass through a tunnel which is a good 50 metres (165 ft) long.

Perched high above the left bank of the Salzach stands **Schloss Goldegg**, built in the 12th century by the counts of the Pongau in the centre of their area of feudal jurisdiction, in their capacity as ministers of the prince-bishops of Salzburg. The present-day fortress and its outer wards both date from 1320–23. In 1527 the castle passed into the possession of Graf Christoph von Schernberg. He had it decorated with frescoes and tempera paintings on wood and canvas. Today the castle houses the Pongau Museum of Local History.

Radioactive spas

The largest and also the wealthiest of the side valleys of the Salzach is the **Gastein Valley**. It is a district that has always possessed the right basis for wealth at the right moment in time. First of all, gold and silver mined in the area brought the local princes riches and prestige. Later, the healing powers of the

A good time to visit the Pongau is in early January, when the bizarre Perchtenlauf ritual takes place. Men dress up (in costumes and masks) as spirits who bring good fortune and bumper harvests. They parade the streets waving sticks and ringing cowbells.

BELOW: rolling hills in the Pongau.

Map on page 216

local hot springs made the valley famous, and in 1434, when Emperor Friedrich III became the first prominent visitor of his time to take a cure here, its reputation as a spa flourished. In recent years, the snow itself has become a marketable commodity, and the population has put their efforts into the skiing industry. Consequently, the fact that mining is no longer lucrative is unimportant.

The "Court at Gastein", as **Bad Hofgastein** (30 km/18 miles south of St Johann) was originally called, belonged first of all to the dukes of Bavaria, subsequently to the counts of Pongau and finally to the diocese of Salzburg. Even in the 16th century the bishops were able to have gold and silver extracted here. Hofgastein first became known as a spa town in 1828, following the laying of water mains to divert some of the thermal waters from Badgastein itself.

Nonetheless, **Badgastein** ❾, 8 km (5 miles) to the south, remains pre-eminent as the centre of spa facilities in Austria. Its thermal springs contain radon – the therapeutic waters are drunk and used for bathing, and the steam is inhaled. Particularly favoured are the steam baths in the radioactive thermal tunnels, where the water temperature climbs as high as 41°C (106°F). A little train transports patients and visitors down into the tunnels, where they inhale the rare radon gas. Unfortunately, scientists now consider radon to be carcinogenic.

In spite of its position at an altitude of more than 1,000 metres (3,280 ft), Badgastein seems in some respects to have many of the characteristics of a miniature international metropolis, with its tall hotel buildings, elegant shops and bustling atmosphere. The spa and congress complex, situated near the upper waterfall, is the centre of activity. It contains the congress centre, pump room, spa pool and museum. The Kaiser-Wilhelm-Promenade is the most attractive place for a stroll, affording fine views of the valley basin.

The numerous chair lifts providing access to the mountains around Badgastein were erected primarily to serve skiing enthusiasts. They also provide an easily-reached starting point for delightful mountain walks. Further up the valley, in **Böckstein**, cars are loaded on to the train for transport through the 8-km (5-mile) Tauern Tunnel, the shortest link between Salzburg and northwest Carinthia or East Tyrol. (However, a tragic fire in the tunnel in 1999 has prompted the authorities to rethink its single-bore design.) In winter, **Sportgastein** – up a tunnelled mountain road from Bockstein – attracts mountain sports enthusiasts with its facilities for ski-touring and downhill and cross-country skiing.

Savoury Krapfen (similar to doughnuts) and smoked trout are specialities of the Pinzgau (the upper Salzach Valley).

BELOW: an Alpine idyll near Goldegg.

Zell am See and the Saalach Valley

Along the entire length of the Upper Salzach Valley there is only one fork that is open at both the northern and southern ends. During the Ice Age this was the only place where the Salzach glacier managed to carve out an exit to the north – a course which the river itself did not follow. The build-up of moraine deposits at this spot prevents the waters of the **Zeller See** from flowing away to the southeast into the Salzach or northwards into the Saalach. Even today, no meltwater flows into the lake; for this reason, in summer the temperature of the water rises exceptionally quickly for an Alpine lake.

Perched on a small alluvial hill in a pretty setting on the western lake shore is **Zell am See** , the principal town in the Pinzgau and a gateway to Hohe Tauern National Park *(see page 224)*. As the epicentre of the so-called European Sports Region Kaprun-Zell-Saalbach it has plenty of attractions to offer – although admittedly most of them are in nearby Saalbach or Kaprun. Within Zell itself there is only the cable-car to the 1,964-metre (6,445-ft) Schmittenhöhe, which nonetheless affords an excellent view of the Pinzgau, and the mighty snow peaks of the High Tauern and the Grossglockner.

The Salzburg monks discovered this picturesque lakeside setting and founded a "Cella in Bisontio" (Pinzgau) in AD 743. This expanded to become an Augustinian priory, whose church – dedicated to St Hippolytus – has been the **Parish Church** since 1217. Its squat fortified tower, dating from the middle of the 15th century, is a local landmark. The interior contains frescoes from the 13th, 14th and 16th centuries, the most impressive of which include the *Madonna in Glory* (13th century) in the apse of the north aisle, and the *Martyrdom of St Catherine* (14th century) in the porch. The delicate tracery on the balustrade of the west gallery dates from 1514, and the fine representations of St George and St Florian on the west gallery wall are from 1520.

In the winter months, Zell am See belongs first and foremost to ski enthusiasts. The snow conditions are ideal from December to April. In summer – apart from the walkers and climbers – it is gliding fans who find optimum conditions here. Thanks to the east–west orientation of the Pinzgau, the southernmost chain of the Kitzbühel Alps provide more than 50 km (30 miles) of south-facing slopes producing the thermals gliders need to attain height. What is more, the pilots of the Alpine Gliding School are willing to take guests up with them.

Between the Gastein Valley and Zell am See is Taxenbach Gorge, which is famous among white-water rafters. Tour operators in Zell am See can arrange trips for you to try a white-knuckle ride for yourself.

BELOW: on the lakeside, Zell am See.

A footpath across 11 peaks

A few miles north of Zell am See, the road meets the Saalach as it flows eastwards from the Kitzbühel Alps. If you follow the course of the river westwards you will arrive in the skiing community of **Saalbach-Hinterglemm** . The local tourist managers take pride in their 60 lifts and 200 km (125 miles) of pistes. From the 2,200-metre (7,205-ft) Schattberg, the intrepid and fit can trek across no fewer than 11 mountain peaks to the Schmittenhöhe, and enjoy stunning views across to the summits of the High Tauern Range.

To the north (and lying immediately to the south of the "German Corner" and Berchtesgadnerland) is **Saalfelden** , which has developed at the point where the Saalach Valley is at its widest. It was once an important market town where horses and cattle were traded. Today it is above all a good starting point for climbing expeditions up the 2,941-metre (9,648-ft) Hochkönig and the vast limestone plateau of the Steinernes Meer. There is a beautiful trek across to the Königsee in Germany, dominated by the mighty, 2,713-metre (8,900-ft) Watzmann, rising almost vertically from its western shore.

East of Saalfelden lies the Urslau Valley, which extends as far as the western slopes of the Hochkönig. The prettiest village in the valley is undoubtedly **Maria Alm**. Its Gothic pilgrimage church houses not only a

Madonna dating from 1480 but also a graceful spire, which at 84 metres (275 ft) is higher than the towers of Salzburg's cathedral.

Further to the north, the Saalach Valley becomes narrower, closed in as it is on the western side by the Leoganger Steinberge and to the east by the precipices of the Hochkalter. Near Weissbach it is worthwhile climbing up to the Seisenbergklamm or visiting the Lamprechtsofenloch.

St Martin bei Lofer is a village of historical interest some 25 km (15 miles) north of Saalfelden. Until 1803 its parish church belonged to the Augustinian Priory of St Zeno in Reichenhall (in Germany). The church, a late conversion to the baroque style, contains fine 17th- and 18th-century altar paintings, the work of Wilhelm Faistenberger, Johann Friedrich Pereth and Jakob Zanusi.

West of St Martin, hidden away at the top of a high-altitude valley, nestles the pilgrimage **Church of Maria Kirchental**. It was built between 1694 and 1701 according to the plans of no less a celebrity than Johann Bernhard Fischer von Erlach. It is interesting above all for the two marble side altars, completed in 1700. The pulpit dates from 1709. An early 15th-century *Madonna in Glory* is venerated as possessing miraculous powers. Of interest to the visitor are the numerous votive gifts. They are collected in an ex voto chapel.

Zell am See to the Grossglockner

The valley of the Fuscher Ache, branching off south of Zell am See near Bruck, is both lonely and wild, but from earliest times it attracted travellers seeking a mountain pass to the south. Even the Romans knew of this particular pass – a 17-cm (7-inch) bronze figure dating from the 1st century AD was found at an altitude of 2,570 metres (8,430 ft), near the Hochtor, during the construction of

Map on page 216

A 4-km (2.5-mile) long funicular train was constructed at Kaprun to provide access to the largest year-round ski slope in Austria – the Schmiedinger Kees, which lies beneath Kitzsteinhorn. This partially underground funicular was the site of a catastrophic fire in November 2000, which claimed the lives of 155 skiers.

BELOW: the Zeller See.

the **Grossglockner Hochalpenstrasse** (High Alpine Road). The south side of the pass was also of interest to the Romans, for they mined gold in the region of Heiligenblut. In the Middle Ages the "Blood Pilgrimage" to Heiligenblut drove the faithful from the Pinzgau into these hostile mountains.

The metre-high walls of snow which border the road until well into the summer relay an unequivocal message. In winter, the snow here lies an average of over 5 metres (16 ft) deep. On approximately 99 days every year a stormy wind blows with gusts of up to 150 kph (93 mph); on 250 days of the year it snows. The climatic conditions along the crest of the Grossglockner Road are equivalent to that of Siberia. The summit of the panoramic road is marked by the Edelweissspitze, at 2,577 metres (8,450 ft), which also offers the best view. Despite the fascination of the Edelweissspitze, this observation post does not mark the southern pass proper. Instead, our journey continues downhill again to the Fuscher Törl, at 2,405 metres (7,890 ft), down again to the Fuscher Lake, and then along the eastern sides of the Brennkogel and uphill again past a long section of scree slopes to the Hochtor Tunnel, at 2,505 metres (8,220 ft).

From the car park at the southern tunnel entrance there is a quite splendid view far to the south, towards Carinthia and East Tyrol: across to the Schober Range and down into the Möll Valley *(see page 237)*.

In the Upper Pinzgau

The main attraction of the European Sports Region around Zell am See is the largest year-round ski slope in Austria – the Schmiedinger Kees, which lies beneath the jagged peak of the 3,203-metre (10,508-ft) Kitzsteinhorn. It has brought renown (at least in the skiing world) to the little Alpine village of

One old chronicle describes the perils of the Grossglockner peaks as they were perceived in medieval times: "There is a region up there where the demons reside, threatening with falling rocks and avalanches every mortal who ventures into the vicinity."

BELOW: the view from the Hochalpenstrasse.

Map on page 216

Kaprun ⑭, which lies a few miles south of Zell am See, at the entrance to the valley of the same name. In order to provide access to this sporting paradise it was necessary to build a glacier cable-car in three sections; it leads via the intermediate stations at the Salzburger Hütte (1,897 metres/6,223 ft) and the Alpine Centre (2,452 metres/8,044 ft) to the Mountain Station (3,029 metres/9,937 ft) on the ridge of the Kitzsteinhorn.

Access to the Pinzgau's most famous mountain provides even visitors without mountaineering aspirations with a spectacular experience of the Alps. From the Mountain Station of the cable car there is a footpath to the summit of the Kitzsteinhorn. Its exposed position affords views of the Glockner massif, the Wiesbachhorn and the Grossvenediger. Lined up to the north stand the Kitzbühel Alps, the Steinernes Meer with the Hochkönig, the Tennengebirge and the Dachstein ranges. Far down below are the vast green reservoirs of the Tauern Hydroelectric Power Station, at the head of the Kaprun valley.

Back in the valley, visitors can tour the power station complex, which includes two huge reservoirs, the higher of which is at 2,036 metres (6,680 ft). Private cars cannot be used all the way – the last stretch is covered by bus. At the upper reservoir, the Mooserboden, the road peters out by the so-called Heidnische Kirche (Heathen Church), claimed by archaeologists to be a Celtic religious site. The high spot – literally – of this impressive mountain tour is the 2,108-metre (6,916-ft) Höhenburg, between the twin dams of the Mooserboden reservoir. From here one can see both lakes at the same time, and there is a breathtaking panorama of the mountain peaks and glaciers flanking the Karlinger Kees.

The Stubachtal, which forks off southwards near Uttendorf, west of Kaprun, has also been exploited by the construction of a power station and cable-cars.

The Tauern Power Station is one of the most ambitious in the Alps. Some 200 million cubic metres (7 billion cubic ft) of water are stored in two vast reservoirs, which are dammed by three barrages, each over 100 metres (328 ft) high. The plant can generate a total of 220,000 kW.

BELOW: the Grossglockner.

CLIMBING THE GROSSGLOCKNER

The first hour of this challenging hike and climb is spent crossing the Pasterze Glacier, passing crevasses up to 25 metres (80 ft) deep. When the surface ice is thawing one must wade the last metres through slush. But that's just the beginning. An exhausting climb of seven and a half hours through the Leitertal to the Salmhütte refuge follows. The overnight hut sits at an altitude of 2,644 metres (8,673 ft); it is advisable to engage a guide for the next day's climb. The remaining 1,000 metres (3,300 ft) include several sections calling for expert climbing skills. The terrain to the "Eagle's Nest" (3,400 metres/11,150 ft) becomes progressively steeper, often with a gradient of 50 percent. After one hour you reach the steep wall below the Eagle's Nest, one of the key sections of the ascent. It takes a good 30 minutes to scale the wall in order to reach the summit ridge, and a further half hour walking along the path – barely 40 cm (16 in) wide – to reach the lowest of the summits of the Grossglockner. After a short rest, continue to the "Little Glockner", separated from the summit proper only by the "roof", a relatively flat ridge. To the left and right, clefts fall away almost vertically. Much of the remaining way is difficult; only the path near the summit flattens out a little before the top at 3,798 metres (12,460 ft) – the highest point in Austria.

On this occasion one can drive right down to the floor of the valley and up to the first stage: the Enzingerboden (1,468 metres/4,816 ft), which is set in spectacularly forested scenery. The Stubach-Weisssee cable-car climbs from here to the Weisssee, at an altitude of 2,323 metres (7,620 ft). The best view can be obtained from the Rudolfshütte, the Austrian Alpine Association Centre on the Hinterer Schafbühel, at 2,352 metres (7,716 ft).

An ancient mountain pass

Further west, the route across the Felber Tauern was an important one for Austrians long before the construction of the 5.2-km (3¼-mile) tunnel. Back in the Middle Ages it was a much-used trade route, crossing the Alpine crest at an altitude of 2,481 metres (8,139 ft) at precisely the point where the St Poltner refuge is situated today. In those days packhorses carried velvets and silks, barrels of wine and citrus fruit northwards and copper, iron, leather and salt in the opposite direction.

Of corresponding significance was the town of **Mittersill** ⓑ, just west of Uttendorf, which marks the start of the climb on the northern side. The town itself came into the possession of the counts of Matrei in the 12th century as a Bavarian fief. They called themselves the counts of Mittersill from 1180, and in 1228 they became subject to the archdiocese of Salzburg. The castle here has been rebuilt complete with massive corner towers and battlements. The triple-bayed Gothic castle chapel was rebuilt in its present form in 1553. It houses a winged altarpiece dating from the middle of the 15th century. The Church of St Leonhard was completed in 1749 and contains interesting stained-glass windows designed by Hans Hauer and Franz Sträussenberger.

Early morning mist near Salzburg.

BELOW: the Hohe Tauern National Park.

HOHE TAUERN NATIONAL PARK

Little of Europe remains wild today, and that makes the presence of Hohe Tauern National Park all the more remarkable. The tremendous variety of mountain, meadow, pasture, forest, riverine and even glacial landscapes here are all worth experiencing.

The park began as a series of relatively small land acquisitions in the Stubach and Amer valleys. Parcels were steadily added in such important areas as the Glockner Massif until, by the 1950s, the growing preserve aroused enough support among locals that they turned out en masse to halt the damming-up of the Krimml River for hydroelectric power. In 1971, leaders of the three provinces within the park's boundaries – Salzburg Province, Carinthia and Tyrol – signed an agreement to create the park.

Hiking and nature-watching are the preferred activities here. The park is home to a wide variety of flowers such as the Alpine aster, alpenrose, edelweiss and orchids; trees include the famous Arolla pine, spruces and firs. Animal life is similarly diverse: you might spot anything from swallowtail butterflies to vultures, wild horses, ibex or lynx. More than a million visitors come to the park each year. Tourist offices in Zell am See, Badgastein and other centres can provide information on hiking trails, flora and fauna.

Even from afar, the **Church of St Anne** stands out from the usual Salzburg baroque by virtue of its curved gable facade. This is hardly surprising, since the architect was Jakob Singer, from Schwaz in Tyrol, who completed the church in 1751. Also a native of Schwaz was Christoph Anton Mayr, who, in 1753, painted the frescoes adorning the interior. The visitor should be sure to see St Anne's Gothic daughter church, **St Nicholas in Felben**, on the outskirts of town, which has a high altar dating from 1631, depicting a series of highly expressive late-Gothic figures of the 14 auxiliary saints.

Beyond Mittersill, the Salzach Valley gradually becomes narrower and more typically Alpine. The peaks fringing the horizon are dominated by the 3,674-metre (12,050-ft) Grossvenediger. There are two ways of approaching this majestic giant. The first is to make the ascent through the Obersulzbach Valley to the Kürsinger Refuge, which lies at 2,549 metres (8,362 ft). This involves a journey on foot of several hours. An easier route is by chair lift from Neukirchen, 20 km (12 miles) west of Mittersill. By this means one is transported to the Alpine Ridge west of the Wildkogel, at a height of 2,093 metres (6,866 ft). From this point one has a perfect view across the Salzach Valley towards the ridge dominated by the Grossvenediger.

Map on page 216

White water at Krimml Falls.

The waterfall of the twelve glaciers

A unique natural phenomenon awaits the traveller in the uppermost reaches of the Salzach Valley, another 12 km (8 miles) west, near the town of Krimml. The **Krimml Falls** ⓰ are the most spectacular in the entire Alps, deserving superlatives on several counts. First, there is the sheer volume of water of the Krimmler Ache, which is fed by no fewer than 12 glaciers in the Venediger Massif to the south. Then there is the total height of the falls, which, divided among the three great cascades, totals 380 metres (1,246 ft), with the longest free-fall being one of 65 metres (213 ft). And finally there is the variety of settings and wealth of natural features which the thundering water passes through on its path. The entire site is marked by well-signposted footpaths which make exploration of the area by foot surprisingly easy. There are observation platforms to get even nearer. As an added bonus, opposition from Alpine hiking and parks groups has so far prevented the exploitation of these magnificently thunderous falls for hydroelectric purposes.

BELOW: the falls at Krimml descend through forest.

Starting at Krimml, the Gerlos Pass Toll Road leads up and over the 1,507-metre (4,944-ft) Gerlos Pass, and descends on the other side into the Ziller Valley in Tyrol *(see page 253)*. On the way up, it describes a large loop around the Tratenköpfl, thereby offering an excellent view of the cascading Krimml Falls.

Shortly after the top of the pass, and just before one reaches the Tyrol border, the traveller can expect to see another remarkable sight. Immediately below the road lies the Durlassboden Reservoir, a place especially popular with watersports. Here, there are sailing and surfing schools and paddle-boat rentals. Dominating the scene, towering proudly above other less lofty peaks, are the soaring summits of the Gerlosspitze and the Reichenspitze. ❏

CARINTHIA AND EAST TYROL

*The country's southernmost province and its remote
western neighbour are relatively unknown outside of Austria,
but they have spectacular lake and mountain scenery*

Map
on pages
230–1

Warm lakes and clear rivers, majestic mountains and secluded valleys, gently rolling meadows and dense woodlands have given the people of Carinthia (Kärnten) a happy disposition which often expresses itself in song. An above-average amount of sunshine makes the snow-clad slopes glisten in winter, melts the ice in spring, warms lake waters – and hearts – in summer, and illuminates golden landscapes in autumn.

Klagenfurt

Today it is hard to imagine that this region was once rough marshland. Legend tells of a winged dragon that struck terror into the hearts of the local inhabitants. Its statue is immortalised as the emblem of **Klagenfurt ❶**, the capital of Carinthia. It stands in the middle of Neuer Platz, which is actually anything but new. Most of the lovely old houses around its perimeter date from the 17th century, as does the Town Hall. A number of picturesque inner courtyards can be glimpsed off Kramergasse and Alter Platz, which adjoin Neuer Platz to the north. In the vicinity are the Trinity Column (1680), the Palais Goess (18th century) and the **Landhaus**, dating from the 16th century, with its famous Grosse Wappensaal (Great Heraldic Hall; open Apr–Oct daily; entrance charge; tel: 0463-57 757-215), which displays 665 coats of arms.

At the western end of Alter Platz is the **Haus zur Goldenen Gans** (Golden Goose), which is listed in records of 1489 and was originally planned as an imperial residence. In return, the emperor handed over his former castle and its park to the estates for the erection of a country house. The estates of the realm was an influential body in Klagenfurt, and at their request, in 1518, the Emperor Maximilian I formally handed over the town to them, a situation unique in German constitutional history. Naturally they cherished their jewel with all their combined strength, creating a chequerboard street layout which was unique at the time, and which characterises the town plan to this day.

Klagenfurt has also retained its traditional function as a shopping centre. Whether you seek traditional costumes or jewellery, gourmet delicacies, fine china, books or exquisite linen, shopping or just browsing through the town's elegant shops is always a delight. There are plenty of cultural attractions too: the Cathedral Church, the Church of the Holy Ghost (14th century), the Parish Church on the Pfarrplatz and, north of town, the 9th-century Carolingian Church in St Peter am Bichl. There are also no fewer than 22 castles within a radius of a few miles.

No-one should fail to visit **Minimundus** (open Apr–Oct daily; entrance charge; tel: 0463-211 940), the miniature world beside Wörther See, 3 km (2

PRECEDING PAGES: the Karawanken Mountains, south of Klagenfurt. **LEFT:** the castle at Strassburg. **BELOW:** this dwarf is a character in local legend.

miles) west of the city. Many thousands of people, large and small, visit the exhibition annually. There are more than 150 replicas of famous buildings, all constructed to a scale of 1:25, as well as a miniature railway and a harbour with model ships.

Wörther See

Klagenfurt's advertising campaign claims that "A town by a lake has twice as much feeling for life". Surveying **Wörther See** ❷, it's difficult not to agree. The town is justifiably proud of the largest lakeside bathing area in Europe and one of the most modern camp sites in the country. In spite of a depth of 85 metres (275 ft) in places, the water temperature can reach 28°C (82°F) – making it irresistible for swimmers.

The five ships of the Wörther See fleet are available for pleasure cruises from the beginning of May until the beginning of October. One of them, the *Thalia*, is the last propeller-driven steamer in Austria. The *Muse of Grace* has had a very varied life since she was launched in 1909. After being destroyed by an explosion in 1945, she was rescued several years later by high-level politics. Restored by the governement, she hosted the US and Soviet ambassadors for the preparatory discussions leading to the SALT-1 agreement.

Heading west from Klagenfurt, the first landing jetty on the north shore is at **Krumpendorf**. The atmosphere of this resort community with 7 km (4 miles) of sunny beaches can best be described as informal. Lakeside promenades, bathing beaches, shady avenues and green parks provide the setting for a restful holiday; the requisite amenities are also all here: water skiing, windsurfing, diving and an 18-hole golf course at nearby Moosburg.

There is no shortage of restaurants in the Carinthian capital. Visitors with a sweet tooth, gourmets, wine buffs and beer drinkers, devotees of spaghetti and chop suey, will all find establishments to suit their tastes. Worthy of particular mention are the café and restaurant in the romantic Hotel Musil, at 10-Oktober-Strasse 14.

BELOW: the Alter Platz, Klagenfurt.

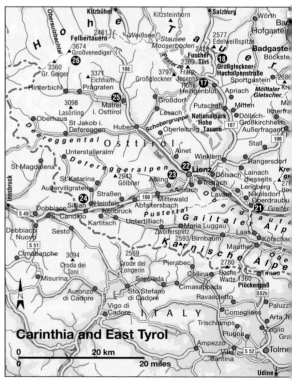

Carinthia and East Tyrol

0   20 km
0   20 miles

The bronzed Adonises of the area can be found at the bathing areas, boulevard cafés or tennis courts in **Pörtschach**, 6 km (4 miles) west. Here a peninsula of land with old trees, flower-bordered paths and little bays juts far out into the lake. Until the middle of the 19th century this was just a sleepy fishing village.

It was the Southern Railway that brought the wealthy citizens of the Habsburg monarchy to Pörtschach and it was here that they built their summer residences in order to escape the bustle of the cities. Johannes Brahms was another summer visitor. Inspired by the beauty of the lake, he composed his 2nd Symphony and celebrated Violin Concerto here. Those wishing to follow in the great composer's footsteps are advised to visit the **Weisses Rössl** – the White Horse Inn. The parlour with his favourite table has not changed since his time.

Velden ❸, the next town west, is the local high-life arena, for it is the resort favoured by the rich and the beautiful. Playground of the jet set, Velden's yacht marina, golf course and casino attract the rich and sporty from across the globe.

The Illyrians, and later Baron von Khevenhüller, had quite different reasons for settling in Velden. The Renaissance **Schloss Velden** the baron built here in 1590 was a favoured rendezvous for the aristocracy at the end of the 16th century. In 1920 it was converted into a luxury hotel. Visitors can sleep in the royal chambers or, at the very least, stroll through the castle park.

Maria Wörth ❹, set on a peninsula on the southern shore of the lake, is an idyllic spot. The character of the village stems from the church, which dominates the peninsula (an island until the water level sank because of the ford on the River Glan). It was built in AD 890 by Bishop Waldo of Freising (in Bavaria) and later extended. The former presbytery church stands on the highest spot; it was rebuilt in the Gothic style following a fire and houses a number of art treasures:

Map
on pages
230–1

Schloss Velden was used as a backdrop for a popular 1980s soap opera, Schloss am Wörther See.

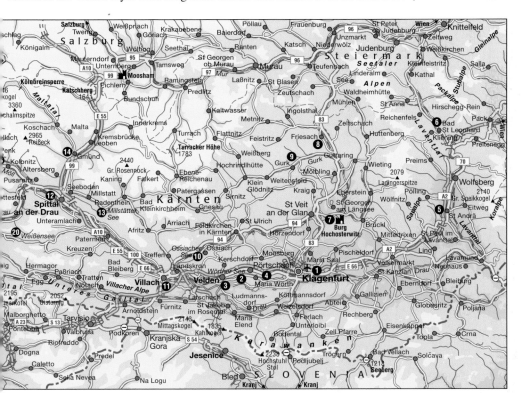

a baroque likeness of St Christopher on the exterior wall, a baroque high altar, an exquisite statue of the Madonna and baroque carved wooden altars. Maria Wörth has enjoyed considerable political and economic importance over the centuries, giving its name to the lake in the process.

More bathing lakes

The Keutschach Valley, just south of Lake Wörther, is the setting for four large lakes. Camp sites and bathing areas fringe the shores of Hafnersee and Rauschelesee. The idyllically situated Bassgeigensee is shaped like its namesake (*geige* means violin). And then there is **Keutschacher See** itself; its 1.4-sq. km (0.5-sq. mile) expanse and water temperatures which reach 26°C (79°F) in the summer entice visitors to swim or hire a rowing, sailing or pedal boat. Its shores are ringed by bathing areas, camp sites, tennis courts, mini-golf ranges and even football pitches. The Keutschacher See Children's Summer is always popular, featuring play festivals, do-it-yourself workshops and "children's gastronomy".

Keutschach, beside the lake, is the focal point of the valley and offers two cultural attractions in the form of its 17th-century baroque castle and the late-Romanesque St George's Chapel, which has a Carolingian-era stone depicting a symbol of the Resurrection. Remains of pile dwellings, neolithic implements and Stone-Age caves bear witness to the region's long history of settlement.

The Lavant Valley

The eastern part of Carinthia is dominated by the idyllic Lavanttal. First stop in the valley en route from Klagenfurt is the ancient diocesan town of **St Andrä ❺**, which grew up around the pilgrimage Church of Maria Loreto. The town

If you're spending some time in Carinthia in the summer, it may be worth paying €32 for a Kärnten Card. Available from tourist offices, it allows free use of all public transport and free entry to the majority of museums and attractions, all for three weeks.

BELOW: the peninsula and church of Maria Wörth.

enchants the traveller with its lovely setting amidst verdant meadows, encircled by castles and palaces. Gourmets flock here in May and June for the so-called Asparagus Sundays. In autumn, fruits are pressed amidst scenes of great merriment, and a culinary walking tour covering local specialities takes place. The Lavant Valley local museum, in nearby St Ulrich, is also worth visiting. It provides a well-displayed insight into the life and traditions of the region.

St Paul im Lavanttal, a 10-km (6-mile) detour down Road 69 to the south, is often referred to by locals as "Carinthia's treasure chest", a name it owes to its **Benedictine Abbey** (open May–Oct daily; entrance charge; tel: 04357-201 922), founded in 1091. The museum here displays collections featuring masterpieces from a number of eras. When the exhibitions are open to the public, guided tours are conducted round the abbey.

In all senses of the word, **Wolfsberg** – about 10 km (6 miles) north of St Andrä – is the centre of the Lavant Valley. Its mountain parks, the Saualpe and the Koralpe, invite the visitor to wander at leisure, to tarry awhile, or to fly – by motorised aircraft, glider or hang-glider.

Bad St Leonhard ❻, further up the valley, offers excellent spa facilities. Its sulphur springs provide rejuvenation and relaxation from mid-May to mid-October. In addition to numerous folklore festivals there is a fine Gothic parish church and, in the surrounding area, 100 km (60 miles) of signposted footpaths leading up to an altitude of 1,800 metres (5,905 ft), plus an excellent network of mountain refuges.

Burg Hochosterwitz

Northeast of Klagenfurt, Road 92 leads to the town of Brückl. Just to the west of Brückl is the stunning fortress of **Burg Hochosterwitz ❼**, a Carinthian landmark (open Apr–Oct daily; entrance charge). The path to the castle up the 160-metre (525-ft) cone-shaped rock passes through no fewer than 14 gate towers. Next to the eighth stands the chapel, with an unusual bronze altar. The castle museum houses an imposing collection of weapons. On the Magdalensberg, south of Hochosterwitz, is the site of the largest archaeological excavations in Austria – a Romano-Celtic town, with an **open-air museum** and display rooms (open May–mid-Oct daily; entrance charge; tel: 04224-2255).

The road from Brückl continues to St Veit an der Glan. Before you reach the latter, there is a fork to the right leading to **St Georgen am Längsee**. The waters of Langsee, nestling between densely wooded mountain slopes, reach summer temperatures of 26°C (79°F). Here are all the ingredients for a varied holiday: sailing, rowing, riding, cycling and fishing, not only for pike and carp, but also zander.

Road 83 from St Veit an der Glan heads north to the old town of **Friesach ❽**. It's worth stopping here awhile. You won't often find three castles, a fort and a still-extant moat in one town, but here they are – testament to Friesach's former importance as a trading post on what was once the main road from Vienna to Venice. The town's basilica is one of half a dozen churches, several with important carvings or altar work.

Map on pages 230–1

It was in Schloss Waldenstein in Preitenegg, north of Wolfsberg, that the Carinthian anthem was composed in the 19th century. This little community on the Packsattel Mountain Road has a late-Gothic parish church with a baroque interior and a small collection of notable paintings.

BELOW: church on the Magdalensburg, near Burg Hochosterwitz.

The unusual Hotel St Veit in St Veit an der Glan was designed by Viennese artist Ernst Fuchs and built in 1998.

BELOW: Gurk Cathedral.

The Gurk Valley

South of Friesach, the entrance to the Gurk Valley at Zwischenwässern is marked by **Pöckstein Castle**, a late-baroque bishop's residence. Its magnificent audience rooms make it a much-visited architectural curiosity. This is also the starting point of the **Gurk Valley Museum Railway**, which puffs westwards to Glödnitz from early June to late September – a unique experience for railway fanatics, romantics and keen photographers. You can even apply for an amateur engine-driver's certificate.

Strassburg, to the west, is dominated by the castle of the same name, which is visible for miles around (open Apr–Oct Mon–Fri; entrance charge). The original building dates from 1131; between the 14th and 17th centuries it was constantly altered and added to, and served as the summer residence of the bishops of Gurk until 1780. Apart from viewing the exquisite arcaded courtyard and the castle chapel, the visitor should not miss the church in the nearby village of Lieding, an architectural gem with a 1,000-year history.

Countess Emma, the consort of the ruler of Carinthia and the region's patron saint, founded the Romanesque cathedral in **Gurk ➒** during the 12th century. The priory courtyard was built in the 15th century. The crypt, supported by 100 pillars, the Gothic paintings and the most important Romanesque series of frescoes in the German-speaking world give it architectural and artistic significance. The celebrated Raphael Donner immortalised his memory with the transept altar and a set of lead reliefs on the pulpit. When the sun is shining brightly, the 13th-century stained-glass windows in the West Porch transform the light into cascades of colour.

Further west, **Weitensfeld** is a village that appeals to the visitor on second sight.

It is a centre in which ancient Carinthian customs, such as the Kranzlreiten (a horserace which takes place at Whitsun), are still observed. The district also has a rich artistic heritage. Austria's oldest item of worked glass, the Magdalene Windowpane, originated in a church in Weitensfeld. The church in the neighbouring village of Zweinitz houses ornate frescoes in the apse which are real jewels of sacred art.

The road soon forks off to the right towards **Flattnitz**, a resort village situated at an altitude of 1,400 metres (4,600 ft). Here, where once the Roman legions crossed the Alps, walkers gather in summer and skiers in winter. The Spitzeralm and the Pfandlhütte are popular goals. The Pass Church contains magnificent frescoes which provide a moving reminder of the faith of early Christians.

Back at the fork, take a left turn instead to reach the road to **Deutsch-Griffen**, the site of one of the few remaining medieval fortified churches in the entire Alpine region. A flight of 200 steps leads up to the sacred edifice, picturesquely situated on a hillside and housing a collection of 15th-century frescoes.

Standing at the point where the Gurk Valley becomes increasingly wild and romantic is **Sirnitz**. Nearby **Albeck Fortress**, today a romantic ruin, experienced its Golden Age at the time of Barbarossa, later becoming the administrative seat of the bishops of Gurk. Visitors are captivated by the octagonal form of the late-Gothic charnel house attached to the medieval parish church. After a detour via Hochrindl, which lies at 1,600 metres (5,250 ft) in the middle of the Gurktaler Alps, the road crosses the Gurk once more near Ebene Reichenau before climbing a gradient of 1 in 4 up to the Turracher Höhe (1,780 metres/5,850 ft), at the top of the valley (see page 189). Here, the spectacular panorama is enlivened by the emerald-green waters of the mountain lakes, and the air seems to taste of the pine woods. There are plenty of choices for a mountain walk. For those preferring not to exert themselves too much, there are two chair lifts climbing to 2,010 and 2,240 metres (6,590 and 7,350 ft). A mineral museum (open Mon–Sat), a summer toboggan run and a total of 800 hotel beds also tempt visitors to stay a day or so.

Ossiacher See

South of Sirnitz, the main road leads to Feldkirchen and then turns southwest to **Ossiacher See ⑩**, a lake that offers sports enthusiasts a wide choice of activities. There are 13 schools of sailing, windsurfing and water-skiing. Bold spirits can even attempt parasailing from a motorboat. Overcoming initial fears will be rewarded by an extra-terrestrial floating sensation and a bird's-eye view of the surrounding countryside. Even the inevitable soft, wet landing is no hardship, for here the water reaches a temperature of 26°C (79°F).

Culture addicts can enjoy the events of the Carinthian summer in the monastery of **Ossiach**, on the south side of the lake. Anglers are in their element catching the catfish, pike, tench, trout, eel and many other fish that abound in the lake. For others there is the attraction of a summer sledging run, while an attractive diversion for the young at heart is **Elli Riehl's Puppenwelt** (Puppet

The area between Magdalensberg and Klagenfurt, known as the Zollfeld, is the historic heart of Carinthia. The Celts and Romans settled here, and it is the site of the Herzogstuhl, a double throne used in medieval times for ducal investiture ceremonies.

BELOW: a Romanesque carving in Gurk.

THE SLOVENES OF CARINTHIA

Official estimates place Austria's Slovene population at around 30,000, making them the country's second largest ethnic group. Most live in southeastern Carinthia, in a strip of land that runs along the Slovenian border from Faakersee, near Villach, to Bleiburg, east of Klagenfurt. There has long been a Slav influence in Carinthia. (Most town names ending -ach are Slavic in origin.) However, when Yugoslavia invaded Carinthia in 1918, tensions between Slovenes and locals rose to a boiling point. They have never completely simmered down. Jörg Haider's ascension to governorship of the province, running on an anti-immigrant platform, is only the most recent manifestation of decades-old unease.

Over the years, the Slovenes have pushed for recognition and autonomy, and in 1955 a treaty granted them official minority status in Austria. Today the various groups in the province speak a number of dialects of their original language – some of them mutually unintelligible. Interestingly, the number of Carinthians who describe themselves as Slovene on census forms has dropped sharply in recent decades, even as their population has held steady – a sign they have become Austrian in their own minds, if not in those of other Carinthians.

World; open Easter–Oct daily; entrance charge; tel: 04248-2395) in Treffen.

South of Ossiacher See is the Drau (Drava) River, and straddling the river is the chic and historically important town of **Villach** ⓫. The Romans built a fort and a bridge here during the first century AD, constructing paved roads as they did so. It was not until 1759 that the town and its surrounding area were ceded to Austria from the Bishopric of Bamberg. They were purchased by Maria Theresa. In the 16th century, when Paracelsus spent his youth here, the town was the economic and cultural centre of Carinthia. He later described the healing power of the springs which were to move Napoleon to rapturous enthusiasm. Even today, the warm waters offer relaxation and healing to guests from all over the world in a number of well-planned cure and bathing centres.

The Kranzlreiten horserace is a survivor from medieval times, when the plague took its toll on the population. Young men would compete in such races to see who could marry the village's surviving virgins.

The Drau Valley

Road 100 leads northwest from Villach through the lower valley of the Drau. Beyond Kellerberg and Feistritz, **Paternion** nestles between sunny mountain slopes and shady woodland, offering a range of amenities for the holidaymaker. Between swimming, fishing, walking, skating, curling and cross-country skiing there is the opportunity to witness the lovely altars of the pilgrimage Church of St Paternianus as well as, on an eminence, a 16th-century castle complex. A rewarding detour away from the main road is the trip up the Weissenbach Valley to Stockenboi to see the remarkable architecture of the local farmhouses.

Back on Road 100, **Spittal an der Drau** ⓬ is an exceptionally pretty little town. It lies on the boundary between the upper and lower Drau valleys. Its fine houses, historic monuments and elegant shops make it worth visiting whether one's interests lie in sightseeing or shopping. Stately **Schloss Porcia** unites the civilizations of past and present: not only does it house a fascinating museum of local history (open Apr–Oct daily; Nov–Mar Mon–Thurs; entrance charge), but its pretty arcaded courtyard serves a as setting for the drama festival held in August and September each year.

BELOW: on the edge of the Millstätter See.

Just north of Spittal, **Millstätter See** ⓭ is idyllically situated amid gentle countryside, offering excellent facilities in addition to its exceptional beauty. Its unspoilt southern shore, densely wooded, is a nature reserve with free access for the public. The sandy beaches and warm, clear waters make the lake ideal for bathing. Parasailing and diving, illustrated lectures and fashion shows, evenings of traditional music and piano recitals are typical of the region's leisure activities. Rounding out the picture is the Kneipp circuit and footpath in Kaning, where six flour mills dating from around 1800 can be seen clattering away within a stretch of 3 km (2 miles), inviting passers-by to a bread-baking session or to a tot of Mühlengeist, the local schnapps.

There is another, slightly longer excursion which all visitors should undertake. Taking the E 55 route from Spittal to **Gmünd** ⓮, the traveller should make a point of pausing for long enough to visit the Porsche Museum (open daily; entrance charge; tel: 04732-2471). Between 1944 and 1950 the revolutionary car designer's workshop was situated here, and in 1948 the legendary Porsche 356 was born on this very spot.

A road branches off to the northwest towards Malta. Beyond the village, a toll-booth marks the beginning of a remarkable section of road between Malta and Hochalm, which passes through the so-called **Valley of Falling Waters**. A new panorama opens up after every hairpin bend – another waterfall, or a glimpse of the 200-metre (656-ft) high wall of the Kölnbrein Barrage, the highest dam wall in Austria. Soon we reach the reservoir, which lies amidst mountain peaks at an altitude of almost 2,000 metres (6,600 ft). A hotel stands beside the dam. A night spent here, with an evening and morning walk, is an unforgettable experience. Walkers can set off after breakfast to the Osnabrück Hut or even go on a wild-animal safari.

The valley of the Möll

Starting back at Spittal, head northwest and then take Road 106 towards the north for an exploration of the **Mölltal ⑮** (Möll Valley), which twists and turns before bringing you eventually to Austria's highest peak. The first diversion in the valley is in Kolbnitz, about 20 km (12 miles) from Spittal. Here it is possible to climb from 800 to 2,000 metres (2,600 to 6,600 ft) without exerting oneself unduly and in a short space of time; or when the weather is fine, take the trip by funicular and underground railway up to the Reisseck-Lake Plateau. You are bound to want to prolong your stay here, so be prepared. The invigorating mountain air, good range of accommodation and signposted walks of all grades of difficulty make Reisseck ideal for a short holiday.

Road 105 branches off at Obervellach towards Mallnitz, a high-altitude resort lying at 1,190 metres (3,900 ft) and marking the southern end of the Tauern Tunnel. Day by day, a car-ferry train system passes on a 10-minute journey through the 8-km (5-mile) tunnel, carrying thousands of cars between Carinthia and Salzburg Province each year.

Castles, glaciers and waterfalls

Continuing up the Möll Valley, castle addicts will be in seventh heaven when they reach **Schloss Groppenstein**, whose roots reach back to the 13th century. It stands majestically over the countryside, next to the waterfall of the same name.

We soon reach **Flattach ⑯** – a small village, but one of the most important centres in the Möll Valley. It is the starting point of the magnificent panoramic road leading up to the Möll Valley Glacier. Every bend opens up new perspectives, each more breathtaking than the last, until, at 2,200 metres (7,210 ft), the road reaches the valley station of a mountain railway. This takes you across the glacier itself up to the mountain station, situated at 2,800 metres (9,180 ft). If you don't feel inclined to jump on your skis (forgetting them is no problem, for all equipment can be rented here) or to climb a 3,000-metre (9,800-ft) peak, you may prefer to enjoy the intoxicating mountain air, the blue sky and the glittering snow from the sun terrace of the mountain restaurant.

Also near Flattach lies the counterpart to the panoramic view of the Möll Valley Glacier: the wildly romantic **Ragga Gorge**, carved over millennia. A meticulously constructed system of bridges and steps

Map on pages 230–1

The road through the Möll Valley leads past the ruins of Schloss Falkenstein, then Obervellach with its pretty townhouses and 16th-century tower. Art connoisseurs will enjoy the 400-year-old parish church with its early Dutch altar paintings and Gothic carvings. Also worth visiting is the baroque Trabuschgen Castle.

BELOW: a statue in Gmund.

permits the visitor to traverse the remarkable site without difficulty, admiring the eight thundering waterfalls formed by the Ragga torrent as it plunges downhill.

Typical of the resorts of the central Möll Valley, beyond Flattach is the village of **Rangersdorf**, which has the ruins of a castle first mentioned in 1278. **Lainach**, too, with its miniature iron and sulphur spring, is a good choice for a restful holiday. **Winklern**, nestling between meadows and fields at the junction with Road 107, lies in a conservation area. The village's landmark, the Toll Tower, was built in about 1500 on foundations which are thought to date back to Roman times.

From this point onwards the course of the cheerfully babbling Möll (the name is of Celtic origin) turns northwards alongside Road 107, passing through pretty villages on the way to **Döllach-Grosskirchheim**. The settlement – known even in Roman times – was the gold-mining centre of the Tauern in the 15th and 16th centuries. As many as 3,000 miners extracted the precious metal from 800 different sites. A museum of gold mining, housed in **Kirchheim Castle**, contains interesting displays on the subject. A walk through the nearby Zirknitz Valley affords views of two magnificent waterfalls, the Neunbrunnen (Nine Springs Falls) and the Gucklöcher des Lindwurms (Dragon's Peepholes).

The Upper Möll Valley Mountain Road leads on from here via various villages to Heiligenblut, where it joins the Grossglockner High Alpine Road.

Before venturing onto the hairpin bends and up the mountain, however, it is worth visiting **Heiligenblut** ⓱. The Gothic **Parish Church of St Vincent** dates from the 15th century. It contains the most important winged altarpiece in Carinthia and an equally renowned, elaborately decorated sacramental shrine.

The discussions are endless as to which high-altitude mountain road is the most beautiful in the world. Definitely deserving of a place on the short list is the **Grossglockner Hochalpenstrasse** ⓲ (High Alpine Road), a curvaceous beauty that is inaccessible for long periods each year, and only open to traffic between May and October. This major project, planned by civil engineer Hofrat Franz Wallack, employed more than 3,000 workers between 1930 and 1935. The impressive result, known at the time as the Dream Road of the Alps, is 50 km (30 miles) long and 7.5 metres (25 ft) wide, with a maximum gradient of 12 percent.

On top of the world

The first spectacular view after you leave Heiligenblut is of the 3,105-metre (10,185-ft) Hoher Sonnblick, topped with the highest weather station in Austria. About 6 km (4 miles) further on, the route forks off to the left on to the glacier road leading to Franz-Josephs-Höhe. From the plateau, which at an altitude of 2,360 metres (7,740 ft) lies above the tree line, you can see across the Pasterze Glacier to the summit of the Grossglockner, Austria's highest mountain at 3,797 metres (12,455 ft).

The Pasterze, the biggest glacier in Austria, is currently about 8 km (5 miles) long and 200 metres (656 ft) deep. However, owing to global warming, it shrinks by about 5 metres (16 ft) in depth and 20 metres (66 ft) in length every year, and the funicular

In Heiligenblut join the local gold- and silver-panning society. This entitles you to search for the precious metals at three different places using the traditional hand-washing method. All equipment is provided and all finds may be kept. There is no doubt about your chances of striking it rich – the mountains behind the Fleisstal are called the Goldberge.

BELOW: a Gmund Gasthof.

Map
on pages
230–1

that once finished at the edge of the glacier is now more than 100 metres (330 ft) above it. If you are wearing suitable shoes, you can venture down to the slippery surface, but the climb back up is quite strenuous.

Another worthwhile excursion is the Gamsberg Nature Path, which can be tackled with ease and leads alongside the Pasterze to an idyllic waterfall. Notice-boards provide information about the glacier and its ecology.

The Upper Drau Valley

If instead of exploring the Mölltal, you continue west from the confluence of the Möll and Drau rivers (12 km/7 miles northwest of Spittal), the Drau Valley soon becomes very narrow, and is known here as the Sachsenburg Defile. Ruins of several castles and fortresses dating from the 13th century testify to the valley's strategic importance in those days.

Greifenburg ⓳, 20 km (12 miles) west, is known as the Heart of the Upper Drau Valley. As early as the 2nd century, this market town in the shadow of its castle was an important staging post on the Roman road to Gurina. Today, there is a newly constructed artificial lake for summer bathing, with a 400-metre (1,310-ft) beach.

The **Weissensee** ⓴ in the hills southeast of Greifenburg, has its own distinctive charm. The fact that the two ends of the lake are not connected by road makes it a quiet and peaceful holiday destination. The crystal-clear waters are a shimmering turquoise hue due to the white sandy shores – which also gave the lake its name. In the shallow sections near the bank one can see the stems of the water lilies right down to the lake bed – an unusual sight, also due to the white sand. Lying at an altitude of 930 metres (3,050 ft) above sea level, the Weis-

Even in summer there may be times when the Grossglockner Hochalpenstrasse is impassable. But visitors who make allowances for its unpredictable conditions – a course strongly recommended in the interests of safety – will be rewarded with a succession of truly unforgettable vistas.

BELOW: the High Alpine Road.

*The Hochtor, at
2,575 metres
(8,450 ft) above sea
level, is the boundary
between Carinthia
and Salzburg
Province. The
Grossglockner Road
continues through the
unique Hohe Tauern
National Park, the
largest continuous
stretch of unspoiled
countryside in
Austria (see page
224).*

RIGHT: a view of the
Grossglockner and
glacier from the
Alpine Road.

sensee is the highest Alpine lake in which bathing is still possible; the waters reach temperatures of 25°C (77°F) in summer.

The best amenities are available on the western approaches, on the Techendorf shore. Apart from fishing, sailing and water-skiing there are also archery and canoeing facilities. A local speciality is *schlurfen*, a sort of water-borne cross-country skiing on polystyrene boards. There is also golf in summer and curling in winter. The countryside here was used as a location in the James Bond film *Licence to Kill*.

Berg im Drautal, back in the Drau Valley and west of Greifenburg, appeals to even the most discriminating traveller, offering a good choice of hotels with indoor and outdoor swimming pools and a wide variety of restaurants. For walking enthusiasts there are the Gaisloch and Ochsenschluchtklamm, two unspoiled, romantic gorges nearby. Adventurous souls might enjoy a boat trip on the Drau in an inflatable raft.

A short distance further on, a minor road branches off to the right towards **Irschen**, an attractive resort village on the southern slopes of the Kreuzeck Range. The local Parish **Church of St Dionysius**, originally Romanesque in style, was rebuilt in the 15th century. It contains an exceptionally fine winged altarpiece and murals dating from the 14th century.

Oberdrauburg ㉑, a few kilometres west, is the last bastion of the Carinthian section of the Drau Valley before the border with East Tyrol. A market town lying at the foot of the Lienzer Dolomites, Oberdrauburg was first settled in the 13th century. Today it offers the traveller a number of historic sights as well as a full range of tourist amenities. The castle on the eastern side of the town dates from the 16th century. It was badly damaged during World War II and sub-

sequently rebuilt, losing much of its original character in the process. However, the Church of St Leonard, in the village of Zwickenberg, north of town, houses a 16th-century winged altarpiece and 15th-century murals, and has retained its aura of historic charm.

Into East Tyrol

West of Oberdrauburg, the main road follows the Drau Valley into East Tyrol (Osttirol). This remote region was once connected to Tyrol, its more famous namesake, but became separated when South Tyrol was ceded to Italy in 1919. Since then the province's connections with the rest of Austria have been improved by the construction of new transport links such as the Felbertauern Tunnel.

Nikolsdorf marks the beginning of the East Tyrolean section of the Drau Valley on the way to Lienz. There is a woodland swimming pool where you can splash and sunbathe in glorious, natural surroundings. Not far beyond, **Lavant** – a detour south off Road 100 – is recognisable from a distance by its pretty Pilgrimage Church of St Peter and St Paul. Since 1948, the foundations of settlements dating from various different eras have been discovered here. A kilometre or so further on lies **Aguntum**, an excavated Roman town and a diocesan city until 622. Many rare and interesting exhibits are on display here Thermal baths and public buildings have been unearthed.

Not far away is **Dölsach**, a resort village at 740 metres (2,430 ft) above sea level. Like the villages of Amlach and Tristach – situated on a pretty little lake just west of it – Dölsach lies in the Lienzer Dolomites resort area, the starting point in summer for delightful mountain walks and in winter for skiing trips, curling and cross-country skiing.

Map on pages 230–1

There is a hefty toll imposed for use of the Grossglockner Road. The frequent buses that make trips along the road include a small fraction of the toll in the cost of a ticket.

BELOW: mountain pastures near the Weissensee.

Lienz  **22** is the capital of East Tyrol. It was an Illyrian settlement as long ago as 500 BC. In fact, at several points in history the region surrounding Lienz acquired considerable importance. Between 1250 and 1500, the counts of Görz resided at **Schloss Bruck** (open June–Oct Tues–Sun; entrance charge; tel: 04852-62 58083) near Lienz. At this time the town was subject to planned development. Later, it passed to the counts of Wolkenstein and finally to the Convent of Halle. In 1798 the town centre was destroyed by a major fire; only on the right bank of the Isel did there remain traces of the old city defences.

The Puster Valley

Southwest of Lienz, beyond the Lienz Defile, is the **Puster Valley**. One way of getting a preview of this breathtaking countryside, is to climb the Sternalm – the first half of the ascent as far as Hochstein is accessible by twin chair lift – from which you will have a magnificent panoramic view. Shortly after Leisach the mountain road forks off to Bannberg; from here, a toll road leads almost as far as the Hochstein refuge. **Assling 23**, the largest village in the area, also lies on the "sun terrace" on the mountain road, further up the valley. It has a **Game Park** with rare native animals (open May–Oct daily; entrance charge). In winter, Assling can offer a ski area that includes a 1,300-metre (4,260-ft) lift.

Down in the valley again, on Road 100, is **Thal**. Here the Gothic parish church of **St Korbinian**, dedicated in 1486, contains a late-Gothic Crucifixion group dating from 1490, three altars of considerable artistic merit and two paintings by Pacher (*circa* 1500). On the sunny north slopes of the valley nestle four idyllic villages: Unterried, Wiesen, Anras and Asch. Accessible by means of a narrow road, they all lie at altitudes of 1,000 metres (3,280 ft) or more.

Lienz's war memorial chapel in the cemetery of the Parish Church of St Andrä was built by Clemens Holzmeister and contains the tomb of the painter Albin Egger-Lienz, as well as that of artist Franz Defregger – a native of East Tyrol.

BELOW: footsteps in the snow.

Traversing Strassen, with its late-Gothic church of St James, the road reaches Heinfels and Panzendorf. The name of **Schloss Heinfels**, the valley landmark and the property of the ancient Görz family, is derived from the Hunnenfels – Huns' Rock. During the Venetian Wars, Emperor Maximilian I surrounded it with a defensive wall to protect the arsenal.

Sillian ㉔ is a sports resort dominating the end of the Austrian section of the Puster Valley. Only a short distance beyond lies the Italian border, which already makes its presence felt here in the mild climate. Each season has its own particular charms: the magnificent colours of the blossom in spring, the luxuriant green of the mountain pastures in summer, the riot of rusts and golds in autumn and the picture-postcard whiteness of the snow in winter. The village itself, with a population of 2,000, presents a broad range of leisure amenities.

Matrei

About 30 km (18 miles) northwest of Lienz, in a spectacular setting against the background of the High Tauern mountains, is the little town of **Matrei** ㉕. Majestically dominating the scene from a high crag is the landmark **Schloss Weissenstein**, which dates from the 12th century but was modified in the 19th. Standing in solitary splendour is the 800-year-old **Church of St Nicholas**, which houses some remarkable Romanesque wall paintings. *The Healing* evokes memories of the frescoes in the cathedral of Gurk. In the tower are three stone sculptures dating from the first half of the 15th century. The impressive Parish Church originally dates from the 14th century, but acquired its present form between 1768 and 1784, when it was rebuilt by Wolfgang Hagenauer.

Every year in September the charming St Matthew's Market takes place in Matrei, but most visitors actually come for the mountains. Over 100 with peaks above 3,000 metres (9,840 ft) can be tackled from here. The Mountain Climbing Advisory Office on Rauterplatz offers guided tours of the entire region and provides information, touring tips and meteorological information. The mountaineering tradition is an important part of life here. On 11 August 1865 an expedition starting in Matrei conquered the **Grossvenediger** ㉖ (3,674 metres/12,055 ft) from its most attractive side – via the Innergschlöss-Alm. Nowadays the "Grossvenediger Adventure" is offered as part of a package in a number of variations by the Mountain Climbing Office.

Matrei has more to offer than just mountain walks: trekking to the isolated High Tauern miners' huts, mountain biking, paragliding, climbing and kite flying are just some of the attractions in this pretty village community. Alpine rafting on the River Isel is a classic adventure for lovers of water sports. Fly-fishing enthusiasts can also indulge in their hobby here. Information can be obtained at the Hotel Rauter on Rauterplatz.

Visitors who would like to try one of these activities, but have left their equipment at home, will be delighted to discover that the Mountain and Sports Gear Rental Service can supply most needs. Another pleasant surprise is the kindergarten for visitors' children situated in Schloss Goldried. ❑

One of Austria's best restaurants, the Kellerwand, is in the town of Kötschach-Mauthen, in the Gail Valley 14 km (9 miles) south of Oberdrauburg. It specialises in authentic local cuisine.

BELOW: waterfall in the Virgental, west of Matrei.

Map on pages 230–1

TYROL

The precipitous mountains and ski resorts of this famous western region draw millions of visitors each winter, but peace can still be found during the summer months

Maps:
City 246
Area 252

According to a popular song, **Innsbruck** , the capital of Tyrol (Tirol), is a "beautiful Alpine town". As long as one restricts one's observations to its breathtaking location surrounded by mountains and to the medieval Old Town itself, the description holds true. Now, as during the reigns of the Emperor Maximilian and Empress Maria Theresa, the encircling chain of unspoiled peaks ensures that nothing changes much: the town is contained by the Karwendel Range to the north, towering more than 2,000 metres (6,600 ft) above the town itself, and the twin landmarks in the south, the Patscherkofel and the Nockspitze.

It was no less a personage than Emperor Maximilian I who first recognised the many-faceted charms of this town nestled in the mountains. Although the residence of the Tyrolean branch of the Habsburgs was transferred from Merano (in what is now Italy) to the River Inn as early as 1420, Maximilian was the first monarch really to hold his court here, when he ascended the throne in 1493. He left his most lasting mark on the city in the magnificent Renaissance funerary monument he commissioned for himself in the Hofkirche. Maria Theresa also brought the splendour of court life to Innsbruck. She had the ancient royal residence (the Hofburg) extended and had the Triumphal Arch erected to mark the marriage of her son.

LEFT: forest and mountain in the Zugspitze range.
BELOW: the Goldenes Dachl.

Tyrolean idol

The year 1805 marked the beginning of a dark but heroic period of history, after the Habsburgs had been forced to cede Tyrol to Bavaria in the Treaty of Bratislava. The Tyroleans, under Andreas Hofer, rebelled and in 1809 made Innsbruck the seat of a civilian government following their victory in the Battle of Bergisel. Andreas Hofer ruled Tyrol "in the name of the Emperor". The resistance was broken in November 1809, and a year later, the Tyrolean popular hero was betrayed and shot in Mantua. Since then the Bergisel Mountain on the southern boundary of the town has symbolised the Tyrolean love of freedom.

Innsbruck's late-Gothic centre has been preserved largely intact. Pedestrians can easily explore the compact area between the River Inn and the beginning of Maria-Theresienstrasse. Herzog Friedrichstrasse, enclosed by arcades, fans out in front of the famous **Goldenes Dachl** (Golden Roof), providing an insight into the intimacy that must have characterised life at court. This magnificent balcony was built to provide a fitting stage for the ruling family to see and be seen. It was erected on the orders of Emperor Maximilian I and completed in 1500. The balustrade of

The Ottoburg.

BELOW: the
Domkirche.

the upper section, which juts out slightly, is decorated on the front and sides with carved reliefs. The two middle sections represent Maximilian with his two wives, Maria of Burgundy and Maria Bianca Sforza, and Maximilian with his chancellor and court jester. The remaining panels portray Morris dancers. The structure was the work of Nikolaus Türing the Elder, the Innsbruck court builder. It is to him that the balcony owes its gold-plated, copper tiled roof.

Diagonally opposite the Goldenes Dachl is the **Helblinghaus** Ⓑ, a late-Gothic building to which a rococo facade was added in the 18th century by Anton Gigl. The window frames, oriels and tympana are painted in pastel colours and lavishly decorated. A little further on, near the River Inn, stands the **Goldener Adler** Ⓒ (Golden Eagle) – the oldest inn in the town – dating from the 16th century. The German poet Goethe (1749–1832) stayed here twice. The **Ottoburg** Ⓓ, diagonally opposite, was originally built as a residential tower in 1495.

The **Domkirche St Jakob** Ⓔ (Cathedral of St James) is hidden away to the north of the Goldenes Dachl. It was completed in the baroque style in 1722 in accordance with plans drawn up by Johann Jakob Herkommer. The interior space is enclosed by a series of domes: three domed vaults spanning the nave and a dome with lantern above the chancel. The frescoes adorning the vaulting – dedicated to St James the Intercessor – are the work of Cosmas Damian Asam, whilst the stucco was decorated by his brother, Egid Quirin.

The **Hofburg** Ⓕ, extended during the reign of Maria Theresa, adjoins the cathedral on the north side (open daily; entrance charge; tel: 0512-587 186). Inside, the Riesensaal (Giant's Hall), over 30 metres (100 ft) long, is one of the main attractions. Its walls are clad with magnificent stucco panels with a marble finish. The grand ceiling was painted in 1776 by Franz Anton Maulbertsch.

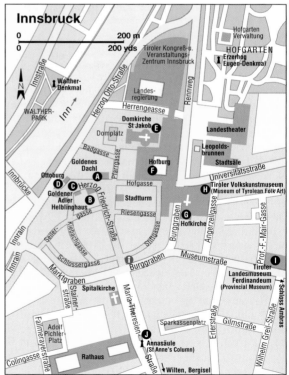

Austria's greatest Renaissance monument

Opposite the southeast corner of the Hofburg, the **Hofkirche** ⓖ (open daily; entrance charge; tel: 0512-584 302) was completed in 1563. It was built in the late-Gothic style with a Renaissance porch, and was designed to house the Tomb of Emperor Maximilian I, the Habsburg whose talents as a matchmaker ensured that there was a member of his family in every royal house in Europe at his death. In 1502, 17 years before he finally expired, the emperor commissioned his own mausoleum. It was to become the most outstanding work of art in Tyrol, and the most moving imperial monument in the Western world.

Gilg Sesselschreiber, a Munich artist, was asked to produce sketches for the tomb. He proposed a bronze edifice with 40 larger-than-life statues of the most important ancestors and kinsmen of the emperor. The ensemble was to be completed by two rows of statuettes and busts of patron saints of the Habsburgs and Roman emperors. Of the 40 statues originally planned, 28 were actually cast, between 1509 and 1550. The two most famous represent King Arthur and Theodoric and were cast in 1513 in Nuremberg by Peter Vischer. It was not until 1550 that the idea arose of erecting a cenotaph bearing the statue of Maximilian as the focal point of the monument. Its construction, in accordance with the design of Alexander Colin, was completed in 1583.

Beside the Hofkirche is the **Tiroler Volkskunstmuseum** ⓗ (Museum of Tyrolean Folk Art; open daily; entrance charge; tel: 0512-584 302), which contains an important collection of local costumes, tools and peasant furniture. Nearby, on Museumsstrasse, the newly refurbished **Tiroler Landesmuseum Ferdinandeum** ⓘ (Provincial Museum; open May–Sept daily; Oct–Apr Tues–Sun; entrance charge) records the development of painting and sculpture in Tyrol.

Maria-Theresienstrasse runs south from the Old Town. It is dominated by **St Anne's Column** ⓙ, erected in 1706 in memory of the retreat of the Bavarian troops from Tyrol during the War of the Spanish Succession. Surmounting the slender pedestal is a statue of the Virgin Mary. St Anne stands next to St George (the patron saint of Tyrol), and St Vigilius and St Cassianus (the patron saints of the dioceses of Trent and Bressanone), symbolise the political unity of Tyrol. The southern end of the street is marked by the Triumphal Arch.

If you continue south you soon reach Wilten, a district of Innsbruck and once the site of the Roman town of Veldidena. **Wilten Abbey** was founded in 1128 under the jurisdiction of the Premonstratensians. Until 1180 they controlled the entire area as far as the Inn. Only after this date did they permit settlers to leave the northern bank of the Inn and to make their homes in what is now the Old Town. The present Abbey Church is a baroque edifice dating from the 17th century, with an imposing façade completed in 1716.

Nearby **Wilten Parish Church** was completed in 1756 in accordance with the plans of the Tyrolean priest-architect Franz de Paula Penz. Its rococo interior was the work of Franz Xaver Feichtmayr, the stuccoist of the Wessobrunn school, and Matthäus Günther, the Augsburg painter. The high altar has a statue of the Virgin under a baldachin supported by

Map on page 246

The bobsleigh run at Igls, just south of Innsbruck, was used in the 1976 Olympics.

BELOW: Wilten Abbey Church.

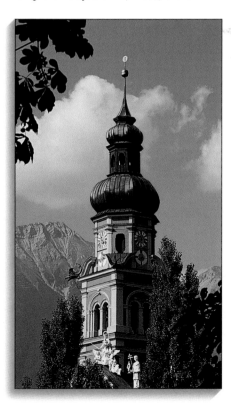

Hiking near Innsbruck

Set at the heart of some of Austria's most spectacular scenery, Innsbruck is home to the national hiking club, virtually all the major trail associations, an Alpine school and an astonishing range of useful, well-organised programmes for visitors.

Hotel guests in Innsbruck or the adjacent towns of Igls and Patsch are eligible for a free "Club Innsbruck Card". From early June until the end of September, this card gives access to mountain walks, shuttle buses into the mountains, a guidebook and equipment such as walking shoes and rucksacks.

The Austrian Alpine Club (Oesterreichischer Alpenverein; Wilhelm-Greil-Strasse 15, 6010 Innsbruck, tel: (0512) 587828) teams up with the local Innsbruck Alpine School to guide trips such as the Sunrise-Mountain Hut Trek, offered every Tuesday and Thursday, from July to September. On this guided tour through the Karwendel nature reserve, you climb the 2,250-metre (7,380-ft) Nordkette and the 2,215-metre (7,065-ft) Stempeljoch, visit a mining museum and sleep in a mountain hut.

Day hikes from Innsbruck start at 8.30 each morning. Alpine School guides take guests on moderate three-to-five-hour walks chosen from more than 40 routes in the Stubai, Tuxer, Karwendel and Mieminger ranges. Children are welcome – indeed the Monday Hiking Day programme is designed specifically for them. Parents and children are paired with guides for local nature walks, a picnic and a camp fire.

For an alternative family outing, the Zirbenweg trail is an easy walk through pine forests. Another easy option is to take the cable-car up to the 2,000-metre (6,600-ft) Patscherkofel station, which has great vistas of the Inn Valley. If you have time while you're here, check out the Alpine Garden Patscherkofel, Europe's highest botanic garden, with 400 kinds of tree, flower and other mountain plant life (open June–Sept: daily; free). It is a quite easy 7-km (4-mile) walk from the cable-car station.

The most romantic option is a Lantern Walk. These take place every Tuesday and Thursday night in the summer. Present your club card at a depot in Innsbruck or Igls, then ride a free bus to the trailhead, where, led by guides bearing lanterns, you ascend in a quiet, easy hike to a rustic lodge, where a hut party with food and drink awaits. You are ferried back to your hotel before midnight. The pick-up point in Innsbruck is just outside Congress Innsbruck at 7.45pm. The shuttle stops at about 8pm at the Igls Tourist Office.

Note that, while guided hiking programmes are free, if you put together your own itinerary, the cost of train journeys can add up. Consider buying a hiking pass for unlimited passage on the Patscherkofel and Nordkette mountain railways, and discounted lifts up the Axamer Lizum and the Glungezer.

If you're here in winter, there are free ski shuttles to downhill and cross-country resort areas, reductions on ski passes, day tickets and single-run prices, and cheap family tobogganing programmes. ❏

LEFT: a hiker looking towards the Sonnenspitze.

marble columns. "Our Lady of the Four Pillars" has been venerated as a source of miraculous powers since the Middle Ages.

Wilten is overlooked by the **Bergisel** hill, site of the famous battle. Today it features a ski jump originally erected for the 1964 Winter Olympics and completely renovated in 2002. The Imperial Light Infantry Memorial here commemorates the élite Tyrolean corps disbanded in 1919.

Perched on a mountainside southeast of the centre is **Schloss Ambras**, the favourite residence of Archduke Ferdinand and his lovely wife Philippine Welser (open Apr–Oct daily; Dec–Mar limited; entrance charge; tel: 0512-348 446). Ferdinand had the castle extended to its present size from 1564. Today visitors can admire a comprehensive arms collection, an exhibition of paintings and curios and the Spanish Hall, with its magnificent Renaissance coffered ceiling.

The Bergisel Panorama, situated near the Hungerberg funicular station north of the town centre, depicts the Battle of Bergisel as a moment of glory for the freedom fighters of the province.

Leaving the capital

The prosperity of the salt-water spa of **Hall in Tirol ❷**, northeast of Innsbruck, comes from its salt deposits. The latter are guarded by **Hasegg Castle**, in which Archduke Ferdinand II set up the first mechanical mint in 1567. For this reason the fortress's distinctive tower is known to this day as the Mint Tower. The parish church of **St Nicholas** was completed in 1437 and remodelled in the baroque style in 1752. The nearby village of **Wattens** is home to the popular **Swarovski Kristallwelt** (Crystal World), a series of sound-and-light installations and a showcase for the nearby Swarovski cut-glass factory (open daily; entrance charge; tel: 01-525 24745).

A further 18 km (11 miles) to the northeast, alongside the Inn River, is the town of **Schwaz**. At the beginning of the 16th century there were 20,000 miners working underground here. The town's parish church dates from this period. It was begun in 1460 and completed after 1492 by Erasmus Grasser, the Munich architect. The largest Gothic hall church in Tyrol, it has a roof covered in 15,000 hammered copper tiles and is known as the Mountain Blessing.

Around 7 km (4 miles) to the northeast is **Schloss Tratzberg** (open Apr–Oct daily; entrance charge). It was built in 1296 as a stronghold on what was then the Bavarian frontier. The extensive complex consists of four main wings and received its present form during the 16th and 17th centuries at the instigation of the Fugger banking family. Beyond Tratzberg the fortresses of Matzen and Lichtwer recall the era of medieval chivalry. Unfortunately they are closed to the public.

Family fortune

Rattenberg ❸, another 11 km (7 miles) to the northeast, owes its prosperity to the mining rights that Maximilian awarded to the Fugger family. From here they controlled all silver mining operations in the entire province. The town itself has managed to retain its medieval splendour. The late-Gothic Parish Church

Maps:
City 246
Area 252

Fresco on the outside of the parish church in Eben, north of Tratzberg.

BELOW: Schloss Ambras.

of St Virgil, which has a magnificent baroque interior, testifies to the great wealth Rattenberg once enjoyed.

Kramsach lies on the opposite bank of the Inn, a village surrounded by a trio of lakes that are all ideal for bathing: the Buchsee, the Krummsee and the Reintaler See. The nearby Brandenberg Valley is delightful walking country, and includes the Kaiserklamm Gorge and the Archduke Johann Hermitage. A chair lift from Kramsach provides access to the Rofan Mountains.

Further to the northeast lies the little hamlet of **Kundl**, which had a church as long ago as 788. Nonetheless, the most interesting religious building here is not really the Parish Church of the Assumption itself but rather the pilgrimage **Church of St Leonhard in the Meadows**, lying just outside the village proper. Reputedly founded by Heinrich I in 1012, it was dedicated in 1020 by Pope Benedict VIII. The present building dates from 1512. Walkers will enjoy the wild and romantic footpath through the Kundlerklamm, which affords direct access to the Wildschönau Mountains.

Carry on in the direction of Kufstein and you will come across the busy little town of **Wörgl ④**, the centre of the Tyrolean Lowlands. The baroque parish church houses the Virgin of Wörgl, dating from about 1500. Perched up on a terrace above the village stands the medieval castle and chapel of **Mariastein**. The Chapel of Miracles containing a venerated image of the Virgin is tucked away on the upper floor.

Kufstein ⑤ lies just on the Austrian side of the border with Bavaria, 16 km (10 miles) northeast of Wörgl. The town itself changed hands between Tyrol and Bavaria on many occasions. Maximilian was the first to fortify the stronghold, first mentioned in 1205, to any great extent. At his behest the Kaiserturm

The keep of the castle of Mariastein, with its pentagonal ground plan, was built in around 1350 to defend the Inn Valley route, which in those days ran past its door.

BELOW: a peaceful Tyrol velley.

(Emperor's Tower) in **Kufstein Fortress** acquired walls which were up to 7.5 metres (25 ft) thick. Today the fortress houses a museum of local history and the Heroes' Organ, the largest in the world, built in 1931 in memory of the Tyrolean freedom fighters (open daily; entrance charge).

Map on page 252

Sporting Kitzbühel

The reputation of **Kitzbühel** ❻ (40 km/25 miles southeast of Kufstein) as a chic winter sports centre dates at least from the triple Olympic victory of local boy Toni Sailer – the "Kitz Comet" – in the 1956 Winter Games in Cortina. Apart from that, the famous Hahnenkamm Races ensure that the Kitzbühel skiing area attracts top enthusiasts from all over the world. It has more than 50 slopes and countless first-rate descents.

The mountains surrounding Kitzbühel have contributed most to the town's sporting reputation, especially the Kitzbüheler Horn to the east and the Hahnenkamm to the west. In summer, the relatively tame Kitzbühel Alps afford a range of mountain walks. For those who prefer it steeper, rockier and more challenging, there are the vast limestone peaks of the Wilder Kaiser to the north. The charms of the broad Kitzbühel Basin can best be experienced when the wall of mountains are lit by the setting sun and reflected in the dark waters of the moorland Schwarzer See, just north of town.

divers in the clear waters of a Tyrol lake.

The Parish Church, dating from 1435, is a relic of Kitzbühel's earlier period of prosperity. The triple-naved Gothic structure with its slender tower and over-hanging single roof blends in harmoniously with its Alpine setting. The nearby **Church of Our Lady** has an unusual two-storey design. The lower church is mentioned in records as early as 1373. The upper storey was adorned in the baroque manner in 1735. Its most attractive feature is the series of frescoes by Simon Benedikt Faisten-berger, thought to be his finest work. The painting adorning the high altar is a copy of *Our Lady of Suc-cour*, the Lukas Cranach (1472–1553) masterpiece in Innsbruck Cathedral. The rose grille in front of the high altar was created in 1781.

BELOW: pastures in the Kitzbüheler.

Barely 8 km (5 miles) south of Kitzbühel, the parish church of **Jochberg** also contains frescoes by Fais-tenberger. The apostles St Peter and St Paul, and St Wolfgang are portrayed as vividly as in a Rubens painting. Works by the same artist can also be seen in the **Parish Church of the Assumption** in **St Johann in Tirol** ❼, a scattered village lying in the valley between the Kitzbüheler Horn and the sheer face of the Wilder Kaiser, 10 km (6 miles) north of Kitzbühel. The church's most notable feature is the protruding west front, completed in 1728 and flanked by twin towers capped by baroque cupolas.

St Johann is first and foremost the central starting point for walking and mountaineering in the Wilder Kaiser. Those seeking a grandstand view of the region can take the route from Griesenau into the Kaiserbach Valley, and from there up to the Griesener Alm. From here one has only to climb a further 580 metres (1,905 ft) to the legendary Stripsenjoch. Those who prefer more romantic scenery can travel west to the pic-turesque Hintersteiner See.

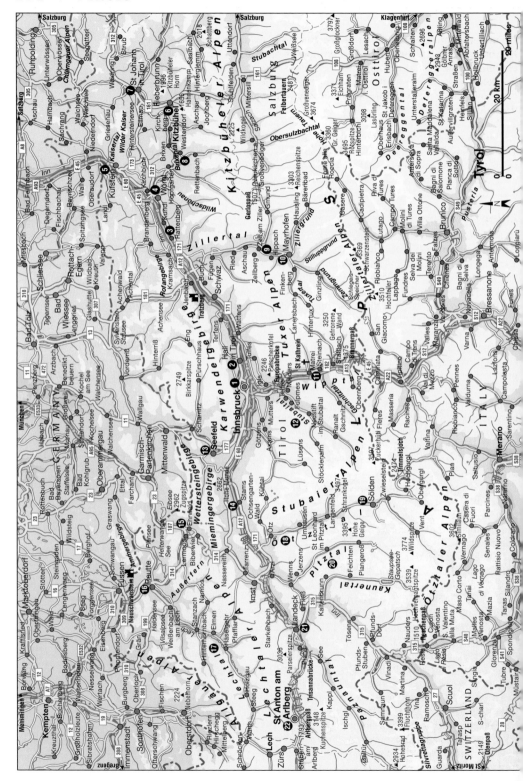

There is more art and culture in the **Brixental** (Brixen Valley), west of Kitzbühel. In **Kirchberg**, the first village in the valley, the baroque parish church houses some fine ceiling frescoes by Faistenberger. That **Brixen im Thale**, 5 km (3 miles) west, was once a prosperous place is apparent from the twin-towered Parish Church of the Assumption, which has a nave roofed by three domes. It was constructed by the master-builder Andrä Hueber between 1789 and 1795.

The third important church in the Brixen Valley is in **Hopfgarten**. Begun in 1758 by Kassian Singer, it was completed by Andrä Hueber. Once more we see a twin-towered facade with an extravagantly curved gable. The ceiling frescoes here are the work of Johann Weiss. It is known locally as the "Peasant's Cathedral".

Ziller Valley contrasts

Heading back west towards Innsbruck, the first important valley south of the Inn is that of the Ziller. There is no other region that has become so associated with Tyrol as the **Ziller Valley**, and this despite the fact that the area has only been part of Tyrol since 1816. Previously it had belonged to the Duchy of Salzburg. At the end of the 17th century Archbishop Johann Ernst of Salzburg erected a hunting lodge in Floitengrund. Today the valley is one of the best-known in the entire Alps. But while Mayrhofen, at the head of the valley, offers more hotel beds than Salzburg, the valley still contains many remote nooks which remain unspoilt. The glaciers, precipitous mountain faces and razor-edge ridges, combined with the height of the mountains have ensured that the beauty of this pristine landscape has remained intact.

The valley extends some 30 km (18 miles) in a north–south direction, from Strass on the Inn River to Mayrhofen. Over this distance, however, it only rises some 100 metres (330 ft). This gentle incline made it possible to open up the valley by means of a narrow-gauge railway, still sometimes served by a steam train.

Near **Strass**, you will be able to view the remains of early 14th-century frescoes in the late-Gothic parish church of Fügen, and the Pilgrimage Church of St Pancratius, built above the village at the end of the 15th century; its altars date from the 17th century.

Further up the valley, the Zillertal Mountain Road branches off to the west and weaves its way at a height of 1,700–2,000 metres (5,600–6,600 ft) along the side of the valley, offering the best panoramic views of the main ridge of the Zillertal Alps and its remarkable glaciers. Access points are from Ried, Aschau, Zellberg and Hippach, so that visitors can plan their ascent and descent via different routes if they so wish. The highest point on the road (2,050 metres/6,725 ft) lies just below the summit of the Arbiskopf (2,130 metres/7,000 ft). From here you will experience the best view of the main Alpine ridge.

Zell am Ziller ❾, the principal village in the valley, lies at the junction with the road to Gerlos Pass. Its name is derived from the monk's cell which was reputedly founded here in the 8th century by St

Ensuring that mountaineering addicts are not left in the lurch in the Brixen Valley is the Hohe Salve, accessible by cable-car and providing the best views of the Wilder Kaiser.

BELOW: the Zillertal.

Rupert. The present parish church was finished in 1782 by the Kitzbühel master-builder Andrä Hueber. The main construction is rococo, although the pointed tower was retained from the original Gothic building.

Mayrhofen , further up the valley, stands at the head of the four Gründe, as the highest mountain valleys are known. The Zillergrund stretches from Mayrhofen for 15 km (10 miles) in a southeasterly direction as far as the Bärenbad Hut (1,450 metres/4,760 ft). The Stilluppgrund is the most deeply eroded and sparsely inhabited of the four mountain valleys.

The Tuxer Grund is the most accessible of the four valleys. It has the most inhabitants and is popular among skiers as the Hintertux Glacier affords fine opportunities until well into the summer. The last valley, the Zemmgrund, leads into the heart of the Zillertal Alps. The construction of the Schlegeis reservoir means that there is now a good road leading up to the Dominikus Refuge in the Zamser Valley. The latter branches off from the Zemmgrund near the Breitlahner Hut, thus enabling the traveller to drive right up to the reservoir, which lies at 1,780 metres (5,850 ft).

Whilst the Ziller, Stillupp and Zemm high-altitude valleys have remained virtually untouched, the Tuxer Grund has become a lively tourist centre. Tux, Lanersbach and Hintertux have developed rapidly since the construction of the Hintertux Glacier Railway. The cable-car opens up good skiing opportunities until well into the summer, and after that it provides access to an extensive high-altitude region for mountain tours, including the Hoher Riffler (3,230 metres/10,600 ft), the Olperer (3,475 metres/11,400 ft) and the Hoher Wand (3,060 metres/10,035 ft). Those who prefer rather warmer temperatures than these heights afford will enjoy the radioactive thermal spring.

On the first weekend of May, Zell am Ziller marks the beginning of summer with the 400-year-old Gauderfest. Folk rituals, processions and contests are accompanied by the consumption of huge amounts of lethal Gauder beer.

BELOW: the soaring Zillertal Alps seen from the Zillertal Mountain Road.

From the Wipp Valley to the Stubai

Map on page 252

South of Innsbruck, between the Tux Alps in the east and the Stubai Alps in the west, the Wipptal leads to the **Brenner Pass** (1,375 metres/4,510 ft), the lowest-lying cleft in the entire Alpine Ridge and as such the easiest and also the oldest Alpine pass. The Illyrians used a mule track here, and the Romans had a chariot road. In the Middle Ages the pass was used by emperors and kings on pleasure journeys or with their armies.

A brilliant example of modern technology is the **Europa Bridge**, which crosses the valley of the Sill near Schönberg. With a span of 800 metres (2,625 ft) it stands at over 190 metres (625 ft) high, making it the second tallest motorway bridge in Europe.

The first village in the Wipp Valley, **Matrei ⑪**, is also the oldest. Oriel-windowed houses with overhanging roofs, Gothic entrances and ground-floor vaulted ceilings characterise the appearance of this typical linear village. The parish church, which dates from the 12th century, was refurbished in the 18th century with brightly coloured baroque frescoes.

The spectacular Europa Bridge was built between 1959 and 1963.

The Navis Valley branching off to the left beyond Matrei, contains the **Chapel of St Kathrin**, built on the remains of Aufenstein Castle. The chapel houses the two oldest known wooden statues in Tyrol, dating from the early 14th century.

Following a major fire in Steinach in 1853, only the chancel remained of the old parish church but it was integrated into the new construction. Its most impressive feature is the fine altar by the South Tyrol artist Johann Perger.

The Gschnitz Valley leads off westwards from Steinach. North of Trins, the first village in the valley, a road climbs towards the Blaser (2,245 metres/7,360 ft), the Tyrolean mountain with the richest carpet of flowers in spring.

BELOW: in the Stubaitaler Alps.

About 10 km (6 miles) south of Innsbruck is the beginning of the **Stubaital ⑫** (Stubai Valley), the largest subsidiary valley leading off the Wipp. It leads eventually to the massive Stubai Glacier, a year-round skiing area with a wide range of pistes. By taking the Stubai Glacier Railway summer visitors can venture onto the icy surface.

In the valley, Mieders, Telfes, Fulpmes and Neustift are not merely lively tourist villages. They all have parish churches built during the 18th century by Franz de Paula Penze, the parish priest of Telfes. The loveliest of his churches is in Neustift. Fulpmes was in former times the home of the most famous iron workers in Tyrol. Their hammers were driven by hydraulic power derived from the Plövenbach stream. Even today, a few riverside workshops continue to ply their trade. Ice axes and crampons from Fulpmes are famous the world over.

Heading back towards Innsbruck, the northern exit of the Wipptal is marked on the eastern side by the Patscherkofel and to the west by the Nockspitze. At their feet extends a broad upland plateau with sleepy villages like Mutters and lively ones like Axams. Between the two, in Götzens, stands what rates as perhaps the loveliest baroque parish church in Tyrol. It was completed in 1780 by Franz Singer. Colourful late-rococo frescoes by Matthäus Günther enhance the master-builder's fine stucco.

The Karwendel

North of Innsbruck are the gigantic cirques and grey limestone walls of the Karwendel Range, which runs from Achensee in the east to the Seefeld Ridge in the west. To the north, the foothills peter out into the Bavarian uplands. To the south, the 2,000-metre (6,600-ft) peaks plunge steeply into the Inn Valley.

The highest mountain in the range is the Birkkarspitze (2,749 metres/9,019 ft). The most convenient cable-car access is via the Northern Cable-Car from Innsbruck, which climbs to the peak of the Hafelekar (2,330 metres/7,645 ft). The Karwendel covers an area of 900 sq. km (350 sq. miles) all told, two-thirds of which lie within the boundaries of Tyrol.

The mountainous region is subdivided by four long mountain ranges running from west to east. Correspondingly long are the valleys in between, some deeply eroded and all inaccessible to traffic. For this reason the Karwendel has remained as it always was: a remote and lonely mountain region with precipitous limestone cliffs, silent high-altitude cirques and numerous pine-fringed Alpine meadows. The threat to the ecology of the area has been averted by the establishment of a national park covering the entire area.

Forest life and death

Many of the trees in the Alps look perfectly healthy, and herds of chamois give the impression that there are no real dangers. Appearances are deceptive, however. Even here, every other tree suffers from a fatal disease, the pine trees no longer give off their characteristic scent and the crystal-clear streams are not infrequently as acid as dilute car battery fluid. And yet, the Karwendel remains an apparently unspoilt mountain wilderness offering walkers, mountaineers and

The Stubaier Höhenweg is a highly recommended eight-day hiking tour that circles the Stubai Valley and offers unparalleled views. Some sections are fairly challenging, but each night is spent in a well-equipped alpine hut. Enquire in Innsbruck for details.

BELOW: winter in the Wetterstein Mountains.

Map on page 252

climbers a high-altitude experience which is second to none.

Despite the almost 3,000 metres (9,840 ft) attained by the Zugspitze, its highest peak, the Wetterstein Range, to the west, has less to offer the visitor. It consists of a single vast mountain ridge, of which only the south side lies in Tyrol. This is actually no real disadvantage, for the Mieminger Mountains, with the prominent Hohe Munde (2,662 metres/8,733 ft), rise up parallel to the Wetterstein Range to the south. This, in conjunction with the western slopes of the Karwendel, creates a high-altitude triangle in which the austerity of the mountain scenery is interspersed by rolling hills, idyllic lakes and vast tracts of unspoilt natural beauty.

Seefeld

The centre of this plateau is marked by **Seefeld ⑬**, famous as a winter sports resort and the Tyrolean centre for Nordic skiing. During the summer months, mountain walkers will find extensive touring routes of all grades here.

Zugspitze is the highest peak in the Wetterstein.

Back in the Inn Valley southwest of Seefeld is the Cistercian abbey at **Stams ⑭** (open May–Sept Mon–Sat; entrance charge; tel: 05263-6242). Together with Göttweig and Melk, it is one of the finest monastery complexes in Austria. Founded in 1268 to mark the death of Konradin, the last of the Hohenstaufen, the monastery became so important within the next century that in 1362 Charles VI had the Imperial jewels deposited here for safe-keeping. The abbey church, 80 metres (265 ft) long, was rebuilt in 1699 and has recently been superbly restored, displaying a breathtaking array of stucco, ornamentation, colourful frescoes and finely worked choir stalls. The high altar features a limewood Tree of Life, carved with the figures of Christ, the Virgin, Adam and Eve, and 84 saints.

BELOW: a fresco at Stams Abbey.

Travel about 35 km (22 miles) northwest and a unique high-altitude basin opens up at a height of 1,000 metres (3,280 ft), on the periphery of which lies a succession of resorts: Biberwier, Lermoos and **Ehrwald ⑮**. All three are excellent starting points for extended mountain tours. Here, a completely flat meadow unfolds like a single bright-green clover leaf between the rock walls of the Mieminger Range, the Zugspitze, the Daniel and the Grubigstein. Dark forested slopes rise up continuously on all sides, surmounted by 1,000-metre (3,300-ft) high limestone cliff faces: the western escarpments of the Schneefernerkopf and the Zugspitze Massif. From Ehrwald it is possible to reach the Tyrol side of the Zugspitze by cable-car.

Head northwest again and you enter a region known as the Ausserfern. The focal point here is the village of **Reutte ⑯**, set beside the Lech River. The village grew up as a typical ribbon development along the valley road. Even today, it is dominated by the squat, low-lying houses with overhanging gables. Particularly noteworthy are the elaborately painted outside walls, dating from the 18th century, the work of the Zeillers, a family of local artists. The highly decorative and figurative murals on the Zeiller family house were painted by Franz Anton Zeiller. Johann Jakob Zeiller executed the vast ceiling fresco in the Parish Church of St Nicholas in Elbingenalp, further up the Lech Valley.

The Lech Valley

The main "landgrabber" in the Tyrolean stretch of the **Lechtal** (Lech Valley) is the untamed Lech itself. The torrent acquired this nickname from the inhabitants, for stretches of the valley have frequently been flooded by detritus which centuries of carefully tended meadowland have only been able to cover after a fashion.

An idyllic lake in the Lechtaler Alps.

At first glance, this region, the Ausserfern, may not look interesting, but in geological terms it is fascinating. To the northwest the valley is hemmed in by the Allgäu Alps; to the south lie the Lechtal Alps. Whilst only the southern and southeastern slopes of the Allgäu mountains belong to Tyrol – and the northern section disperses into Bavaria – the Lechtal Range forms the longest independent mountain ridge in the northern limestone Alps. The summits form a single ridge of countless 2,000-metre (6,560-ft) peaks, except for one single 3,000-metre (9,800-ft) mountain – the Parseier Spitze, at 3,036 metres (9,955 ft).

The best view of this unique mountain ridge can be gained from the summit of the Valluga (2,810 metres/9,220 ft), accessible by cable car from St Anton *(see page 261)*. From this vantage point one can begin to comprehend the forces which once pushed the layers of rock across each other and into a vertical position, and how the subsequent weathering gouged out cracks and clefts, thus forming the jagged mountain peaks. This is ideal countryside for a high-level walk across the peaks and ridges since the latter are uninterrupted by deep valley clefts, and the shelters lie at convenient distances from each other.

Meadows and lakes

BELOW: a Schloss in the Lechtal.

The position on the north side of the Lech Valley is quite different. Here the terrain is dominated by flysch, which consists of alternating layers of clay, slate, marl and limestone, which, lightly weathered, acquires a less jagged profile. Verdant meadows, dense forests, marshy water meadows and highland moors are the external characteristics of this "soft", easily weathered stone.

Limestone also contributes to the appearance of the mountain world of the Allgäu. The variety of rocks explains the wealth of flora, for different plants flourish on different geological foundations. Only in the Allgäu, where the mountains are clothed up to their summits in a thick carpet of grass and the alpine meadow flora blooms in such a riot of colours, can such myriad species be found.

The most attractive part of the Tyrolean section of the Allgäu Alps lies behind the Gaicht Pass (1,095 metres/3,590 ft), accessible via Weissenbach am Lech, which is about 6 km (4 miles) southwest of Reutte. On the other side of the pass is a valley where turquoise lakes contrast with green pastures and ochre-coloured dolomite rock. Two lakes, the Haldensee and the Vilsalpsee, are as yet virtually unknown but offer an ideal starting point for an expedition into the Tannheim Mountains or along the Allgäu Jubilee Path.

The Ötztal Alps

Retracing your route back to the River Inn, head for the **Ötztal** (Ötz Valley), the Inn's longest and most imposing side valley. Obergurgl, at the far end, is at least 50 km (30 miles) from the valley mouth. The difference in altitude, 1,235 metres (4,050 ft), corresponds to that of quite a considerable mountain ascent. The valley opens up like a staircase in distinct steps which mark the stages of the retreating glaciers. Steep narrow sections with a deeply cut river bed alternate with broad, almost level fertile valley areas, on which villages and agricultural lands are located.

The village of **Ötz** is dominated by the silhouette of the parish church, which overshadows historic houses with painted façades. The most attractive of the latter is the Gasthof Stern, whose frescoes date from 1573. High above the village is the popular bathing spot of Piburger See.

The most important spa in the Ötztal – thanks to its sulphur springs – is **Langenfeld**. Here, too, is the highest church tower in the valley (75 metres/ 245 ft). The late-Gothic parish church was completed in 1518.

Sölden ⑲, which lies at an altitude of 1,380 metres (4,525 ft) about 30 km (18 miles) south of Ötz, is primarily a winter sports resort. Skiers come in hordes to **Hochsölden**, which lies 700 metres (2,300 ft) higher still, and to the glacier road to the Rettenbachferner, where skiing is possible well into the summer.

In the upper reaches of the valley, at Zwieselstein, the Ötztal divides into two: the Gurgltal and the Ventertal. Here lie the two highest villages in the eastern Alps: Obergurgl (1,920 metres/6,300 ft) and Vent (1,895 metres/6,215 ft). **Vent** is popular with mountaineers. From here they can easily reach many of the surrounding 3,000-metre (9,840-ft) peaks. Both valleys continue upwards until they reach the glaciers of the main Alpine ridge. It was here, by the Italian border, that the famous "Ötzi", a Celt who died in this icy region 5,500 years ago, was discovered in 1991.

Map on page 252

On the other side of the valley from Langenfeld stands a votive chapel erected in 1661 to commemorate local plague victims.

BELOW: the Ötztal, with the village of Ötz in the foreground.

Obergurgl and nearby **Hochgurgl** are both ski resorts. From here cable-cars fan out in all directions towards the surrounding peaks. The toll road to the Timmelsjoch, the 2,474-metre (8,115-ft) pass connecting the valley with Italy, begins in Hochgurgl. The best view can be had from Windegg, at 2,080 metres (6,822 ft), which affords a panorama extending over the entire Gurgl Valley and part of the Gurgler Ferner. To the north one can see extensive sections of the Ötz Valley.

Since the Ötz Valley merely marks the eastern boundary of the Ötztal Alps, the **Pitztal** ⑳ (Pitz Valley) – which branches off from the upper Inn Valley some 8 km (5 miles) to the west – provides the first route into the heart of the mountains themselves. The Pitzal Valley is a perfect hiking region. For long stretches it is a forbiddingly narrow gorge, only occasionally opening out into a sunny basin. The villages of Wenns, Jerzens and St Leonhard owe their new prosperity to skiing enthusiasts and the Glacier Road, constructed to provide access to the Mittelbergferner.

The Kauner Valley in the west runs in a north–south direction through the Ötztal Alps. It branches off from the Inn Valley in an easterly direction south of Landeck near Prutz, soon turns towards the south and offers at its far end – near the Gepatsch reservoir – another glacier with skiing facilities beneath the slopes of the Hochvernagtspitze (3,539 metres/11,610 ft).

In the valley, the parish church in **Kaltenbrunn** was a place of pilgrimage as long ago as 1285, where initially it was the location of a chapel. The Gothic chancel was completed in 1502, and the nave contains a domed Chapel of Miracles with a carved votive statue of the Madonna with Child (1400).

The principal sight in the Pitz Valley is the Platzhaus in Wenns, which is adorned with fine Renaissance murals.

BELOW: Ötz church.

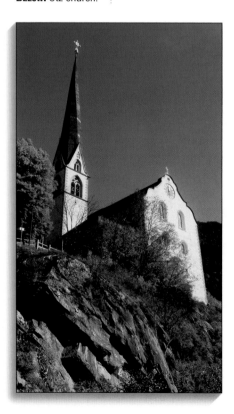

From Landeck to the Arlberg

Even in pre-Roman times there was a settlement at present-day **Landeck** ㉑, at the confluence of the rivers Sanna and Inn. During the 13th century, Duke Meinhard II of Tyrol had the existing fortress rebuilt in its present form. The fortress chapel, which dates from the same period, was adorned with frescoes during the first half of the 16th century. Today the castle houses a **museum** (open June–Oct Tues–Sun; entrance charge). The most important architectural monument in the town is the parish church, in the Angedair district. The elaborate tracery of its windows and the network vaulting make this the most harmonious Gothic church in Tyrol. Inside there is the late-Gothic Schrofenstein Altarpiece.

Beyond Pians, a few kilometres west, the valley forks again; to the left opens up the Paznaun Valley with the Trisanna River, whilst the Rosanna Valley leads straight ahead, climbing towards the Arlberg. At the river confluence, the railway crosses the valley at a height of 85 metres (280 ft) by means of the famous Trisanna Bridge. In former times the Paznaun Valley was virtually cut off from the rest of the world. Nowadays, thanks to the tourism within the region, it has been opened up with the construction of the Silvretta Alpine Road (with a pass at an altitude of 2,035 metres/6,675 ft), and the development of skiing around Ischgl.

The Arlberg

Skiers have also brought world fame to the **Arlberg**, which was once just a mountain with pine-covered slopes, Today it is a gigantic winter sports paradise, including **St Anton am Arlberg** ㉒ (30 km/18 miles west of Landeck), Zürs (15 km/9 miles further west) and Lech (5 km/3 miles beyond Zürs).

A hundred years ago the rural, farming existence – which for centuries had functioned satisfactorily on the Arlberg – was on the verge of extinction. Only technology and the development of skiing as a sport brought about the region's renaissance. First came the construction of the railway through the Arlberg, followed by the building of the Flexen Road (which reached Lech in 1900). But it was really the invention of skiing which led to the boom. A priest named Müller, from the Lech Valley, was the first to try out the new sport. Progress in the footsteps of the daring priest was rapid. The Arlberg Ski Club in St Christoph was founded in 1901, and Hannes Schneider from Stuben started to adapt techniques from Scandinavia to suit Alpine conditions. Stefan Kruckenhauser developed the parallel turn – now practised all over the world – and the wedel (a short, rapid turn), which makes skiing seem like child's play.

The skier's delight was until recently the bane of the driver. In winter the Arlberg Pass, which lies at 1,795 metres (5,885 ft), was frequently closed due to snowdrifts or the danger of avalanches. Only since the end of 1978 has the road tunnel, almost 14 km (9 miles) long, provided a year-round link.

So now motor travellers, too, can enjoy, in peace, the broad Alpine meadows as well as the tunnels and avalanche galleries on the Flexen Road. They can also enjoy breathtaking views down into the Klostertal and towards the pretty village of Stuben am Arlberg *(see page 301).* ❑

Map on page 252

Skiing, which arrived at the beginning of the 20th century, was the economic saviour of the population of the Arlberg

BELOW: mountaineering in the Ötztaler Alps.

Rotes
Haus

VORARLBERG

Reaching from the shores of the Bodensee to the Silvretta peaks, this small province – Austria's western outpost – is home to many religious buildings and wonderful mountain scenery

Map on page 264

For the Irish missionary Columban, who came to **Bregenz ❶** on the Bodensee (Lake Constance) in AD 610 to convert the region to Christianity, the town of Brigantium lay "as in a golden dish". What he described so vividly in words is the same impression gained by a modern-day traveller approaching Bregenz in one of the ships of the Lake Constance Line, or surveying the town, lake, Rhine Valley and Swiss Alps from the summit of the Pfänder.

The capital of Vorarlberg lies on a gently rising terrace on the shores of a wide bay on the Bodensee. To the east the shell-shaped intrusion is sheltered by the slopes of the Pfänder. To the southwest lies the Rhine, which once provided the necessary protection against enemy attack from the plains beyond. It was precisely this protected position which encouraged the Celts to settle on the site. Their village, Brigantioi, later became Brigantium under Roman occupation, complete with forum, basilica, baths and temple. The Romans were the first to build a fortified harbour. Following attacks by the Alemanni in the 3rd century the Romans withdrew up the hillside to the strategically more easily defensible site of what is now the Upper Town; here they built themselves a new fort.

After the retreat of the Romans in the middle of the 5th century, the Alemanni captured the town and with it the main and subsidiary valleys of the Rhine. The new conquerors did not, however, establish their rule from the town itself but chose Feldkirch, to the south, where – as the counts of Montfort – they built a fortress, the Schattenburg. In 1860 Bregenz became the nominal capital of Vorarlberg, by virtue of the creation of the first local parliament for the region, which at that time was still a part of Tyrol. Only in 1918, however, did Bregenz become the official capital of the province.

LEFT: the Rotes Haus in Dornbirn. **BELOW:** strolling in a Bregenz park.

The Lower Town

Bregenz's greatest claim to fame – and one for which the town is now known all over the world – is the annual Bregenz Festival, held on a specially constructed floating stage *(see page 267)*. A different opera is performed every second year.

Nearby, the Lower Town huddles on a mound of land deposited by the lake. Apart from the railway station, it is characterised by a series of neoclassical local government buildings, the regional military headquarters and the **Museum of Vorarlberg** (Kornmarkt 1; open Tues–Sun; entrance charge). In the Middle Ages the lake waters actually reached as far as the foundation walls of the **Seekapelle** (Lake Chapel), at the junction of Rathausstrasse and Anton-Schneider-Strasse. In 1445 the first memorial to the fallen soldiers of the Appenzell Civil War was erected here.

The present church was built in 1698 according to the plans drawn up by Christian Thumb. Externally its most remarkable feature is an octagonal tower with an onion dome; inside, its high altar is an unusual example of late-Renaissance craftsmanship. The work, completed in 1615, has a central shrine decorated with a Crucifixion group; on the upper section you can see the figures of St John the Baptist and St John the Evangelist. A granary was built on to the north side of the chapel in 1686 by Hans Kuen. The chapel was then converted into the Town Hall, completed in 1810. Only in 1898 did the broad front acquire its present-day neo-Renaissance façade.

The most impressive building in the Lower Town is the **Herz-Jesu-Kirche** (Sacred Heart Church). It stands near the Pfänder cable-car station and is characterised by twin pointed spires. The largest neo-Gothic building in Vorarlberg, it was built under the supervision of Stuttgart architect Joseph Cades, and was completed in 1908. The harmonious design of the west front reveals the inspiration of the medieval brick churches of north Germany. Within, too, the architect has followed these examples, constructing a basilica with ribbed vaulting in accordance with the strict rules laid down by the church designers of the past.

Boat tours of the Bodensee are popular with visitors to Bregenz. Highlights along the German shore are the cathedral at Überlingen and the flower island of Mainau. On the Swiss side, St Gallen is away from the lake but worth the trip for its fine cathedral and library.

The Upper Town

If you stroll along Maurachgasse towards the Upper Town, you will pass the site of the former Roman port. Passing through the Unteres Tor gateway, you will enter the medieval town centre. Haug von Tübingen, later known as Hugo of Montfort, had this area laid out in a regular pattern on the ruins of the Roman fortress. Sections of the town wall which formed part of medieval Bregenz have survived to this day.

The most notable building in the Upper Town – **Martinsturm** (St Martin's Tower; open May–Sept daily; entrance charge) – also serves as the local landmark. The first count of Bregenz used it as a tithe barn – in other words, as his tax office. During the 14th century two storeys were converted into a double chapel. Finally, by 1601, Benedetto Prato from Roveredo had added the flamboyant canopy to the tower and topped it with its lantern-festooned onion dome. On the upper floor of this 13th-century tower is a local military museum.

Passing along the Meissnersteige, we come down to the Thalbachgrund, opposite which stands the **Parish Church of St Gall**. Its origins date from an early church founded here by the missionaries St Gall and St Columban. The present building was completed by 1737 under the supervision of Franz Anton Beer, using some structural elements from the older edifice. The West Tower, constructed in 1480, acquired its baroque gable in

Map on page 264

1673. The single-naved interior seems exceptionally wide because of its relatively low ceiling; it was elaborately decorated in the rococo style by Abraham Bader.

The location of the Upper Town betrays the fact that, at least in early times, the citizens of Bregenz had no strong links to the lake in spite of the town's picturesque situation on the eastern bay. No important buildings were erected on the lake shore, and at the end of the 19th century few protests were voiced when a jungle of railway tracks wormed their way on to the land between the town and the lake. Since that time, those wishing to visit the lakeside or board one of the white ships of the Lake Constance Line must use the only railway crossing. A 9-km (5-mile) path along the lakeshore from Lochau in the north to the mouth of the Bregenzer Ache in the west has proved little compensation.

Nestled in the meadowland to the west of town (and beyond the Seebühne) is the former Cistercian **Abbey of Mehrerau**, founded in 1097 and a bastion of the Counter-Reformation. The neo-Romanesque abbey church, rebuilt in 1962, is a high-ceilinged hall with a transept and a semicircular chancel, impressive in its simplicity. The right aisle wall is broken up by three chapels, each containing an important work of art: a triple portrait of St Anne (*circa* 1515), an Annunciation (second half of the 15th century) and a triptych with Crucifixion scenes from the end of the 15th century.

In the Bregenzerwald

In 830 the abbot of Reichenau Abbey, Wahlafried Strabo, described the Bregenz hinterland and the primeval forests along the Bregenzer Ache as far as the Hochtannberg Pass as a "wilderness devoid of human habitation". It was not until the middle of the 10th century that the counts of Bregenz started to use

Empress Maria Theresa donated 1,500 Gulden for the high altar in the Parish Church. As a token of gratitude, one of the shepherdesses in the altarpiece of the Adoration of the Magi was painted in her likeness.

BELOW: a pier over the Bodensee in Bregenz.

these forests as hunting grounds and permitted settlers to make their homes here.

In the first half of the 19th century a systematic network of footpaths was finally created, although proper access was not guaranteed until 1912, when the Bregenzerwald Railway reached as far as Bezau. The present-day road network was not built until after World War II. Today it is possible to drive from Dornbirn across the Bödele to Schwarzenberg, across the Furka Ridge or the Faschina Ridge to Damüls or from the Lech Valley across the Hochtannberg into the Valley of the Bregenzer Ache. From Bregenz there is a direct link across the gorge of the Schwarzbach torrent to Alberschwende, which sits at the base of the Brüggelekopf. The village square in front of the church is adorned by a linden tree that is reputedly 1,000 years old.

Hittisau, which possesses more than 100 privately-owned meadows, and **Sibratsgfäll** – the youngest community in the Bregenzerwald, reached by a 10-km (6-mile) detour southeast – are ideal destinations for holidaymakers in search of a relaxing atmosphere. **Langenegg ❷**, just west of Hittisau, has an exceptionally fine church. Built in 1775, the interior was decorated during the following year by Johann Michael Koneberg. The nave contains murals depicting the Nativity, the Marriage and the Assumption of the Virgin Mary. The fresco under the balcony, depicting Christ expelling the money-changers from the temple, includes (somewhat incongruously) the figure of a woman carrying a basket of eggs and dressed in the unmistakable traditional costume of the Bregenzerwald.

In the village of **Schwarzenberg**, 10 km (6 miles) southwest on the road to the Bödele summit, stands the house where the artist Angelika Kauffmann (1741–1807) lived as a child. She was the daughter of the portrait painter,

Angelika Kauffmann (1741–1807), who spent her youth in Schwarzenberg, was one of the few famous pre-20th-century women artists. At the peak of her success in London, she was a founder member of the Royal Academy and was rumoured to have had an affair with Joshua Reynolds.

BELOW: dawn over the Bodensee.

Joseph Kauffmann. In 1757, when she was 16 years old, she painted the pictures of the apostles on the walls of the nave of the Parish Church of the Trinity. Her father had been entrusted with the interior decoration of the church. These paintings rank amongst her finest work. In 1802 she presented the village church with a picture that adorns the high altar to this day, the *Coronation of the Virgin by the Holy Trinity.*

Map on page 264

The market town of **Bezau**, southeast across the mountain, is one of the principal communities of the Bregenzerwald. Its **Museum of Local History** is worth visiting for its exhibition of folklore. **Mellau**, which lies a little further up the valley, is overshadowed by the lofty summit of the Kanisfluh. Its five rock faces, with a total length of 6 km (4 miles), fall precipitously down to the valley from a height of 1,300 metres (4,265 ft).

The terminus of the Bregenzerwald Railway, long since axed, is marked today in Bezau only by an old steam locomotive.

Damüls ❸, at the foot of the Glatthorn, was first and foremost a Walser settlement. According to a document dated 1313, the Walser people received the mountain valley in fief from the counts of Montfort. In 1484 they had the massive stone **Parish Church of St Nikolaus** built by Rolle Maiger from Röthis. The flat wooden coffered ceiling was decorated in 1693 by Johann Purtscher with scenes from the Life of the Virgin. The walls are a poor man's bible: frescoes on the north wall depict the Passion of Christ; the apse portrays Christ at the Last Judgment with the Sword of Justice; scenes on the south wall depict Miracles of Compassion. The early baroque elements in the church date from 1630 onwards. Erasmus Kern created the high altar and its figures, as well as the Plague Altar in the north wall.

Back on Road 200, the last village of any size in the valley of the Bregenzer Ache is **Schoppernau ❹**. The desolate nature of this upland valley is reflected

BELOW: the Bregenzerwald.

THE SEEBÜHNE

Reaching out onto the Bodensee just behind the Bregenz casino, the Seebühne (lake stage) is famous throughout Austria and one of Europe's most interesting opera venues. The tiered banks of seats, which can accommodate 6,800, rest firmly on dry land, but the square performance space itself floats on the lake – creating a stage with the entire Bodensee (and its weather) as a rather dramatic backdrop to the operas being sung upon it.

In 1946 the director of the Vorarlberg State Theatre constructed the stage on a raft anchored in one of the old harbour basins. Mozart's lyrical drama *Bastien and Bastienne* was performed, as well as a ballet to his *Eine Kleine Nachtmusik*. The little raft was later replaced by a floating stage 60 metres (200 ft) wide and 40 metres (130 ft) deep, some 25 metres (85 ft) from the shore.

The designers here put great care into the construction of sets on the stage, spending months hammering and painting away before unveiling them to appreciative crowds at the Bregenz Festival each summer. In 2005 a spectacular set depicted a huge industrial fortress for the two-year-long run of Verdi's *Il Trovatore*. For more information on programmes and concerts visit; www.bregenzerfestspiele.com

in the name, which means "naked meadows". Even in early times its inhabitants were forced to seek their living elsewhere. Nonetheless, the woodland dwellers had a grand church built during the second half of the 18th century. Its frescoes and stucco date from 1796.

The final hamlet within the valley proper is **Schröcken**, 10 km (6 miles) southeast, which is also an old Walser settlement dating from the 14th century. In 1863 all the buildings were destroyed by a fire – even the church did not remain unscathed. Beyond Schröcken the road winds uphill to the 1,679-metre (5,495-ft) Hochtannberg Pass. On the other side lies Warth, in the Lech Valley, the last village before the Tyrol border. Providing there is no danger of avalanches when you arrive, you can drive from here into the bustling world of the Arlberg.

A Bavarian valley in Austria

The **Kleines Walsertal** ❺, situated north of the Hochtannberg Pass, is accessible from Austria only by foot. By road it can be reached through the Bavarian section of the Allgäu, via Oberstdorf. Because of its location, in 1871 Hungary and the German Reich agreed that the Kleines Walsertal should become part of the German Customs Union. Today the valley appears more German than Austrian in character, although it remains officially part of Austrian territory.

The largest village in the Kleines Walsertal is **Riezlern**, located 18 km (11 miles) southwest of Obertsdorf; it contains a **Museum of Walser History** (open Mon–Sat; entrance charge), a casino and various mountain lifts. Hirschegg and Mittelberg, just southwest, are also primarily tourist centres. The oldest parish church in the valley can be found in **Mittelberg**. Dedicated in 1390, it was extended in 1463 and 1694. Its 15th-century frescoes depict the Creation of the World and scenes from the Life of Christ.

Along the Rhine

The first town up the Rhine from Bregenz is also the biggest and youngest in Vorarlberg. **Dornbirn** ❻ was formed in 1901 by the amalgamation of four villages. For this reason, between townhouses and factories you will repeatedly come across single farms, large gardens and open fields. The name Dornbirn was first mentioned as long ago as 815, when it was known as Torrinpuirron. The present centre is dominated by the **Parish Church of St Martin**, completed in the Neo-classical style in 1840. It has a temple-like porch with six Ionic columns. The fresco in the nave portrays the Last Judgment. Near St Martin's stands the **Rotes Haus** (Red House), the town landmark. Built in 1634, it is a typical Rhine valley dwelling with a brick-built base surmounted by an ornate log-cabin construction.

For nature-lovers Dornbirn can offer two attractions: firstly, the refurbished **Vorarlberg Exhibition of Natural History** (open daily; entrance charge; tel: 05572-23 235) – a remarkable collection explaining the area's geology as well as its wealth of fascinating flora and fauna – and secondly the **Rappenloch Gorge**, a 60-metre (200-ft) deep ravine that was gouged out by the Dornbirner Ache when the Rhine glacier melted.

Every summer, as part of the Bregenz Festival, Schloss Hohenems plays host to a series of concerts. They are performed in the castle's beautiful Renaissance courtyard.

BELOW: the Church of St Martin, Dornbirn.

Map
on page
264

In the early Middle Ages, the Alemanni advanced as far as **Hohenems** ❼ – 7 km (4 miles) southwest on Road 190 – in their struggles against the Rhaeto-Romanic tribes. As early as the 9th century a fortress was built here to guard the frontier. The Emperor Barbarossa gave it to the knight of Ems, who extended it into a mighty Imperial castle. As the castle itself grew in importance, so too did the Ems family, until Marcus Sitticus became prince-archbishop of Salzburg in 1612. As bishop of Konstanz, long before he was summoned to the Salzach, he began to build a new palace in the valley.

The centre section of the present palace, **Schloss Hohenems** was completed in 1576. The two side wings and the curtain wall on the rock side were finished in 1610. The magnificent main facade is divided into 11 sections; the doorway in the centre bears the arms of Marcus Sitticus.

Connected by a passageway to the palace is the Parish Church, completed in 1581. The most important element in its interior is a Renaissance high altar with a late medieval Coronation of the Virgin in the central shrine. **Glopper Castle** is what is left of the former fortress on the mountainside. The late-Gothic complex consists of an inner fortress protected by an outer castle, moat and ramparts. The Town Hall, too, owes its origins to Marcus Sitticus. He commissioned its construction in 1567 as a guesthouse on the occasion of a synod in Konstanz.

A stout door at Schloss Hohenems.

Five kilometres (3 miles) to the south, **Götzis** ❽, first mentioned in 842 as Cazzeses, owed its early economic importance to its trading rights, dispensed by the Montforts. What is known today as the **Old Parish Church** was thus dedicated in 1514. It enchants the visitor even now with its richly decorated frescoed walls. The left wall of the nave displays scenes from the Life of Christ and the choir arch has a rather grim Last Judgment. The tabernacle is the work of Esaias Gruber from Lindau and dates from 1597. The nearby daughter church, dedicated to **St Arbogast**, has a wooden porch containing a cycle of pictures by Leonhard Werder, painted in 1659 and portraying scenes from the legendary life of the saint, who became bishop of Strasbourg and died in 1550.

BELOW: a Schloss Hohenems courtyard.

The market community of **Rankweil** ❾, further south, has grown up around a picturesque hill, which was a holy place for the Rhaetians as long ago as 1500 BC and subsequently supported a Celtic and then a Roman fort. At the start of the 9th century the bishops of Chur had the first chapel built here. From then until the end of the 15th century, it was extended to form the present Castle Church. Its most valuable treasure is the silver cross in the chancel apse.

Medieval Feldkirch

It was Louis, king of the East Franks, who gave the next town, **Feldkirch** ❿, its name. In the year 909 he gave "ad Veldkirichum" – the settlement at the forking of the roads – to the Arlberg and the canton of Grisons to the monastery of St Gallen. The village only began to prosper, however, when Hugo of Montfort moved his residence from Bregenz to Schattenburg Castle in Feldkirch, and then, around the year 1200, had a brand new town built in the shadow of his fortress.

In spite of a colourful political past, Feldkirch has been able to retain its regular medieval plan as well as

the picturesque squares enclosed by ancient houses with creeper-clad arbours. The town wall has suffered from the passage of time since the Middle Ages, but its course can still be made out everywhere by virtue of the numerous towers. The finest example of the old fortifications is the **Cats' Tower**, built in 1500. It is 40 metres (130 ft) high and has a circumference of 38 metres (125 ft). It was originally crowned by battlements, which gave way to a belfry during the 17th century.

The square in front of the cathedral – now one of the busiest centres of life in the town – was until 1380 the site of the local cemetery. The **Cathedral of St Nicholas** is a double-naved late-Gothic construction with an asymmetrically placed tower at the end of the north aisle. The church was completed in 1487 by Hans Sturn, the master-builder from Göfis. The chancel as we see it today has a number of Renaissance features and was added to the church in about 1520. The most notable treasure contained within is a picture showing the Descent from the Cross painted in 1521 by Wolf Huber.

Schattenburg Castle was built by Count Haug von Tübingen in 1185. In 1200, in line with his new place of residence, he changed his name to Hugo of Montfort. He was responsible for the 23-metre (75-ft) high keep which forms the heart of the complex as it stands today. In 1436, after the Montfort family died out, the castle came into the possession of the Habsburgs. Emperor Maximilian I had it extended to its present aspect in about 1500. The castle now houses a **Museum of Local History** (open daily; entrance charge; tel: 05522-71 982).

The bell in the Cats' Tower, weighing 7.5 tonnes, is the largest in the whole province.

BELOW: the cathedral tower, Feldkirch.

The Walgau

Beyond the Ill gorge lies the **Walgau**, the basin-shaped section of the Ill Valley between Feldkirch and Bludenz. Hemmed in to the south by the Rätikon Massif and to the north by the Walser Ridge and the foothills of the Lechtaler Alps, the valley's name recalls the Rhaeto-Romanic tribes who were the first settlers, for they were known to the Alemanni as the Walser. They built their homesteads on the cones of scree deposited by the gushing mountain streams, or on the mountain terraces formed by the glaciers.

The best example of such a settlement is **Göfis**, mentioned in a document of 850 as Segavio. Even in those days it had its own church and was part of the king's property. In 1450 local son Hans Sturn, who built the cathedral in Feldkirch, was allowed to build a new church for his fellow-citizens. In 1972, however, the edifice, with the exception of the chancel, was demolished to make way for a new building. This is a particularly good example of a successful symbiosis between ancient and modern building styles.

Just south on Road 193, once-strategic **Bludenz**  lies at the end of the Walgau, a short distance before the Kloster Valley branches off from the Ill. It was founded by Count Rudolf von Werdenberg, who gained lands in the Grosses Walsertal, in the Kloster Valley and the Montafon when the Montfort family heritage was divided up. To protect his domain he built a fortress in Bludenz and – in the manner established by his relatives in Feldkirch – started to lay out a town according to a regular grid pattern. His goal was to extract certain advantages from the traffic pass-ng through the Arlberg. In 1394 the last of the Werdenbergs was forced to sell his seigneurial rights to the Habsburgs.

The Werdenbergs' fortress stood on the rock which is crowned today by the baroque-style **Schloss Gayenhofen**. It was completed in 1752 by an Austrian governor on the site of the earlier stronghold. Today it houses the district officers' quarters. The prominent position on the castle rock was also chosen as the site of the **Parish Church of St Laurence**. Since the church was mentioned as early as 830, it seems to have an even earlier claim to the place than the castle. The present building was completed in 1514, the tower dating from 1670.

More typical of the historical aspects of the Walgau is the small-scale **Church of St Martin** in nearby Ludesch. Completed in 1480 in the Gothic style, the building has a fascinating collection of treasures which make it one of the most interesting examples of sacred architecture in Vorarlberg. The high altar was created in 1629 and combines various Gothic elements with Renaissance details.

Where the Walser once lived

The high-lying valleys to the west of the Arlberg were inhabited at the beginning of the last millennium by Rhaeto-Romanic farmers and hunters, although their settlements did not extend beyond the valley floors. This pattern did not change until about 1400, when Germanic Walser tribes from the Upper Rhône Valley drove out the Rhaetians, taking possession of their lands and building their own settlements, not only in the valleys but also on the upland slopes.

Many of their villages were situated in the **Grosses Walsertal** ⑫, a valley some 25 km (15 miles) long, which extends in a northeasterly direction from Ludesch. It is demarcated on its sunny side by the Walser Ridge, and on the

Map on page 264

Just north of Bludenz a cable-car climbs to the Muttersberg, which, at 1,384 metres (4,541 ft), affords breathtaking views of the towering Rätikon and Silvretta mountains to the south.

BELOW: a vineyard near Feldkirch.

shadow side by the Lechtaler Alps. The valley gradually climbs from the depths of the Walgau to the 1,850-metre (6,070-ft) Schadona Pass, through which one can reach Schröcken on the Hochtannberg Pass. Two roads provide access to the Grosses Walsertal. One winds along the shadow side of the valley from Ludesch to Raggal; the other opens up the sunny side from Thüringen to the Faschina Ridge and the way to Damüls on the edge of the Bregenzer Wald.

The Priory of St Gerold experienced its Golden Age in the 18th century when it was even able to purchase the High Court from the emperor in Vienna. Today, there are seminars, concerts and theatrical productions put on here.

Up the Walsers' valley

The hamlet of **Raggal**, 7 km (4 miles) north of Bludenz, is one of the Rhaetian settlements which was taken over by the Walser. Its **Parish Church** has its origins in a Rhaetian chapel dating from the 12th century. The Gothic chancel is the result of an extension added in 1460. The stucco ceiling, elaborately decorated with painted creepers, was completed in 1899.

The remote **Priory of St Gerold** is worth a detour. It marks the site of a hermitage to which a nobleman once retired. In the year 949 he was pardoned by the abbot of the Abbey of Einsiedeln (in Switzerland). As a counter-gesture the hermit gave his cell to the abbey, which founded a monastic settlement on the site.

The principal village in the valley is **Sonntag**, which consists of a number of districts, hamlets and isolated settlements. House 17, in the Flecken district, contains the **Grosses Walsertal Museum of Local History**. The furnished rooms and workshops provide an excellent insight into the rural life of the Walser as well as their customs and costumes. Buchburg is the best starting point for mountain walks in all directions. The surrounding area is regarded with good reason as the largest nature conservation area in Vorarlberg.

Here you will still find flower-covered mountain meadows, where edelweiss

BELOW: green pastures in Vorarlberg.

and gentians of every variety grow, and where you may even find wild orchids in bloom. On the rocky slopes above, are the homes of the golden eagle and the chamois – all talk of a threatened ecology seems far away.

The highest settlement in the Grosses Walsertal is the scattered village of **Fontanella**, about 2 km (1¼ miles) north of Sonntag. Until 1806 it formed a part of the parish of Damüls, on the other side of the Faschina Ridge, and prior to the middle of the 17th century its inhabitants had to attend the larger village's church. In 1673, however, they were allowed to build their own place of worship. In recent years the district of Faschina has become a popular ski centre.

The Brandner and Kloster valleys

Brandnertal, which lies south of Bludenz, opposite the Grosses Walsertal, was formerly colonised by the Walser. A community of 12 families received the valley in fief in 1347. They built the hamlet of **Brand**, 10 km (6 miles) south-west of Bludenz and close to the three-country point – where the borders of Austria, Liechtenstein and Switzerland meet. It has become a popular tourist centre thanks to the nearby Lünersee, which lies at an altitude of almost 2,000 metres (6,560 ft), and the 2,965-metre (9,725-ft) Schesaplana, the highest mountain in the Rätikon range.

In spring the cattle are put out to pasture on the lower slopes.

From Bludenz the main valley seems to continue in a straight line southeast. This is true geographically, for the River Ill does indeed spring from this part of the valley. However, it is the shorter **Klostertal** ⓭ (Kloster Valley), which runs from east to west that is the route taken by the railway, the main road and the motorway heading for the **Arlberg Pass**. Only 1,793 metres (5,885 ft) high, the pass was for a long time the only east–west link between the Rhine and the Inn, and the only route from the Austrian motherland to Vorarlberg.

BELOW: the Kleines Walsertal in winter.

It is clear that the traffic to the pass dominated life in the Klostertal from the earliest times. As the way was difficult and dangerous, Hugo of Montfort instructed the Knights of St John of Jerusalem to establish and maintain a hospice near the pass to provide travellers with accommodation and assistance. This hospice was called Klösterle, and soon gave its name to the entire valley and the village which sprang up in its shadow. Heinrich Findelkind followed this good example in 1386 with the foundation of the St Christopher Brotherhood, which organised searches to find travellers who had strayed from the path.

The real link to the modern world came in 1884, when the Arlberg Railway from Bludenz to Landeck was inaugurated. The section between Langen and St Anton required a 10-km (6-mile) tunnel. It provided the first all-weather link between Tyrol and Vorarlberg. The road followed the trail blazed by the railway with the opening of the **Arlberg Road Tunnel** in 1978. Its length of 14 km (9 miles) makes it the longest road tunnel in Austria.

Since the approach road to the Arlberg Road Tunnel is a motorway that bypasses the villages of the Klostertal, the latter have returned to their former tranquillity, affording sufficient leisure to enjoy the sights they have to offer. The first of these can be found in

Braz, the oldest permanent settlement in the valley, just east of Bludenz. The name comes from the Rhaetian Prats, which means "broad meadow". The Parish Church of Innerbraz was rebuilt in the baroque style at the end of the 18th century by Tyrolean artists. The frescoes on the vaulting are the work of the artist Carl Klausner.

Above Stuben, the road finally wends its way to the crest of the Arlberg. To the north, the Flexenpass provides access to Zürs and Lech am Arlberg across almost vertical rock faces.

As long ago as the 9th century, **Dalaas**, to the east, was the centre of the Rhaetian iron mining industry. The Walser took over the excavations, but decided to dig for silver instead. They smelted their finds in Danöfen, further up the valley. The village's name is directly derived from the location "by the ovens".

In **Langen**, another 10 km (6 miles) east, both the railway and the main road disappear into the mountain, leaving **Stuben am Arlberg** ⓮, an attractive, sleepy place, a little further east up the valley. The village's name stems from the room maintained by the Knights of St John as a place where travellers could warm themselves. The little church has a Gothic chancel, a baroque nave and a lovely Madonna dating from about 1630.

The Montafon

If instead of taking the Klostertal you continue up the Ill River southeast of Bludenz, you enter a region known as the **Montafon**, which the commercially-minded Vorarlberg community claims, with some justification, to have made into an Alpine Park. Schruns-Tschagguns, St Gallenkirch, Gaschurn and Partenen sport pretty Montafon-style houses, ski-lifts of all descriptions – and, in every season, an assortment of Austrian and foreign holidaymakers.

BELOW: Lech am Arlberg in the spring.

The Montafon lies directly in front of the impassable barrier formed by the giants of the Silvretta Range. In former times the region was poverty-stricken despite the existence of iron ore and silver deposits in the mountains. The profits from mining filled the coffers of the local feudal lords, the bishops of Chur and the Fugger clan of Augsburg. For this reason the area contains few major architectural masterpieces or works of art.

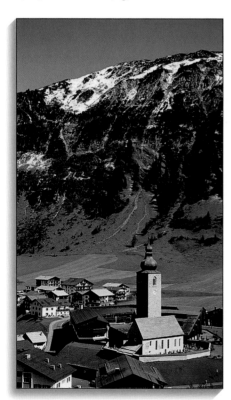

The one exception is the ancient community of **Bartholomäberg** ⓯. Not only is it the oldest village in the region, it also possesses the most important church in the valley. The **Parish Church of St Bartholomew** existed even in Roman times. Its 12th-century processional cross is the most valuable Romanesque work of art in Vorarlberg. The present church is baroque in style and was completed in 1743.

Nearby **Schruns** was the seat of the local court during Maria Theresa's reign. It was also once the terminus of the railway line.

Today this is unused except on special occasions when trips are arranged on old steam engines. There are, however, plenty of cable-cars and hotels in the town. The **Montafon Museum of Local History** (open Tues–Sat; entrance charge) provides an insight into the natural and human history of the valley.

Mule tracks and Alpine roads

The highest permanently inhabited village in the Montafon today is **Gargellen** ⓰, at 1,423 metres (4,669 ft). It is situated in a side valley, about 15 km

Map on page 264

(9 miles) south of Schruns on Road 192. Its name, derived from the Romansch language, means mountain torrent. What was once a miners' summer encampment has become a popular holiday village, bearing not the slightest sign of its former poverty. In any case, the path up to the 2,200-metre (7,220-ft) Schlappinerjoch follows an ancient shepherds' trail, which continues across the Swiss border to Klosters in the Prättigau. The valley and ridge represent the geographical boundary between the Rätikon and Silvretta mountains. There were also once ancient footpaths leading from Partenen, further up the Montafon Valley. One mule track led across the Zeinisjoch to the Tyrol; a second, via the Vermuntpass, into Switzerland.

Hydroelectric power stations are as important to the Montafon as road traffic is to the Klostertal. In 1953 the Montafon and the Paznaun Valley in Tyrol were linked by the Silvretta Reservoir, which lies at an altitude of 2,036 metres (6,680 ft). The reservoir is located exactly on the watershed between the two valleys. Here the River Ill, fed by the Silvretta glaciers, runs precisely along the European watershed between the Rhine and the Danube. As it seemed unable to make up its mind in which direction to flow at this point, it was necessary to construct dams on both sides.

The road built to serve the station, the **Silvretta Hochalpenstrasse** ⓱ (High Alpine Road), has become a real attraction. It is constructed to a very high standard and leads into a magnificent section of the High Alps, where rocks and glaciers form a harmonious unity seldom encountered in these mountains. South of the reservoir no fewer than 74 peaks rise above the 3,000-metre (9,840-ft) mark. The top section of the High Alpine Road is a toll road maintained by the Vorarlberg Ill Power Authority. ❑

The Romans used the Zeinisjoch, whilst Swiss farmers drove cattle across the Vermuntpass to summer pastures in the meadows of the Montafon. Mountain ramblers follow in their tracks to this day.

BELOW: a misty view of the Flexenpass above Lech.

In this ever changing world,
Singapore Girl, you're a great way to fly.

SINGAPORE
AIRLINES

A STAR ALLIANCE MEMBER

singaporeair.co

PENANG · NANJING · FRANKFURT · PERTH · KOLKATA · SAN FRANCISCO · OVER 55 MAJOR CIT

TRAVEL TIPS

T RANSPORT

GETTING THERE
AND GETTING AROUND

GETTING THERE

By Air

Austria's national carrier, Austrian Airlines (www.aua.com), operates direct services to most European capital cities on a several-times-daily basis from Vienna's Schwechat airport, and less frequently from the other principal international gateways of Salzburg, Graz, Linz, Klagenfurt and Innsbruck. Dozens of other carriers, including most European airlines, also fly between Vienna and national capitals. From London, for example, BA (www.ba.com) has several daily London–Vienna flights, with less frequency to Klagenfurt and Graz.

Among budget airlines, Austria's Lauda Air (www.laudaair.com) flies an increasing number of routes from elsewhere in Europe (though not the UK) to Austria at very competitive rates, while Ryanair (www.ryanair.com) offers surprisingly affordable flights from London Stansted to Linz, Graz and Salzburg (Bratislava might also be considered a possibility to reach Vienna) when booked in advance. The low-cost Austrian carrier Niki (www.flyniki.com) flys from London and Manchester to Vienna.

Austrian Airlines' route network is principally within Europe and the Middle East, but it has direct non-stop daily flights to New York's JFK airport and Atlanta's Hartfield International as well as less frequently to Tokyo. A host of other airlines also connect the US and Vienna, with a change of planes in Germany or Switzerland. Lufthansa connects New York with Munich.

Schwechat airport is located

Cut Your Carbon

Air travel produces a huge amount of carbon dioxide and is one of the main contributors to global warming. If possible, take the train to your destination as this produces less CO_2 (see www.raileurope.co.uk for sample fares). However, certain travellers may find it impossible to do this and will end up flying (especially from places such as the US). Although nothing can repair the immediate damage the trip will cause, it is possible to offset your "carbon load" by, for example, having trees planted as a "carbon sink". A number of organisations can do this for you and many have online "carbon calculators" which tell you how much you need to donate. In the UK travellers can try www.climatecare.org or www.carbonneutral.com, in the US log on to www.climatefriendly.com or www.sustainabletravelinternational.com

15 km (9 miles) to the east of the city (25 minutes' drive on the motorway). Its terminals were modernised in 1988, and its information booth – tel: 01-7007 22233 – in the arrival hall is open 24 hours daily. An express bus service that operates approximately every half hour from 5am–midnight, links the airport with Vienna's two main railway stations and the City Air Terminal next to the Hilton Hotel. For information, tel: 01-9300 02300. A train service operates between the Südbahnhof and the airport approximately every hour from 6am to 9.30pm (see also the CAT opposite).

By Train

For travellers from the UK and northern Europe, there are two options. If you're travelling by Eurostar to Paris, the Orient Express night train leaves Paris-Est station at 5.49pm each evening and pulls into Vienna at 8.30am the next morning. If you're travelling via Belgium, the Donauwalzer departs from Brussels at 7.10pm every evening, arriving in Vienna at 10.58am the following morning. Bookings from London are made through DER, tel: 020-7290 1111.

Other major international trains include the Prinz Eugen (Hamburg and Hannover to Vienna), the Donauwalzer's Amsterdam leg and the CityNightLine Donau Kurier (Dortmund, Bonn and Frankfurt to Vienna).

There are two main stations in Vienna: the Westbahnhof serves Germany, France, Belgium and Switzerland, and the Südbahnhof serves Italy, the Balkans, Greece and Hungary. For passenger information in Vienna tel: 051-717.

By Road

By Bus/Coach

If you want to make the journey by bus, it's a brutal 22-hour haul from London to Vienna for approx £100/$150 return. Another alternative is to travel to Munich (at roughly the same fare), then use local services to connect to Salzburg or elsewhere. Not all these long-distance services operate daily, however. Contact Eurolines in the UK, tel: 08705-143 219 or www.eurolines.com, for the latest schedule and pricing details.

Tour Suggestions

The following itineraries offer breathtaking views of the Austrian countryside for either fit cyclists or drivers:

A tour across the Alps

Away from the major routes, along the ridge of the Alps from Bregenz to Vienna, you can organise a spectacular trip across the country as follows:
Bregenz – Bregenzer Wald – Schröcken – Hochtannenbergpass – Lechtal – Holzgau – Reutte – Leermos – Ehrwald – Fernpass – Nassereith – Mieminger Plateau – Innsbruck – Hall – Schwaz – Zillertal – Gerlos-Pass Strasse – Krimml – Zell am See – Saalfelden – Mühlbach am Hochkönig – St Johann im Pongau – Radstadt – Schladming – Gröbming – Admont – Hieflau – Mariazell – Lilienfeld – Vienna.

Vienna

Höhenstrasse: The road to Klosterneuburg with city views.

Carinthia

Villacher Alpenstrasse: This road from Villach to Rosstratte presents a view of the Dachstein and the Grossglockner.

Salzburg

Grossglockner-Hochalpenstrasse: The Bruck–Heiligenblut (Carinthia) road with a view of Grossglockner and Edelweiss peaks.

Tyrol

Timmelsjoch-Hochalpenstrasse: High road from Sölden to Meran (Italy); views of the Ötztal Alps.

Vorarlberg

Arlberg-Pass-Strasse: The road from Langen to St Anton (Tyrol).

By Car

Travelling to Austria by car from northern Europe is a long and arduous journey, best achieved via Germany's excellent toll-free motorway network. Beware of attempting to enter the country via the less busy Alpine passes, which may be closed at night and in winter. To drive on motorways in Austria you need to buy a "vignette", which you then attach to your windscreen. A vignette can last anything from 10 days to a year, with a 10-day pass costing around €8. They can be bought at petrol stations, post offices and tobacconists. A Green Card for insurance purposes is not mandatory, but it is advised; a red accident triangle, seat-belts, a reflective safety vest and first aid kit are mandatory, however, for all vehicles travelling on Austrian roads. Petrol and diesel prices are similar to those in the rest of Europe.

GETTING AROUND

Public Transport

By Train

The Austrian Federal Railway System (www.oebb.at) maintains approximately 5,800 km (3,600 miles) of track and is connected with both the Eastern and Western European railway networks.

Trains travelling between Vienna and Graz, and between Vienna and Salzburg, depart at one-hour intervals; between Vienna and Innsbruck, and Vienna and Villach they leave at 2-hour intervals. Children up to seven go free if they don't need their own seat. There are also family tickets available. Nearly all day trains have dining cars; night trains have sleeping compartments and *couchettes*. For local train details, dial 051-717 in any city.

By Boat

From the beginning of April until the end of October boats operate on regular schedules along the Danube River. Vienna is connected to Budapest and Passau.

There are also boats running on a regular basis on all larger lakes in Austria. Along the stretch from Vienna to Budapest, the Donau-Dampfschiffahrts-Gesellschaft Blue Danube (the Danube Steamship Company), Friedrichsrasse 7, operates the hydrofoil to Budapest. The hydrofoil makes three trips form Vienna to Budapest and three return Budapest–Vienna trips daily. For details, tel: 01-588 800, or visit www.ddsg-blue-danube.at

DDSG also offer a Vienna–Bratislava hydrofoil service. Boats leave Vienna at Reichsbrücke from Wednesday to Sunday at 9am and 9.30am and arrive in Bratislava at 10.30am and 11am. The hydrofoil leaves Bratislava at 5pm and 5.30pm, arriving in Vienna at 6.45pm and 7.15pm.

By Bus

Some 70 international bus lines connect Austria to other countries. The Austrian public bus service primarily links places not served by the railway network. Nearly all tourist areas offer bus excursions into the surrounding countryside.

Transport in Vienna

Vienna's proverbial easy-going charm disappears when it comes to driving. Mercilessly pushing and shoving their way forwards, each driver fights their way ahead. The one-way system in the centre of the city has been specifically designed to discourage cars from entering at all. Parking spaces are rare, multi-storey garages expensive and the parking restrictions awkward.

So, don't drive in Vienna; if arriving by car, leave it on the city outskirts or at your hotel. Vienna's public transport is exemplary, comprising rail, underground, tram and bus. These have all been integrated into one system with many convenient and clearly labelled interchanges. All forms of transport arrive regularly and run late.

The S-Bahn

From whichever direction you approach the city by S-Bahn (suburban railway), you will find interchange stations where you can transfer to the underground. Many popular destinations in the countryside surrounding Vienna can be reached conveniently by taking the S-Bahn, and then changing to the local railway system.

The CAT

The most convenient, and quickest, way from Schwechat Airport to the city centre is on the CAT (City Airport Train; www.cityairporttrain.com). This takes 16 minutes from the airport to Wien Mitte/Landstrasse from where you can take the tram or U-bahn lines 3 and 4. From the city trains run from 5.38am to 11.08pm, and from the airport from 6.05am to 11.35pm. It is cheaper to buy a return than two single tickets.

The U-Bahn

The five U-Bahn (underground railway) lines are an ideal, and easy, way of getting into and around the city centre. They are:
U1: Kagran–Stephansplatz–Karlsplatz–Reumannplatz
U2: Schottenring–Volkstheater–Karls-platz
U3: Erdberg–Stephansplatz–Ottakring
U4: Hütteldorf–Karlsplatz–Schwed-enplatz–Heiligenstadt
U5: Heiligenstadt–Westbahnhof–Mei-dling–Philadelphiabrücke

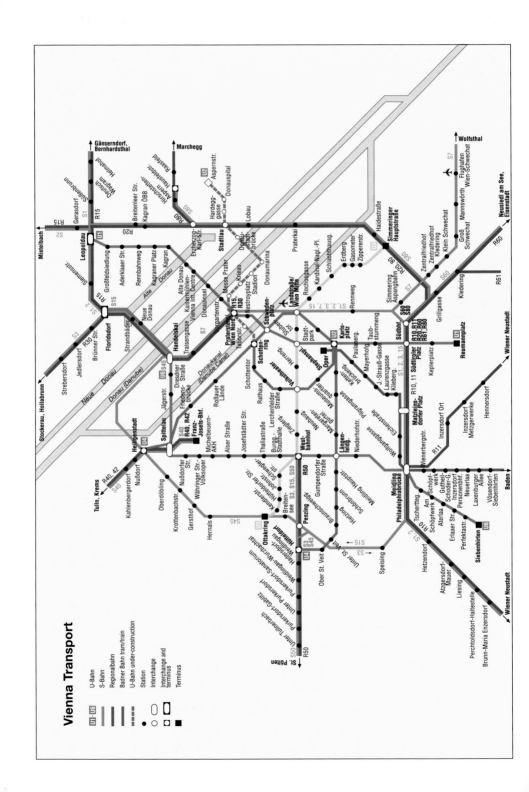

Vienna Transport

Travel by Tram

Vienna's tram system is very extensive and runs to almost all areas of the city; however, the most useful lines for visitors are:
1 and 2 around the Ringstrasse
31 and 38 from Schottentor to Grinzing and Stammersdorf
52 and 58 from the West Bahnhof to the city centre

Travel by Bus

Like the trams, the bus network is very extensive. The principal lines in the city centre are:
1a: Schottentor–Stephansplatz
2a: Burgring–Graben
3a:Schottenring–Schwarzenbergplatz.

Seven days a week, there is a special night-bus service from 12.30am, when the other public transport closes down, until 4am. The buses leave Schwedenplatz along various routes marked at bus stops by a sign bearing the letter N followed by a number.

Tickets and Price Reductions

Within the central area (zone 100, or Kernzone) you can use a validated ticket to travel as far as you like, changing as often as necessary as long as you continue to travel in the same basic direction.

Children under the age of 6 go free of charge, and children under 15 pay half the adult fare. During the local school holidays (July and August) they can travel free of charge; the same rule applies to foreign children with proof of identity and age.

Tickets for individual journeys (called *Einzelfahrscheine*), and reduced tickets for children and short journeys (known as *Halbpreisfahrscheine*), can be purchased from ticket machines at U-Bahn stations, or from many Tabak stands; they must be validated immediately. Keep your ticket as inspectors do make regular checks on passengers.

A much cheaper way of getting around is to purchase a multi-journey ticket *(Streifenkarte)* for 4 or 8 journeys. This type of ticket is also more convenient if you are planning on doing a lot of travelling around the city. One strip should be validated for each separate journey. Ticket offices also sell reduced-price tickets for pensioners *(Senioren)* on the production of proof of age.

In addition, there are special season tickets at a reduced rate, which permit unlimited travel for periods of either 24 hours or 72 hours. Both tickets are valid for all forms of public transport within the central area. A Vienna Shopping ticket allows travel in zone 100 for one day from 8am to 8pm. The Vienna Card, which entitles you to reductions on admission fees to museums and galleries, is also valid for all forms of public transport for 72 hours.To purchase a season ticket for either a week or a month, you will need a passport-type photo.

Private Transport

Taxis

All taxis are equipped with calibrated meters. They park at taxi stands and cannot be hailed from the street.

By Car

Driving in Austria

Traffic regulations in Austria correspond to those of other continental European countries. Driving is on the right. In snowy conditions (mid-November–mid-April) winter tyres, chains or studded tyres are required. ARBÖ (Austrian Motoring Association) and ÖAMTC (Austrian Automobile, Motorbike and Touring Club) run over 100 agencies throughout the country from which you can rent chains for your car. On main roads the speed limit is 100 kph (about 60 mph), on motorways 130 kph (80 mph), and in populated areas 50 kph (30 mph).

The blood alcohol limit is 0.5 parts per thousand; a driver caught exceeding this limit can expect to have his or her licence suspended and be fined at least €600. It is illegal for children under the age of 12 to sit in the front seat, and wearing a seat-belt is mandatory. Drivers must have proof of liability insurance; a Green Insurance Card is advisable. In many cities where you are required to pay a fee for short-term parking, it is first necessary to obtain a parking certificate, available at tobacconists, banks and petrol stations.

The police must be called to the scene of all car accidents in which any persons are injured. Foreigners should fill out the accident form entitled *Comité Européen des Assurances*. ÖAMTC and ARBÖ maintain vehicle breakdown services along the most important thoroughfares; non-members may also take advantage of these services for a somewhat higher price than members.

Traffic reports are broadcast on Channel 3 (Ö3) every hour following the regular news bulletin. Programmes on this channel may be interrupted by announcements about especially nasty traffic conditions.

Car Rental

Most international car rental agencies have offices in Austria. In addition to these, there are also a number of local rental businesses which tend to offer cheaper rates. You'll find offices located in larger cities, at airports and in main railway stations.

International firms in Vienna to try include:
Avis, 1, Opernring 5 and airport, tel: 01-587 6241, www.avis.com
Budget, 3, Vienna Hilton and airport, tel: 01-7146 5650, www.budget.com
Europcar, 1, Schubertring 9, tel: 01-714 6717, www.europcar.com
Hertz, 1, Kärntner Ring 17, tel: 01-512 8677, www.hertz.com

BELOW: the Vorarlberg bus service is excellent.

ACCOMMODATION

HOTELS AND CAMPSITES

Private Accommodation

On just about every street in tourist-oriented towns you'll find a *Zimmer frei* (vacancies) sign. Alternatively, tourist information offices can give you a list of local private accommodation, probably the most reasonably-priced lodgings you'll find anywhere in Austria.

Hotels

Austrian hospitality enjoys worldwide recognition (many hotels throughout the world are under Austrian management). Even the country's smallest inns offer excellent service.

Hotels in Austria are divided into five categories, each distinguished by a number of stars. In the following list you'll find hotels belonging to the top three categories, plus Vienna *pensions*.

In the tourist season (in July and August, and over Christmas and Easter), you should book hotel rooms in advance as most hotels and inns are fully booked. Bookings can be cancelled up to three months before the date of arrival. On shorter notice a cancellation fee will apply.

Besides the excellent hotel industry, Austria is known for inexpensive family vacations. These are offered through a system of vacations on farms and in villages, and through the many *pensions*, guest houses and private accommodations throughout the country. The Austrian National Tourist office has two brochures – *Dorfurlaub in Österreich* and

Preisgünstiger Urlaub in Österreich – that list the many possibilities.

Hotels in Vienna are more expensive than elsewhere in the country and, with the number of international institutions in the city and a large volume of tourists, accommodation is at a premium. It is advised to book in advance if you want to make sure of getting in to the hotel of your choice.

Prices

The hotels below are arranged alphabetically and given the following price categories for a double room in high season:
€€€€ = more than €300
€€€ = €140–300
€€ = €90–140
€ = less than €90

ACCOMMODATION LISTINGS

HOTELS

Vienna

Altstadt
7, Kirchengasse 41
Tel: 01-522 6666
Fax: 01-523 4901
www.altstadt.at
Cool, modern and non-smoking rooms in a great *fin-de-siècle* building. Communal areas are decorated with

contemporary works of art and the hotel is within easy walking distance of the MuseumsQuartier. €€

Arenberg
1, Stubenring 2
Tel: 01-512 5291
Fax: 01-513 9356
www.arenberg.at
The doyen among *pensions* (part of the Best Western group), with a plush, elegant atmosphere and excellent location. All rooms have satellite TV and direct-dial telephones. €€

Astoria
1, Kärntnerstrasse 32–34
Tel: 01-515 770
Fax: 01-515 7782
www.austria-trend.at
A civilised old hotel immediately behind the Staatsoper. Some rooms are accessible to physically disabled guests. €€€

Hotel Austria
1, Am Fleischmarkt 20
Tel: 01-515 23
Fax: 01-5152 3506
www.hotelaustria-wien.at
Newly reconditioned rooms

in a very centrally placed hotel; those without bath are cheaper. An elegant, friendly and quiet hotel. €€

Biedermeier im Sünnhof
3, Landstrasser Hauptstrasse 28
Tel: 01-716 710
Fax: 01-7167 1503
www.dorint.com
A unique, attractive set of restored Biedermeier-style buildings, with original shopping arcade. Specially outfitted rooms for guests with disabilities. €€€

Bristol
1, Kärntner Ring 1
Tel: 01-515 160
Fax: 01-5151 6550
www.starwoodhotels.com
An art nouveau building dating from 1884 that is rather more intimate than many other five-star hotels. Its restaurant, the Korso, is known for its light Viennese cuisine and distinguished wine list. There are non-smoking rooms and wheelchair facilities for guests. €€€€

Haydn
6, Mariahilfer Strasse 57–59
Tel: 01-5874 4140
Fax: 01-586 1950
www.haydn.hotel.at
Simple, mid-range *pension* in a noisy area. Only a few minutes from the city centre by U-Bahn. There is cycle storage space available to guests, and breakfast is included. €

Hollman Beletage
1, Köllnerhofgasse 6
Tel: 01-961 1961
Fax: 01-9611 96033
www.hollmann-beletage.at
It is hard to recommend this small (only seven large rooms) hotel enough. It is very central, and the rooms are modern, chic and beautifully kept. It has a laid back feel, the reception shuts down at night, leaving the guests to help themselves at the bar. It is excellent value, and a good breakfast is included in the price. €€

Imperial
1, Kärntner Ring 16
Tel: 01-50 100
Fax: 01-501 0410
www.starwoodhotels.com
Official guests of state, actors and leading pop stars stay in the Imperial, with its 128 elegant rooms and suites. Definitely the place to be seen, and the restaurant is one of the best and most expensive in Vienna (the café isn't bad either). All rooms can accommodate guests with wheelchairs. €€€€.

Kärtnerhof
1, Grashofgasse 4
Tel: 01-5121 9230
Fax: 01-5132 22833
www.karntnerhof.com
Pleasantly quiet, despite its central location. A range of services is offered by the multilingual staff. Though the hotel is very popular, some might find the hand-held showers to be as outdated as the furniture. All rooms have satellite TV and telephones; some are outfitted for wheelchairs. €€

König von Ungarn
1, Schulerstrasse 10
Tel: 01-515 840
Fax: 01-515 848
www.kvu.at
Centrally located only metres from the Stephansdom, and over 400 years old, this hotel is full of old-fashioned charm. It has everything you would expect of a four-star hotel, and the glass-roofed inner courtyard is particularly attractive. All rooms are wheelchair-friendly and guests with cycles have access to repair and storage facilities. €€€

Kugel
7, Siebensterngasse 43
Tel: 01-5233 3550
Fax: 01-5233 3555
www.hotelkugel.at
Good location in the middle of the shopping district, and small, clean rooms. Enthusiastic owners make the experience more enjoyable. Some rooms are outfitted for wheelchair use. €

Mailbergerhof
1, Annagasse 7
Tel: 01-512 0641
Fax: 01-5120 64110
www.mailbergerhof.at
An old building with a modern interior, in the pedestrian area of the city centre. A full breakfast is included in the rate. €€€

Meridien
1, Opernring 13
Tel: 01-588 900
Fax: 01-5889 09090
www.vienna.lemeridien.com
Five star luxury in a row of converted Ringstrasse buildings. The interiors have been beautifully designed, with clean modern lines. The restaurants are pretty good as well. €€€€

Nossek
1, Graben 17
Tel: 01-533 7041

ABOVE: modern comfort at the Beletage.

Fax: 01-535 3646
www.pension-nossek.at
Small, cosy *pension* in the heart of Vienna's shopping district. Credit cards are not accepted and reservations are highly recommended in the high season. Also available is an apartment for those wishing to stay longer. €–€€

Palais Coburg
1, Coburgbastei 4
Tel: 01-518 180
Fax: 01-518 181
www.palais-coburg.at
Horribly expensive but wonderfully opulent, this mid-19th century palace has been converted into a series of luxury suites. Everything is, as you would expect, very smooth, with a good restaurant, pool and city centre garden. €€€€

Parkhotel Schönbrunn
13, Hietzinger Hauptstrasse 12
Tel: 01-878 040
Fax: 01-8780 43220
www.austria-trend.at
Very close to the palace and gardens of Schönbrunn, this hotel formerly housed the emperor's guests and is still redolent of the Imperial past. Amenities include an indoor pool, satellite TV, and phones with voice mail as well as some rooms outfitted for wheelchair use. Rates include a generous breakfast. €€€

Penta Renaissance
3, Ungargasse 60
Tel: 01-711 750
Fax: 01-7117 58145
www.marriott.com
One of the city's architecturally most striking hotels (with a lavish

PRICE CATEGORIES
€€€€ = more than €300
€€€ = €140–300
€€ = €90–140
€ = less than €90
Prices are for a double room in high season; off-season rates are often considerably lower.

reception area), but slightly off the beaten track, 10 minutes by tram from the Ringstrasse. All rooms can accommodate wheelchair users, and there are telephones, satellite TVs and minibars in all rooms. €€€

Pertschy
1, Habsburgergasse 5
Tel: 01-534 490
Fax: 01-534 4949
www.pertschy.com
A friendly small hotel right in the middle of the Innere Stadt. The rooms are very comfy in a kitsch Viennese sort of way (which is all part of the charm) and breakfast is included in the cost. €€

Plaza Vienna
1, Schottenring 11
Tel: 01-313 900
Fax: 01-31390 22009
www.vienna.crowneplaza.com
A recently built and very elegant art nouveau-style hotel. Catering to the business traveller, rooms are equipped with modems and satellite TV. Wheelchair users can be accommodated in any room. €€€

Rathaus
8, Lange Gasse 13
Tel: 01-400 1122
Fax: 01-4001 12288

www.hotel-rathaus-wien.at
Inexpensive quiet rooms right in the middle of the lively Josefstadt district, with its many small bars. Each room is named after an Austrian wine maker, and samples of their wines are found in the minibar. €€

The Rooms
22, Schlenthergasse 17
Tel: 0664-431 6830
Fax: 01-2636 70215
www.therooms.at
This lovely bed and breakfast is a little way out of the centre in the Donaustadt district (near to Kagran U-bahn). Just three rooms (1 single and 2 doubles), which are beautifully furnished, with views on the garden. Cash only. €

Sacher
1, Philharmonikerstrasse 4
Tel: 01-514 560
Fax: 01-5145 7810
www.sacher.com
Archdukes, ministers and senior army officers used to stay here, and the Sacher is still the city's most famous hotel. Past its heyday, perhaps, but you can still be sure of top-class service. Some rooms are accessible to wheelchair users. €€€€

Schild
19, Neustift am Walde 97–99
Tel: 01-4404 0440
Fax: 01-444 000
www.hotel-schild.at
This 20-room hotel is a paradise for wine lovers, since it is surrounded by *Heurigen*. The country location is also appealing to cyclists as the hotel offers cycle storage and repair facilities. Wheelchairs are welcome in some rooms. €€

Schweizerhof
1, Bauernmarkt 22
Tel: 01-5331 9310
Fax: 01-533 0214
www.schweizerhof.at
Relatively inexpensive, despite its very central position. A generous breakfast buffet is served with salmon and champagne on Sunday. All rooms have en-suite facilities and satellite TV. €€

Style Hotel Vienna
1, Herrengassse 12
Tel: 01-227 800
01-227 8077
www.stylehotel.at
Very central, chic and well-designed, this modern "style" hotel is a great place to stay. Plus, it is not quite as expensive as it first appears (check out their "specials"). €€€

Wandl
1, Petersplatz 9
Tel: 01-534 550
Fax: 01-534 5577
www.hotel-wandl.com
Located immediately behind the Peterskirche, and thus very much at the hub of things. Nice rooms and moderate rates. €€–€€€

Wild
7, Lange Gasse 10
Tel: 01-4065 1740
Fax: 01-402 2168
www.pension-wild.com
A popular *pension* in Josefstadt with large modern and very clean rooms with or without en-suite facilities. There are kitchenettes on every floor for light meals and breakfast (included) is served on the ground floor. A good place to stay for gay and lesbian visitors. €

Zur Wiener Staatsoper
1, Krugerstrasse 11
Tel: 01-5131 2740
Fax: 01-5131 27415
www.zurwienerstaatsoper.at
Newly renovated and, as its name suggests, close to the opera. Small rooms, most with en-suite facilities, all facing a quiet, residential street. Advance reservations are recommended. €€

BELOW: reception at the Palais Coburg.

Lower Austria

Krems

Gästehaus Freisleben
Steiner Landstrasse 16
Tel: 02732-85 169
16th-century inn located outside Krems in Stein with recently renovated rooms. Near ferry terminal. Longer stays are encouraged. Cycle storage. €

Gourmet-Hotel Am Forthof
Donaulände 8
Tel: 02732-83 345
Fax: 02732-833 4540
email: hotel.foerthof@netway.at
The only Krems hotel overlooking the Danube, this civilised inn is festooned with pretty window-boxes. Ask for one of the off-street rooms for peace and quiet. There is also a restaurant for gourmets, as the name of the hotel implies. €€–€€€

Hotel Unter den Linden
Schillerstrasse 5
Tel: 02732-82 115
Fax: 02732-821 1520
email: hotel@udl.at
www.udl.at
Spacious rooms with antique wooden beds and shiny parquet floors. There's an extra charge for one-night stays. €

Kremsleithenhof-Familie Felsner
Kraxenweg 15
Tel: 02732-85 671
Apartments with cooking facilities and home-made schnapps. Parking is available. €

Melk

Gasthof Wachauerhof
Wienerstrasse 30
Tel: 02752-52 235
Fax: 02752-522 3523
email: wachauerhof@pvg.at
Large, comfortable inn with spacious rooms. €

Gasthof Goldener-Stern
Sterngasse 17
Tel: 02752-52 214
Fax: 02752-522 144
A good resting place for cyclists, this *pension* features clean rooms with shared facilities. €

Gasthof zum Fürsten
Rathausplatz 3–5
Tel: 02752-52 343
Fax: 02752-523 434
email: cafe.madar@netway.at
Small, family-run hotel with

a view of the town square and abbey. €

Durnstein

Romantik Hotel Richard Löwenherz
Tel: 02711-222
Fax: 02711-22 218
email: loewenherz@duernstein.at
www.richardloewenherz.at
Run by the same family since 1884, on the site of a former convent on the banks of the Danube. Affords wonderful views, excellent cuisine and plentiful art. €€€

Hotel "Sänger Blondel"
Tel: 02711-253
Fax: 02711-2537
email: saengerblondel@aon.at
www.saengerblondel.at
Traditional hotel next to the abbey, family-run since 1901, 15 individual rooms, a pleasant garden and live zither music. €€

St Pölten

Gasthof Graf
Bahnhofplatz 7
Tel: 02742-352 757
Fax: 02742-3527 5740
email: hotel-graf@wirie3100.at
Facing the train station, this hotel is a good, clean place convenient for early-morning departures. €

Hauser Eck
Schulgasse 2
Tel: 02742-73 336
Fax: 02742-78 386
email: hausereck@kstp.at
Warm, inviting hotel close to the station. All rooms are furnished with TV and direct-dial phones. €

Metropol
Schillerplatz 1
Tel: 02742-707 000
Fax: 02742-7070 0133
email: metropol@austria-trend.at
www.austria-trend.at
Modern, city-centre hotel with standard, comfortable rooms equipped with TV and air conditioning. Some rooms for use by guests in wheelchairs. There's also a golf course available to hotel residents. €€€

Semmering

Panoramahotel Wagner
Hochstrasse 267
Tel: 02664-25 120
Fax: 02664-251 261
email: biowelt@panoramahotel-wagner.at
Small and tidy, with a good restaurant. €€–€€€

Panhans Grand Hotel
Hochstrasse 32
Tel: 02664-8181
Fax: 02664-818 1513
email: hotel@panhans.at
www.panhans.at
Built in 1888, the Panhans has a majestic outlook and large recreational facilities. €–€€

Burgenland

Eisenstadt

Gasthof Familie Ohr
Rusterstrasse 51
Tel: 02682-62 460
Fax: 02682-624 609
email: info@hotelohr.at
www.hotelohr.at
Golden stucco hotel run by a friendly family. Close to transport links and city centre. On-site restaurant. €€

Hotel Burgenland
Franz Schubertplatz 11
Tel: 02682-6960
Fax: 02682-65 531
email: burgenland@austria-hotels.at
Modern structure featuring doubles as well as apartments, and cycle hire and breakfast are included. €€€

Neusiedl am See

Hotel Wende
Seestrasse 40–42
Tel: 02167-8111
Fax: 02167-811 1649
email: anfrage@hotel-wende.at
www.hotel-wende.at
Lakeside family-run hotel that's great for health-conscious and active guests – there are cycles for hire and swimming and fitness facilities. €€

Rust

Mooslechners Rusterhof Restaurant-Hotel
Rathausplatz 18
Tel: 02685-60 793
Fax: 02685-607 9311
email: office@mooslechners.at
www.mooslechners.at
Old baroque town-centre house with top-class gourmet restaurant and apartments. €€€

Hotel Sifkovits
Am Seekanal 8
Tel: 02685-276
Fax: 02685-36 012
email: hotel@sifkovits.at

www.sifkovits.at
Small, lakeside hotel with large, comfortable rooms. Pets welcome and credit cards are accepted. €€

Styria

Graz

Hotel Erzherzog Johann
Sackstrasse 3
Tel: 0316-811 616
Fax: 0316-811 515
email: office@erzherzog-johann.com
Charming grand hotel in the centre of town with 19th-century furnishings. Spacious rooms with high ceilings. Excellent restaurant. €€€

Hotel Daniel
Europaplatz 1
Tel: 0316-711 080
Fax: 0316-711 085
email: daniel@weitzer.com
www.hoteldaniel.com
Extensive remodelling has created Austria's first "lifestyle" hotel and a member of design hotels. Unfussy, modern stylised interiors, by main railway station. €€

Hotel Ohnime di Gallo
Purbergstrasse 56
Tel: 0316-391 143
Fax: 0316-3911 4319
email: ohnime@ohnime.at
www.ohnime.at
A modern, peaceful retreat a little way from the city centre in the green Mariatrost district. Serves local and international cuisine and has a cycling and walking trail nearby. €

Gasthof Pension "Zur Steirerstub'n"
Lendplatz 8
Tel/Fax: 0316-716 855
email: office@pension-graz.at
www.pension-graz.at
A centrally-located, family-run guesthouse with views of the Clock Tower, the restaurant specialises in traditional local food. €

TRANSPORT

ACCOMMODATION

EATING OUT

ACTIVITIES

A – Z

LANGUAGE

Mariazell

Hotel Schwarzer Adler
Hauptplatz 1
Tel: 03882-28 630
Fax: 03882-286 350
email: info@schwarztradler.at
Posh hotel with four fully functioning apartments for travellers needing longer stays. Great views of the cathedral and town. Good facilities for guests in wheelchairs. €€–€€€

Bauernhof Stockreiter
Sandbühel 14
Tel: 0644-531 2388
Situated on the edge of the village,and close to the famous basillica, this farmhouse offers accommodation in holiday apartments.

Upper Austria

Freistadt

**Austria Classic
Hotel-Goldener Adler**
Salzgasse 1
Tel: 07942-721 120
Fax: 07942-721 1244
email: goldener.adler@hotels-freistadt.at
A pale-yellow building containing just 80 beds,

BELOW: coffee at breakfast.

but lots of amenities such as a pool and gym. At the on-site restaurant, you're advised to skip the main menu and go straight for the legendary desserts. €

Gasthof Deim Zum Goldener Hirschen
Böhmergasse 8–10
Tel: 07942-722 580
Fax: 07942-722 5840
email: goldener.hirsch@hotels-freistadt.at
Historic, hospitable hotel. The bright, airy reception hall's stonework and vaulted ceilings lend it a medieval look. Bikes are available to guests as well. €€

Pension Pirklbauer
Höllgasse 2/4
Tel: 07942-72 440
Fax: 07942-724 405
email: pension.pirklbauer@aon.at
The Pirklbauer is well situated for sightseeing and famous for its breakfasts (which you must order ahead). All of the rooms are equipped with a shower and toilet. €

Linz

Goldenes Dachl
Hafnerstrasse 27
Tel: 0732-775 897
email: goldenesdachl@gmx.at
This fairly spacious *pension* is not particularly exciting but provides value for money and is centrally located. Friendly management. €

Hotel Drei Mohren
Promenade 17
Tel: 0732-772 6260
Fax: 0732-772 6266
email: hotel@drei-mohren.at
www.drei-mohren.at
An excellent location and modern rooms – all complete with toilet and shower – make for a pleasant stay at this 300-year-old hotel. Great breakfast buffet. €€

Hotel Mühlviertlerhof
Graben 24
Tel: 0732-772 268
Fax: 0732-7722 6834
email: office@hotel-muhlviertlerhof.at
Modern hotel centrally located in the downtown area. Amenities include all en-suite rooms. €

Pension Wilder Mann
Goethestrasse 14
Tel/Fax: 0732-656 078
This homely *pension* has a great location – a 10-minute walk from the railway station – and cosy rooms. Breakfast costs extra. €

Steyr

Gasthof Bauer
Josefgasse 7
Tel: 07252-54 441
Fax: 07252-51 936
email: bauers.gasthof@aon.at
Inexpensive rooms some distance away from the city centre. €

Landhotel Mader
Stadtplatz 36
Tel: 07252-533 580
Fax: 07252-533 586
email: mader@landhotels.at
This central Renaissance building has quite small rooms but the restaurant is outstanding and there is a traditional German wine bar on site. €€–€€€

The Salzkammergut

Bad Ischl

Goldenes Schiff
Stifter-kai 3

Tel: 06132-24 241
Fax: 06132-242 4158
email: office@goldenes-schiff.at
Riverside hotel offering comfortable rooms, some with pleasant balconies, all recently renovated. €€€

Haus Stadt Prag
Eglmoosgasse 9
Tel: 06132-23 616
email: stadt-prag@aon.at
Pink building not far from the station. Spacious rooms; most with balconies (which cost extra). €

Waldesruh
Kaltenbachstrasse 43
Tel: 06132-24 558
email: ignaz.bruendl@gmx.at
Contemporary chalet-hotel not far from the centre. En-suite rooms throughout the building. €

Fuschlsee

Hotel Schloss Fuschl
5322 Hof bei Salzburg
Tel: 06229-22 530
Fax: 06229-2253 1531
email: schloss.fuschl@arabellasheraton.com
Smart hotel in a stone complex overlooking the pretty lake of Fuschl See, with short but scenic golf course adjacent. €€€

Hallstatt

Gasthof Zauner Seewirt
Markplatz 51
Tel: 06134-8246
Fax: 06134-82 468
email: zauner@hallstatt.at
A historical hotel with all the modern conveniences. €

Gasthof Simony
Wolfengasse 105
Tel/Fax: 06134-8231
email: susanna.scheutz@multikom.at
Small, lakeside hotel with some rooms sharing shower facilities. Friendly management. Good-value restaurant on premises. €

Mondsee

Gasthof Schwarzes Rössl
Raisnerstrasse 32
Tel: 06232-22 35
Fax: 06232-22 355
In addition to its good location – not far from the centre – this comfortable hotel offers great value for money. €

Hotel Seehof
Loibichl am Mondsee
Tel: 06232-5031

TRANSPORT

ACCOMMODATION

EATING OUT

ACTIVITIES

A – Z

LANGUAGE

Fax: 06232-503 151
email: seehof@nextra.at
Lakeside luxury hotel that looks like a farmhouse. Breakfast buffet, beach access. €€€

Seegasthof-Hotel Lackner
Gaisberg 33
Tel: 06232-2359
Fax: 06232-235 950
email: office@seehotel-lackner.at
A pristine location on the lake is the setting for this family-run resort. Features cycles and sailboats for guests, and non-smoking rooms. €€

St Gilgen

Parkhotel Billroth
Billrothstrasse 2
Tel: 06227-2217
Fax: 06227-221 825
email: office@billroth.at
www.billroth.at
Luxury resort within spacious park. Facilities include tennis courts and massage/sauna. €€–€€€

Pension Falkensteiner
Salzburger Strasse 11–13
Tel: 06227-2395
Fax: 06227-7298
email: pension-falkensteiner@aon.at
Pleasant family-run *pension* featuring comfortable rooms, some of which are en-suite. Relax in the adjacent garden or hire a cycle from reception. €

Salzburg (City)

Amadeus
Linzergasse 43–45
Tel: 0662-871 401
Fax: 0662-871 4017
email: salzburg@hotelamadeus.at
www.hotelamadeus.at
Good location on busy Linzergasse, this hotel offers functional en-suite rooms and has a lift. €€

Bergland
Rupertgasse 15
Tel: 0662-872 318
Fax: 0662-872 3188
email: kuhn@berglandhotel.at
www.berglandhotel.at
A hotel run by gracious hosts who provide rooms ranging from comfortable to posh. You can choose rooms with just toilet, just shower or (more expensive) both. €

Best Western Hotel-Restaurant Elefant
Sigmund-Haffner-Gasse 4
Tel: 0662-843 397
Fax: 0662-8401 0928
email: reception@elefant.at
www.elefant.at
Partake of the breakfast buffet included in the rate. Children are well catered for by staff attendants who will help supervise them while you shop. Catch up on local and international news via the TVs that are supplied in every room. €€€

Blaue Gans
Getreidegasse 41–43
Tel: 0662-841 910
Fax: 0662-841 3179
email: office@blauegans.at
www.blauegans.at
The location is this hotel's finest feature – it is firmly entrenched in the Altstadt. But following close behind are the simply appointed rooms – decorated in warm tones and with contemporary art – which come with or without private toilet and shower. €€–€€€

Cordial Theater-Hotel
Schallmooser Hauptstrasse 13
Tel: 0662-881 681
Fax: 0662-8816 8692
email: chsalzburg@cordial.at
Staff ensure you're well looked after here, and a variety of amenities, such as an Austrian-style breakfast, are included in the rate. There's a restaurant and bar, a non-smoking public area, lift, parking, TVs, sauna, solarium, suites and studios. €€–€€€

Goldener Krone
Linzergasse 48
Tel: 0662-872 300
Fax: 0662-8723 0066
Expect a warm welcome at this relaxed family hotel. Ask for a quiet room if you want to sleep, and a room without a toilet or shower if you're on a budget. €

Haus Ballwein
Moostrasse 69
Tel/Fax: 0662-824 029
Pleasant bed-and-breakfast establishment featuring farm-style accommodation outside the city limits. Rooms range from the simple, with the use of shared bath facilities down the hall, to those featuring basic cooking facilities for longer stays. If you don't have a car, you'll have to rely on the buses (No. 1 from station and No. 16 from F-Hanusch-Platz) to get there. €

Hinterbrühl
Schanzlgasse 12
Tel: 0662-846 798
Fax: 0662-841 859
email: hinterbruehl@sbg.at
This hotel just east of Alstadt is good value and is often full. Situated near the bus station and the Salzburg Festival. Don't expect en-suite facilities in the plain but functional rooms. €

Hotel Restaurant Weisses Kreuz
Bierjodlgasse 6
Tel: 0662-845 641
Fax: 0662-845 6419
email: weisses.kreuz@eunet.at
Small hotel located at the foot of Hohensalzburg Castle with a good restaurant featuring food from the Balkans. €

Hotel Bristol
Makartplatz 4
Tel: 0662-873 5570
Fax: 0662-873 5576
email: hotel.bristol@salzburg.co.at
www.bristol.salzburg.at
Located in a stately building and flanked by gorgeous gardens, and with an impressive façade, this hotel fulfills your every need with a comprehensive series of services ranging from childcare to a beauty parlour. The hotel's considerable luxuries extend to antique furnishings and wonderful thick pile carpets. €€€€

Hotel Goldener Hirsch
Getreidegasse 37
Tel: 0662-80 840
Fax: 0662-843 349
email: welcome@goldenerhirsch.com
www.goldenerhirsch.com
This hotel frequently serves as the meeting point for the stars of the Salzburg Festival, which is reflected in the prices. The glamorous and wealthy are attracted by comfortable yet old-fashioned furnishings and the staff's attention to detail. Expect to be pampered, and an air-conditioned room complete with TV. €€€€

Institut St-Sebastian
Linzergasse 41
Tel: 0662-871 386
Fax: 0662-8713 8685
email: office@st-sebastian-salzburg.at
www.st-sebastian-salzburg.at
The St Sebastian is located in the centre, on Linzergasse, and is complete with kitchens, laundry facilities and private rooms with balconies overlooking the city. Be sure to confirm reservations in advance at this hotel. €

Pension Adlerhof
Elisabethstrasse 25
Tel: 0662-875 236
Fax: 0662-873 663
email: adlerhof@pension-adlerhof.at
Great location for early-morning trains because the hotel is very close to the Hauptbahnhof. The furnishings are a mixed bag, ranging from the modern to the traditional. There is also the option of cheaper rooms without private facilities. €

Schloss Mönchstein
Mönchsberg Park 26
Tel: 0662-848 5550
Fax: 0662-848 559
email: salzburg@monchstein.at
www.monchstein.at
Fairy-tale castle, overgrown with vines and overlooking the city. Nestled in a garden with sculptures and a winding path, this hotel serves those for whom money is no object. Features include tennis courts and meals tailored to meet individual dietary needs. €€€€

Überfuhr
Ignaz-Rieder-Kai 43
Tel: 0662-623 010
Fax: 0662-623 0104
email: ueberfuhr.sbg@aon.at
Not close to town, but in a peaceful setting. Welcoming rooms with and without private facilities. €

PRICE CATEGORIES
€€€€ = more than €300
€€€ = €140–300
€€ = €90–140
€ = less than €90
Prices are for a double room in high season; off-season rates are often considerably lower.

Salzburg Province

Zell am See

Gasthof Schmittental
Schmittenstrasse 60
Tel: (06542-72 332
Fax: 06542-723 328
email: info@schmittental.at
www.schmittental.at
Traditional Austrian chalet
with window-boxes. Relax
in adjacent garden.
Rooms are all en-suite.
€

Hotel Lebzelter
Dreifaltigkeitsstrasse 7
Tel: 06542-7760
Fax: 06542-72 411
email: zell@hotel-lebzelter.at
www.hotel-lebzelter.at
Hotel in city centre
with large, comfortable
rooms, en-suite
facilities and TV.
€

Salzburgerhof
Auerspergstrasse 11
Tel: 06542-765
Fax: 06542-76 566
email: 5sterne@salzburgerhof.at
www.salzburgerhof.at
Full-facility resort nestled
in the mountains. Good
for active travellers,
as it provides bicycles,
a spa and health-
related courses such
as yoga. €€€–€€€€

Carinthia and East Tyrol

Klagenfurt

Hotel Musil
10-Oktober-Strasse 14
Tel: 0463-511 660
Fax: 0463-511 6604
email: reservation@musil-hotels.co.at
This pleasant hotel is in a
romantic spot and has a
good restaurant attached.
€€€

Moser-Verdino
Domgasse 2
Tel: 0463-57 878
Fax: 0463-516 765
email: moser-verdino@arcotel.at
Guests staying here on
business have internet
access, satellite TV and
decent bathrooms, which
make this hotel
recommended for any
working traveller. €€€

Blumenstöckl
10-Oktober-Strasse 11
Tel: 0463-57 793
Fax: 0463-577 935
email: mail@blumenstoeckl.at
www.blumenstoeckl.at
Great central location with
en-suite facilities, satellite
TV and attractive courtyard.
€

Sandwirt
Pernhartgasse 9
Tel: 0463-56 209
Fax: 0463-514 322
email: hotel@sandwirth.com
www.sandwirth.com
An idyllic lakeside location
and newly renovated. €€€

Hotel-Pension Aragia
Völkermarkter Strasse 100
Tel: 0463-31 222
Fax: 0463-312 2213
email: hotel@aragia.at
This wheelchair-friendly
pension is some distance
from the city centre and
isn't particularly
spectacular, but it does
have a restaurant. €€

Lienz

Hotel Haidenhof
Grafendorfer Strasse 12
Tel: 04852-62 440
Fax: 04852-624 406
email: info@haidenhof.com
Country manor some
distance from the city
centre but close to the
natural beauty of the
Tyrolean green hills and
golden meadows. €

Romantikhotel Traube
Hauptplatz 14
Tel: 04852-64 444
Fax: 04852-64 184
email: hotel.traube@tirol.com
Four-star hotel includes
many extras such as bike
rentals, great restaurant,
swimming pool and very
comfortable rooms.
Located right on the main
square. €€

Matrei

Hotel Rauter
Rauterplatz
Tel: 04875-6611
Fax: 04875-6613
email: info@hotel-rauter.at
www.hotel-rauter.at
Full-service resort for

BELOW: a well-decorated *Gasthof* in Ötz in the Tyrol.

sports-oriented guests.
€€€€

Villach

Hotel Goldenes Lamm
Hauptplatz 1
Tel: 04242-24 105
Fax: 04242-241 0556
email: office@goldeneslamm.at
www.goldeneslamm.at
Centrally located,
comfortable hotel with
annexe containing less
expensive rooms with fewer
amenities. Facilities
available for wheelchair
users. €€

Hotel Mosser
Bahnhofstrasse 9
Tel: 04242-24 115
Fax: 04242-2411 5222
email: info@hotelmosser.at
www.hotelmosser.at
Upmarket, friendly
establishment that caters
for those seeking
straightforward rooms and
spa treatments. There are
also non-smoking rooms.
€€–€€€

Tyrol

Innsbruck

Austria Classic-Hotel Zach
Wilhelm-Greil-Strasse 11
Tel: 0512-589 667
Fax: 0512-589 67666
email: info@hotel-zach.at
www.hotel-zach.at
City centre hotel with large,
well-decorated rooms.
Abundant breakfast buffet,
and televisions and
telephones in all rooms.
€€

Binder
Dr-Glatz-Strasse 20
Tel: 0512-334 360
Fax: 0512-334 3699
email: office@binders.at
www.binders.at
Twee little hotel with simple
rooms in a good location.
Hospitable reception. €

City Hotel Goldene Krone
Maria-Theresien-Strasse 46
Tel: 0512-586 160
Fax: 0512-580 1896
email: info@goldene-krone.at
www.goldene-krone.at
Contemporary, central hotel
but with small rooms. €€

Goldener Adler
Herzog-Friedrich-Strasse 6
Tel: 0512-571 1110
Fax: 0512-584 409
email: office@goldeneradler.com
www.goldeneradler.com

Grand Austrian hotel
featuring large, comfortable
rooms and a convenient
central location. €€€

Hotel Helga
Brandlweg 3
Tel: 0512-261 137
Fax: 0512-261 1376
email: hotel.helga@tirol.com
Not close to town, but
rooms have TVs and en-
suite facilities. Pool. €€

Internationales Studenten
Haus
Rechengasse 7
Tel: 0512-5010
Fax: 0512-501 905
email: office@studentenhaus.at
www.studentenhaus.at
Large, dorm-like rooms,
open July–Oct. Accepts all
credit cards. €

The Penz Hotel
Adolf Picher Platz 3
Tel: 0512-575 6570
Fax: 0512-575 6579
email: office@thepenz.com
www.the-penz.com
Situated a few steps
from the old town, this is
Innsbruck's finest designer
hotel. Wonderful views
from the roof terrace.
€€€

Weisses Kreuz
Herzog-Friedrich Strasse 31
Tel: 0512-594 790
Fax: 0512-594 7990
email: hotel@weisseskreuz.at
www.weisseskreuz.at
Though the exterior of this
Altstadt hotel has been
preserved for greater
authenticity, the rooms
have been renovated to
modern standards. Choice
of en-suite or shared
facilities in the hall. Guests
can use storage rooms for
winter sports equipment.
€€

Kitzbühel

Hörl
Josef-Pirchler Strasse 60
Tel/Fax: 05356-63 144
Inexpensive hotel near the
station, good for early
morning departures. It's
cheaper still if you choose
a room with facilities down
the hall. €

Hotel Weisses Rössl
Bichlstrasse 5
Tel: 05356-625 41
Fax: 05356-63 472
email: info@weisses-roessl.com
www.weisses-roessl.com
Central locale whose wide

range of bright, tasteful
rooms (that include a
separate sitting area)
is reflected in the diversity
of prices. Features a
restaurant, indoor pool
and bar. €€€–€€€€

Vorarlberg

Bregenz

Hotel Deuring Schlössle
Ehre-Guta-Platz 4
Tel: 05574-47 800
Fax: 05574-478 0080
email: deuring@schloessle.vol.at
A classy hotel that is
popular with the casino
crowd. Rooms feature
contemporary art. Rooms
for non-smokers available.
€€€

Hotel Garni Bodensee
Kornmarktstrasse 22
Tel: 05574-423 000
Fax: 05574-45 168
email: hotel.bodensee@telemax.at
Comfortable
accommodation at
affordable prices, this
central hotel has a
restaurant and parking. €€

Pension Sonne
Kaiserstrasse 8
Tel: 05574-42 572
Fax: 05574-425 724
email: office@bbn.at
Pleasant, affordable rooms
(more expensive in
summer) in the centre of
Bregenz's pedestrian zone.
€

Feldkirch

Best Western Hotel
Alpenrose
Rosengasse 6
Tel: 05522-72 175
Fax: 05522-721 755
email: hotel.alpenrose@cable.vol.at
A uniquely shaped rose-
coloured building that has
wheelchair-friendly rooms, a
restaurant/bar, cycles and
a posh penthouse suite.
€€–€€€

Hotel-Gasthof Löwen
Kohlgasse 1
Tel: 05522-35 830
Fax: 05522-358 355
email: loewen.hotel@aon.at
www.hotel.loewen.at
This hotel, housed in a
cheery building, offers
guests special touches
including a shuttle service
from the station, cycles
and a breakfast buffet.
€–€€

Lech am Arlberg

Hotel Berghof
Tel: 05583-2635
Fax: 05583-26 355
email: info@derberghof.at
This is a chalet-like hotel
catering for active
travellers, especially skiers.
The Berghof doubles its
rates accordingly in the
winter. Amenities include a
restaurant/bar, exercise
room, cycles and golf
course. €€–€€€€

Hotel Restaurant Aurelio
Tel: 05583-2214
Fax: 05583-3456
email: aurelio@aurelio.at
The Aurelio is a pleasant,
mid-range hotel with clean,
comfortable rooms, many
of which have sitting areas.
Open from December to
April only. €

Haus Brunelle
Tel: 05583-2976
email: brunelle@aon.at
This is a simple but
acceptable *pension* for
travellers sticking to a
budget. Breakfast included
in the rate. Open in
summer and
December–April only. €

CAMPSITES

The Austrian Tourist Office
Publicity Department, tel:
01-0587 2000, will send
you out a detailed map of
all the country's camping
sites on request. If you are
planning to travel with a
caravan, you should
ascertain in advance the
roads and passes on which
these vehicles are
prohibited. Trailers need a
carnet de passage. For
more information contact:
**Österreichischer Camping
Club (öcc)**, 1, Wien,
Schubertring 1–3
Tel: 01-713 6151

PRICE CATEGORIES

€€€€ = more than €300
€€€ = €140–300
€€ = €90–140
€ = less than €90
Prices are for a double
room in high season; off-
season rates are often
considerably lower.

TRANSPORT

ACCOMMODATION

EATING OUT

ACTIVITIES

A – Z

LANGUAGE

E ATING OUT

RECOMMENDED RESTAURANTS AND CAFÉS

WHERE TO EAT

Austrian cooking is generally rich and wholesome *(see pages 59–65)*. Almost every large town has several nationally known restaurants. Listed here are some of the top dining establishments.

Vienna

Vienna's restaurant offerings are simply astounding; anything from continental to Asian food can easily be located. But try to sample the local cuisine. You will find a *Beisl*, or little local bar/restaurant, on just about every street corner in Vienna. Their simplicity reflects the uncomplicated culture and traditions of Vienna; the wine is basic table wine; the food is good home cooking; and the prices won't break the bank.

Some have developed into fashionable bars and top-class restaurants in recent years, but others remain affordable and low-key. The best way to recognise a real *Beisl* is to check whether the owners do the cooking and pull the beer themselves, and whether the menu is written on a slate.

Although a number arenow very touristy it is also well-worth paying a visit to a *Heuriger*. Both *Heurigen* and *Buschenschanken* are places where new wine is sold by the wine-grower, and are recognisable by the wreaths or branches hanging outside the door. They often have beautiful gardens in which you can sample the latest vintage in the shade of chestnut trees or under the actual grapevine; most have music and a buffet.

Don't miss the wonderful open-air Naschmarkt (4, Linke und Recht Weinzeile, Karlsplatz), open Mon–Fri 6am–6pm, Sat 6am–5pm; this market has plenty of food stalls where you can either sit down or get food to take away.

Viennese Coffee Houses

Bräunerhof
1, Stallburggasse 2
tel: 01-512 3893
Open Mon–Fri 7.30am–8.30pm, Sat 7.30am–6pm, Sun 10am–6pm
Popular city-centre café with a wide selection of Torten.

Central
1, Herrengasse 14
tel: 01-533 3763-38
Open Mon–Sat 8am–11pm, Sun 10am–6pm.
Busy but cosy, with a splendid neo-Gothic painted ceiling.

Demel
1, Kohlmarkt 1
tel: 01-535 1717
Open daily 10am–7pm
Very popular with tourists, but allegedly the best *Torten* in town

Diglas
1, Wollzeile 10
tel: 01-512 5765-0
Open daily 7am–midnight
Old coffee house with huge *Torten* in the window, near Stephansplatz.

Frauenhuber
1, Himmelpfortgasse 6
tel: 01-512 8383
Open Mon–Sat 8am–midnight, Sun, holidays 10am–10pm
A classic Viennese café.

Griensteidl
1, Michaelerplatz 2
tel: 01-5352 6920
Open daily 8am–11pm
Light and airy café in traditional style, next door to the Hofburg.

Hawelka
1, Dorotheergasse 6
tel: 01-512 8230
Open Mon, Wed–Sat 8am–2am, Sun 4pm–2am. A former artists' café.
The famed *Buchteln* (yeast dumplings) are served after 10pm.

Imperial
1, Kärntner Ring 16
tel: 01-5011 0389
Open daily 7am–11pm. Opulent and set in the Hotel Imperial.

Landtmann
1, Dr-Karl-Lueger-Ring 4

tel: 01-5320 6210
Open daily 8am–midnight
A grand café, popular with politicians and business people, next to the Burgtheater.

Museum
1, Friedrichstrasse 6
tel: 01-586 5202
Open daily 8am–midnight
Popular with arts students and lecturers, with an Alfred Loos interior.

Prückel
1, Stubenring 24
tel: 01-512 6115
Open daily 9am–10pm
A long-standing café with a superb 1950s interior. Weekend piano entertainment.

Sperl
6, Gumpendorfer Strasse 11
tel: 01-586 4158
Open Mon–Sat 7am–11pm, Sun 11am–8pm. Large but still cosy, with a distinctively Viennese atmosphere.

RESTAURANT LISTINGS

Vienna

Beim Czaak
1, Postgasse 15
Tel: 01-513 7215
Open 11am–midnight
Mon–Sat
A friendly *Beisl* with helpful staff. There is good food, particularly the *Tafelspitz*, sinful desserts and an excellent selection of beers. €–€€

Braunsperger
19, Sieveringer Strasse 108
Tel: 01-320 3992
Open daily Jan and alternate months.
3pm–midnight
If you have a particular interest in genuine local grape varieties, then don't miss this *Heuriger*. *Weissburgunder*, *roter Zweigelt* and *Grüner Veltliner* are among those on offer, while *Gemischter Satz* is a blend of different grape varieties that are picked and pressed together. €–€€

Cantinetta Antinori
1, Jasomirgottstrasse 3–5
Tel: 01-5337 7220
Open daily
11.30am–midnight
A unique restaurant located in the meat district but specialising in exquisite fish dishes. Closely packed tables are not for non-smokers or the shy. Try the wines produced by the owners. €€–€€€

Enrico Panigl
8, Josefstädter Strasse 91
Tel: 01-406 5218
Open daily
5.30pm–1.30am
Arty and media types flock here for the Italian food and bar snacks, eaten at long communal tables. €–€€

Esterhazy Keller
1, Haarhof 1
Tel: 01-533 3482
Open 11am–11pm
Mon–Fri, 4–11pm Sat–Sun
A *Stadtheurigen* in a dark cellar; take the winding stairs down from the small doorway. Typical gut-busting food and local wines. Fine and atmospheric in a very

Viennese sort of way. €

Feuervogel
9, Alserbachstrasse 21
Tel: 01-317 5391
Open daily
5.30pm–midnight Mon–Sat
Excellent food from the Ukraine – most customers are recent arrivals from the Kiev area. €€€

Figlmüller
1, Wollzeile 5
Tel: 01-512 6177
Open daily 11am–10.30pm
Most famous for its *Wienerschnitzel* but now very touristy. However, the *Schnitzel* are certainly large and tasty and the wine is excellent. €€

Fuhrgassl-Huber
19, Neustift am Walde 68
Tel: 01-440 1405
Open Mon–Sat
2pm–midnight, Sun, holidays noon–midnight
If you fancy a rustic setting, don't miss the earthy atmosphere of this *Heuriger*. On days when it's too cold to sit outside in the magnificent garden, warm yourself indoors with a plate of suckling pig, grilled chicken or other choice items from the buffet. €–€€

Gasthaus Wild
3, Radetzkyplatz 1
Tel: 01-920 9477
Open daily 10am–1am
This *Beisl* has been beautifully restored, keeping the original character. The food, which includes typical Viennese dishes, is excellent, as is the selection of beers and wines. €€

Gerhard Klager
21, Stammersdorfer Strasse 14
Tel: 01-292 4107
Open daily 1pm–midnight, every other month
This *Heuriger* is particularly good for children, who can play in the playground while the adults sample fine wines and high-quality food. If you're driving, try the delicious low-alcohol grape *must*. €–€€

Glacis Beisl
7, Breitegasse 4
Tel: 01-526 5660
Open daily 11am–2pm

ABOVE: a cheese plate at Steiereck.

Part of the Museums-Quartier complex, a busy modern space that serves up great Viennese food. Very popular so you might want to book. €€

Immervoll
1, Weihburggasse 17
Tel: 01-513 5288
Open daily midday–midnight
A tiny, vaulted restaurant and café that has been carefully renovated. Popular at lunch time with local workers, it serves up lovely Viennese classics and has a good range of drinks. €–€€

Karls
4, Karlsplatz 5
Tel: 01-505 3839
Open Sun–Thur 11am–2am, Fri–Sat 11am–4am
Down a flight of stairs besides the Musikverein is this bar and restaurant. Friendly staff bring modern Viennese dishes and an excellent range of drinks. €€€

Kervansaray/Hummerbar
1, Mahlerstrasse 9
Tel: 01-5128 8430
Open noon–midnight, closed Sun
Said to be one of the best fish restaurants in Vienna, with a fresh catch flown in

every day. Lobster is a speciality, as are the fish soups. €€–€€€€

Korso bei der Oper
1, Kärntner Ring 1
Tel: 01-5151 6546
Open Sun–Fri noon–3pm, 6pm–1am; closed Aug
A standard bearer for new Austrian cuisine, Korso offers an impressive range of dishes, from potato goulash and tripe to experimental creations such as skate wings and morel ravioli. Korso also has a good range of Austrian wines. €€€€

Ma Pitom
1, Seitenstettengasse 5
Tel: 01-535 4313
Open daily 5pm–3am, Fri–Sat until 4am
Ma Pitom combines Israeli and Italian cuisine – hummus and pitta bread pitted against *zuppe pavese* and lasagne. More

PRICE CATEGORIES

€€€€ = €50–120
€€€ = €25–50
€€ = €12–25
€ = Less than €12
Prices are based on an average three-course meal for one.

a part of the youthful Vienna *szene* than a restaurant. €€–€€€

Nordsee
1, Kärntner Strasse 25; also at Kohlmarkt, Naschmarkt and Mariahilfer Strasse
Open daily 9am–9pm
Café-style joint specialising in fresh seafood, including succulent salmon, prepared in a variety of ways. Service is fast and friendly and the locations are well placed whenever you need a quick bite. €–€€

Österreicher im MAK
1, Stubenring 5
Tel: 01-714 0121
Open daily 11.30am–11.30pm
The revamped café and restaurant of the Museum of Applied Arts has been beautifully designed and turns out excellent modern takes on Austrian classic dishes. €€–€€€

Palmenhaus
1, Burggarten
Tel: 01-533 1033
Open daily, food served 10am–11pm
A spectacular *Jugendstil* glass house, now a

restaurant and café. Good modern European dishes and a few Viennese classics.€€

Pfudl
1, Bäckerstrasse 22
Tel: 01-512 6705
Open daily 10am–11.30pm
A rural atmosphere and finely prepared traditional Viennese cuisine, and speedy service. €–€€

Reinthaler
1, Dorotheergasse 4 and 1, Gluckgasse 5
Tel: 01-512 1249/01-512 3366
Open (Dorotheergasse) daily 11am–11pm, (Gluckgasse) Mon–Fri 9am–11pm
Classic city centre *Beisln*, very popular with the Viennese for the hearty portions and quality of the food. €–€€

Rosenberger
1, Maysedergasse 2
Tel: 01-512 3458
Open daily 7.30am–11pm
Popular Innere-Stadt self-service restaurant for salads, soups, juices and coffee. Choose your meal from assorted food stations. €

Schnattl

BELOW: a game motif at Glacis Beisl.

8, Lange Gasse 40
Tel: 01-403 3400
Open Mon–Fri 11.30am–2.30pm, 6–11pm
Superb modern Austrian dishes with fresh and delicate flavours. The interior is a pleasant and airy traditional space and the wines are excellent. €€€

Schweizerhaus
2, Prater 116
Tel: 01-728 0152
Open daily Mar–mid-Nov, 11am–midnight
Huge portions of gut-busting pork served up in a very busy and popular eating house; you can also relax with a draught beer in the tree-shaded garden. €

Silberwirt
5, Schlossgasse 21
Tel: 01-544 4907
Open daily, lunch, dinner–midnight.
Very popular *Beisl* at weekends. Good, traditional dishes at a decent price. €–€€

Stiegen-Beisl
6, Gumpendorfer Strasse 36
Tel: 01-587 0999
Open daily 6pm–1am
Classic Austrian fare in this simple, cosy and comfortable *Beisl*. €–€€

Steiereck im Wien
3, Am Heumarkt 2a
Tel: 01-713 3168
Open (restaurant) Mon–Fri midday–3pm, 7–10pm, (Meierei) Mon–Fri 9am–10pm, Sat 9am–11pm, Sun 9am–7pm
One of Austria's top restaurants, now relocated to a beautifully designed modern building overlooking the Stadtpark. It specialises in creative twists on Austrian classics. For a taster try the cheaper lunch menu, or sample the phenomenal range of cheeses in the Meierei. €€€–€€€€

Trzesniewski
1, Dorotheergasse 1
Tel: 01-512 3291
Open Mon–Fri 8.30am–7.30pm
Featuring the beloved Viennese open-faced sandwich, with toppings such as egg, red onion, salmon or crab. Diners cluster around chest-high

tables and eat standing up; beer is the traditional drink here. €

Weingut Reinprecht
19, Cobenzlgasse 22 (in Grinzing)
Tel: 01-3201 4710
Open daily Mar–Nov, 3.30pm–midnight
Everything that a *Heuriger* should be: excellent local wines, a large and varied buffet including grilled meats, traditional Viennese melodies in the background and a large terraced garden. €–€€

Witwe Bolte
7, Gutenberggasse 13
Tel: 01-523 1450
Open daily 11.30am–midnight
Viennese home cooking in one of the city's oldest and most basic *Beisln*. In the interesting Spittleberg district. €–€€

Wrenkh
1, Rauhensteingasse 12
Tel: 01-513 5836 and Bauernmarkt 10
Tel: 01-533 1526
Open daily 11.30am–midnight
A place for vegetarians and healthy eaters. First-class food, excellent wines and a cosy atmosphere. €€

Zu den 3 Hacken
1, Singerstrasse 28
Tel: 01-512 5895
Open Mon–Sat 9am–midnight, closed public holidays
A good place for lovers of traditional Viennese cuisine. The menu is big, and so are the portions. Very popular with the locals, so advance booking is essential. €–€€

Zu den drei Husaren
1, Weihburggasse 4
Tel: 01-512 1092
Open daily noon–3pm, 6pm–1am
Luxurious meals served by candlelight, complete with waltz music and a stylish interior. The starters and desserts are particularly recommended. €€€€

Zum Altes Fassl
5, Ziegelofengasse 37
Tel: 01-544 4298
Open Sun–Fri 11.30am–3pm, 6pm–1am, Sat 6pm–1am
Beisel featuring al fresco eating in atmospheric

courtyards shaded by enormous chestnut trees. €–€€

Zum Schwarzen Kameel
1, Bognergasse 5
Tel: 01-5338 1250
Open Mon–Sat
8.30am–11.30pm
Delicatessen and art nouveau restaurant that's full of history – Beethoven used to eat here – good for Viennese food. €

Zwölf-Apostel-Keller
1, Sonnenfelsgasse 3
Tel: 01-512 6777
Open daily
4.30pm–midnight, closed July
This well-known city-centre *Heuriger* has an historic wine cellar on two floors, and serves good wines and hot (though average) food. €€

Lower Austria

Joching

Weingut Josef Jamek
Tel: 02715-2235
Open Mon–Thur lunch, Fri and Sat lunch and dinner. Atmospheric restaurant attached to one of Austria's most famous little vineyards. €€–€€€

Kleinwien

Schickh
Klein Wien 2
Tel: 02736-72 180
Intimate venue for hearty food. Open daily for lunch and dinner. €€

Krems

Gasthof Jell
Hoher Markt 8–9
Tel: 02732-83 128
Gourmet restaurant for hearty Austrian fare. Sample some locally produced wine with your meal. €

Nordsee
Obere Landstrasse 20
Tel: 02732-82 045
Chain fish joint, open Mon–Sat; good value. €

Restaurant Gozzoburg
Margarethenstrasse 14
Tel: 02732-85 247
www.gozzoburg-krems.at
Celebrated local restaurant in pretty location. €

Orth an der Donau
Uferhaus
Uferstrasse 20

Tel: 06641-800 322
www.uferhaus.at
A favourite amongst Viennese fish-fanciers, directly on the river. Try the speciality – Serbian-style carp. Open Oct–May

Mautern

Bacher
Südtiroler Platz 2
Tel: 02732-82 937
Open Wed–Sun, lunch, dinner
Chef Lisl Wagner-Bacher shows why she was awarded three tocques in the *Gault-Millau* guide. €€€€

Melk

Hotel-Restaurant Zur Post
Linzer Strasse 1
Tel: 02752-52 345
Posh eatery featuring *haute cuisine* Austrian style. €€€

Restaurant zum "Alten Brauhof"
Linzer Strasse 25
Tel: 02752-52 296
Sit and relax at outdoor tables while savouring heavy *Wienerschnitzel* or fresh greens from the salad bar. €

Burgenland

Eisenstadt

Café Esterházy
Esterházy Platz 5
Tel: 02682-62 819
Smart restaurant with an after-hours bar. €€€

Haydnbräu
Pfarrgasse 22
Tel: 02682-63 945
www.haydnbraeu.at
Try the beer, micro-brewed on site, to go with the basic pub fare. €

Neuseidl am See

Rathausstüberl
Kirchengasse 2
Tel: 02167-2883
Open 10am–10pm
A terrace that's especially pleasant in summer, and a kitchen featuring local fish and wine. €€

Podersdorf

Gasthaus Zur Dankbarkeit
Haupstrasse 39
Tel: 02177-2223
Weekends only in winter
This is a tiny, family-owned place featuring great

ABOVE: eating out in Naschmarkt

Jewish regional cookery. €–€€

Rust

Romerzeche
Rathausplatz 11
Tel: 02685-332
A popular restaurant. Savour goulash for dinner at shared wooden tables in a flowery courtyard. €

Zum Alten Haus
Raiffeisengasse 1
Tel: 02685-230
Well-located restaurant serving *Schnitzel* and other Austrian fare. €

Schützen am Gebirge

Taubenkobel
Hauptstrasse 33
Tel: 02684-2297
Open Wed–Sun lunch and dinner
Good for local fish, lamb and vegetable dishes. €€€–€€€€

Weiden am See

Blaue Gans
Seepark
Tel: 02167-7510
Closed winter. Fine Alsatian cuisine a long way from Alsace. €€€–€€€€

Styria

Graz

Café Erzherzog Johann
Sackstrasse 3-5
Tel: 0316-811 616
Viennese-style coffee

house, serving pastries and snacks. €€€

Mangolds
Griesgasse 11
Tel: 0316-718 002
Open Mon–Fri 11am–8pm; Sat 11am–4pm.
Vegetarian self-service. €

Stainzerbauer
Bürgergasse 4
Tel: 0316-821 106
www.stainzerbauer.at
One of the oldest restaurants in Graz. Local Styrian cooking, served in a Renaissance courtyard.

Mariazell

Gasthof zum Jägerwirt
Hauptplatz 2
Tel: 03882-2362
Traditional Austrian restaurant, good for meat-based dishes. €€

Upper Austria

Freistadt

Café Vis à Vis
Salzgasse 13
Tel: 07942-74 293
Jovial beer garden for hearty, local fare such as "farmer's soup". €€€

PRICE CATEGORIES

€€€€ = €50–120
€€€ = €25–50
€€ = €12–25
€ = Less than €12
Prices are based on an average three-course meal for one.

Goldener Adler
Salzgase 1
Tel: 07942-72 112
Good-value hotel
restaurant; standard main
dishes, great desserts.

Linz

Gelbes Krokodil
Dametzstrasse 30
Tel: 070-784 182
Open Mon–Fri 11am–1am
Sat–Sun 5pm–1am
Eclectic dining at this
everything-under-one-roof
entertainment/dining
complex in the Moviemento
Cinema. Varied menu
(including lots of vegetarian
options) can be savoured
while watching an avant-
garde film. €€
Mangolds
Hauptplatz 3
Tel: 0732-785 688
Popular, self-service
vegetarian cafeteria. Most
of the food is organic,
including the eggs. Juices
and salad-bar offerings are
the stars. €€
Ursulinenhof
Landstrasse 31
Tel: 0732-774 686
Open Mon–Sat lunch,
dinner
Exquisite, creative cuisine,
bland interior. €€€

Steyr

Zu den drei Rosen
Hotel Mader Stadtplatz 36
Tel: 07252-533 580
Closed Sunday
Local cuisine served on the
sunny terrace in a
venerable restaurant
attached to a posh hotel.
Good Tagesmenü (daily
special). €€€

The Salzkammergut

Bad Ischl

**Restaurant Goldenes
Schiff**
Stifter-kai 3
Tel: 06132-24 241
Excellent restaurant
specialising in locally
caught fish dishes. Sit on
the terrace in sunny
weather. €€–€€€
**Wirsthaus zum Blauen
Enzian**
Salinenplatz
Tel: 06132-28 992
Upmarket restaurant
serving a variety of pastas

and salads. €€€
Café Zauner
Pfarrgasse 7
Tel: 06132-233 1020
Open daily
8.30am–6.00pm
You'd be remiss to pass
through Bad Ischl without
trying one (or two) of the
delectable pastries on offer
at this venerable café. Also
hot dishes and salads
served on the river terrace
at the Esplanade location. €

Hallstatt

Gasthof Zur Mühle
Kirchenweg 36
Tel: 06134-8318
Good-value eatery in a
guesthouse. Try the pizza –
the cheapest meal in this
tourist town. €

Mondsee

Café-Restaurant Lido
Robert Baum Promenade
Tel: 06232-3370
Open for lunch, dinner until
10pm
Good place for dependable
favourites such as boiled
beef and Wienerschnitzel.
Savour an ice cream on the
serene lakeside terrace.
€€€
Pizzeria Nudelini
Marktplatz 5
Tel: 06232-4193
Pizzas and salads in a
central location. €€
La Farandole
Schlössl 150/Tiefgraben
Tel: 06232-3475
You'll be well cared for at
this gourmet establishment
that specialises in its own
Austrian, French and Swiss
dishes. €€€€

St Gilgen

Gasthof Kendler
Kirchenplatz 3
Tel: 06227-2223
Fresh cuts of meat grace
the menu at this welcoming
guesthouse. Vegetarians
can opt for standards such
as spinach dumplings.
€–€€

St Wolfgang

Pizzeria Mirabella
Pilgerstrasse 152
Tel: 06138-2353
Basic pizza parlour with a
menu that includes pastas.
Good value in a very
touristy location. €€

Salzburg (City)

Augustiner Bräu
Kloster Mülln
Augustinergasse 4
Tel: 0662-431 246
Open Mon–Fri 3–11pm,
Sat, Sun, holidays
2.30–11pm
Huge beer hall with outdoor
garden that becomes very
rowdy at weekends.
Choose Austrian dishes
from self-service counter.
€–€€
Café Bazar
Schwarzstrasse 3
Tel: 0662-874 278
Open Mon–Sat
7.30am–11pm Charming
café on Salzach River with
terrace overlooking
Altstadt. A cup of coffee
entitles you to an afternoon
of people watching. €€
Goldener Hirsch
Getreidegasse 37
Tel: 0662-80 840
Elegant hotel restaurant
featuring fine Austrian
cuisine. €€€–€€€€
Nordsee
Getreidegasse 27
Tel: 0662-842 320
Open Mon–Sun 9am–8pm
Good, quick seafood meals
for those who need to
maximise sightseeing time.
€–€€
Zum Fidelen Affen
Priesterhausgasse 8
Tel: 0662-877 361
Open Mon–Sat 5pm–
1am
Pub in heart of Linzergasse
district with convivial
atmosphere, outdoor
seating and efficient
service. Serves hearty
dishes such as
Hungarian goulash and
Wienerschnitzel. €–€€

Salzburg Province

Zell Am See

Moby Dick
Kreuzgasse 16
Tel: 06542-73 320
Open Mon–Fri 9am–6pm,
Sat 8am–1pm
Fish (some from the
adjoining lake) dominates a
simple but satisfying menu
at this unpretentious
restaurant. €
Schloss Prielau
Hofmannsthalstrasse
Tel: 06542-729 110

Dine like royalty in this
castle, where the menu
specialises in traditional
Austrian fare. Some non-
smoking dining rooms;
reservations
recommended. €€€
Zum Hirschen
Dreifaltigkeitsgasse 1
Tel: 06542-7740
Hotel restaurant
demonstrating a light touch
with the local specialities.
€€

Carinthia and East Tyrol

Klagenfurt

Da Luigi
Khevenhüllerstrasse 2
Tel: 0463-516 651
Open Mon 6–10pm,
Tues–Sat 11.30am–2pm
6–10pm
An Italian restaurant with
the emphasis on fresh
produce. Particularly
recommended for its
seafood. €€€
Dolce Vita
Heuplatz 2
Tel: 0463-55 499
Closed Sat and Sun
Small but highly rated
Italian restaurant.
€€–€€€
Maria Loretto
Lorettoweg 54
Tel: 0463-24 465
About 5 km (3 miles)
west of Klagenfurt, the
Maria Loretto is right
on the edge of the lake
and has a balcony, terrace
and garden, with lovely
views over the water.
The emphasis is on fish,
but there is a range of
Austrian and international
dishes. €€–€€€

Kötschach-Mauthen

Restaurant Kellerwand
Tel: 04715-269
A gourmet restaurant
listed among the country's
best eating establishments
– proprietor Sissy
Sonnleitner has picked up
numerous national awards.
€€€€

Lienz

Gästhof Neuwirt
Schweizergasse 22
Tel: 04852-62 101
Tyrolean restaurant known
for its fish dishes. €€€

Matrei

Restaurant-Hotel Rauter
Rauterplatz 3
Tel: 04875-6611
Well-prepared Austrian
cuisine for the hungry
hiker. €€

Villach

Restaurant Mosser
Bahnhofstrasse 9
Tel: 04242-24 115
Located in Hotel Mosser,
this restaurant offers
no surprises on the
schnitzel-heavy menu.
Good, simple fare.
€€

Tyrol

Innsbruck

Alstadtstüberl
Riesengasse 13
Tel: 0512-582 347
Open Mon–Sat, lunch,
dinner
In a busy pedestrian
area, this restaurant
serves filling Tyrolean
meals such as *Tiroler
Gröstl* and tender
Tafelspitz. €€€

Philippine
Müllerstrasse 9
Tel: 0512-589 157
Open Mon–Sat, lunch &
dinner
An oasis for vegetarians
with an innovative menu
that's not restricted to
Filipino cuisine, despite
the name. €€

Stiftskeller
Burggraben 31
Tel: 0512-583 490
Good for fish, especially
trout. Quiet, affordable
restaurant in the centre
of the tourist area near
Hofburg. €€

Thai-Li
Marktgraben 3
Tel: 0512-562 813
Book early for this
exceptional Thai restaurant
featuring favourites such
as green curries and *pad
Thai*. A refreshing change
from heavy Tyrolean fare.
€€–€€€

Kitzbühel

Chizzo
Josef-Herold Strasse 2
Tel: 05356-62 475
Good selection of Tyrolean
cuisine. Attractive seating
outside. €€

Vorarlberg

Bregenz

**Restaurant Deuring-
Schlössle**
Tel: 05574-47 800
One of the classiest
restaurants in Bregenz,
ideal for those who have an
expansive budget. €€€

Zum Goldenen Hirschen
Tel: 05574-42 815
Open 10am–midnight
(closed Tues)
Homely Austrian pub
serving local favourites as
well as Austrian takes on
international classics such
as chili con carne. €€

Feldkirch

Restaurant-Gasthof Löwen
Dortstrasse 28
Tel: 05522-38 005
Restaurant affiliated to a
hotel, featuring solid
Austrian fare. €€€

**Pizzeria-Trattoria La
Taverna**
Vorstadtstrasse 18
Tel: 05522-79 293
Open daily 11.30am–2pm,
5pm–midnight
Typical Italian pizza and
pasta with some choice for
vegetarians. €€

Lech am Arlberg

Charly's Cantina
Tel: 05583-2339
Open daily 11am–2pm,
4pm–midnight, closed June
Popular with skiiers and
others for Tex Mex
highlights. €

Restaurant-Hotel Krone
Tel: 05583-2551
Reservations
recommended at this
classy *après-ski* eatery.

DRINKING NOTES

Austria has a long tradition
of viticulture. The Romans
tended vineyards in the old
region of Vindobona, a
tradition re-established by
local monasteries 1,000
years later. More than a
third of the total area used
for the cultivation of grapes
is devoted to the tangy and
slightly peppery Grüner
Veltliner. Blaufränkische, a
hearty, fruity red wine, is
also very popular. Wine in

ABOVE: a table at Gasthous Wild.

Austria is separated into
four categories: *Landwein*
(table wine), *Qualitätswein*
(wine of certified origin and
quality), *Kabinettwein* (high-
quality white) and
Prädikatswein (special
quality).

Vineyards are primarily
cultivated in four provinces:
Vienna, Lower Austria,
Burgenland and Styria. In
most vineyard areas you
can pay a visit to one of the
wine cellars for a little
sampling. Or, better still, sit
out in the open, under the
shade of old trees and
have the wine-grower
himself serve you a glass.

For further details of
wine in Austria, contact
your nearest tourist office
(see page 307).

White Wine

Riesling – a lively, piquant
wine with a flowery
bouquet; grown in Wachau.
Grüner Veltliner – full-
bodied, fruity and piquant;
produced in Lower Austria
and Burgenland.
Traminer – aromatic.
Zierfandler – a rich
bouquet.

Müller-Thurgau – light and
sweet with a flowery
bouquet.
Welschriesling – finely full-
bodied; from Burgenland
and Styria.
Weisser Burgunder – a
nutty bouquet.
Neuburger – full and
hearty; grown in Lower
Austria and Burgenland.

Red Wine

Zweigelt blau – fine and
fruity.
Blauer Portugieser – mild;
produced in Lower Austria.
Blauer Burgunder – fiery,
with a nutty bouquet; found
in Lower Austria and
Burgenland.
Schilcher – fruity and
sharp; the Styrian
speciality, produced in the
western region of the
province.

PRICE CATEGORIES

€€€€ = €50–120
€€€ = €25–50
€€ = €12–25
€ = Less than €12
Prices are based on an
average three-course meal
for one.

A CTIVITIES

MUSIC, NIGHTLIFE, WINTER SPORTS, SUMMER SPORTS AND SHOPPING

THE ARTS

Music

Vienna

Klangforum Wien, www.klangforum.at
Klangforum are Vienna's top
contemporary music ensemble,
giving always exciting, and often
unusual, concerts.
Musikverein, www.musikverein.at
The city's premier, gilt-encrusted,
concert hall *(see page 137)*.
Radio Symphonieorchester Wien,
www.rso-wien.orf.at
The very accomplished orchestra of
the state broadcaster, ÖRF.
Wiener Konzerthaus, www.konzerthaus.at
A complex of three concert halls,
with varied and exciting programming.
Wiener Philharmoniker,
www.wienerphilharmoniker.at
Quite simply, one of the world's
greatest orchestras, with an
illustrious history *(see their website
for more details)*.
Wiener Staatsoper,
www.wiener-staatsoper.at
One of the world's top opera houses,
for which, fittingly, the Wiener
Philharmoniker is the orchestra.
Wiener Symphoniker,
www.wiener-symphoniker.at
The rival to the Philharmoniker, the
Wiener Symphoniker is an
exceptional ensemble.
Volksoper, www.volksoper.at
The city's second opera house, with
a reputation for daring and innovative
productions.

Graz

Grazer Oper, www.buehnen-graz.com/oper
The city's opera house has an
excellent reputation, putting on
sparkling performances of standard
repertory and more unusual works.

Linz

Brucknerhaus, www.brucknerhaus.linz.at
This superb modern concert hall
holds concerts throughout the year.
Bruckner Orchester,
www.bruckner-orchester.at
The city's resident orchestra is the
star of the annual Brucknerfest.

Festivals

Vienna

Donauinselfest
Summers see the Donauinsel play
host to up to 500,000 revellers at
one of the largest free concert
events in Europe.
**Summer Fesival in Schönbrunn
Palace Theatre** (Sommerspiele im
Schönbrunner Schlosstheater),
1, Fleischmarkt 24, tel: 01-512
0100, www.wienerkammeroper.at
Mid-July–mid-August.
Vienna Easter and Summer Music
(Osterklang and Klangbogen),
6, Linke Wienzeile 6, tel: 01-5883
0660, www.theater-wien.at
Orchestral works, chamber music
and opera. Easter and mid-July–
mid-August.
Vienna Festival
(Wiener Festwochen),
6, Lehargasse 11, tel: 01-589 2222,
www.festwochen.at
A key event on the music scene:
orchestras, opera and dance
companies from around the world
converge on the city for a month of
performances. Mid-May–mid-June.
Viennale Film Festival,
7, Siebensterngasse 2,
tel: 01-526 5947,
www.viennale.at
Two weeks from mid-October.

Lower Austria

Baden Summer Operettas (Badener
Operettensommer), Stadttheater

Baden, tel: 02252-48547,
www.stadttheater-baden.at
Mid-June–early September.
Midsummer's Night,
Wachau region, tel: 02713-300
6060, email: urlaub@donau.com
Bonfires and dances celebrating the
summer solstice. Late June.

Burgenland

Haydn Festival (Haydn Festspiele),
Eisenstadt (Schloss Esterházy),
tel: 02682-61 866, email:
office@haydnfestival.at,
www.haydnfestival.at
Second week of September.
Mörbisch Lakeside Festival
(Seefestspiele Mörbisch), Mörbisch,
tel: 02685-8181, www.seefestspiele-
moerbisch.at
Operettas on a stage built out over
the Neusiedler See, with each
performance ending in a firework
display over the water. Mid-July–
late August.
St Margarethen Summer Opera
Staged in an atmospheric Roman
quarry. Every five years they stage a
Passion Play.
St Martin's Day
Day of feasting and drinking to
honour the patron saint of pubs
and inns; roasted goose, red
cabbage and plenty of spirits. 11
November.
Thousand Wine Festival, Eisenstadt
Vintners from around Burgenland
congregate here to offer wines of the
region. Late August.
www.burgenlandische-weinwoche.at

Styria

Feast of St Barbara, Leoben
Processions, ballads, dancers and
church services honouring the patron
saint of miners. Mid-December.
Mid Europe, Schladming,
tel: 07753-2645,

www.mideurope.com
Courses and concerts. August.
Styriarte Graz, Graz
tel: 0316-825 000,
www.styriarte.com
A summer festival of music in Graz
founded in 1985. Early June–end
July.
La Strada
www.lastrada.at
Annual festival of street theatre for
all the family, with musicians and
performance artists. First week of
August.

Upper Austria
International Brucknerfest,
Linz, tel: 0732-775230,
www.brucknerhaus.linz.at
A celebration of Bruckner's music.
Last three weeks of September.
Operetta Festival (Operettenwochen
Bad Ischl),
Bad Ischl, tel: 06132-23 839,
www.leharfestival.at
July–early September.
Upper Austrian Monastery Concerts
(OÖ Stiftskonzerte),
Linz, tel: 0732-776 127,
www.stiftskonzerte.at June–July

Salzkammergut
Corpus Christi, Hallstatt. Also in
Lungau (Salzburg Province).
Processions of firemen, pensioners,
women wearing garlands, and flowery
boats on the lake, combined with
much singing. Early June.

Salzburg and Salzburg Province
Mozart Dinner Concerts (Mozart
Serenaden), Salzburg, tel: 0662-436
870 or 828 695
Candlelight concerts. Easter to the
end of the year.
Mozart Week (Mozart-Woche),
Salzburg, tel: 0662-873 154,
www.mozarteum.at
Major orchestras and chamber music
groups play Mozart favourites and
less well-known works. Fourth week
of January.
Perchtenlauf, St Johann im Pongau
Townsmen dress as spirits and
parade through town, blessing
houses as they go. Early January.
Salzburg Culture Days (Salzburger
Kulturtage), Salzburg, tel: 0662-845
346 Last 2 weeks of October.
Salzburg Festival (Salzburger
Festspiele), Salzburg, tel: 0662-804
5500, www.salzburgfestival.at
The world-famous annual tribute to
Mozart in his home town, when
music lovers from all over the world
come to celebrate. Mid-July–August.
Salzburg Fortress Concerts
(Salzburger Festungskonzerte),
Salzburg, tel: 0662-825 858
Chamber concerts are held in the

Salzburg Fortress. Year-round.
Salzburg Palace Concerts
(Salzburger Schlosskonzerte),
Salzburg, tel: 0662-848 5860,
www.salzburger-schlosskonzerte.at
All year round, chamber concerts are
held in Schloss Mirabell.

Carinthia
Carinthian Summer (Carinthischer
Sommer), Ossiach, tel: 04243-2510,
www.carinthischersommer.at
July–August.
International Music in Millstatt
(Internationale Musikwochen in
Millstatt), Millstatt,
tel: 04766-202 235,
www.musikwochen.at
May–October.
Villach Kirchtag, Villach
Annual birthday party for the village
turns into a night of non-stop drinking
and revelry. Early August.

Tyrol
Alpabtrieb, Zell am Ziller
Merriment to mark the moving of
local cattle to lower pastures. Early
October.
Ambras Palace Concerts (Ambraser
Schlosskonzerte), Innsbruck, tel:
0521-571 032, www.altemusik.at
July–early August.
Hahnenkamm Ski Race, Kitzbühel
Famous ski race on frighteningly
steep downhill course. January.
Innsbruck Festival of Early Music,
www.altemusik.at
Famous musicians congregate for a
week of authentic performance.
August.
**International Summer Dance
Festival**, Innsbruck
Virtuoso dancers of various styles
from around the world converge for
two weeks of performance. Early July.

Vorarlberg
Bregenz Festival (Bregenzer
Festspiele), Bregenz, tel: 05574-
4076, www.bregenzerfestspiele.com
A major opera production, symphony
and chamber concerts, and lavish
theatrical productions. Mid-July–mid-
August.
Schubertiade, Schwarzenberg,
tel: 05576-72 091, www.schubertiade.at
Prestigious chamber music festival.
June and late August.

Theatre

For the non-German speaker,
Viennese theatre will have limited
appeal. However, there are a few
English-speaking theatre groups, and
the Burgtheater is worth visiting for
its splendid interior.
Burgtheater
1, Dr-Karl-Lueger-Ring 2,

tel: 01-5144 44440
Vienna's most prestigious theatre,
staging serious drama. Spectacular
foyer and staircases.
International Theatre
9, Porzellangasse 8,
tel: 01-319 6272
This is where expats put on plays,
both on the main stage and in the
smaller, more intimate room
downstairs.
Vienna's English Theatre
8, Josefsgasse 12,
tel: 01-4021 2600, www.englishtheatre.at
The well-established English Theatre
(founded in 1963) attracts visiting
groups from the UK and the US, as
well as putting on its own shows.

Cinema

In Vienna, several cinemas screen
films in English. The website www.film.at
gives current listings – click the "OV"
box for English-language versions.
These are some of the best venues:
Artis Kino-Treff, 1, Schultergasse/
Jordangasse, tel: 01-535 6673
With six screens, a bar, and plenty of
seating, showing mainstream hit
films in their original English.
Breitenseer Lichtspiele
14, Breitenseerstrasse 21
tel: 01-982 2173
Opened in 1909, this is one of the
oldest cinemas in the world, as the
wooden seats testify. Screens
English films with subtitles.
Burgkino
1, Opernring 19, tel: 01-587 8406,
www.burgkino.at
Cosy, centrally-located cinema with a
small café downstairs. The place to
see The Third Man (again). It has
screened it on a regular basis for
more than a quarter of a century.
Haydn English Cinema
6, Mariahilfer Strasse 57
tel: 01-587 2262
Set on the city's main shopping
street, here you can see mainstream
Hollywood and British films in its
three rooms.
  There are also cinemas in
Salzburg (Daskino) and Innsbruck
(Metropol) that regularly show films
in English.

NIGHTLIFE

Vienna's club scene is rather
limited but there are plenty of
late-night drinking spots, mainly
concentrated in the centre and in
the area between Karlsplatz and
Naschmarkt. The majority of the
city's clubs are bars which
sometimes have live bands.

Elsewhere in Austria, nightlife is rather more subdued. To find out what's going on locally, ask at the tourist office.

Vienna
B72
8, Hernalser Gürtel
Stadtbahnbögen 72–3
tel: 01-409 2128
Anything from live local indie talent to drum 'n' bass or soul DJs, all happening under a railway arch.
First Floor
1, Seitenstättengasse 5
tel: 01-533 7866
An interesting mix of aquariums and 1930s fittings attracts a well-dressed, affluent crowd.
Flex
Am Donaukanal, Abgang Augartenbrücke
tel: 01-533 7525, www.flex.at
Vienna's largest, and possibly most happening club, in a great position by the Donaukanal.
Jazzland
1, Franz Josephs-Kai 29
tel: 01-533 2575
Vienna's main trad-jazz venue.
rhiz
8, Lerchenfelder Gürtel
Gürtolbögen 37–8
tel: 01-409 2505
Cutting-edge club also offering multimedia events such as book readings.
Volksgarten
1, Burgring 1
tel: 01-532 0907
Well-established club; varied mix of soul, funk, hip-hop and house; for young people
Wirr
7, Burggasse 70
tel: 01-524 6825
Herbal tea and food on the ground floor; lounge music and a very alternative crowd downstairs.

Graz
Bier Baron
Heinrichstrasse 56
A large "pub" serving German, Austrian and Czech beer on tap.
3 Monkeys
Elisabethstrasse 31
Wild cellar hangout for the local student crowd, playing dance music.
Miles Jazz-Club
Mariahilferstrasse 24
Cosy cellar club with live music and friendly atmosphere

Linz
Aquarium
Altstadt 22
Lively late-night bar.
Posthof

Environmental Impacts

Skiing is in danger of becoming a victim of its own popularity and visitors should be aware of its impact on the mountian environment. Slopes are artificaly graded; ski edges destroy underlying flora (which leads to both a degradation of the biodiversity and increases erosion); wildfe is disturbed by the huge influx of visitors; resorts are developing at ever higher altitudes and environments become increasingly fragile the higher you go; snow machines use chemicals and deplete water supplies (the increased snow melt also heightens erosion); there is a huge amount of littering which remains for years on the slopes; flying adds greatly to global warming; and, while some money does enter the local economy the jobs created are temporary and many are taken by itinerant workers rather than locals. There is also a trend for rich foreigners to buy up chalets, which would otherwise have been used by local people, that are only in use during the ski season. Last but not least, ski lifts litter the mountain slopes and impact greatly on the visual beauty of the area.

A number of organisations can help you book through responsible tour operators, which aim to limit their impact on the environment (*see* www.responsibletravel.com; www.tourismconcern.org.uk; and www.skiclub.co.uk). Certain measures are a matter of common sense: don't fly but take the train to the ski area you are staying in; avoid resorts that use snow machines; don't throw litter (and pick up any you see); don't ski off-piste; and stay and eat in locally owned and staffed hotels and restaurants.

Posthofstrasse 43
Live music and dance DJs at trendy arts centre.

Salzburg
Rock House
Schallmooser Hauptstrasse 46
Club nights and touring bands.

Klagenfurt
Fun Factory
Südring-Gerberweg 46
Club with predominantly techno sounds, plus occasional theme nights.

Innsbruck
Innkeller
Innstrasse 1
Bar on the west bank of the river with a young crowd and good, up-to-date music.

WINTER SPORTS

Skiing

Austria is the home of modern skiing. At the beginning of the 20th century, in the little village of Lilienfeld in Lower Austria, the ski pioneer Matthias Zdarski invented the now world-famous stem turn which even today causes every fledgling skier so many problems.

Since then Austria has become one of the finest winter sports centres in the world. The resorts are strung out like pearls on a necklace right across the Alps: Lech am Arlberg, St Anton, Innsbruck, Kitzbühel, Saalbach, Obertauern, Schladming. Only Switzerland can look back on a similarly long tradition of winter sports. But in Austria, skiing is not just a winter sport. The country possesses the greatest density of all-year-round glacial ski regions. Areas like the Dachstein, the Kaunertal, the Pitztal or the Mölltal offer skiing with all amenities whatever the weather. It is possible to ski in a swimming costume in the summer.

In 2000, in Kitzbühel, aficionados celebrated the 60th anniversary of the notorious Hahnenkamm downhill race on the Streif Run, the most difficult and dangerous descent in the world. In skiing circles a victory in this race is more prestigious than a gold medal in the world championships. All great downhill skiers have stood on the starting line at the top of the run, which is over 2 km (1½ miles) long.

The winners' names have gone down in the annals of skiing history: Toni Sailer, the first man to win a gold medal in all three Alpine ski disciplines, Karl Schranz, the Austrian downhill champion of the 1960s, and the Olympic medallist from Carinthia, Franz "The Emperor" Klammer, who once completed the course just one-thousandth of a second faster than the famous Italian skier, Gustav Thoeni.

During the past decade, off-piste skiing in powder snow has become increasingly popular in Austria. Ski touring was for many years treated with derision as the hobby of a handful of extremists; but today it is definitely considered one of the most exciting winter sports. However, its environmental impact is extremely damaging. It should always be undertaken in the company of experienced guides; in view of the high risk of avalanches in the Austrian mountains, it would be extremely dangerous to venture out without their help.

The Dachstein offers the country's best off-piste skiing (see below). Remember that, to avoid damaging young saplings when skiing in this fashion, try not to use the sides of your skis more than necessary. Trees in the central Alps are of vital importance; they provide avalanche protection in winter and prevent mountainslides and mudflows in summer. Austria claims the highest number of deaths from avalanches in the world.

Snowboarding and "rafting"

During the past few years the innovative branch of the ski industry has invented a number of demanding alternatives to alpine skiing.

The fun element is undoubtedly greater in the case of the snowboard. Wearing normal mountain boots, one stands in overshoes which are mounted directly on the snowboard. Centrifugal force enables the expert snowboarder to take spectacular curves, braking with fists; on humpbacked slopes even leaps in the air. Both items of equipment are suitable for beginners. For some years now, virtually all Austrian ski schools have offered courses in snowboarding, and an increasing number of resorts are installing half-pipe runs (grooved trails specifically for snowboarders) to capture the young market segment that craves the sport.

It's interesting to note the trend towards more exotic and dangerous outdoor sports. Specialists such as the Dachstein-Tauern Region Adventure Club have abandoned alpine skiing altogether. Apart from the snow sports mentioned above they also provide an introduction to snow rafting, in which the boldest sports enthusiasts hurtle down the pistes in huge inflatable rafting boats. The descent takes place at breakneck speed, but unfortunately there is absolutely no way of steering the snow raft. Every excursion inevitably ends with a tumble. Canyoning, equally foolhardy (see page 302) is one of the more recent thrills to have been adopted.

Ski Resort Areas

People don't only come to Austria just for conventional skiing these days. In addition to "just skiing", they come to go tobogganing, bobsledding, cross-country skiing, curling, and to take classes to learn how to manage a snowboard at one of the 190 snow resort areas. Tourist information centres can provide you with further information.

Salzburg Province
Bad Gastein (51 lifts, 200 km/125 miles of piste)
Spa town with a surprising range of long-run pistes and expert slopes.
Obertauern (26 lifts, 150 km/93 miles of piste)
Block of holiday flats built to take advantage of reliable snow high atop Tauern pass; most runs are short and of medium difficulty. Cross-country sking as well.
Saalbach-Hinterglemm (60 lifts, 200 km/125 miles of piste)
Many types of piste and good snow in a rustic setting; plenty of tracks.
Saalfelden (5 lifts, 14 km/8 miles of piste)
Favoured as a cross-country ski resort possessing some 80 km (50 miles) of track.
St Michael in Lungau (11 lifts, 60 km/38 miles of piste)
Modern resort near foot of Katschberg mountain and tunnel towards Italy.
West Dachstein/Tennengau (61 lifts, 195 km/122 miles of piste)
Series of resorts including St Martin and Annaberg. More than 200 km (125 miles) of cross-country tracks as well.
Zell am See-Kaprun (55 lifts, 130 km/80 miles of piste)
Beautiful lake town featuring steep and intermediate runs.

Tyrol
Innsbruck/Igls (7 lifts, 25 km/

15 miles of piste)
Really more of a hiking destination, but a few lovely runs here as well.
Kitzbühel (60 lifts, 158 km/98 miles of piste)
Attractive and popular resort town with much to do off the mountain; range of medium pistes. Not the most difficult skiing.
Neustift (28 lifts, 68 km/42 miles of piste)
Rustic village in Stubai Valley; famous for glacier skiing through to summer. Snowboarding also popular.
St Anton am Arlberg (37 lifts, 260 km/160 miles of piste)
World-famous resort; excellent après-ski, annual World Cup event, and some rather expert pistes.
St Johann in Tirol (18 lifts, 60 km/38 miles of piste)
Pretty village with ski and snowboard schools and lively nightlife. Not the most difficult pistes.
Seefeld in Tirol (14 lifts, 25 km/15 miles of piste)
More notable as a cross-country ski destination, with more than 100 km (62 miles) of track.

Vorarlberg
Lech am Arlberg (85 lifts, 260 km/160 miles of piste)
Pretty, expensive resort of medium-difficulty skiing; backcountry routes as well. Famous après-ski scene.
Zürs (29 lifts, 110 km/68 miles of piste)
Chic resort for jet-setters only; quite remote, above Flexenpass road from the Bodensee. Lively at night.

Summer Skiing
Styria
Dachsteingletscher, 2,300–2,700 metres (7,545–8,860 ft)
tel: 03687-81241
www.planai.at
Salzburg Province
Kitzsteinhorn, 2,450–3,030 metres

Off-Piste Skiing in Dachstein

Austria's best – and perhaps most challenging – off-piste skiing (though see the box opposite on its environment impact) is probably in the Dachstein, and it should only be attempted by seasoned skiers.

Take the first cable-car of the day up to the Dachstein glacier, as it is a long haul to reach the starting point. At the top trudge uphill through deep snow for over an hour to a snowy gully just 100 metres (320 ft) below the Dachstein peak. The incline is steeper than 60 percent, and a mixture of deep

drifts of powder snow and ice. The gully is about 50 metres (160 ft) wide, bordered by high walls of rock and littered with jagged rocky outcrops and ridges.

Lean backwards as far as possible, and making short, rapid swings to left and right in order not to gain too much speed. Usually one guide leads the group whilst a second brings up the rear, ready to assist those who need help. The deep-snow will last all of 10 minutes, during which you may often sink up to your neck.

(8,040–9,940 ft)
tel: 06547-8700/8621

Carinthia
Mölltaler Glacier, 2,700–3,100
metres (8,860–10,170 ft)
tel: 04785-8110

Tyrol
Kaunertal, 2,750–3,100 metres
(9,020–10,170 ft)
tel: 05475-5566
Pitztaler Glacier, 2,840–3,440
metres (9,315–11,282 ft)
tel: 05413-86288
Ötztaler Glacier, 2,800–3,200
metres (9,185–10,500 ft)
tel: 05254-508
Stubaier Glacier, 2,600–3,200
metres (8,530–10,500 ft)
tel: 05226-8141/8151

On the Ice
Austria has a long history of skating.
Skating rinks such as Engelmann, or
the Stadhalle or the Southern Ice
Rink in Vienna or the stadia in Graz,
Klagenfurt or Villach, are well
patronised during the winter months.
But Austria's lakes provide the most
exciting skating to be had.
When there is a hard frost
Neusiedler See is transformed into a
huge ice-sheet, frozen to a depth of
several metres and offering an area
of almost 40 sq km (15 sq miles) for
skating and other ice sports. From
the end of December until the
beginning of February you can usually
skate across the lake from Pamhagen
to Rust. Neusiedler See also serves
as the national centre for ice-sailing.
Although they are fragile vessels
weighing only a few kilograms and
supported on blades, ice yachts can
reach top speeds of more than 80 km
(50 miles) an hour in a good wind,
which makes them faster than any
other form of sailing boat. Ice-sailing
requires a high degree of technical
proficiency as a sailor. The sport is
not without hazard for participants;
dangers include sudden gusts of wind
and a capsize if the ice sheet
suddenly gives way.
Once a year the Weissensee in
Carinthia is transformed into the
setting for the Carinthian Ice
Marathon, during which skaters must
complete a course of over 200 km
(125 miles) on ice.
South of the main Alpine ridge, ice
hockey is the most popular sport.
The matches of KAC (Klagenfurt) and
their perpetual challengers from
Villach always attract large crowds.
Anyone and everyone can try
their skill at curling. This sport has
many thousands of enthusiasts,
especially in the western provinces

of Austria. There are two kinds of
curling: firstly, long-distance curling,
in which the aim is to slide the
curling stone – a metal plate
weighing some 5 kg (11 lbs) with a
handle – as far as possible across
the ice. The present world record is
held by an Austrian, who achieved a
distance of over 200 metres (650
ft). In the more sophisticated
version of the game the curling
stone must be placed as close as
possible to the tee. In winter the
Sunday curling match is one of the
highlights of the week. Most tourist-
oriented villages have a curling pitch
where visitors may join in.
Much smaller, and therefore more
exclusive, is Austria's circle of
bobbers. Nonetheless, the Austrians
often occupy top places in the world
rankings. The real heroes of
Innsbruck are, however, the skeleton
riders. The steep walls of the
Innsbruck run result in record times.
The public particularly appreciates
races on natural toboggan runs,
which are usually narrow defiles or
forest tracks with an artificial surface
of ice. Here the sledges achieve top
speeds of over 60 km (38 miles) per
hour. Throughout Austria, sledging is
a popular alternative to skiing as well
as a much-loved après-ski pastime.
Many an evening of merrymaking in
one of the numerous ski huts
culminates in a toboggan ride by
torchlight along woodland paths to
the valley.
One of the newest winter sport
trends, dog sledging imported from
Canada and the US, has become one
of the most popular spectator sports
in Austria. The country's mushers are
some of the continent's best. Horst
Maas, the sportsman-adventurer
from Linz, was the first man to cross
the Himalayas with a dog sledge and
also one of the few European dog
sledgers to take part in the notorious
Iditarod race in Alaska.

SUMMER SPORTS

Besides the obvious national pastime
of skiing, Austria offers a huge
variety of outdoor activities, from
hiking in the Alps to the latest white-
knuckle adventure pursuits. The
listings below are a selection of what
is available around the country, with
contact details of specialist
operators and agencies.

Balloon Trips
Balloons have long been a popular
way to see Austria. Some of the
balloon companies include:

**Helmut Tucek Balloon & Airship
Company**
5360 St Wolfgang
tel: 06138-3027
www.freiheit.at
Dachstein Tauern
8972 Ramsau a. D.
tel: 03687-80863
www.dachstein-tauern-balloons.at
Othmar Pircher Balloonfahrten
6952 Tlittis
tel: 05513-6374
www.heissluft.at

Bicycle Tours
The Burgenland, Austria's
easternmost province, is the ideal
setting for a cycling tour. The region
offers a well-developed network of
cycle tracks with inns and service
stations offering special services for
cyclists. Well-maintained tracks also
run along the Danube, from the
Strudengau in Upper Austria, and
through the Wachau – Austria's
most famous wine-growing area – to
Vienna. In Upper Austria cycling
tours are organised whereby
luggage is transported to the next
overnight stop whilst the visitors
cycle unencumbered along the
Danube valley.
The mountain-bike boom has
taken Austria by storm. There are
plenty of opportunities for mountain
biking in all regions of Austria,
although the owners of some private
woods have banned bikes; in the
province of Salzburg, on the other
hand, many forest tracks and paths
have been made available. Their use
is permitted in most woods
managed by the Federal Forestry
Commission.
The Austrian Federal Railway has
bicycles to rent at various railway
stations; they can then be returned
to any station. The rental price is
reduced by 50 percent if you've
arrived by train. Contact the Austrian
National Tourism Office for further
inforrmation and a brochure
on cycling. The most popular
trails include:
Danube Bicycle Route: Passau-
Vienna, 300 km (186 miles). Classic
riverside trail, framed by castles and
vineyards.
Neusiedlersee Bicycle Route:
Mörbisch-Rust-Neusiedl-Illmitz, 70 km
(45 miles). Option of dipping into
Hungary briefly.
Pinzgau Bicycle/Walking Route: Zell
am See-Kaprun-Mittersill-Neunkirchen
am Grossvenediger, 50 km (30
miles). Quite a workout.
Inn Valley Bicycle Route: Innsbruck-
Hall-Wattens-Schwaz-Brixlegg-
Kufstein, 75 km (46 miles).
Spectacular scenery.

TRANSPORT

Ziller Valley Bicycle Route: Fügen-Zell am Ziller-Mayrhofen and back, 30 km (18 miles). More spectacular mountains, and not so crowded in summer as in winter.

Canoeing

Canoeing or rafting along Austria's many rivers have developed into popular sporting activities. Equipped with an inflatable raft (small and light enough to be transported in a knapsack), with or without a guide, you drift or paddle through white-water rivers. There are maps and literature available to inform you of the degree of difficulty of any particular river. The most popular rivers include the Zwettl (in Lower Austria), the Enns (in Styria), the Lämmer and Salzach (in Salzburgerland), and the Inn and the Lech in Tyrol. There are many more choices, as well.

Hang-glliding

During the summer, thousands of brightly coloured hang-gliders hurl themselves down the steep rock faces, but when it comes to popularity, paragliding has long overtaken hang-gliding in Austria. The paragliding centres are Kössen in Tyrol and the Garstner Valley in the Phyrn-Priel region. The sport is practised all over the country, however. Other favourite starting points are the mountains surrounding Hallstatt in the Salzkammergut or the Zettersfeld, near Lienz in East Tyrol. Scattered across the country are more than 30 hang-gliding and paragliding schools.

Horse Riding

There are a number of horse-riding centres all around Austria. For information, contact **Reitarena Austria**, Mairhof 4–5, 4121 Altenfelden, tel: 07282-5992, www.reitarena.at This office can direct the traveller to specific stables and instructors.

Mountaineering

Austria is one of the cradles of mountaineering. During the 19th century, most of the country's 3,000-metre (9,850-ft) peaks were conquered for the first time by English climbers, but native mountaineers more than made up for this in the 20th century. Some of them – Habeler, Fritz Morawetz, Heinrich Harrer and Edi Koblmüller – have achieved world fame; together, they have conquered all the 8,000-metre (26,250-ft) giants of the Himalayas. All the country's climbing heroes began with the mountains on

their back doorstep, the peaks of the Eastern Alps, the Karawanken or the Totes Gebirge. Most of them passed their first baptism of fire on difficult sections such as the south wall of the Dachstein. All of them have tackled the king of Austrian mountains, the Grossglockner.

At 3,798 m (12,460 ft) the Grossglockner is the most majestic of all the country's peaks. It is notorious above all for its rapidly changing weather conditions as well as the panoramic road completed during the 1930s, the first of its kind in the world. It enabled the general public to penetrate the heart of the Austrian Alps. Yet the Alpine Highway is actually just the approach road to the real world of the Grossglockner.

To really explore the area you should park your car at the Franz-Josephs-Höhe near the Pasterze Glacier – at the spot where hordes of tourists in sensible shoes clamber out of their air-conditioned coaches to gaze at the marmots. Apart from the Glockner, mountaineers should head for the Grossvenediger, the Silvretta group, the Dachstein, the Ötscher in Lower Austria, the Wilder Kaiser and the precipitous peaks of the Karawanken in Carinthia.

Another variation is ice or waterfall climbing. Equipped with two ice axes and crampons, experienced climbers ascend frozen waterfalls and ice-covered mountain slopes. Their only grip is by means of the axes embedded in the ice; the crampons only serve to support some of their weight. The main ice climbing centre is the Gastein valley. Here, at temperatures many degrees below zero, the frozen waterfalls offer a variety of climbing opportunities.

Learning to climb

Climbing is taught in many mountain-eering schools. The Alpine School in Kaprun is run by the Austrian Climbing Association. It lies in a picturesque high mountain valley by the top reservoir of the Kaprun hydroelectric scheme. The school uses the rock faces of the Glockner as practice walls and is famous for its children's courses, which give youngsters a first taste of alpine sports.

Austria's mountaineering schools also offer courses in rock climbing, a popular pursuit in the Alps. Rock climbers are drawn to the tricky faces in one of Austria's increasing number of climbing parks (one of the best known is in Bad Ischl in the Salzkammergut). Most routes are in the limestone Alps, in the Gastein Valley or in the Salzkammergut.

Mountain Climbing Schools

Mountain climbing in Austria is serious and should not be attempted without previous training and a clean bill of health from your doctor. There are countless instruction schools, though not all teach classes in English; it's best to call in advance of your stay in order to learn more about the programmes on offer.

Styria
Bergsteigerschule Dachstein-Tauern
8972 Ramsau am Dachstein 273
tel: 03687-81 424/282
www.bergsteigerschule.net

Upper Austria
Alpinschule Laserer
4824 Gosau
tel: 06136-8835

Salzburg Province
Club Alpin Extra
5441 Abtenau
tel: 06243-2939
Alpin und Bergsteigerschule Oberpinzgau, 5742 Wald
tel: 06565-6574

Carinthia
Alpinschule Viktor Steiner
9822 Mallnitz
tel: 0676-8314 1788

Tyrol
Alpinschule am Wilden Kaiser, 6352 Ellmau
tel: 05358-3062
Club Alpin
6481 St. Leonhard im Pitztal
tel: 05413-85 000
Bergschule "High Live"
6733 Fontanella-Faschina.
tel: 05510-322

Vorarlberg
Bergschule Kleinwalsertal
6993 Mittelberg
tel: 05517-30 245

Watersports

The most famous sailing regions are Neusiedler See in Burgenland, the Attersee and Wolfgangsee in the Salzkammergut, the Bodensee in Vorarlberg and the Achensee in Tyrol. Small, agile sailing dinghies are the most popular as they adapt more quickly to the wind conditions, which often tend to extremes. The national windsurfing centre is on Neusiedler See.

Windsurfing has overtaken sailing in popularity throughout Austria; many stars of the international windsurfing scene first tacked into the wind across Neusiedler See. Another popular venue is the "New" Danube in the Lobau, whose mirror-

TRANSPORT

ACCOMMODATION

EATING OUT

ACTIVITIES

A – Z

LANGUAGE

calm waters and stable wind conditions make it ideal for beginners.

For decades now Austria has been one of the European white-water centres. The most attractive rivers for kayak and canoe trips are the Enns, the upper reaches of the Salzach, the Isel in East Tyrol, the Drau, the Gail, the Steyr and the Kamp in the Waldviertel of Lower Austria. Numerous white-water schools have been set up along the banks of all these rivers; all offer instruction as well as touring programmes. Adequate training is essential, especially in spring, when the melting snows make the country's mountain torrents highly dangerous and difficult to navigate.

During the past few years rafting has overtaken canoeing in popularity. The formula for what may well be the most exciting adventure on Austria's mountain rivers is a heavy-duty rubber dinghy, nine people, nine wooden paddles, steel safety helmets, life jackets, wet suits and a raging torrent. Even this, however, is not extreme enough excitement for some.

A variation on rafting is canyoning, whereby participants swim down the rushing torrent with only a life jacket or light raft to keep them afloat. It is a sport that requires considerable courage – or at least foolhardiness. In Switzerland in 1999 a flash flood swept down a steep gorge and killed 21 canyoners caught in the valley. But there is little sign of the sport's popularity waning.

The lovely, crystal-clear Alpine lakes offer some of Europe's finest diving experiences. A wide variety of freshwater fish, an unspoilt underwater world and the remarkable flora may not compare with the wealth of colour of tropical coral reefs, but diving in mountain lakes at heights of 2,000–2,500 m (6,550–8,200 ft) can present a challenge of quite a different sort. Diving centres in Austria include the Hallstätter See, which is home to the most famous diving school in Austria, run by the Zauner family. Other centres include the Attersee, the Grundlsee, the Fernsteinsee near the Fernpass in Tyrol and the Erlaufsee in Lower Austria, near the pilgrimage village of Mariazell.

Rafting

Rafting is becoming increasingly popular in mountainous parts of the country. Popular destinations include:

Styria
Pruggern (Enns)
tel: 03685-22 245
www.bac.at
Schladming (Enns)
tel: (03687) 23 372

Upper Austria
Bad Goisern (Traun, Lammer, Koppentraun)
tel: 06135-8254

Salzburg Province
Abtenau (Salzach, Lammer)
tel: 03612-25 343
Taxenbach, tel: 06543-5352

Carinthia
Mallnitz (Möll)
tel: 0664-204 0814

East Tyrol
Lienz (Isel)
tel: 04853-5231

Tyrol
Haiming (Inn, Ötztaler Ache)
tel: 05266-88 606
Ötz (Ötztaler Ache)
tel: 05252-6721
Gerlos (Lech, Gerlos, Salzach)
tel: 05284-52 440

Vorarlberg
Lech (Lech)
tel: 05519-340

Walking

The Austrian passion for hiking began in 1825, when an official at the Viennese court by the name of Josef Kyselak applied for absence, shouldered his rucksack and set off to walk the length and breadth of the land. Wherever he arrived he wrote his name to prove the point – on walls, on rocks, on towers, churches and bridges. He went on to write up his experiences in a two-volume work. It was the first book to describe the pleasure of walking in Austria and was published simultaneously in Europe and the United States.

Many people have followed in his footsteps. The slogan invented a few years ago by the National Tourist Authority – "Austria is wanderbar!" – is not so much a challenge as a statement. During holidays or sunny weekends large numbers of Austrians leave the towns for the countryside; they are joined in their wanderings by many of their country's numerous visitors.

Any list of suggestions for mountain walks will inevitably lead to disagreement, but particularly recommended are the Bregenzer Wald and the Montafon in the

Vorarlberg and the Kitzbühel Alps in Tyrol. In Salzburg province, the best hiking areas include the Österhorn Mountains (between the Salzkammergut and the Dachstein), the Pinzgauer Mountains (Saalbach, Zell am See, Uttendorf) and the head of the Rauris Valley (Kolm-Saigurn), where gold mining and glacier trails have been devised.

In Carinthia, the gently rolling Nockberg Mountains are worth a mention, as are the Low Tauern, the Hochschwab and the Koralpe in Styria. In Upper Austria, favourite recommendations include the Warscheneck Mountains in the Totes Gebirge, the Salzkammergut and the hills of the Muhlviertel. Popular in Lower Austria are the Otscherland, the Ybbstal Alps and the Waldviertel.

One route that is especially rewarding is the footpath from the Bokstein in Salzburg province (Gastein Valley) across the Korntauern Mountains to Mallnitz in Carinthia. Parts of the pass have existed for 5,000 years. On the north side of the steep, narrow pass the ascent is via steps formed by flat stone slabs that were probably placed there by the Celts.

There are a few precautions to remember before setting out on any walk. Always seek advice in the local tourist office as to a walk's degree of difficulty (staff are well-informed); some mountain footpaths are steep tracks over rocky terrain requiring surefootedness and a head for heights.

One of the pleasures of walking in Austria are the mountain refuges offering high-altitude refreshment and accommodation. In some regions, however, especially in Styria, the refuges in the medium altitude districts close in mid-September because hunting takes priority. Otherwise, long periods of fine weather make the early autumn an ideal time.

SHOPPING

What to Buy

Look for Tyrolean costumes and walking sticks in the Innsbruck area, local wine in Lower Austria and Burgenland, bottles of pumpkin-seed oil and hand-blown glassware in Styria and *Mozartkugeln* in Salzburg. Salzburg's north-of-the-river streets and the pedestrianised Maria-Theresien-Strasse in Innsbruck are also good for browsing.

Where to Shop

To shop in Austria generally means to go to Vienna, where the best choices are within the Ring. The shopping district in most other towns and cities will be compact and often close to the railway station. Shops generally close at 6pm on weeknights, 7pm or later on Thursday, 5pm Saturday. On Sunday you will find little open.

Vienna

The winding streets of Vienna's Inner City – especially between the Hofburg, Graben and Kärntnerstrasse – are the best places to find something. Some of the world's finest cakes and pastries abound at confectioners such as Demel and Gerstner; and Adolf Loos-inspired furnishings and fixtures are well in evidence throughout the Inner City. Elsewhere, Mariahilferstrasse is the other main shopping area: a long series of shops which only peter out at the Westbahnhof. Smaller shopping districts can be found in the university district (near the Votivkirche) and Siebensterngasse, where a younger crowd takes over. The city's best market is on Naschmarkt.

Books

British Bookshop
Weihburggasse 24, tel: 01-512 1945
www.britishbookshop.at
Open Mon–Fri 9.30am–6.30pm, Sat 9.30am–6pm
A long-standing Viennese institution with a good range of English-language publications (there is a second branch at Mariahilferstrasse 4).

Shakespeare & Company
Sterngasse 2, tel: 01-535 5053
www.shakespeare-company.biz
Open Mon–Sat 9am–7pm
Vienna's best source of English-language publications on Vienna, Austria and Central Europe, as well as an excellent selection of Austrian works in translation.

Fashion

Helmut Lang
Seilergasse 6, tel: 01-513 2588
www.helmutlang.com
Open Mon–Fri 9.30am–6.30pm, Sat 9am–5pm
This is the flagship store of Vienna's superstar designer.

Loden-Plankl
Michaelerplatz 6, tel: 01-533 8032
www.loden-plankl.at
Open Mon–Fri 10am–6pm, Sat 10am–5pm
The place for superb quality *Tracht* (traditional Austrian clothing), especially heavy, felted woollen coats. It is also possible to order them by post or online.

Ludwig Reiter
Mölkersteig 1, tel: 01-5334 20422
www.ludwigreiter.com
Open Mon–Fri 10am–6.30pm, Sat 10am–5pm
Beautiful handmade shoes (also at Führichgasse 6 and Wiedner Hauptstrasse 41, and with branches in Linz, Salzburg, Graz and Klagenfurt).

Modus Vivendi
Schadekgasse 4, tel: 01-587 2823
www.modus-vivendi.at
Open Mon–Fri 10am–7pm, Sat midday–4pm
Pretty and eminently wearable clothes for women and good tailoring for men.

Mühlbauer
Seilergasse 10, tel: 01-512 2241
www.muehlbauer.at
Open Mon–Fri 10am–6.30pm, Sat 10am–6pm
Beautifully-made millinery, from the traditional to the new and exciting (also at Seilergasse 5 and Landstrasser Hauptstrasse 3).

Steffl
Kärntnerstrasse 19, tel: 01-514 310
www.kaufhaus-steffl.at
Open Mon–Fri 9.30am–7pm, Sat 9.30am–6pm
Vienna's answer to Harvey Nichols; a large department store with fashion, cosmetics and a top-floor bar.

Wolford
Kärntnerstrasse 29, tel: 01-512 8731
www.wolford.com
Open Mon–Fri 9.30am–6.30pm, Sat 9am–6pm
High-quality Austrian-made hosiery and lingerie (there are a number of other shops around the city).

Food and Drink

Demel
Kohlmarkt 14, tel: 01-5351 7170
www.demel.at
Open daily 10am–7pm
These were the k.u.k bakers, and the proof is in the eating – an excellent selection of exquisite *patisserie*.

Gerstner
Kärntnerstrasse 13–15, tel: 01-512 4963
www.gerstner.at
Open Mon–Sat 8.30am–8pm, Sun 10am–6pm
Are these the finest cakes in the city, or those from Demel? There is only one way to find out…

Heiner
Kärntnerstrasse 21–3, tel: 01-512 6863
www.heiner.co.at
Open Mon–Sat 8.30am–7pm, Sun 10am–7pm
Another superb *Konditorei*. So many cakes, so little time… (also at Wollzeile 9).

Meinl am Graben
Kohlmarkt 1, tel: 01-532 3334
www.meinlamgraben.at
Open Mon–Wed 8am–7.30pm, Thur–Fri 8.30am–8pm, Sat 9am–6pm
A temple of gastronomy, with a superb range of high quality Austrian goodies. The restaurant on the first floor is extremely good.

Oberlaa
Neuer Markt 16, tel: 01-5132 9360
www.oberlaa-wien.at
Open daily 8am–8pm
Excellent *patisserie*, made with the finest ingredients (also in other locations across the city).

Wein & Co
Jasomirgottstrasse 3–5, tel: 01-539 0916
www.weinco.at
Shop open Mon–Sat 10am–midnight, Sun 11am–midnight
This wine bar and shop is just one of a number across the city (see thier website for details of other stores). The selection of Austrian wines is excellent. Also in Linz, Graz, Salzburg, Innsbruck and Bregenz.

Viennese Design

Augarten
Stock-im-Eisen Platz 3, tel: 01-512 1494
www.augarten.at
Open Mon–Wed, Sat 10am–6pm, Thur–Fri 10am–7pm
Some of their exquisite porcelain designs date back 300 years (also in Linz, Salzburg and Graz).

Backhausen
Schwarzenbergstrasse 10, tel: 01-514 040
www.backhausen.com
Open Mon–Fri 9.30am–6.30pm, Sat 9.30am–5pm
Wiener Werkstätte textiles and interior design.

Lobmeyr
Kärntnerstrasse 26, tel: 01-512 0508
www.lobmeyr.at
Open Mon–Fri 10am–7pm, Sat 10am–6pm
Glass makers to the imperial court. They still produce Josef Hoffmann's iconic black-and-white drinks service (also in Salzburg).

Woka
Palais Breuner, Singerstrasse 16, tel: 01-513 2912
www.woka.com
Open Mon–Fri 10am–6pm, Sat 10am–5pm
Founded in 1977 to make replicas of lamps from classic Adolf Loos and Wiener Werkstätte designs. They are not cheap, but are wonderful artefacts, all beautifully made.

A – Z

A HANDY SUMMARY OF PRACTICAL INFORMATION, ARRANGED ALPHABETICALLY

Addresses and Phones

Vienna has 23 numbered districts. The district number *precedes* the street name; the house number comes after the street name. You can ascertain the district of any given address from the postcode – the middle two numbers represent the particular district. A single street number can refer to a number of adjacent buildings. Phone numbers don't all have the same number of digits, and extensions are often included as part of the number. In this book, any digits following a hyphen refer to an extension number.

Business Hours

In general, shops and businesses are open Monday–Friday 8am–6pm and on Saturday 8am–5pm. Banks are open Monday–Friday 8am–12.30pm and again from 1.30–3pm, often to 5.30pm on Thursday.

Children

Travelling With Kids

Children are highly regarded in Austria – some trains even have playrooms – and they tend to go on the same sort of outings as their parents. There are a number of child-geared attractions throughout the country, of course – everything from Vienna's Prater amusement park to an array of zoos, nature parks and slightly kitschy attractions such as Minimundus in Klagenfurt.

There is a children's hospital in Vienna with emergency services: **St Anna Kinderspital**, 9, Kinder-spitalgasse 6, tel: (01) 401 700.

Climate

The Alps cover most of the land in Austria and play a decisive role in determining the country's different climatic conditions. The weather on the northern edge of the Alps is Central-European for the most part, which means that even during the usually lovely summers you can expect quite a bit of precipitation. South of the Alps, in Carinthia, the climate is almost Mediterranean – warmer temperatures and less rainfall. In the Alps themselves summers are hot and winters are cold and snowy, closing many routes; proceed with caution whenever driving in the high mountains. Also note that late winter and early spring bring dangerous avalanches to the mountains. The eastern part of the country has a continental climate – Burgenland is under the influence of the Panonian Plain, which causes hot summers and freezing winters.

Customs Regulations

Austria applies the same customs regulations as those in other European Union nations. There is no limit – within reason – on what you can bring in from, or take out to, another EU country.

Entering from a non-EU country the following free import allowances are for persons over 17: 200 cigarettes or 50 cigars or 100 cigarillos or 250 gr tobacco. 2 litres of alcohol max. 22 vol. percent, or 1 litre of more than 22 vol. percent, and 2 litres of wine. 50g of perfume and 0.25 litres of toilet water.

Visitors entering Austria by car are not required to obtain any special customs documents for their vehicles. The import and export of Austrian and foreign currency is unrestricted, although sums above

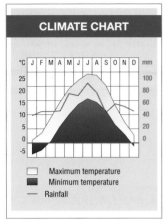

CLIMATE CHART

☐ Maximum temperature
■ Minimum temperature
— Rainfall

€10,000 must be declared if they are not to be used for tourist purposes.

D isabled Travellers

With its excellent public transport system Austria is generally an easy country to get around. The ÖBB (state railways; www.oebb.at) offers a discount card (the VORTEILScard Spezial) to disabled travellers and also has a 24-hour helpline (tel: 05-1717) which travellers with disabilites can use to plan all aspcts of their journey. Some stations have special wheelchair lifts to help travellers onto trains.

The Vienna Tourism website (www.wien.info) has a very useful section on services, transport and accommodation for disabled people with downloadable factsheets.

E mergencies

Ambulance *(Rettung)*
Tel: 144
Fire *(Feuerwehr)*
Tel: 122

Embassies Abroad

Australia: 12 Talbot St, ACT 2603, Canberra, tel: 02-6295 1533.
Belgium: Place du Champ de Mars 5, 1050 Brussels, tel: 02-289 0700.
Canada: 445 Wilbrod Street, Ottawa, K1N 6M7, tel: 613-789 1444.
Denmark: Solundsvej 1, 2100 Copenhagen, tel: 3929 4141.
France: 6 Rue Fabert, F 75007 Paris, tel: 01-4063 3063.
Germany: Stauffenbergstrasse 1, 10785 Berlin, tel: 030-20287-0.

Great Britain: 18 Belgrave Mews West, London, SW1X 8HU, tel: 020-7235 3731.
Italy: Via Pergolesi 3, 00198 Rome, tel: 06-844 0141.
Netherlands: Van Alkemadelaan 342, The Hague, 2597 AS, tel: 070-324 5470.
Switzerland: Kirchenfeldstrasse 77–79, 3006 Bern, tel: 031-356 5252.
USA: 3524 International Court NW, Washington DC 20008, tel: 202-895 6700.

Police *(Polizei)*
Tel: 133

F oreign Embassies

Australia
Mattiellistrasse 2–4, Vienna
Tel: 01-506 740
www.australian-embassy.at
Canada
Laurenzerberg 2, Vienna
Tel: 01-5313 83000
www.dfait-maeci.gc.ca
Ireland
Rotenturmstrasse 16–18, 5th Floor, Vienna
Tel: 01-715 4246
www.foreignaffairs.gov.ie
New Zealand
Salesianergasse 15/3, Vienna
Tel: 01-318 8505
www.nzembassy.com
South Africa
Sandgasse 33, Vienna
Tel: 01-3206493
www.saembvie.at
United Kingdom
Jauresgasse 12, Vienna
Tel: 01-716 130
www.britishembassy.at
USA
Boltzmanngasse 16, Vienna
Tel: 01-313 390
www.usembassy.at

G ay and Lesbian Visitors

The Austrian city with the liveliest gay and lesbian scene is Vienna (recently voted one the most gay-friendly cities in Europe). The year's two big events are the Rainbow Parade (held in July; www.hosiwien.at) and the Life Ball (held in May; www.lifeball.org). The Rainbow Parade is a gay-pride march while the Life Ball started off as an AIDS awareness event and has turned into one of the country's premier social events with many politicians and celebrities (gay and straight) making an appearance.

Gay and lesbian visitors should encounter little trouble in Vienna, but elsewhere in the country, although it is unlikely people will be hostile, attitudes tend to be much more traditional.

In Vienna one of the best places to meet up and find further information is the café/restaurant, **Rosa Lila Villa** (Wienzeile 106; www.villa.at). The city authorities also produce a **Queer Guide** for gay and lesbian visitors (it can downloaded at www.wien.info).

H ealth and Insurance

Austria is, generally speaking, a very safe, clean and healthy country; no special vaccinations are necessary, water won't need to be boiled, and healthcare is free to EU residents. Nevertheless, it's always prudent to buy health and travel insurance with medical cover prior to a trip – especially since reimbursement for medical expenses involves mounds of paperwork.

If you are going to ski, hike, do water sports, etc, check that your insurance covers accidents in such sports – you may need to purchase a "rider" covering these activities. The same holds true for travel with a laptop computer. Bring proof of your insurance policy in case you need to show it to doctors, police, hospital attendants, etc. Also carry a list of emergency numbers in your wallet or purse *(see above)*.

Medical Treatment

Austria's standard of medical care is generally good. If you need help, visit the local pharmacy for minor aches, pains and sniffles; most stay open to 6pm weekdays and noon on Saturday and usually post a list of 24-hour pharmacies nearby.

For more serious matters, call the emergency number (141) or go straight to a hospital. In Vienna, lots of hospitals maintain 24-hour walk-in emergency services – the Allgemeines Krankenhaus (AKH), an enormous hospital at Alserstrasse and Spitalgasse with its own U-Bahn stop, is excellent:
Währinger Gürtel 18–20, Vienna
Tel: 01-404 000
www.akhwien.at

M edia
Press

There's only one regular English-language publication in all of Austria, and it's certainly not comprehensive: *Austria Today* is

ABOVE: a bronze ibex at Krimml.

now only available online
(see Websites) but whether
the subscription is worth it is
debateable. Various foreign-
language newspapers, are
available early in the morning
from newsstands. Newsagents,
called *Tabak Trafik*, are
recognisable by the sign of a
red ring with a cigarette in the
middle. In addition to newspapers
and magazines they also sell
stamps and bus and tram
tickets.

Radio

The Austrian Radio Network
broadcasts a brief daily news
report in English and French on
Channel 1 (01) at 8.05–8.15am.
FM4 is in English in the mornings
and has news reports in English
on the hour all day.

Public Holidays

- **1 January** New Year's Day
- **6 January** Epiphany
- **April** Easter Monday
- **1 May** May Day
- **May** Ascension Day
- **May/June** Whit Monday
- **May/June** Feast of Corpus
  Christi
- **15 August** Day of Assumption
- **26 October** National Holiday
- **1 November** All Saints' Day
- **8 December** Day of the
  Immaculate Conception
- **25 December** Christmas Day
- **26 December** St Stephen's Day

Television

There are two official channels,
(ORF1 and ORF2), both of which are
German-language, plus a cable
package, largely controlled by the
Telekabel consortium, that
includes some programmes in
other languages. Your hotel might
well subscribe to the package that
includes CNN and BBC World News.
There's a glut of German TV with
its focus on sport, business news
and slightly racy films, as well as
some programming from France
and Switzerland. The advent of
satellite television in a growing
number of higher-priced Austrian
hotels improves your chances of
catching news and sport in
English.

Money

In January 2002, the Austrian
Schilling was replaced by the
European single currency, the Euro
(€), which was made equivalent to
13.76 Schillings. 1 Euro equals 100
cents. Banknotes are available in
denominations of 500, 200, 100,
50, 20, 10 and 5 Euros. The coins
come in denominations of 2 and 1
Euro, and 50, 20, 10, 5, 2 and 1
cent. Coins minted in the different
countries will match on one side but
differ on the other. However, they can
all be used in all EU countries.

The main credit cards and
travellers' cheques are widely
accepted by major hotels and most
shops in cities. Otherwise, ATMs
(Bankomats) are by far your best

option for obtaining local currency;
cash dispensers at most banks
accept the major European debit
cards. When travelling to remote
destinations in rural areas you might
need to change money at a railway
station. Banks (usually open
Monday–Friday 8am–12.30pm and
1.30–3pm, often to 5.30pm
Thursday) and exchange offices will
change foreign currency at the
current rate of the Viennese stock
exchange.

There is no limit to how much
local money visitors may bring into or
take out of Austria.

Postal Services

Post offices are open 8am–noon and
2–6pm. Railway post offices in the
main cities are open 24 hours,
though not all services may be
available around the clock. In Vienna,
the Main Post Office is at
Fleischmarkt 19, tel: 05 77677-
1010, open 24 hours.* Courier
services are also available in major
cities. In Vienna, try **Der Bote**, tel:
(01) 310 7373, or **Blitzkurier**, tel:
(01) 409 4949-0.

Religious Services (Vienna)

Anglican, 3, Jaurésgasse 12,
tel: (01) 714 8900.
Catholic Mass (in English)
Votivkirche, 11am,
tel: (01) 402 1830.
Jewish, 1, Seitenstättengasse 4,
tel: (01) 531 040.
Methodist,
15, Sechshauserstrasse 56/2/6,
tel: (01) 895 8175.
Viennese Islamic Centre, 21, Am
Hubertusdamm 17–19,
tel: (01) 263 0922.

Security & Crime

Austria is uniformly safe, except for a
few areas in Vienna – and the chief
threat here is the pickpocket. Keep a
hand on your hip in such crowded
and/or seedy areas as the
Westbahnhof, Naschmarkt, the Prater
and especially Karlsplatz – a noted
haunt of thieves and drug-dealers at
night. Keep valuables in your hotel
safe.

Telephones

Austria has a modern
communications network and
direct dialling is available to the
majority of countries. In addition
to telephoning from your hotel,
you can also make international calls
from post offices or from many

telephone booths. Note that, when dialling Vienna numbers from outside the city, you must include the area code 01 (within Austria) or 1 (outside Austria).

Tipping

It is customary to leave a 10–15 percent tip for good service. Bills at hotels and restaurants include a service charge but porters and maids expect a gratuity. Taxi drivers, tour guides, cloakroom attendants and hairdressers also expect a 10 percent tip. In general, rounding up the bill seems to be good form.

Tourist Information

There are a number of Tourist Information offices in Vienna. The two main ones are: Information-City, Albertinaplatz; and Information-South, Triestestrasse. There are also information offices at main railway stations, at the airport and by the motorway exits. The three government tourism websites are also useful (www.wien.gv.at, www.info.wien.at and www.austria-tourism.at). The Vienna Tourist Board is at Obere Augartenstrasse 40 (tel: 211 140), and there is a Stadtinformation office in the Rathaus (tel: 52550).

Transport information offices

The public transport system's information offices, which all give information on prices and provide maps, are open as follows: Karlsplatz, Stephansplatz, Praterstern, Philadelphiabrücke and Volkstheater.

V isas and Passports

Austria relies heavily on tourism, and immigration and customs formalities are fairly relaxed. Citizens of most European nations are not required to possess a visa in order to enter the country, only a valid passport. Non-European visitors also require a passport, but many (from Canada, the US and Australia for example) don't need a visa; contact the Austrian embassy in your home country for specific details (www.bmaa.gv.at).

Visa information for US citizens is available at www.traveldocs.com.

W hat to Wear

Bring comfortable clothes and sensible shoes. More formal wear is expected at the theatre and concerts. Those walking in the mountains should be well prepared with proper footwear and equipment.

Be prepared for weather fluctuations that are normal in a country with such a varied topography. Pack something light for Vienna or Carinthia in summertime, as it can get quite hot, but also bring sweaters and perhaps an emergency waterproof if you'll be in the high mountains whatever the season. The Alps require cold-weather gear of the highest order in winter, as well as appropriate expertise. Most parts of the country (other than the south) get a fair amount of rain, so bring an umbrella and a bit of rain gear.

Websites

www.alpenverein.at
The Austrian Alpine Club is the top mountaineering organisation in Austria, their website (in German only) contains much useful information, including a list of huts (hütten).
www.austria.info
The website of the Austrian tourist board with a great deal of information including accommodation and weather updates (it also has links to regional tourist organisations including: www.burgenland.info; www.salzburg.info; www.tirol.info; and www.wien.info).
www.wien.gv.at
This is the web portal of the Vienna Municipality with a huge amount of information on the city, from how to get your bins emptied to history.
www.events.at
If you want to know what's on, this is the place to find it, from clubbing to classical music.
www.aeiou.at
This site, of the Ministry for Education, Science and Culture, gives a superb overview of the country's cultural achievements.
www.austria-today.at
The country's only English-language newspaper has now become a web-only project. It has some useful freeview information but to get the whole thing you must subscribe.
www.austria.org
The website of the Austrian Embassy in Washington DC with a great deal of general infomation on the country.
www.austrianmap.at
A searchable and printable map database that zooms in and out and covers the whole country.

Women Travellers

In general women will encounter few problems travelling around Austria on their own, and you will only need to follow common sense rules that apply anywhere. Vienna is one of the safest cities in Europe, but at night you might want to avoid the noted drug-haunts of Karlsplatz U-bahn station and the Prater if you are on your own. The city also has women's taxi service (Lady-Taxi, tel: 60160, www.ladytaxi.at).

BELOW: the Hundertwasserhaus

LANGUAGE

UNDERSTANDING THE LANGUAGE

Language Tips

The Austrian national language is German, which is spoken by about 100 million people world-wide. As well as Austria, Germany, parts of Switzerland and some small German enclaves in eastern Europe, there are also German-speaking communities in North America, South America and South Africa. German and English both belong to the West Germanic language group, together with Dutch, Frisian, Flemish and Afrikaans, but while a Dutch speaker and a German may be able to communicate quite effectively, an English speaker and a German are unlikely to make much progress. A glance at the numbers from one to 10 (see page 309) will prove that point.

If you learned Latin at school you'll be familiar with some of the difficulties that German presents: nouns have three genders and four cases, verbs are conjugated, pronouns are followed by one of three cases, word order is governed by some complicated rules and there

Compound Words

The German language can be restructured to create new words simply by linking words together, and very often it is, producing tongue-twisting words on schedules, street signs and the like. One good example is the firm which runs regular ferries up the Danube River from Vienna to Krems and beyond. Its name – Donaudampfschiffsfahrtsgesell-schaft – means Danube steamship company. Better to call it DDSG.

are five different ways of saying "the". Pronunciation, thankfully, is perfectly consistent with spelling.

Although many young Austrians speak English and are always keen to try it out, there are many parts of the country where a smattering of German will prove very helpful.

Even if you are fairly confident in German, you may encounter some difficulties in rural Austria, as there is a remarkable diversity in regional accents and dialects. There are strong links between Austrian German and the dialects of German spoken in Bavaria, yet within Austria some dialects are not understood by fellow Austrians. While it may sometimes be difficult to understand Austrians when they are speaking to each other, almost all can switch to High German when necessary.

Words and Phrases

General

Hello *Gruss Gott*
Good morning *Guten Morgen*
Good afternoon *Guten Nachmittag*
Good evening *Guten Abend*
Good night *Gute Nacht*
Goodbye *Auf Wiedersehen*
Goodbye (informal) *Servus, Pfiat di*
Do you speak English? *Sprechen Sie Englisch?*
I don't understand *Ich verstehe nicht*
Could you please speak slower? *Könnten Sie bitte etwas langsamer sprechen?*
Can you help me? *Können Sie mir helfen?*
yes/no *Ja/Nein*
please/thank you *Bitte/Danke*
sorry *Entschuldigung*
How are you? *Wie geht's?*
Excuse me *Entschuldigung Sie, bitte*
You're welcome *Bitte schön*

The Alphabet

Learning how to pronounce the German alphabet will enable you to spell your name:
a = ah, **b** = bay, **c** = tsay,
d = day, **e** = eh, **f** = eff,
g = gay, **h** = har, **i** = ee, **j** = yot,
k = kar, **l** = el, **m** = em,
n = en, **o** = oh, **p** = pay,
q = koo, **r** = air, **s** = es,
t = tay, **u** = oo, **v** = fow,
w = vay, **x** = icks, **y** = upsilon,
z = tset

It doesn't matter *(Es) macht nichts*
OK *Alles klar*
What a pity *Schade*
Thank you for your help *Besten Dank für ihre Hilfe*
See you later *Bis später*
See you tomorrow *Bis morgen*
What time is it? *Wie spät ist es?*
10 o'clock *zehn Uhr*
half past ten *halb elf*
This morning *heute morgen*
this afternoon *heute nachmittag*
this evening *heute abend*
Let's go! *Los!*
Leave me alone *Lass mich in Ruhe*
Clear off *Hau ab*
Where are the toilets? *Wo sind die Toiletten?*
large/small *gross/klein*
more/less *mehr/weniger*
now *jetzt*
later *später*
here *hier*
there *dort*

On Arrival

station *Bahnhof*
bus station *Busbahnhof*
bus stop *Bushaltestelle*
Will you tell me when to get off the bus? *Können Sie mir sagen,*

wann ich aussteigen muss?
Where can I get the bus to the Adler Hotel? *Wo fährt der Bus zum Hotel Adler weg?*
Does this bus go to the town centre? *Fährt dieser Bus zur Stadtmitte?*
Which street is this? *Welche Strasse ist das?*
How far is it to the station? *Wie weit ist es zum Bahnhof?*
Do you have a single room? *Haben Sie ein Einzelzimmer?*
Do you have a double room? *Haben Sie ein Doppelzimmer?*
Do you have a room with a private bath? *Haben Sie ein Zimmer mit Bad?*
How much is it? *Wieviel kostet das?*
How much is a room with full board? *Wieviel kostet ein Zimmer mit Vollpension?*
Please show me another room *Bitte zeigen Sie mir ein anderes Zimmer*
We'll (I'll) be staying for one night *Wir bleiben (Ich bleibe) eine Nacht*
When is breakfast? *Wann gibt es Frühstück?*
Where is the toilet? *Wo ist die Toilette?*
Where is the bathroom? *Wo ist das Badezimmer?*
Where is the next hotel? *Wo ist das nächste Hotel?*

Travelling

Where is the airport? *Wo ist der Flughafen?*
Where is platform one? *Wo ist Bahnsteig eins?*
Can you call me a taxi? *Können Sie mir ein Taxi rufen?*
Where do I get a ticket? *Wo kann ich eine Fahrkarte kaufen?*
departure/arrival *Abfahrt/Ankunft*
When is the next flight/train to ...? *Wann geht der nächste Flug/Zug nach ...?*
to change (flights/trains) *umsteigen*
Have you anything to declare? *Haben Sie etwas zu verzollen?*
close/far *nah/weit*
free (of charge) *kostenlos*
price *Preis*
fee *Gebühr*
Have you got any change? *Können Sie Geld wechseln?*
bridge *Brücke*
Customs *Zoll*
entrance *Eingang, Einfahrt*
exit *Ausgang, Ausfahrt*
height/width/length *Höhe/Breite/Länge*
no stopping *Halten verboten*
one-way street *Einbahnstrasse*
picnic area *Rastplatz*
travel agency *Reisebüro*

Driving

Petrol (gas) station *Tankstelle*
I have run out of petrol *Ich habe kein Benzin mehr*
My car has broken down *Ich habe eine Autopanne*
Could you give me a push/tow? *Könnten Sie mich bitte anschieben/abschleppen?*
Can you take me to the nearest garage? *Können Sie mich zur nächsten Werkstatt bringen?*
Can you find out what the trouble is? *Können Sie feststellen, was das Problem ist?*
Can you repair it? *Können Sie es reparieren?*
The road to ... ? *Die Strasse nach ...?*
left *links*
right *rechts*
straight on *geradeaus*
opposite *gegenüber*
Where is the nearest car-park? *Wo ist der nächste Parkplatz, bitte?*
over there *da drüben*
Turn left/right after the bridge *Biegen Sie hinter der Brücke links/rechts ab*
Here is my driving licence *Da ist mein Führerschein*
Here are my insurance documents *Hier sind meine Versicherungsunterlagen*
brakes *Bremsen*
bulb *Glühbirne*
by car *mit dem Auto*
dead end *Sackgasse*
diesel *Diesel*
give way *Vorfahrt beachten*
headlights *Scheinwerfer*
jack *Wagenheber*
map *Strassenkarte*
no parking *Parken verboten*

one-way street *Einbahnstrasse*
petrol *Benzin*
road/street *Strasse*
slow/fast *langsam/schnell*
unleaded *bleifrei*
water/oil *Wasser/Öl*
windscreen wipers *Scheibenwischer*

On the Telephone

I must make a phone call *Ich muss telefonieren*
Can I use your phone? *Kann ich Ihr Telefon benutzen?*
Can I dial direct? *Kann ich direkt wählen?*
Please connect me with ... *Bitte verbinden Sie mich mit ...*
What is the code for Great Britain? *Was is das Vorwahl für Grossbritannien?*
Who is speaking? *Wer spricht da?*
The line is engaged *Die Leitung ist besetzt*
I'll call again later *Ich rufe später wieder an*

Shopping

Where can I change money? *Wo kann ich Geld wechseln?*
Where is the pharmacy? *Wo ist die Apotheke?*
What time do they close? *Wann schliessen sie?*
Where is the nearest bank? *Wo ist die nächste Bank?*
Where is the nearest post-office? *Wo ist die nächste Post?*
I'd like ... *Ich hätte gern ...*
How much is this? *Was kostet das?*
Do you take credit cards? *Akzeptieren Sie Kreditkarten?*
I'm just looking *Ich sehe mich nur um*
Do you have ...? *Haben Sie ...?*

Numbers

0	*null*	1st	*erste(r)*
1	*eins*	2nd	*zweite(r)*
2	*zwei*	3rd	*dritte(r)*
3	*drei*	4th	*vierte(r)*
4	*vier*	5th	*fünfte(r)*
5	*fünf*	6th	*sechste(r)*
6	*sechs*	7th	*siebte(r)*
7	*sieben*	8th	*achte(r)*
8	*acht*	9th	*neunte(r)*
9	*neun*	10th	*zehnte(r)*
10	*zehn*	11th	*elfte(r)*
11	*elf*	12th	*zwölfte(r)*
12	*zwölf*	13th	*dreizehnte(r)*
13	*dreizehn*	20th	*zwanzigste(r)*
20	*zwanzig*	21st	*einundzwanzigste(r)*
21	*einundzwanzig*	22nd	*zweiundzwanzigste(r)*
30	*dreissig*	30th	*dreissigste(r)*
40	*vierzig*	40th	*vierzigste(r)*
50	*fünfzig*	50th	*fünfzigste(r)*
100	*hundert*	100th	*hundertste(r)*
1,000	*tausend*	200th	*zweihundertste(r)*
1,000,000	*eine Million*	1,000th	*tausendste(r)*

That'll be fine. I'll take it. *In Ordnung. Ich nehme es.*
No, that is too expensive *Nein, das ist zu teuer*
Can I try it on? *Kann ich es anprobieren?*
Do you have anything cheaper? *Haben Sie etwas Billigeres?*

Sightseeing

Where is the tourist office? *Wo ist das Fremdenverkehrsbüro?*
Is there a bus to the centre? *Gibt es einen Bus ins Stadtzentrum?*
Is there a guided sightseeing tour? *Gibtes geführte Besichtigungstouren*?*
When is the museum open? *Wann ist das Museum geöffnet?*
How much does it cost to go in? *Was kostet der Eintritt?*
art gallery *Kunstgalerie*
castle *Schloss*
cathedral *Dom*
church *Kirche*
exhibition *Ausstellung*
memorial *Denkmal*
old part of town *Altstadtviertel*
tower *Turm*
town hall *Rathaus*
walk *Spaziergang*
Roman *Römisch*
Romanesque *Romanisch*
Gothic *gotisch*
open daily *täglich*

Eating out

Do you know a good restaurant? *Kennen Sie ein gutes Restaurant?*
A table for one/two *Ein Tisch für eine Person/zwei Personen, bitte*
Could we order a meal, please? *Können wir bitte bestellen?*
Can we have the bill, please? *Können wir bitte bezahlen?*
evening meal *Abendessen*
lunch *Mittagessen*
children's portion *Kinderteller*
snack *Jause, Imbiss*
menu *Speisekarte*
soup/starter *Suppe/Vorspeise*

main course *Hauptgericht*
dessert *Nachspeise*
beer/wine *Bier/Wein*
bread *Brot*
bread roll *Brötchen, Semmel*
cake *Kuchen*
coffee *Kaffee*
milk *Milch*
mineral water *Mineralwasser*
mustard *Senf*
salt/pepper *Salz/Pfeffer*
sugar *Zucker*
tea *Tee*
wine list *Weinkarte*
tip *Trinkgeld*

Breakfast Frühstück

Brot **bread**
Semmel/Brötchen **roll**
Eier **eggs**
Fruchtsaft **fruit juice**
hartgekochtes Ei **hard-boiled egg**
heiss **hot**
kalt **cold**
Marmelade/Konfitüre **jam**
Orangensaft **orange juice**
Pumpernickel **black rye bread**
Rühreier **scrambled egg**
Schinken **ham**
Schwarzbrot **brown rye bread**
Speck **bacon**
Weissbrot **white bread**

Soups Suppen

Eintopf **thick soup**
Erbsensuppe **pea soup**
Fritattensuppe **consommé with strips of pancake**
Gemüsesuppe **vegetable soup**
Griessnockerlsuppe **semolina dumpling soup**
Gulaschsuppe **goulash soup**
Hühnersuppe **chicken soup**
Nudelsuppe **noodle soup**
Ochsenschwanzsuppe **oxtail soup**
Zwiebelsuppe **onion soup**

Starters Vorspeisen

Austern **oysters**
Froschschenkel **frogs' legs**
Gänseleberpastete **pâté de foie**
Geeiste Melone **iced melon**
Rollmops **rolled-up pickled herring**

Schnecken **snails**
Spargelspitzen **asparagus tips**
Wurstplatte **assorted cooked meats**

Meat Courses Fleischgerichte

Backhuhn **roast chicken**
Blutwurst **black pudding**
Bockwurst **large frankfurter**
Bratwurst **fried sausage**
Currywurst **pork sausage with curry powder**
Deutsches Beefsteak **minced beef/hamburger**
Stelze **knuckle of pork**
Ente **duck**
Fasan **pheasant**
Fleischlaibchen **meatballs**
Fleischpastetchen **rissole**
Gulasch **goulash**
Hähnchen/Huhn **chicken**
Kalbsbries **veal sweetbreads**
Kümmelfleisch **pork stew with cumin**
Lamm am Spiess **lamb on the spit**
Lammbraten **roast lamb**
Leberknödel **liver dumplings**
Ochsenschwanz **oxtail**
Räucherschinken **cured ham**
Rehrücken **saddle of deer**
Rind **beef**
Rinderbraten **roast beef**
Rinderfilet **fillet of beef**
Sauerbraten **braised pickled beef**
Schweinebauch **belly of pork**
Schweinebraten **roast pork**
Schweinefilet **loin of pork**
Serbisches Reisfleisch **diced pork, onions, tomatoes and rice**
Speck **bacon**
Szegediner Goulasch **goulash with pickled cabbage**
Tiroler Bauernschmaus **various meats served with sauerkraut, potatoes and dumplings**
Wienerschnitzel **breaded escalope of veal**
Zigeunerschnitzel **veal with peppers and relishes**
Zunge **tongue**

Fish Fisch

Austern **oysters**
Barbe **mullet**
Bismarckhering **filleted pickled herring**
Fischfrikadellen **fishcakes**
Fischstäbchen **fish fingers**
Forelle **trout**
Garnelen **prawns**
Hecht **pike**
Heilbutt **halibut**
Heringstopf **pickled herrings**
Hummer **lobster**
Jakobsmuscheln **scallops**
Kabeljau **cod**
Krabbe **shrimps**
Lachs **salmon**
Makrele **mackerel**
Muscheln **mussels**

Emergencies

Help! *Hilfe!*
Stop! *Halt!*
Please call a doctor *Holen Sie einen Arzt*
Please call an ambulance *Rufen Sie einen Krankenwagen*
Please call the fire-brigade *Rufen Sie die Feuerwehr*
Where is the nearest telephone box? *Wo ist die nächste Telefonzelle?*
I am ill *Ich bin krank*
I have lost my wallet/hand-bag *Ich habe meine Geldtasche/ Handtasche verloren*
Where is the nearest hospital? *Wo ist das nächste Krankenhaus?*
Where is the police station? *Wo ist das nächste Polizeiwache?*
Where is the British consulate? *Wo ist die britische Konsulat?*

Sardinen **sardines**
Schellfisch **haddock**
Schwertfisch **swordfish**
Seebarsch **sea bass**
Seezunge **sole**
Thunfisch **tuna**
Tintenfisch **squid**

Dumplings & Noodles Knödel

Semmelknödel/Serviettenknödl
bread dumplings
Leberknödel **liver dumplings**
Kasnocken/Kässpätzle/
Kasnödel **pasta balls with
cheese**
Kartoffelknödel **potato dumplings**
Knödel **dumplings**
Maultasche Swabian **ravioli**
Nockerl **gnocchi**
Nudeln **noodles**
Spätzle **grated pasta**

Vegetables Gemüse

Bohnen **beans**
Bratkartoffeln **fried potatoes**
Champignons **mushrooms**
Erdäpfel **potatoes**
Kartoffelpuree **creamed potatoes**
Kartoffelsalat **potato salad**
Knoblauch **garlic**
Kohl **cabbage**
Kopfsalat **lettuce**
Linsen **lentils**
Pommes (frites) **chips/French fries**
Rohnen **beetroot**
Salat **salad**
Sauerkraut **pickled cabbage**

Desserts Nachspeisen

Apfelkuchen **apple cake**
Apfelstrudel **flaky pastry stuffed
with apple**
Auflauf **soufflé**
Bienenstich **honey-almond cake**
Eis **ice cream**
Eisbecher **ice cream with fresh
fruit**
Fruchttörtchen **fruit tartlet**
Gebäck **pastries**
Kaiserschmarrn **sugared pancake
with raisins**
Käsetorte **cheesecake**
Linzer Torte **cake spread with jam
and topped with cream**
Marillenknödel **apricot
dumplings**
Mandelkuchen **almond cake**
Mohnkuchen **poppyseed cake**
Mohr im Hemd **chocolate pudding
with chocolate sauce**
Obstkuchen **fruit tart**
Palatschinken **pancakes**
Pofesen **stuffed fritters**
Rote Grütze **raspberries or
redcurrants cooked with
semolina**
Sacher Torte **chocolate cake
with jam and chocolate icing**
Schwarzwälder Kirschtorte
Black Forest gateau

Days, Months and Seasons

Monday	Montag
Tuesday	Dienstag
Wednesday	Mittwoch
Thursday	Donnerstag
Friday	Freitag
Saturday	Samstag/Sonnabend
Sunday	Sonntag
January	Januar/Jänner
February	Februar/Feber
March	März
April	April
May	Mai
June	Juni
July	Juli
August	August
September	September
October	Oktober
November	November
December	Dezember
spring	Frühling
summer	Sommer
autumn	Herbst
winter	Winter

Slang

a right mess eine Schweinerei
bastard Arschloch, du blöde Kuh, du
Schweinehund
bloody hell! verdammt noch mal!
great, magic klasse, super, toll,
Spitze, leiwand
oh my God! du lieber Gott!
pissed besoffen, fett, voll
pissed off sauer, grantig,
angefressen
shit Scheisse, Mist
stupid doof, blöd, deppert, narrisch
wow! Mensch! Mah! Wahnsinn!

Loan Words

With Austria standing at the heart of
Europe, its language has been
subjected to numerous and varied
foreign influences. For centuries,
there was a large Jewish community
within the Empire, and they brought
many Hebrew words into regular
usage. Words such as Massel (good
luck), vermasseln (to make a mess
of things), messchugge (crazy) and
Mischpoche (rabble) are now part of
everyday language.

During the 17th century, the
Huguenots introduced many French
words into German, such as those
used to describe food (eg Ragout fin,
Roulade, Frikassee, Püree, Eclair,
Petits fours). The late 17th/early 18th
century rivalry between France and the
Habsburgs also left a Francophone
mark, especially in Vienna.

More recently, English has
infiltrated the German language,
mainly in popular culture. English

ABOVE: in Vienna's MuseumsQuartier.

speakers will be on familiar ground in
the worlds of sport and leisure, pop
music, entertainment and computers
(words such as Fitness, Feedback,
Snowboard, Mountain-bike, Disco,
Video recorder, Groupie, Entertainer,
Software and Byte, amongst others,
are used and heard frequently in
everyday conversation). Some of
these loan words are more unfamiliar
to the "lenders" than the borrowers;
what English speaker thinks of a
mobile phone as a Handy?

False Friends

False friends are words that look like
English words, but actually mean
something different. Ich bekomme
ein Baby, for example, does not
mean "I am becoming a baby", but "I
am having a baby"; ein Berliner is a
jam doughnut and also doesn't mean
"also", but usually "so" or
"therefore". Some loan words can be
very confusing, too. Aktuell means
"up-to-date" or "fashionable", not
"actual", and Ich komme eventuell
could mean that I am not coming at
all. A good translation would be "I
might come". Ein Knicker is a
scrooge and ein Schellfisch is a
haddock.

TRANSPORT

ACCOMMODATION

EATING OUT

ACTIVITIES

A–Z

LANGUAGE

FURTHER READING AND LISTENING

General

Journeys, by Jan Morris. Oxford University Press, 1984, and Replica Books, 2000. Collection includes a jaundiced essay on Vienna.
Austrian Cooking, by Gretel Beer. André Deutsch, 1999. Treasure-trove of traditional recipes; not for light eaters.

History

The Austrians, by Gordon Brook-Shepherd. Harper Collins, 1997. A fascinating and very readable account that moves from 800 to 1994; particularly interesting on the post-World War I period.
Schubert's Vienna, by Raymond Erickson (Ed). Yale University Press, 1997. An examination of the history, politics and social conventions of the times.
The Fall of the House of Habsburg, by Edward Crankshaw. Penguin, 1983. Entertaining scholarly history of one of Europe's most significant dynasties.
The Austrian Mind: An Intellectual and Social History 1848–1938, by William M Johnstone. University of California Press, 1983. Comprehensive treatment of the psychologists, artists and other figures assembled in Vienna during an historical moment.
Dissolution of the Austro-Hungarian Empire, by J.W. Mason and Neil Macqueen. Addis, 1997. A textbook-sized tome on the ups and downs of the Habsburgs.
Freud and Beyond: A History of Modern Psychoanalytic Thought, by Stephen A Mitchell and Margaret J Black. Basic Books, 1996. Comprehensive, readable history of the social science Freud founded.
A Nervous Splendor: Vienna, 1888–1889, by Frederic Morton. Viking, 1980. One of the better snapshots of flourishing late-period Vienna, just before the end of the empire.
The Dollfuss/Schuschnigg Era: A reassessment by Gunter Bishof (Ed). Transaction Publishers, 2003. A look at the political and economic problems in Austria in the years before the annexation.
Guilty Victim: Austria from the Holocaust to Haider, by Hella Pick. IB Tauris. A fascinating look at 60 years of Austrian and international politics, highlighting the degree of sympathy with and support for the Nazis within the country.
Fin-de-Siècle Vienna: Politics and Culture, by Carl E. Schorske. Vintage, 1981. Remains a key, rather academic text on the Vienna of Freud, Schnitzler, Klimt and Schoenberg.
The Siege of Vienna, by John Stoye. Birlinn, 2000. A vivid account of the summer of 1683 when the Turks surrounded Vienna.

Biography

Maria Theresa, by Edward Crankshaw. Longman, 1970. Biographies in English of the great Empress are hard to find, but this one is well worth seeking out.
Prophets Without Honour: Freud, Kafka, Einstein, and Their World, by Frederic V Grunfeld. Kodansha International, 1996. Collection of essays recounting famous Austrian-related figures.
Mozart: A Cultural Biography, by Robert W. Gutman. Harcourt Brace, 1999. Massive (almost 900-page) volume, but an accurate portrait.
The Reluctant Empress, by Brigitte Hamman. Ullstein, 1998. Scholarly but readable account of the brilliant, beautiful and tragic Sisi, wife of Franz Joseph.
Diaries: 1898–1902, by Alma Mahler-Werfel. Cornell University Press, 2000. Fascinating extracts from the diaries of Mahler's wife, an artist and socialite in her own right. Gives new insight into swinging Vienna.
W.A. Mozart: Letters, edited by Hans Mersmann. Hippocrene, 1987. Just what it promises: largely unadorned letters of the troubled composer.
Thunder at Twilight, by Frederic Morton. Methuen, 2001. With a cast that includes Stalin, Trotsky, Freud and Hitler, this presents a vivid and sympathetic portrait of the Archduke Franz Ferdinand and his ferocious struggle for peace that ended with his assassination at Sarajevo.
Twilight of the Habsburgs, by Alan Palmer. Phoenix, 1998. A full and rounded biography of Franz Joseph, ruler of the Austrian Empire from 1848 to 1916 and husband of Sisi, the Empress Elizabeth.
Emperor Francis Joseph, by John Van Dor Kiste. Sutton Publishing, 2005. A critical look at the life and times of Austria's longest-serving Monarch.
1791: Mozart's Last Year, by H.C. Robbins Landon. Thames and Hudson, 1999. An interesting reconstruction of Mozart's last year.
Uncrowned Emperor: The Life and Times of Otto Von Habsburg, by Gordon Brook-Shepherd. Hambledon & London. 2004. The first English-language biography of the heir apparent to the Habsburg throne.
Last Waltz in Vienna, by George Clare. Pan, 2002. The true and tragic story of a Jewish family in Vienna at the time of the Anschluss.

Art & Architecture

Baroque Art and the Architecture of Central Europe, by E Hempel. Penguin. Austria's baroque treasures are covered admirably.
Viennese Design: And the Wiener Werkstätte by Jane Kallir. George Brazillier, 1986. An introduction to the artists and architects in fin-de-siècle Vienna.
Vienna 1900: Architecture and Painting, by Christian Nebehay. Full treatment of the art of Vienna's Golden Age.
Art in Vienna 1898-1918, by Peter Vergo. Phaidon, 1993. Comprehensive and well illustrated review of Vienna's most exciting artistic years.
Klimt, by Frank Whitford. Thames and Hudson, 1998. A short biography of one of the key figures in Vienna's great artistic development at the turn of the 20th century.

Fiction

The Third Man, by Graham Greene. Penguin, 1999. Classic novel of intrigue set in uneasy post-war Vienna, later to become Orson

Welles' classic film.

Madensky Square, by Eva Ibbotson. Arrow, 1998. A delightful and funny novel about life in Vienna in 1911, seen through the eyes of a fashionable dress-maker.

Dream Story, by Arthur Schnitzler, Penguin, 2000. Inspiration for Kubrick's *Eyes Wide Shut*: an exploration of desire in *fin-de-siècle* Vienna.

Embers, by Sandor Marai. Penguin Viking, 2001. A story of lost love and broken friendship set in imperial Vienna and the vast country estates of the aristocracy.

The Opal and Other Stories by Gustav Meyrink. Dedalus, 1994.Dark fantasies satirising late imperial civil and military life.

The Man Without Qualities, by Robert Musil. Vintage Books, 1996. Dense work that thoroughly mines the inner and outer worlds of an Austrian in pre-war Vienna.

The Radetzky March, by Joseph Roth. Granta, 2002. Sombre but evocative account of three generations of the empire's servants until World War I.

Auto Da Fe, by Elias Canetti. The Harvill Press, 2005. The story of a reclusive sinologist in Vienna between the Wars. Canetti fled Austria and won the Nobel Prize for Literature in 1981.

Hands Around: A Cycle of Ten Dialogues, by Arthur Schnitzler. Dover, 1995. Another of Schnitzler's morally amibiguous plays, again involving love and lust.

Amadeus, by Peter Shaffer. Harper Collins, 1985. Basis of the film *Amadeus*; a somewhat simplified and romanticised version of the Salzburg composer's life.

The World of Yesterday, by Stefan Zweig. University of Nebraska Press, 1964. Largely autobiographical memoir of old Vienna, and the subsequent horrors of the Anschluss, by one who was there.

Travel

The Sunny Side of the Alps: Year-Round Delights in South Tyrol and the Dolomites, by Paul Hofmann. Henry Holt, 1995. Author's travels in the borderland Alpine region straddling (mostly) Italy and Austria.

Classical Music

Haydn
With around 108 symphonies, 68 string quartets and numerous works for keyboard there is a lot of choice; for starters try the excellent set of symphonies 82–7 recorded by

Nikolaus Harnoncourt and the Vienna Concertus Musicus (Harmonia Mundi).

Mozart
Again, there is a huge amount of choice and these recommendations are in no way definitive. However, Guilini's EMI recording of *Il Nozze di Figaro* with Elizabeth Schwartzkopf is still fabulous; for the piano concertos try Clifford Curzon's performances conducted by Benjamin Britten (Decca); and Alfred Brendel has produced some wonderful recordings of the piano sonatas (Philips).

Beethoven
There are many, many recordings of works by Beethoven, in many competing styles. For complete sets of the symphonies, the Harnoncourt cycle using period instruments is excellent (Teldec), while the Wiener Philharmoniker under Abbado produced some superb playing for his Deutsche Grammophon set. For the piano sonatas some of the greatest performances are the historic recordings by Solomon (various labels), more controversial, modern renditions are those by Stephen Kovacevich (EMI).

Schubert
Perhaps best known for his *Lieder*, Schubert also wrote 9 symphonies and a great deal of piano music. Some of the greatest recordings of his *Lieder* are by Dietrich Fischer-Dieskau, try, especially, *Winterreise* accompanied by Gerald Moore (EMI).

Brahms
With such a huge output it ages to plough through all of Brahms' works. Of his four symphonies, the two cycles by Gunther Wand with the North German Radio Orchestra (RCA) are excellent, as are, if you can get them, the recordings by Rafael Kubelik. For his piano works, try the wonderful historic recordings made by Wilhelm Backhaus (Music & Arts among others).

Bruckner
Bruckner's output is dominated by his symphonies and one of the great masters of these was Herbert von Karajan. To hear him, and the Wiener Philharmoniker, at their best, try his two late recordings of symphonies 7 and 8 (both on Deutsche Grammophon).

Mahler
The other great late-19th century Austrian symphonist. Among the outstanding interpreters of his works are John Barbirolli (try symphonies 5 and 9, both on EMI), Sinopoli (Deutsche Grammophon) and Claudio Abbado, whose on-going live cycle with the Berlin Philharmonic is simply breathtaking (Deutsche Grammophon).

Feedback

We do our best to ensure the information in our books is as accurate and up-to-date as possible. The books are updated on a regular basis, using local contacts, who painstakingly add, amend and correct as required. However, some mistakes and omissions are inevitable and we are ultimately reliant on our readers to put us in the picture. We would welcome your feedback on any details related to your experiences using the book "on the road". Maybe we recommended a hotel that you liked (or another that you didn't), as well as interesting new attractions, or facts and figures you have found out about the country itself. The more details you can give us (particularly with regard to addresses, e-mails and telephone numbers), the better. We will acknowledge all contributions, and we'll offer an Insight Guide to the best letters received.

Please write to us at:
Insight Guides
PO Box 7910
London SE1 1WE
United Kingdom
Or send e-mail to:
insight@apaguide.co.uk

Strauss
Although Strauss isn't stricly Austrian, his long association with Hofmannsthal and at times distinctly Viennese sensibilities merits his inclusion here. His Viennese piece *par excellence* is *Der Rosenkavalier*; Karajan's legendary recording on EMI has yet to be surpassed.

Schoenberg
Perhaps Schoenberg's most interesting pieces are the early Expressionist works; try, for example, *Pierrot Lunaire* (in the outstanding recent version by Boulez on Deutsche Grammophon), or *Erwartung* (again Boulez, Sony Classical).

Berg
The more Romantically inclined of Schoenberg's two great pupils, both of Berg's operas are stunning. In *Wozzeck* listen to Karl Böhm and the Vienna State Opera (Andante), while for *Lulu* it must be Boulez (Deutsche Grammophon)

Webern
All of Webern's works fit onto three CDs and by far the best collected set is by Pierre Boulez, the composer's great champion (Deutsche Grammophon).

ART & PHOTO CREDITS

Austrian National Tourist Office
170
akg-images London 17, 21, 27, 32,
36, 38, 39, 41, 42, 43, 44, 46, 47,
49, 53, 70, 71, 72, 73, 74, 77, 78,
80, 81, 82, 83L&R, 90, 92, 95, 96,
99, 126, 130, 131, 133, 197
Art Archive 14–15, 20, 193
Art & History Collection 24
Augsberg City Archives 18
**Walter Bibikow/The Viesti
Collection** 283
Bodo Bondzio 31,
Bundeskanzleramt 50, 51, 84
Collection Pavel Scheuffler 33
Contrast 226–7, 233, 243, 247T
Corbis 124
Annabel Elston 247, 249T, 254,
255T
Robert Fried front flap bottom,
68–9, 132, 177, 181, 195T, 199T,
272, 273T, 274
Wolfgang Fritz 148–9, 158, 158T,
159, 160, 163, 174, 175, 175T,
181T, 182, 182T, 183, 186, 195,
200, 219, 224T, 225, 231, 234T,
236, 237, 273
Walter Geiersperger/Transglobe
187
Glyn Genin back flap top, 1, 10–11,
91L&R, 97, 113, 115, 117, 118,
120, 122, 128, 129, 143T
Getty Images 34, 48, 52, 54, 55,
75, 76, 79, 85, 86

Britta Jaschinski back cover, spine,
back flap bottom, 2, 4, 6–7, 8–9,
12, 56–7, 58, 59, 60, 61, 62L&R,
63, 64, 65, 93, 98, 100–1, 102–3,
104–5, 106, 110, 111, 114, 114T,
118T, 119, 125T, 127, 127T, 136,
137, 138, 139, 140, 141, 142,
143, 144, 150, 151, 153, 153T,
157, 161, 162, 166, 167, 169,
169T, 170T, 171, 171T, 172, 173,
173T, 174T, 176, 178T, 184, 184T,
188, 190–1, 192, 198, 198T, 199,
201, 201T, 202, 203, 204, 205,
205T, 206, 207, 209, 209T, 210,
210T, 211, 212, 213, 214, 220,
221, 222, 223, 224, 225T, 228,
229, 230, 232, 234, 238, 239,
240, 244, 245, 246, 246T, 249,
251, 251T, 253, 255, 257, 257T,
258, 258T, 260, 262, 263, 265,
267, 268, 269, 269T, 270, 271,
278, 281, 282, 283, 284, 286,
288, 290, 291, 292, 293, 295,
296, 304, 306, 307, 308, 311,
312
Michael Jenner 185
János Kalmár 45, 123, 154, 154T,
155, 179, 179T, 187T, 204T
Wilhelm Klein 23, 25, 35, 89,
121T, 125
Maria Lord 121, 133T
Dieter Maier 19, 189, 217, 235,
248
MAK 139T

Ludwig Mallaun/Transglobe 242,
250, 266, 275
Österreichische Galerie Belvedere
88, 94
Andrea Pistolesi 196T
Topham Picturepoint 16, 30,
37L&R, 40
US Press 156
Wolfgang Simlinger/Contrast 196
Evelyn Tambour 241
Transglobe front flap top 215, 218,
256
Vienna City Museum 26, 29
Vienna Tourist Board 87, 123T, 145
WARCH 28, 116

PICTURE SPREADS

66–7 All Britta Jaschinski, except
for 67R Glyn Genin.
146–7 All Britta Jaschinski.
164–5 Clockwise from top: Austrian
National Tourist Office; Walter
Geiersperger/Transglobe; Robert
Fried; Robert Fried; Robert Fried.

Every effort has been made to trace the
copyright holders, and we apologise in
advance for any unintentional omissions.

Map Production:
Dave Priestley and Mike Adams
© 2006 Apa Publications GmbH & Co.
Verlag KG (Singapore branch)

INSIGHT GUIDE
austria

Cartographic Editor **Zoë Goodwin**
Design Consultant
Klaus Geisler
Picture Research **Hilary Genin**

INDEX

Register with
HotelClub.com
and get £15!

At **HotelClub.com**, we reward our Members with discounts and free stays in their favourite hotels. As a Member, every booking made by you through **HotelClub.com** will earn you Member Dollars.

When you register, we will credit your account with **£15** which you can use for your next booking! The equivalent of **£15** will be credited in US$ to your Member account (as **HotelClub Member Dollars**). All you need to do is log on to **www.HotelClub.com/insightguides**. Complete your details, including the Membership Number and Password located on the back of the **HotelClub.com** card.

Over 2.2 million Members already use Member Dollars to pay for all or part of their hotel bookings. Join now and start spending Member Dollars whenever and wherever you want – you are not restricted to specific hotels or dates!

With great savings of up to 60% on over 20,000 hotels across 97 countries, you are sure to find the perfect location for business or pleasure. Happy travels from **HotelClub.com!**

www.insightguides.com

TRULY ADVENTUROUS

TRULY ASIA

**Limerick
County Library**

In the heart of Asia lies a land of many cultures, wonders and attractions. Especially for the adventure seeker to whom fear is not a factor. There are hundreds of thrills to experience. Mount Kinabalu. Mulu Caves. Taman Negara. These are just a few places where you'll always find that rewarding adrenaline rush. Where is this land, so challenging and exhilarating? It can only be Malaysia, Truly Asia.

Malaysia
Truly Asia